Understanding Pupil Behaviour in Schools: A diversity of approaches

The companion volumes in this series are:

Inclusion and Behaviour Management in Schools: Issues and Challenges, edited by Janice Wearmouth, Ted Glynn, Robin C. Richmond and Mere Berryman

Addressing Pupils' Behaviour: Responses at District, School and Individual Levels, edited by Janice Wearmouth, Robin C. Richmond and Ted Glynn

These three volumes constitute part of a course jointly developed by the Open University in the UK and the University of Waikato in New Zealand. The Open University course is E804 *Managing Behaviour in Schools*. The University of Waikato course comprises three modules: HDCO534 - Theorising Behaviour in Schools; HDCO535 - Behaviour Assessment and Intervention in Schools; HDCO536 - School Behaviour Policies

The Open University Course E804 - *Managing Behaviour in Schools*

The course is offered within the Open University Master's Programme in Education. The Master's Programme provides great flexibility. Students study at their own pace and in their own time anywhere in the European Union. They receive specially prepared study materials, supported by face-to-face tutorials where they can work with other students.

The MA is modular. Students may select modules from the programme which fit their personal and professional interests and goals. Specialist lines of study are also available and include special and inclusive education, management, applied linguistics and lifelong learning. The attainment of an MA entitles students to apply for entry to the Open University Doctorate in Education Programme.

How to apply

If you would like to find out more information about available courses, please write, requesting the Professional Development in Education prospectus, to the Call Centre, PO Box 200, The Open University, Walton Hall, Milton Keynes, MK7 6ZW, UK (tel: 0 (0 44) 1908 653231). Details can also be viewed on our web page http://www.open.ac.uk.

The University of Waikato *Postgraduate Diploma in Managing Behaviour in Schools PGDip (MBS)*

This postgraduate diploma is offered within the University of Waikato Master of Education programme, and utilises the same specially prepared study materials, supported by face-to-face classes and tutorials offered flexibly through summer school sessions and intermittent Saturday sessions. Each module is offered as a Master's level course, and can be credited towards a Master's degree in Education. The PGDipMBS requires one additional course in research methodology (on-line options available). Holders of the Postgraduate Diploma are able to complete a one-year Master's Degree in Education by thesis or course work, across a wide range of areas, such as inclusive education, Maori and bilingual education, educational policy and educational leadership.

How to apply

If you would like to find out more about the PGDipMBS and other available courses, please contact the Administrator, Graduate Studies in Education, School of Education, University of Waikato, Private Bag 3105, Hamilton, New Zealand (tel: 64-7-838-4500 or fax 64-7-838-4555). Details can also be accessed via e-mail: educ_grad@waikato.ac.nz or viewed on our website: http://www.waikato.ac.nz/education/grad

Understanding Pupil Behaviour in Schools: A diversity of approaches

Janice Wearmouth, Robin C. Richmond, Ted Glynn and Mere Berryman

David Fulton Publishers
London

in association with
The Open University and
the University of Waikato

The
University
of Waikato
Te Whare Wānanga
o Waikato

The Open
University

David Fulton Publishers Ltd
The Chiswick Centre, 414 Chiswick High Road, London W4 5TF

www.fultonpublishers.co.uk

First published in Great Britain in 2004 by David Fulton Publishers

10 9 8 7 6 5 4 3 2 1

British Library Cataloguing in Publication Data
A catalogue record for this book is available from the British Library.

David Fulton Publishers is a division of ITV plc.

ISBN 1 84312 230 8

Typeset by RefineCatch Limited, Bungay, Suffolk
Printed in Great Britain

Contents

Part 3: Psychological perspectives 149

Part 4: Medical perspectives 325

Acknowledgements

We would like to thank all those who have contributed chapters to this reader or have approved their reprinting from other publications. Grateful acknowledgement is made to the following sources for permission to reproduce material in this book. Chapters not listed have been newly written.

Chapter 3: Messiou, K. (2002) 'Marginalisation in primary schools: listening to children's voices', *Support for Learning*, 17(3), 117-21. Blackwell Publishing Ltd.

Chapter 5: Osborne, J.W. (2001) 'Academic disidentification: unravelling underachievement among Black boys', in R. Majors (ed.) *Educating Our Black Children: New Directions and Radical Approaches*. London: RoutledgeFalmer, pp. 45-58.

Chapter 6: Wright, C., Weekes, D. and McGlaughlin, A. (2000) 'Teachers and pupils - relationships of power and resistance', in *'Race', Class and Gender in Exclusion from School*. London: Falmer, pp. 37-62.

Chapter 7: Braithwaite, J. (2001) 'Youth development circles', *Oxford Review of Education*, 27(2), 239-51.

Chapter 8: Bishop, R. and Glynn, T. (1998) 'Achieving cultural integrity in education in Aotearoa/New Zealand', in K. Cushner (ed.) *International Perspectives on Intercultural Education*, pp. 38-70. Mahwah, NJ: Lawrence Erlbaum Associates.

Chapter 10: Greenhalgh, P. (1994) *Emotional Growth and Learning*. London: Routledge, pp. 21-43.

Chapter 11: O'Brien, T. and Guiney, D. (2001) 'Self-esteems and emotional differentiation', in T. O'Brien and D. Guiney *Differentiation in Teaching and Learning*. London: Continuum, pp. 132-55.

Chapter 12: McLeod, J. (1998) 'Cultural and historical origins', in J. McLeod *An Introduction to Counselling*. Buckingham: Open University Press, pp. 12-30.

Chapter 13: Boxall, M. (2000) 'The nurture group in the primary school', in M. Bennathan and M. Boxall (eds) *Effective Intervention in Primary Schools: Nurture Groups* (2nd edn). London: David Fulton, pp. 19-38.

Chapter 16: Glynn, T. (1982) 'Antecedent control of behaviour in educational contexts'. *Educational Psychology*, 2(3), 215-29.

Chapter 19: Rigby, K. (2000) 'Why bully?', in K. Rigby *New Perspectives on Bullying*. London: Jessica Kingsley, pp. 147-70.

Chapter 20: Cornwall, J. (1999) 'Pressure, stress and children's behaviour at school', in T. David (ed.) *Young Children Learning*. London: Paul Chapman.

Chapter 21: Place, M., Wilson, J., Martin, E. and Hulsmeier, J. 'Attention deficit disorder as a factor in the origin of behavioural disturbance in schools'. *British Journal of Special Education*, 30(1).

Preface

Understanding pupil behaviour in schools: A diversity of approaches

Janice Wearmouth

Across the world there is a drive towards the inclusion of all students in mainstream education, including those whose behaviour is seen as difficult to manage. Professionals' views of the causes of challenging behaviour among students vary considerably. In many situations these views have considerable influence over how behaviour considered as problematic is addressed. It is crucial, therefore, to consider ways of viewing student behaviour that have the potential both to enable all students to participate in schools' communities of practice (Lave and Wenger, 1991; 1999) and to support a sense of professionalism among teachers and other educators.

This volume outlines different ways of carrying out research in schools and of understanding behaviour viewed as difficult to manage or problematic in some way in schools across the UK, in New Zealand and internationally. In doing so it comprises discussion of cultural issues, including those of ethnic diversity and power dynamics, a range of psychological models of behaviour seen as challenging to teachers, medical perspectives and sociological issues. These last issues include tensions related to the inclusion of students whose behaviour may be seen as undesirable, challenging or threatening to the social order in schools.

In the introductory part of the book, Wearmouth and Connors in chapter 1 adopt a view of the human mind as dependent on its evolution within a social context and that context as highly influential in shaping children's thinking and learning. They outline a range of ways of interpreting behaviour and relate them to particular psychological models which are seen as cultural constructs, not as universal givens. In chapter 2, McCall goes on to draw out the implications of a range of perspectives on behaviour for multi-disciplinary and multi-agency approaches to addressing student behavioural issues.

In Part 1, *Research*, Messiou's chapter discusses a research project on the marginalisation of children in primary schools and outlines a number of research techniques which were appropriate for eliciting information relevant to the work: interviews, participant observation, development of classroom sociograms and analysis of children's drawings. The following chapter by Wearmouth describes a very powerful projective technique, 'Talking Stones', which can be used in schools to engage with the views of disaffected young people. Discussion of the technique includes provisos on its use which relate to the ethics of putting such a technique into practice without consideration of issues of confidentiality and sensitivity to what might be in students' best interests.

Part 2, *Cultural issues*, opens with Chapter 5 by Osborne which reviews three important theoretical perspectives which suggest that particular minority ethnic students are at risk of academic disidentification: stereotype threat, a socio-ecological framework and 'Cool Pose'. Wright, Weekes and McGlaughlin's chapter then summarises part of an ethnographic research study into race, class and gender in four inner-city schools. In particular it focuses on aspects that relate to students' resistance to schools and school learning. In chapter 7, Braithwaite raises the question of whether restorative justice circles might effectively address a range of problems such as drug abuse and homelessness experienced by young people in the transition from school to work. Bishop and Glynn, in chapter 8, outline the historical development of the New Zealand education system and the position of Māori students within it. They pose the question of how a multi-ethnic country can organise and direct its education system to address the needs of both immigrant and indigeneous populations while preparing all its young people for a global society. Berryman and Glynn, in chapter 9, describe and discuss a whole-school intervention programme 'Eliminating Violence' that was designed to reduce the incidence of undesirable student behaviour in the context of a primary school in a Māori community in New Zealand.

In Part 3, *Psychological perspectives*, Greenhalgh adopts a view that it is through individual students' emotional inner world that they develop personal constructions of outside 'reality' and discusses the link between emotional 'safety' and learning. Chapter 11 by O'Brien and Guiney goes on to relate issues associated with the emotional context for learning to notions of differentiation in the school curriculum. It focuses particularly on self esteem, the nature of 'Self' and the teaching and learning experience. In chapter 12, McLeod traces the history of counselling as a response to emotional distress and problematic behaviour and points to its origins in the social forces that have shaped contemporary culture and society. Boxall's chapter goes on to discuss the rationale underpinning the concept of 'nurture groups' for children in the early years. She draws on principles of 'attachment theory' (Bowlby,

1944; 1951) to show how schools can adopt a structured, educational approach to fostering the emotional growth and well-being of young children whose early life experiences may have been very traumatic. In chapter 14, Wearmouth takes an eclectic approach in explaining the success of strategies associated with 'circle time' with reference to a number of different, and in some ways conflicting, psychological paradigms. Hesketh and Olney, in chapter 15, show how principles derived from systems theory and exemplified in, for example, family therapy, can be used in schools by suitably qualified and experienced staff to address problematic student behaviour in ways that draw on and recognise the expertise and knowledge of both families and school professionals. Chapter 16 by Glynn takes a behavioural approach to demonstrating how the characteristics of settings in which student behaviours are performed may have just as powerful an influence over those behaviours as do the consequences which act to reinforce them. This is a particularly important factor to consider in designing learning activities and environments in ways that will promote and foster students' academic learning and positive interactions with peers. Proactivity at the planning stage may be more effective in the long term than reactivity subsequent to poor behaviour. In chapter 17, Hufton and Elliott offer an outline review of motivation theory and conclude that there should be an investigation of ways in which aspects of the process of educating students at the level of the education system, the school and the classroom should be brought into line with each other to maximise motivation to learn. Chapter 18, by Dwivedi, draws on the theory of self management training from a cognitive perspective to discuss ways in which schools might address issues of persistent antisocial, aggressive or defiant behaviour at the level of the individual student. In chapter 19, Rigby looks at an area of behaviour that is currently of international concern to teachers and other educators associated with schools, that of bullying. He discusses three kinds of explanations for bullying behaviour: supernatural, biological and environmental, and draws out the implications of each for addressing such behaviour in schools. In the final chapter of Part 3, Cornwall discusses the effects of stress on student behaviour and outlines a number of strategies which have the potential to support students to manage excessive levels of stress in their lives.

Part 4, *Medical perspectives*, opens with chapter 21 in which Place, Wilson, Martin and Hulsmeier focus on Attention Deficit/Hyperactivity Disorder (AD/HD) as a way of viewing behaviour from a medical standpoint. They discuss its diagnosis and interventions commonly associated with it and highlight the importance of early identification. In the final chapter, Sheehy discusses 'autism' and outlines diagnostic criteria in common use, a range of explanations for behaviour seen as autistic, and a number of approaches for addressing such behaviour in schools.

References

Bowlby, J. (1944) 'Forty-four juvenile thieves: their characters and home life', *International Journal of Psycho-Analysis*, **25**, 19–52, 107–27.

Bowlby, J. (1951) *Maternal care and mental health*, World Health Organisation, London: HMSO

Lave, J. and Wenger, E. (1991) *Situated learning: legitimate peripheral participation*, Cambridge: Cambridge University Press

Lave, J. and Wenger, E. (1999) 'Learning and pedagogy in communities of practice', in J. Leach and B. Moon (eds) *Learners and Pedagogy*, London: Paul Chapman

Chapter 1

Understanding student behaviour in schools

Janice Wearmouth and Bushra Connors

Introduction

Professionals' views of the root cause of students' behaviour have considerable influence over how behaviour considered as problematic is addressed. For example, there is considerable research evidence to suggest that teachers' ways of thinking about, and emotional reactions to, behaviour perceived as disturbing bear a strong relation to their 'intentional' and 'actual behaviour' (Poulou and Norwich, 2002, p. 111). Internationally there is a drive towards the inclusion of all students in mainstream education. It is crucial, therefore, to consider ways of viewing student behaviour that can both enable all students to derive the maximum benefit from their education and add to and support a sense of professionalism among teachers and other educators.

Clearly, the behaviour of a student whose interactions in classrooms are often disruptive to the education of peers might be interpreted in a wide variety of ways and we discuss a number of common interpretations. However, in this chapter our major focus is a view of the human mind as dependent on its evolution within a social context and that context as highly influential in shaping children's thinking and providing a 'cultural toolkit' (Bruner, 1996) for organising meaning in ways that can be communicated to others. We outline a number of interpretations of behaviour and relate them to particular psychological models which we view as cultural constructs, not as universal givens. The assumptions associated with these models are important because they have been used to underpin much of the provision and/or interventions that have been devised in the area of student behaviour management.

Common explanations

In schools teachers are surrounded by different kinds of explanations for student behaviour, some of which can be detrimental to active engagement with students' best interests (Watkins and Wagner, 2000). Common explanations include:

> 'They're that sort of person'
> 'They're not very bright'
> 'It's just a tiny minority'
> 'It's their age'
> 'This is a difficult neighbourhood'

(Watkins and Wagner, 2000, p. 3)

'That sort of person' is a classic deficit model of the person. The use of 'prevalent stereotypes' is problematic in a number of ways (Watkins and Wagner, 2000). It is inadequate to explain the behaviour of the individual student and can be used to justify the school abnegating its responsibility for the welfare and progress of the individual student.

'They're not very bright' implies an innate lack of ability in certain students and therefore justifies some schools' lack of preparedness to find ways to engage with the students' learning.

'A tiny minority' implies that 'they' are very different from 'we', that is, the majority, and therefore hard to understand. There is an incentive to remove the miscreants before they contaminate the majority. In addition, where the 'tiny minority' has been removed, 'new members have emerged to fill the deviant roles' (Watkins and Wagner, 2000, p. 7).

The explanation 'it's their age' is used largely to apply to secondary-aged students. Biological determinism in the form of 'it's their hormones' or adolescent moodiness and unpredictability is often used to explain the higher incidence of disaffection amongst students at secondary compared with primary level.

Explaining difficult behaviour as emanating from a difficult neighbourhood does little to illuminate individual students' patterns of behaviour. Socio-economic factors have a great deal of influence on school populations. There is differential distribution of educational success along lines of social class (Gewirtz et al, 1995). However, research outcomes do not support the application of a simple cause and effect model of student disaffection and disruptive behaviour caused by economically impoverished neighbourhoods (Mortimore et al, 1988; Hargreaves, 1984; OFSTED, 2000; 2003). The structure and organisation of schools can make a difference to student behaviour even in disadvantaged areas (Rutter et al, 1979).

A number of researchers have noted that student behaviour perceived by others as unacceptable is influenced at three levels: individual student, teacher in the classroom and whole-school. The most effective interventions intended to reduce the risk of unacceptable behaviour are those that operate at all three levels, given that:

   a) Some individuals are more likely than others to misbehave
   b) Some teachers are more likely than others to produce higher levels of misconduct in their classroom by their management and organization practices
   c) Some schools more often than others fail to control student behaviour
               (Gottfredson et al, 1998, p. 182 quoted in Watkins and Wagner, 2000, p. 17)

Student behaviour and culturalism

Different ways of conceptualising the human mind, the development of learning and the way this impacts on behaviour also lead to different approaches to the education of young people and the development of children's learning (Bruner, 1996) and different interventions for dealing with issues of behavioural concerns in schools. One view that can account for the processes of human meaning-making and which is sensitive to context is what Bruner terms 'culturalism' (Bruner, ibid) with its rather different implications for addressing issues of learning and behaviour. 'Culturalism' assumes that the development of the human mind depends on its evolution within a society where the 'reality' of individual experience is represented through a shared symbolism, for example verbal or written language. The cultural context in which a child is reared shapes his/her thinking. Meaning-making is situated in a cultural context as well as in the prior conceptions that learners bring with them into new situations as a result of previous learning in other contexts. New learning is a product of the 'interplay' between them. Bruner raises a number of issues relevant to a consideration of student behaviour. For example:

- where learning is assumed to occur through engagement in society, pedagogy needs to be interactive and 'intersubjective' to take account of individual meaning-making and allow for the production of shared task outcomes;
- educational policies and practices need to take account of the fact that schools exist in societies where issues of power, status and rewards are very influential;
- schooling plays a critical part in shaping a student's sense of 'Self', that is in his/her belief in his/her ability, responsibility and skill in initiating and completing actions and tasks. The way in which schools mediate success and failure are crucial to the development of a sense of personal agency. School is an integral part of the culture, not simply a way of preparing for entry. Teachers should therefore reflect continuously on the impact of school processes and practices on young people's sense of agency and ability;

- failing to support the development of students' understanding and ability to act in a cultural context risks marginalising and alienating young people and rendering them incompetent, with the consequent threat to the stability of society as a whole.

Among the salient features of this socio-cultural approach are an emphasis on the 'indivisibility' of human action, both internal to the individual and external, and of the context in which it occurs (Davies, 2004). Learning is viewed as taking place through 'participation' and as transforming the individual learner's identity. The sense of belonging to, or marginalisation from, a community affects every aspect of participation and, therefore, learning within it, and necessarily affects a student's behaviour and self perception. Notions of 'inclusion' can be interpreted as the extent to which students are able to participate in the school community. From this viewpoint a sense of belonging and acceptance in a social group which shows care and respect for its members is a basic human need. The identity of community members is influenced by the extent to which interactions within the group engage and acknowledge them. It may not be easy to engage with and acknowledge students whose behaviour in schools is experienced as challenging or threatening, but nevertheless they have the same basic needs as any other individual.

As Bruner (1996) notes, one of the prime responsibilities of schools is to support the construction of a student's sense of Self through an acknowledgement of agency and the development of self esteem. Within an institution, both educators and students are defined by that institution's social practices. Participation in a community is 'transformative' both to participants and to the group (Davies, 2004). It is essential, therefore, to examine the way in which school practices contribute to a student's sense of agency and personal esteem and, therefore, to the construction of a concept of Self, and his/her feelings about being able to cope with the world both during and after the years of compulsory schooling. 'Formalised education, commencing at the age of five years, imposes a whole range of requirements' (BPS, 1996, p. 13). It is inevitable that students who experience difficulties in meeting these demands must face 'a range of social, educational and psychological consequences' which will be 'compounded by personal unhappiness' (ibid).

In recent years, the relative under-achievement of students from particular minority ethnic groups and the proportionately high exclusion rate among the same students has been a focus of investigation – in the educational research of some countries for a considerable time (Rampton, 1981; Swann, 1985; Bishop, 1996; Smith, 1995). Findings from the Youth Cohort Study (YCS) of England and Wales indicate a trend of growing gaps by gender and ethnicity (DfE, 1994a):

> The YCS data paint a clear picture of growing inequalities of achievement between the white group and pupils from several minority ethnic backgrounds. Only two of the

different ethnic categories covered in the study enjoyed a year-on-year improvement: the white and Indian groups. The consequence is a growing gap between the majority white group and pupils classified as 'Black', 'Pakistani' and 'Bangladeshi'.

(Gillborn and Youdell, 2000, p. 38)

As Gillborn and Youdell go on to point out in the context of UK research, inequalities in achievement between ethnic groups were mirrored by growing gaps between the social classes. They conclude that:

> It is clear that social class remains a hugely important factor associated with significant and increasing inequalities of achievement.

(Gillborn and Youdell, 2000, p. 40)

Osborne (2001) and Blair (2001) have attempted to understand and explain perceived school underachievement of some racial minorities, particularly African or Caribbean Black boys. Both writers comment that causes have been attributed to the students themselves and their cultures. Osborne argues that all children enter school with positive attitudes, what he refers to as 'identification with academics', but Black boys are at high risk of developing a resistance to, or 'disidentification' with, school as the result of poor academic results, and retreat into a negative group stereotype. He examines three theoretical areas within social psychology to support his argument. A stereotype threat theory (Steele, 1992; 1997) proposes that the school environment is aversive to members of groups with negative group stereotypes. A cultural-ecological theory (Ogbu, 1997) distinguishes between members of a minority culture whose forebears chose to live in the predominant culture and who seek education as the path to success, and involuntary immigrants. These latter, it is claimed, are more likely to develop social or collective identity in opposition to the predominant culture. A 'cool pose' theory on the other hand (Majors and Billson, 1992) claims that survival in an environment of social oppression and racism leads to the adoption of flamboyant and non-conformist behaviour leading to punishment in school settings.

Osborne concludes that disidentification is more likely from Black boys and is a developmental process. Resistance to school, hence removal from the source of frustration and 'negative evaluation', reduces anxiety and improves self esteem. Successful outcomes are related to identification with school learning. The social dynamics of an environment, for example acceptance of difference, can affect academic outcomes.

It is perhaps this third conclusion that comes closest to the factors with which Blair is concerned: the effect of an 'aversive' school environment. She accepts that Black students who behave badly, as with any other adolescents, are placed in lower academic sets. However, she is more concerned with why students behave badly in a particular school. Blair refers to 'cultural dissonance' in saying that white teachers may not understand Black youngsters or their learning styles. She claims that the school has a responsibility to respond to the culture, experiences, interests and needs of the whole range of students, hence the notion that, for Black youngsters, racism is structural to an institution.

In considering steps that could be taken to address the issues, the two writers have a different emphasis. Osborne highlights responses to 'resistance' and Blair 'inclusive schooling'. As part of a strategy for respecting all cultures, Blair describes a successful school which provided six-week courses of Afrikaans and Irish studies for all students to develop understanding and respect across the school. She notes the commitment of the school to work with Black parents and the strong relationships forged between the school and the Black community with consultation on policies and school governance. Blair puts strong emphasis on a school climate and ethos in which the views of Black students along with all students are listened to and respected. The essential factor is teachers who respect diversity and are open to learn and understand the issues that affect the students including their political and social concerns. Students' needs and concerns as adolescents will be recognised alongside needs arising from ethnic and racial identities.

In contrast Osborne criticises 'ethnic studies' additions to Eurocentric curricula. In a 'true' multicultural curriculum, he claims, the contributions of people of colour are infused throughout. However, Osborne also implies changing the attitudes and behaviour of Black students through the teaching of the Black values in Europe (Afro-centric socialisation): 'cooperation, mutual respect, commitment and love of family, race community and nation' in contrast to white European culture which is perceived as individualism and competition.

Osborne also suggests interventions in Black communities to change community and family norms, emphasise academic achievement and encourage Black students to identify with school learning: 'accommodation without assimilation'. Respected members and leaders of the community might reinforce attitudes and behaviours that lead to academic success alongside attitudes and behaviours that maintain ethnic identity. The community ought to demonstrate, through examples, that academic achievement is valued equally with other activities such as sporting achievements. Members of the community, usually people who have voluntarily moved into the dominant culture, who use their academic success to leave, should be encouraged to remain within the community.

Psychological interpretations of behaviour

Individual cultures have their own ways of constructing reality. Interpretations of behaviour underpinned by particular psychological models can be seen as cultural constructs (Bruner, 1996) and not as universal givens. This is a very important issue in schools because different psychological approaches carry their own assumptions about human learning and behaviour and legitimise different ways of engaging with students and attempting to change their behaviour.

Behavioural approaches

Most work in response to issues of individual students' behaviour that is perceived as disturbing by teachers has been based 'on behavioural management approaches (which employ strategies such as positive reinforcement, response cost, extinction and so on) where the reinforcing conditions or consequences of a behaviour are adjusted in order to moderate its frequency' (Dwivedi and Gupta, 2000, p. 76). Often, the kind of conditioning assumed to influence human behaviour is 'operant'. The individual operates on the environment to cause an effect. It performs 'operants'. Translating this interpretation of behaviour into the context of the behaviour of students in schools, behaviour perceived as disturbing has been learned through positive reinforcement in some way. One way to address undesirable behaviour is to identify and alter the stimulus context in which that behaviour occurs. Changing the setting can prove very effective in modifying students' behaviour. Another way is to ensure that whatever is rewarding and reinforcing it is removed so that the behaviour will be extinguished. Further, whenever the individual behaves in ways that are seen as more appropriate, s/he should be rewarded in a way that clearly recognises the greater acceptability of the new behaviour in settings where it occurs.

In operant conditioning terms, the opposite of positive reinforcement is negative reinforcement. In negative reinforcement, desired behaviour is encouraged through putting a stop to something unpleasant. For example, student compliance may be reinforced through avoidance of punishment. 'Contingencies of reinforcement', on the other hand, as noted previously, are assumed to 'shape' behaviour by serving to reinforce behaviour after the event and thus make it more likely that the particular behaviour that has been reinforced will re-occur. Good planning prior to events in schools and classrooms to ensure that things will go well is likely to be more time-efficient than subsequent actions driven by the need to restore good order.

Behaviour management is not simply about increasing and decreasing behaviours, but also about discriminating between settings (times and places) where certain behaviours are appropriate and acceptable, and other settings where they are not. Key to training students in what constitutes appropriate behaviour is making clear what is unacceptable and modelling, rehearsing and reinforcing what is acceptable.

Behavioural approaches are often criticised for failing to take adequate account of the emotions. Inappropriate use of praise for what Hanko (1994) calls 'discouraged students' can be damaging to some individuals:

> Discouraged children, trapped in a self-concept created by past experiences of failure, will lose out in a particularly disheartening way when a praising teacher fails to understand, and thus to address, the effects of such painful experiences on their low self-image as learners. Consequently, a praise-refusing student's determination not to be lured into the risks of failing yet again may be further reinforced.
>
> (Hanko, 1994, p. 166)

Cultural differences are also crucial here. Where teachers are from different cultural groups from their students, they may 'mis-cue' in their application of reinforcement. For example, in New Zealand with Māori students, to reward an individual and thereby elevate him/her above the group may be to introduce an aversive consequence. Māori teachers instead may reward individuals' positive contributions to the well-being and/or the performance of the group.

Cognitive-behavioural approaches

The cognitive-behavioural approach has emerged from behavioural psychology (see above) and has a number of additional key characteristics:

> a problem-solving, change-focused approach to working with clients; a respect for scientific values; and close attention to the cognitive processes through which people monitor and control their behaviour.
>
> (McLeod, 1998, p. 62)

This approach encompasses a wide range of cognitive processes: perception, language, problem-solving, memory, decision-making and imagery. A number of researchers have opened up the concept of meta-cognitive awareness, that is awareness of one's own thinking, feelings and emotions, into the area of emotional regulation, or self management in order to cope with feelings such as violence, bullying, disaffection or isolation (Meichenbaum and Turk, 1976; Shapiro and Cole, 1994). In the school situation there is an assumption that when students begin to pay attention to 'the stream of automatic thoughts which accompany and guide their actions, they can make choices about the appropriateness of these self-statements, and if necessary introduce new thoughts and ideas' (McLeod, 1998, p. 72), which lead to behaviour that is more appropriate to the school context and that leads to a higher level of academic achievement. Teaching self management skills aims to encourage independence and self reliance. It can therefore address the ethical concerns associated with a behavioural approach of teachers managing students' behaviour to serve their own interests rather than those of the students themselves (Dwivedi and Gupta, 2000; Shapiro and Cole, 1994).

In recent years there has been a recognition that 'the emotional and behavioural difficulties which people experience in their lives are not caused directly by events but by the way they interpret and make sense of these events' (McLeod, 1998, pp. 71–72). The cognitive-behavioural approach has extended into constructivism with its focus on ways in which individuals construct their understanding of the reality in which they live:

> First, the person is regarded as an active knower, as purposefully engaged in making sense of his or her world. Second, language functions as the primary means through which the person constructs an understanding of the world. Constructivist therapists are therefore particularly interested in linguistic products such as stories and metaphors, which are seen as ways of structuring experience. Third, there is a developmental dimension to the person's capacity to construct their world.
>
> (McLeod, 1998, pp. 81–82)

From this approach there is a clear implication for schools to take seriously the issue of how to encourage student self-advocacy.

The ecosystemic approach

In contrast with individualistic approaches, the ecosystemic approach shifts the focus away from an assumption that problem behaviour lies within the student to a view that such problems are symptomatic of dysfunctions in the family system, dysfunctions in the school system, or dysfunctions in the family–school relationship system (Campion, 1985; Dowling and Osbourne, 1985). Cooper and Upton (1991) describe the nature of this approach:

> The ecosystemic approach is based on the idea that human interactional structures, such as families, schools and other organisations, are self-regulating systems, which function in a way which is analogous to the natural ecosystem. Such systems are sustained by repeating interactional patterns among the participants (subsystems), which are shaped and continually modified by the survival needs of the system as a whole. Systems are in continual interaction with other systems which form elements in their environment (the social ecosystem). Changes in any one part of the ecosystem have the result of changing the whole ecosystem. Difficulties for individuals arise when they become caught up in interactional patterns which serve the needs of the system as a whole at their personal expense.
>
> (Cooper and Upton, 1991, p. 23)

There is an overt recognition that behaviour perceived as problematic does not stem from within the individual who displays the behaviour, but results from the interaction between that individual and others. Individuals therefore have:

a rational basis for behaving as they do, based on their perception of the situation. Individuals' views of a situation are often related to specific goals they have. Different parties, therefore, have different perspectives on the same situation, which can lead to conflicting views as to what is rational, justifiable behaviour. No one perception of a situation is the true definition. This implies a rejection of the idea that problem behaviour originates from within the individual, and indicates that all parties in an interaction are involved in the maintenance of problem situations. There are many valid viewpoints, and it is often possible for a particular interpretation of events to be found that will serve the interests of different parties, without need for conflict.

A further implication of this viewpoint is that opposition gives rise to opposition. For the more one party in a conflict attempts to reject and supplant the other's view, owing to its wrongness or illogicality, the more the other resists the injustice of such an assault.

(Cooper and Upton, 1991, p. 23)

Any intervention must be based on an assumption that everyone taking part in the interactions associated with the problem behaviour is also contributing to the problem situation. Anyone, therefore, whose actions do not help to solve the problem must be a part of the cause of the problem behaviour. 'There is no neutral position' (ibid). One common intervention based on an ecosystemic view is that of family therapy, which is in widespread use internationally (Minuchin, 1974).

Attachment theory

One theory that has been highly influential over what is seen to constitute an appropriate educational response to young children whose behaviour is a focus of teacher concern is that of attachment theory (Bowlby, 1952). Central to Bowlby's work is the view that:

children deprived of maternal care … may be seriously affected in their physical, intellectual, emotional and social development … Bowlby asserts that 'prolonged separation of a child from his mother (or mother substitute) during the first five years of life stands foremost among the causes of delinquent character development' (Bowlby, 1944; 1952).

(Holmes, 1993, p. 39)

Bowlby's work draws together two different traditions: child psychiatry and ethology, the study of animal behaviour. As a child psychiatrist he made the connection between the lack of consistent and caring relationships in early childhood and later emotional insecurity manifesting itself as 'behaviour difficulties'.

Despite the criticisms of Bowlby's hypotheses from psychoanalytic circles and from others, the scientific study of early childhood is now well established. It is accepted that babies quickly attach themselves emotionally to their adult carers and go through well-recognized stages of development towards maturity.

Attachment theory has been used to justify the development of 'nurture groups' in some infant schools. The underlying assumption of the nurture group is that as a result of early childhood experiences, some children need extra emotional support and appropriate learning opportunities before they can learn in a normal school setting. The emphasis is 'on growth not on pathology'. In this way the issue is addressed as a means to develop, not as a deficit label to justify ignoring, development and learning. The nurture group attempts to provide opportunities to develop trust, security, positive mood and identity through attachment to a reliable attentive and caring adult and to develop autonomy through the provision of secure, controlled and graduated experiences in a familiar environment. It is assumed that more mature appropriate behaviour will develop in the child.

Biological/medical explanations of behaviour

Difficult behaviour, from a medical perspective, is the result of an underlying condition or disease which an individual has and which requires treatment. In some cases this may involve the use of medicine, which, in the context of schools, has obvious ethical considerations. Explanations involve a process of diagnosis based on the symptoms to identify the existence of an underlying condition or illness and then intervention or treatment to provide a cure. However, because behaviour is defined within the context of a social grouping, establishing the existence of a condition or disease of 'difficult behaviour' or 'emotional disorder' is fraught with problems.

Among the explanations of behaviour experienced as challenging to teachers and (often) to parents also is the notion of attention deficit/hyperactivity disorder (AD/HD), described by Norwich et al. (2002):

> AD/HD is a medical diagnosis of the American Psychiatric Association. It is characterised by chronic and pervasive (to home and school) problems of inattention, impulsiveness, and/or excessive motor activity which have seriously debilitating effects on individuals' social, emotional and educational development, and are sometimes disruptive to the home and/or school environment. Between two and five per cent of British school children are believed to experience this condition (BPS, 1997). The coming of this diagnosis has revived traditional conflicts between medical and educational perspectives on EBD, which affect the way in which practitioners approach problems surrounding childhood attention and activity problems...
>
> (Norwich, Cooper and Maras, 2002, p. 182)

The 'defining features' of AD/HD is behaviour which 'appears inattentive, impulsive and overactive to an extent that is unwarranted for their developmental age and is a significant hindrance to their social and educational success' (BPS, 1996, p. 13). In Britain and Europe, unlike the USA, the tradition has been 'to use the diagnostic systems of the International Classification of Diseases (ICD) published by the World Health Organisation' and to assume a 'hyperkinetic disorder'. There is a strict requirement for 'pervasiveness and persistence' which means that behaviour seen largely in one context only does not constitute grounds for a diagnosis.

Autism is another explanation of behaviour that relates very closely to a medical model of disability:

> **What are the characteristics of autism?**
> All people with autism have impairments in social interaction, social communication and imagination. This is referred to as the triad of impairments.
>
> **Social interaction** (difficulty with social relationships, for example appearing aloof and indifferent to other people).
> **Social communication** (difficulty with verbal and non-verbal communication, for example not really understanding the meaning of gestures, facial expressions or tone of voice).
> **Imagination** (difficulty in the development of play and imagination, for example having a limited range of imaginative activities, possibly copied and pursued rigidly and repetitively).
>
> In addition to this triad, repetitive behaviour patterns are a notable feature and a resistance to change in routine.
>
> (National Autistic Society, 2004)

Commonly some form of behaviour modification is designed to address the behaviour seen as associated with autism.

Oakley (2002) has noted how the tensions between medicine and educational practice and the differing professional roles can clash. Behavioural rating scales are an accessible, expedient way to quantify adult perception of students' behaviour and, in the case of AD/HD may result in a prescription for 'Ritalin'. However, assessment of behaviour which is intended to lead to an educational intervention needs to take account of a comprehensive range of factors that influence the student's behaviour in the context of school. In addition, as McLeod (1998) notes, in any relationship where the role of a professional is to influence the behaviour of others, there is an important question of ethics. This is particularly the case where the administration of mind-influencing medicines is involved. 'Underpinning ethical codes are a set of core moral principles: autonomy, non-maleficence, beneficence, justice and fidelity' (McLeod, 1998, p. 289).

Summary

There are many ways in which behaviour seen as problematic in schools may be interpreted. Different interpretations imply different interventions. However, in order to take clear account of the principles of inclusion for all students it is clearly important to take account of the basic human need for a sense of rootedness and acceptance in a social group which shows care and respect for its members. The sense of belonging to, or marginalisation from, a community affects every aspect of participation within it, including learning, behaviour and self perception. Failure to acknowledge, respect and engage students and fulfil universal basic needs may result in alienation from the education system of students from any social or cultural group.

References

Bishop, R. (1996) 'Addressing issues of self determination and legitimation in kaupapa Māori research', in B. Webber (ed) *He Paepae Kōrero Research Perspectives in Māori Education*, 143–160, Wellington: NZCER.

Blair, M. (2001) 'The education of Black children: why do some children do better than others?', in R. Majors (ed) *Educating Our Black Children: new directions and radical approaches*, 28–44, London: Routledge Falmer.

Bowlby, J. (1944) 'Forty-four juvenile thieves: their characters and home life', *International Journal of Psycho-Analysis*, **25**, 19–52, 107–27.

Bowlby, J. (1952) 'A two-year-old goes to hospital', *Proceedings of the Royal Society of Medicine*, 46, 425–427.

British Psychological Society (1997) *Attention Deficit Hyperactivity Disorder (ADHD): a psychological response to an evolving concept*, Leicester: BPS.

Bruner, J. (1996) *The Culture of Education*, London: Harvard University Press.

Campion, J. (1985) *The Child in Context: family systems theory in educational psychology*. London: Methuen.

Cooper, P. and Upton, G. (1991) 'Controlling the urge to control: an ecosystemic approach to behaviour in schools', *Support for Learning*, 6 (1), 22–26.

Davies, S. (2004) 'Barriers to belonging: students' perceptions of factors which affect participation in schools', in J. Wearmouth (ed) *Inclusion and Behaviour Management in Schools: issues and challenges*, London: Fulton.

Department for Education (1994) *Youth Cohort Study*, London: DfE.

Dowling, E. and Osbourne, E. (eds) (1985) *The Family and the School*, London: Routledge Kegan Paul.

Dwivedi, K. and Gupta, A. (2000) ' "Keeping cool": anger management through group work', *Support for Learning*, 15(2), 76–81.

Gewirtz, S., Ball, S. J., and Bowe, R. (1995) *Markets, Choice and Equity in Education*, Buckingham: Open University Press.

Gillborn, D. and Youdell, A. (2000) *Rationing Education: policy, practice, reform and equity*, Buckingham: Open University Press.

Gottfredson, D. C., Gottfredson, G. D. and Skroban, S. (1998) 'Can prevention work where it is needed most?' *Evaluation Review*, 22 (3), 315–340.

Hanko, G. (1994) 'Discouraged children: when praise does not help', *British Journal of Special Education*, 21 (4), 166–168.

Hargreaves, D. (1984) *Improving Secondary Schools*. London: ILEA.

Holmes, J. (1993) *John Bowlby and Attachment Theory*, London: Routledge.

Majors, R. and Billson J. M. (1992) *Cool Pose: the dilemmas of black manhood in America*, New York: Lexington Books.

McLeod, J. (1998) *An Introduction to Counselling*, 2nd edn, Buckingham: Open University Press.

Meichenbaum, D. and Turk, D. (1976) 'The cognitive-behavioural management of anxiety, anger and pain', in Davidson, P. O. (ed), *The Behavioural Management of Anxiety, Anger and Pain*, 1–34, New York: Brunner/Mazel.

Minuchin, S. (1974) *Families and Family Therapy*, Cambridge, Mass.: Harvard University Press.

Mortimore, P., Sammons, P., Stoll, L., Lewis, D. and Ecob, R. (1988) *School Matters. The Junior Years*, Wells: Open Books.

National Austistic Society (2004) 'What is autism?' downloaded on 19.01.04 from http://www.nas.org.uk/nas/jsp/polopoly.jsp?d=211

Norwich, B., Cooper, P. and Maras, P. (2002) 'Attentional and activity difficulties: findings from a national study', *Support for Learning*, 17 (4), 182–186.

Oakley, A. (2002) 'Social science and evidence-based everything: the case of education', *Educational Review*, 54 (3), 277–286.

OFSTED (2000) *Improving City Schools*, London: OFSTED.

OFSTED (2003) *Excellence in Cities and Education Action Zones: management and impact*, London: OFSTED.

Ogbu, J. U. (1997) 'Understanding the school performance of urban Blacks: some essential background knowledge', in H. Walberg, O. Reyes and R. Weissburg (eds) *Children and Youth: interdisciplinary perspectives*, London: Sage Productions.

Osborne, J. W. (2001) 'Academic disidentification: unravelling underachievement among Black boys', in R. Majors (ed) *Educating our Black children: new directions and radical approaches*, 45–58, London: Routledge Falmer.

Poulou, M. and Norwich, B. (2002) 'Cognitive, emotional and behavioural responses to students with emotional and behavioural difficulties: a model of decision-making', *British Educational Research Journal*, 28(1), 111–138.

Rampton, A. (1981) *West Indian Children in Our Schools*, Cmnd 8273, London: HMSO.

Rutter, M. *et al.* (1979) *Fifteen Thousand Hours: secondary schools and their effects on children*. London: Open Books.

Shapiro, E. S. and Cole, C. L. (1994) *Behaviour Change in the Classroom: self-management interventions*, New York: The Guilford Press.

Smith, G. (1995) 'Whakaoho whanau: new formations of whanau as an innovative intervention into Māori cultural and educational crisis', *He Pukenga Korero: A Journal of Māori Studies*, 1(1), 18–35.

Steele, C. (1992; 1997) 'A threat in the air: how stereotypes shape intellectual identity and performance', *American Psychologist*, 52, 613–629.

Swann, Lord (1985) *Education for All: final report of the Committee of Enquiry into the education of children from ethnic minority groups*, Cmnd 9453, London: HMSO.

Watkins, C. and Wagner, P. (2000) *Improving School Behaviour*, London: Paul Chapman.

Chapter 2

Perspectives on behaviour

Colin McCall

Introduction

The word behaviour has several meanings. First, it is used to describe capability. In this sense we speak of competent and incompetent behaviour. This implies the application of knowledge, skills and understanding in ways that are effective or inefficient. Second, we use behaviour as a descriptor of reaction. This can be social or anti-social actions, aggressive or non-aggressive responses, conforming or non-conforming dispositions. A third use of the term is to portray emotions. This may be in the form of a general connection, whereby we refer to behaviour that is determined by emotion rather than reason, or the link may be to a specific expression of an emotional nature – for example, a tendency to exhibit behaviour that is fearful or zealous. A fourth is to actions that can be interpreted as indications of particular traits of personality. Thus an individual may exhibit anxiety, extroversion/introversion, depression or self-actualisation. A fifth, and for most people the most worrying feature of the range of human response, is when actions are experienced by others as troublesome. Thus, we may speak of abnormal behaviour, challenging behaviour, delinquent behaviour, violent behaviour, and so on.

This plethora of meanings arises from a number of influences:

- the interest there has been down the centuries to describe, classify, explain, control and utilise the myriad of human characteristics referred to as 'behaviour';
- the obvious fact that a variety of motives, actions and functions may underlie a specific 'manner of behaving';
- the need in social settings, such as the home, school and community to promote behaviour that is regarded as positive, self-preserving and respectful of social conventions;

- linked with the previous point, the desire to cure or support those whose behaviour is judged to be troublesome to themselves or others, or at least to prevent its further manifestation as a later and perhaps more enduring problem for other people.

Historical and cultural roots

The subject of behaviour is both long in historical connections and multi-disciplinary in nature. For centuries it has been in close focus and has permeated the thoughts and theories of anthropologists, philosophers, politicians, psychologists, sociologists and theologians. Everyone has a view of what behaviour is, how it should be regarded and what constitutes behaviour that is acceptable and non-acceptable. However, these viewpoints, dispositions and parameters of acceptability are in themselves not static conditions. They change from culture to culture, and from one generation to the next. They do this because of shifting values and changed reactions to perceived or actual crises. These crises in themselves emanate from our attempts to put political, social and tribal beliefs into practice.

The nature of behaviour and reactions to it also tend to fluctuate along a wide continuum of tolerance. At one end is the libertarian bias that seems to stand against any suggestion of restricting individual freedom of choice, an almost total 'rights zone' that is free of any balancing responsibilities. At the other end is the early Spartan ethic, that individuals should be trained in the services of the collective good, which in this case was the needs of a military society, 'responsibility writ large' with little room for individual rights. Somewhere in between comes the argument that individual expression must not be stifled nor allowed to roam free and uncontrolled – rather, human behaviour has to be shaped until its holder reaches some position of accepting self-discipline and the equilibrium of personal rights balanced with personal responsibilities.

One strong cultural factor, prevalent in most societies, has been the inclination to describe behaviour that is normal and thereby to contrast normal features with other behaviours labelled abnormal. O'Brien (1998) also sees powerful assumptions underlying how the topic of behaviour, including 'challenging behaviour', is perceived and defined. These assumptions rest on a range of interacting factors that need to be taken into consideration if useful understanding is to be exercised by those who design and implement intervention:

> These factors include individual and school pathology, gender, social, economic and cultural factors. Psychological and biological factors must also be considered. The term also indicates that the challenge can be caused by the effect that the behaviour has on the lives of others.
>
> (O'Brien, 1998, p.5)

Until recent decades, the conceptualisation of behaviour and behaviour difficulties has been focused largely on the individual and the individual perspective. Questions such as why does she behave like that? – or, why can't he control this behaviour? – have been centre stage. Answering them has been approached either by viewing behaviour as pathology, that is, a disorder stemming from early experiences trapped in the unconscious or subconscious mind, or as caused by physical factors, or by focusing on how exhibited behaviour has been learned and how it may need to be ameliorated and restructured. The psychodynamic practitioners lead the former approach, behavioural psychology the latter. The focus on 'abnormal' behaviour has led to what has come to be known as the 'medical model' of human functioning. The notion of 'disorder' has resulted in a whole range of therapies for treating behaviour that is troublesome for the individual or the community. The concept of disorders is at the extreme end of the troublesome spectrum, and the idea of psychosomatic conditions is at the milder end. Though much earlier somatic therapy has been abandoned, as the power of the medical model has lessened under the influence of new insights and new approaches, many perceived behavioural abnormalities or behavioural difficulties are still treated using chemotherapy, electrical stimulation techniques and surgical intervention. There is now renewed energy to examine associations between behavioural difficulties and prevailing diet, allergies and biochemical changes, the latter occurring through exposure to the environment and the ageing process. Coupled with this renewal, is a growing tendency to more readily approve of such interventions as antidepressants, electroconvulsive therapy, hypnosis, psychotherapy and somatic inhibitors and stimulants. For some commentators, the far end of this tendency is the controversial idea of a risk-free, no-blame culture. Here, the perpetrator of an unacceptable act is seen as equally blameless as the victim. S/he was caught up in responding to forces s/he could not control or was demonstrating difficult behaviour that should have been identified and managed much earlier.

An equally strong cultural influence has been an approach to behaviour education and behaviour management known as the learning model and associated with behavioural or cognitive-behavioural psychology. This views troublesome and aberrant behaviour as emanating from faulty learning or insufficient learning. This view has led to a close examination of how (a) learning is modelled by parents and others, and (b) to consider how far personal dispositions such as acting out, anxiety, conduct difficulties, eating disorders, irrational beliefs, obsessive-compulsive actions and severe helplessness are learned responses. In turn, this approach has led to interventions that emphasise new learning or reconstructed learning. Techniques used include behaviour shaping, cognitive conceptualisation, desensitisation training, modelling, drama, role-play and social skills training.

The assumption underlying the early work in all these schools of thought has been that behaviour resides largely, if not entirely, 'within' the individual and to 'cure it' or 'resolve it' requires finding the right treatment or process of intervention. This assumption has also been prevalent in many models of group interaction, since despite the fact that a group may be brought together for a session of therapy, encounter or reflection, the approach is still person-centred therapy as opposed to examining 'collective influence' and the 'effects of institutions'.

A shift from a focus on the individual to the dynamics of social systems came about from the 1940s forward, largely under the influence of four major trends. These were:

- a move away from a 'within the child' perspective to look at problems that may reside in relationships and a 'family's system' of interaction (Kohut 1977);
- the development of the concept of 'ecosystems' and its application to human behaviour, resulting in stronger recognition that both inner body and outer environmental influences affect behaviour (Bronfenbrenner 1979);
- a focus within the social sciences and philosophy on 'systems analysis/therapy' and the implications for managing 'whole institutional' responses to individuals and the needs of communities as a whole (Foucault 1980, Kelly 1966 and Walker 1991);
- the development, in particular within anthropology and sociology, of social constructivist approaches, whereby the individual and group are examined as far as possible through understanding the norms and values of their culture, as opposed to imposing methods of observation and intervention drawn from other rules and other societies (Berger and Luckman 1967, Said 1994, Stainton Rogers 1992).

Both approaches, individual focus and systems focus, have resulted in intervention regimes that can be seen in some guise or other in operation in schools and other institutions. These interventions include the Antecedent-Behaviour-Consequence functional analysis model based on behaviourist principles (Wheldall and Merrett 1984), Assertive Discipline in educational settings (Canter and Canter 1976), personal and social education through the use of Circle Time (Goldthorpe 1998), client centred therapy (Rogers 1959), the operation of merit systems and reward schedules and positive behaviour modelling for the individual using situational analyses and role play.

Close consideration of the operation of situational factors, social conditions and institutions as systems tend to be found in those approaches that see the demands of learning, behaviour, community living and emotional development as intertwined in many ways. Thus attention may be focused on implementing behaviour policies (DES, 1989) differentiation within teaching and learning (Visser, 1993), the promotion of effective environments (Brighouse and Woods 1999), the development of emotional literacy (Goleman 1996), the characteristics of effective practice in schools and other settings that demonstrate good discipline and successful anti-bullying regimes (Watkins and Wagner 2000, Rigby 2002), the development of large-scale frameworks for intervention (Birmingham City Council 1998), the consideration of pastoral influences (McCall and Lawlor 2002), the encouragement of pupils' courts and school councils (Braithwaite, 1997), helping young people to understand and cope with the context of social changes they are experiencing (Lloyd 1997), the use of nurture groups in early education (Bennathan 2000 and Boxall 1976) and victim-offender reconciliation programmes (Woolpert 1991).

Contemporary thinking

Whether the focus is upon understanding behaviour and its effects by examining an individual's behavioural repertoire of itself, or the manner in which that behaviour is supported or sustained in different settings, a common approach now seems to be that any difficult behaviour is the result of the interaction between the individual and the environment. The emphasis tends to be on working from a positive attitude towards individuals (Cava 1990). In practical terms this assumption implies a far-reaching and demanding stance. For example, it suggests that:

- there has to be co-operation with others at international, national, regional and institutional levels, to define and formulate shared values, behavioural standards and a behavioural code;
- the code should extend across the 'rights–responsibilities' continuum;
- any arising charters and policies related to behaviour should be framed positively and optimistically, rather than in draconian form with the focus on just lists of sanctions;
- labels or categories for behaviour that becomes troublesome have to be better defined than they are currently; they need to refer explicitly to the nature of the behaviour, its antecedents and consequences;
- the manner and means by which adults regard each other and communicate with one another should model respect and value for the other party, a ready acceptance that the real meaning of any message in its day-to-day medium of transmission, in schools and elsewhere, is that it is no longer possible to adopt the 'do as I say, but not as I do' approach, it now has no credence;

- tackling difficult behaviour requires acting together so that the behaviour does not become strongly reinforced because the responsible team or lead community, or some of its key members, pass the buck;
- acting together implies establishing agreement about the rules, the boundaries and the 'highway code' that should direct the management of behaviour.

(Thomas 1997)

Implications for multi-disciplinary and multi-agency approaches

A variety of professionals in the course of their daily practice encounter people with behavioural needs and/or troublesome behaviour. Increasingly one professional group has to work with others to design a suitable policy and programme to carry forward the focus and nature of intervention and support. For example, at the school interface alone, a team response may involve teachers, learning support assistants, clinical psychologists, educational psychologists, educational welfare officers, school medical officers, social workers, therapists and counsellors, and other staff with psychiatric oversight. The management of these contributions may be invested in (i) a single lead service, (ii) the co-ordination of different management perspectives and agendas through regular review meetings, or (iii) there may be no united approach and those 'engaged in multi-agency work' may have to pull together the disparate professional skills and expertise as best they can. There may be an oversight group or steering group to whom the different professionals and the team as a whole are accountable, or the quality assurance arrangements may not be so formalised.

The nature of multi-disciplinary and multi-agency perspectives and the consequent actions may be further complicated by the exact nature of the service being delivered. In general, with the trend to focus as much as possible on preventative work, the location for intervention and the duration of that intervention, in terms of attendance and contact time, may vary significantly. Individuals and teams of professionals may find themselves working in or supporting one or more contexts. These may include:

- holding/containing centres;
- base support centres;
- community service teams;
- outreach work to sustain attendance and development within a host school, hospital or support agency;
- in-home education or in-house support to a programme of personal development.

Conclusion

The different potential disciplinary perspectives, the different team compositions and the different locations for engaging with the individual or the group who need support implies a conceptual structure in place and a set of procedures that are understood and workable across the various teams and the different contexts. This necessitates:

- a common understanding of the meaning that is attached to behaviour and an appreciation of the values and assumptions that underpin it;
- a conceptualisation of how the working model of behaviour interconnects with the broader political and social context, e.g. the inclusion debate;
- a coherent model of behaviour education and behaviour support (including taking into account competing ideologies);
- the incorporation of that model within operating wider policy initiatives (e.g. at the levels of the local education authority, the health trust, etc.);
- an agreement on the balance of focus in intervention – for example, sustaining existing provision, preventative work, action-based research, the level of multi-agency involvement;
- some declaration of 'realistic entitlement' for clients and staff in terms of what services/resources can be provided;
- agreed referral procedures;
- a framework to translate intentions into working structures and practices;
- a common approach to the use of rewards and sanctions;
- the development of any necessary team-building and team maintenance activities;
- a framework to evaluate the efficacy of the work done.

References

Bennathan, M. (2000) 'Children at risk of failure in primary schools', chapter 1 in M. Bennathan and M. Boxall *Effective Intervention in Primary Schools: nurture groups*, 2nd edn, London: David Fulton Publishers.

Berger, P. L. and Luckman, T. (1967) *The Social Construction of Reality: A Treatise in the Sociology of Knowledge*. Garden City, NY: Anchor Books.

Birmingham City Council (1998) *Behaviour in Schools: framework for intervention*. Birmingham Education Department.

Boxall, M. (1976) *The Nurture Group in the Primary School*, London: ILEA.

Braithwaite, J. (1997) *Restorative Justice: Assessing an Immodest Theory and a Pessimistic Theory*. Australian Institute of Criminology, Australian National University.

Brighouse, T. and Woods, D. (1999) *How to Improve Your School*, London: Routledge.

Bronfenbrenner, U. (1979) *The Ecology of Human Development*, Cambridge, Mass.: Harvard University Press.

Canter, L. and Canter, M. (1976) *Assertive Discipline: a take charge approach for today's education*, Santa Monica, CA: Lee Canter Associates.

Cava, R. (1990) *Dealing with Difficult People*, London: Piatkus Publishers Ltd.

DES (1989) *Discipline in Schools* (the Elton Report). London: HMSO.

Foucault, M. (1980) *The History of Sexuality* (trans. R. Hurley), Vol. 1. New York: Vintage Press.

Goldthorpe, M. (1998) *Effective IEPS through Circle Time*, Cambridge: LDA.

Goleman, D. (1996) *Emotional Intelligence: why it matters more than IQ*, London: Bloomsbury.

Kelly, G. A. (1966), quoted in B. A. Maher (ed) (1979) *Clinical Psychology and Personality: the selected papers of George Kelly*. Huntington, NY: Kreiger.

Kohut, H. (1977) *The Restoration of the Self*. New York: International Universities Press.

Lloyd, T. (1997) *Let's Get Changed Lads: developing work with boys and young men*, London: Working with Men.

McCall, C. and Lawlor, H. (2002) *Leading and Managing Effective Learning*, London: Optimus Publishing.

O'Brien, T. (1998) *Promoting Positive Behaviour*, London: David Fulton Publishers.

Rigby, K. (2002) *New Perspectives on Bullying*, London: Jessica Kingsley Publishers Ltd.

Rogers, C. R. (1959) 'A theory of therapy, personality and interpersonal relationships, as developed in the client-centred framework', in S. Koch (ed) *Psychology: a study of science*, Vol. 3, 184–526, New York: McGraw-Hill.

Said, E. (1994) *Orientalism: Western conceptions of the Orient*, Harmondsworth: Penguin.

Stainton Rogers, R. (1992) 'The social construction of childhood', in

Stainton Rogers, W., Hevey, D., Roche, J. and Ash, E. (eds) *Child Abuse and Neglect: facing the challenge*, 23–29, London: Batsford/The Open University.

Thomas, L. (1997) 'Managing pupil behaviour', in Craig, I. (ed) *Managing Primary Classrooms*, London: Pitman Publishing.

Visser, J. (1993) *Making It Work*. Tamworth: NASEN.

Walker, G. (1991) *In the Midst of Winter: systematic therapy with families, couples and individuals with AIDS*, New York: Norton.

Watkins, C. and Wagner, P. (2000) *Improving School Behaviour*, London: Paul Chapman.

Wheldall, K. and Merrett, F. (1984) *Positive Teaching: the behavioural approach*, London: Allen and Unwin.

Woolpert, S. (1991) 'Victim–offender reconciliation programs', in K. G. Duffy, J. W. Grosch and P. V. Olczak (eds) *Community Mediation: a handbook for practitioners and researchers*, 276–297, New York: Guilford Press.

PART 1
Research

Chapter 3

Marginalisation in primary schools: listening to children's voices

Kyriaki Messiou

Introduction

Children's views about educational practices have often been neglected, perhaps because of assumptions of their inability to give accurate information about what is happening in schools. In this chapter I argue that children's voices should be taken into consideration in relation to the development of inclusive practices. This is not simply because of children's right to be heard but, more importantly, because their perspectives can help us to move forward in relation to improvements in the field.

Inclusive education and the direction of this research

Inclusive education refers to the education of all children within their local community in their neighbourhood school (Sebba and Ainscow, 1996; Udvari-Solner and Thousand, 1995). But more importantly, as Farrell (2000) emphasises, the term inclusion involves a focus on the quality of education provided for students. Advocates of inclusion come, therefore, to talk about a school's competence to include each child effectively. Though initially inclusion was associated only with children defined as having special needs, nowadays some authors see inclusion in even broader terms. For example, Booth and Ainscow (1998) suggest that:

> ... inclusion or exclusion are as much about participation and marginalisation in relation to race, class, gender, sexuality, poverty and unemployment as they are about traditional special educational concerns with students categorised as low in attainment, disabled or deviant in behaviour.
>
> (Booth and Ainscow, 1998, p. 2)

Taking this perspective, inclusion is seen as related to notions of special needs, but also in terms of forms of marginalisation that might be experienced by any child in a school. This was the perspective that was followed in this study. For me, inclusive education is more like a puzzle for which each one of us holds some different pieces. Without having all the pieces the picture can never be complete. However, it is possible to go further. Even if we have all the pieces in our hands, we have to put them together to get the full picture.

I am not suggesting that there is a blueprint for the inclusive school. My experience is that the picture for the puzzle is unique in each case. My argument is that unless the views of everybody who is affected are seriously taken into consideration in this process with no limits (Ballard, 1995), then opportunities for development will be overlooked.

This, then, is the rationale on which this study was based: the belief that children hold a big part of the puzzle's pieces. To this end, no matter what policies may say, no matter what resources are available and what changes have been made, those that really experience inclusive or exclusive practices are the children. Consequently, don't they have the right to be heard?

Recently a number of studies have investigated children's perspectives in relation to inclusive practices (e.g. Ainscow, Booth and Dyson, 1999; Allan, 1999; Lewis, 1995; Mordal and Stromstad, 1998; Vlachou, 1997). However, in most of the studies considered so far, which investigated children's perspectives in relation to inclusive practices, the term inclusion was addressed from the angle of special needs. As Ainscow (2000) suggests, focusing only on special needs is very limiting as an agenda. In addition, when the focus is only on special needs there is for me a tension between the theory of inclusion and the practical task of carrying out research. For example, by going into a classroom and singling out individuals for attention, there is a danger that this contributes to marginalisation by reproducing certain stereotypes associated with special needs.

Taking into account these concerns and following a broader definition of inclusion, the study described here had two aims. First of all, it aimed to bring to the surface the voices of children who experience marginalisation in schools, regardless of whether these children are perceived as having special needs or not. In other words, it was an attempt to listen carefully to what children have to say about marginalisation, and explore what they do about it. In such a way I assumed that we might gain better understandings, which could then be used to inform the improvement of more inclusive practices. Second, my aim was to explore methodological issues related to the way that primary age children's views can be captured.

In essence, then, my research questions were:

- How do children explain and define being marginalised?
- How do these children feel about marginalisation?
- How do they respond to it?

To sum up, this study is an effort to add something to the understanding of this complex process, called inclusive education, through attempts to study the way children see and experience their lives in school. It is certainly acknowledged that children's understandings constitute only one of the multiple dimensions involved in the process. As Allan (1999) suggests, 'the pupils' accounts are not essentialized and treated as indicative of how things *really* are' (p. 1). They were therefore viewed as part of the rather complex picture of inclusive practices.

Methodology

The study was carried out in a primary school in the UK that is making efforts towards inclusive practices and was then participating in the ESRC-funded project, 'Understanding and Developing Inclusive Practices in Schools', in collaboration with the University of Manchester. In order to explore the above questions in close detail I decided that it would be better if I concentrated only on one particular classroom. A Year 3 classroom with 32 children was chosen. This classroom included some children with hearing impairments, though the focus was not solely on these pupils.

Theories of inclusion were seen as being central to the development of the methodology. Therefore, children who possibly experience marginalisation were identified in relation to three perspectives:

- children's own views
- my observations in the school
- teacher's point of view.

Taking into consideration all the above perspectives the aim was to make an identification of children who experience marginalisation that would be valid. By combining these three perspectives data were triangulated and therefore final decisions on the children who experience marginalisation can be said to be more valid. Whereas, if this choice was made based only on my observations, for instance, maybe some other dimensions experienced by the children or the teacher could have been missed. One of my concerns before conducting the study was about what I would do if the three perspectives diverged a lot from one another. Since the study had the children at its centre, I decided that the prevailing voices would be theirs, but always taking into consideration the other perspectives. Interestingly, there were no huge discrepancies among the three perspectives.

Qualitative methods were used. In particular, it was decided that since the children's views along with their actual behaviours were of interest, observational methods along with interviews with the children were appropriate. In addition triangulation of the two methods was used to enhance the credibility and trustworthiness of the data. Moreover, I felt that in order for children's views to make sense, these had to be viewed in the context they were coming from. As Maykut and Morehouse (1994) suggest 'in order to understand any human phenomenon we must investigate it as part of the context within which it lies' (p. 68).

The study was divided into two parts. The aim of the first part of the study was to spot children who might experience marginalisation. Open participant observations were carried out in the classroom and in the playground. At the same time semi-structured interviews with all the children in the classroom were carried out. These observations, along with the interviews, served as the platform for more focused observations of particular children.

At the beginning of each interview issues of confidentiality were clarified and children were asked to choose a pseudonym for themselves. The aim of these initial interviews was to allow voices of dissatisfaction to emerge. For ethical reasons it was not possible to ask directly about marginalisation. Moreover, it is a term that would be very difficult for children of that age to understand. So, I had to find a way that would allow 'voices of despair' to be heard but without asking explicitly. Here Davies's (2000) technique of a 'Message in a bottle' seemed appropriate. She used this approach to investigate children's democratic understandings in the primary school. With a variation in the instruction, since the purpose of this research was different, children were asked to write a message which would be sent to another planet, saying what they would like to change at school, if they could change one thing. Then, discussions followed according to the wish each child expressed. In addition, children were asked to say other things they did not really like at school, and things they did like, and to explain why.

The second aim of these interviews was to explore what children thought about other children in their class. Sociometric ratings were used for this investigation. An adaptation of Moreno's (1978), and Hall and McGregor's (2000), method of peer nominations was used. Children were asked to identify three children from their classroom that they would like to work with, three they would not like to work with, three they would like to play with and three they would not like to play with. Figure 3.1 shows the number of nominations that each child got for two of the prompts.

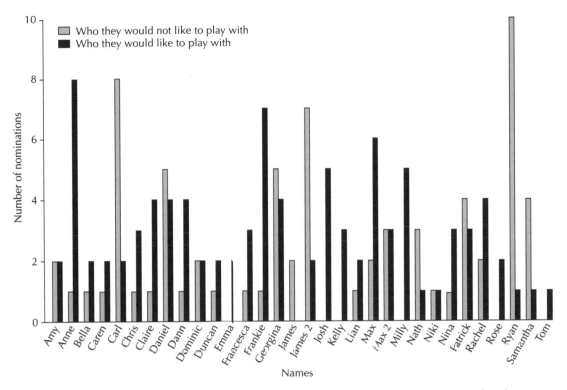

Figure 3.1 Number of nominations that each child got for two of the prompts: who they would like to play with and who they would not like to play with. *Note: Though the total number of children's nominations for each prompt should be 96 (32 × 3), this is not the case, because some children chose to give less than 3 names in some cases.*

From children's nominations sociograms were developed which identified the 'stars' of the class (as referred to by Moreno, 1978), as well as the least accepted children in the class. It should be noted that sociometric measures were also used here as a means for a further exploration of children's choices. Therefore, children were asked to give reasons for these choices and explain in more detail why they made the specific choices.

To sum up, each interview provided three areas of information:

• what children would like to change at school and why
• children's likes and dislikes in relation to school
• children's preferences among their classmates (who to work with, who not to work with, who to play with, who not to play with) and the reasons they made the specific choices.

All the interviews were tape recorded and transcribed. After this first round of interviews with all the children in the class was completed, an analysis of these and of the observations that had been made up to that point followed. This analysis, along with talks that I had with the teacher, led to the identification of four children that I suspected as possibly experiencing marginalisation. Therefore, my final decision was based on this data triangulation which in my view enhanced the validity of the study. What I mean is that if, for example, I had taken into consideration only one of the perspectives mentioned above, then my decisions could have been different. For example, as can be seen in Figure 3.1, Ryan was one of the children that many of his classmates mentioned they would not like to play with, and it could therefore be assumed that he was less accepted and more marginalised by others. However, this was not supported either by my observations or by what the teacher thought. But more importantly Ryan himself did not express any feelings of marginalisation. On the contrary, he said that he had many friends to play with; something that I also confirmed with my observations. Of course, it could be said, why then did all those children say that they did not want to play with him? My assumption is that, because Ryan was sometimes misbehaving in the classroom and the teacher used to tell him off a lot, maybe this created a negative view towards him. However, children did play with him as I found out in my observations. What is important is that this data triangulation enabled me to question and be more critical of the evidence I was collecting.

In the second part of the study, more focused observations followed, with shadowing of the particular children who were identified as possibly experiencing marginalisation. A second round of interviews with those four children followed as well. The aim was to explore whether these children truly experienced marginalisation and, if they did, how they felt about it and how they responded to it. It was explained to all the children that when I heard the tapes of their interviews there were some points that I wanted to clarify with some children and that was why I would interview certain pupils for a second time.

Again, for ethical reasons I could not tell these children directly that I suspected that they were experiencing marginalisation. I therefore chose to use drawing as an elicitation technique and from that starting point explore whether these children truly experienced marginalisation and, if they did, how they felt about it and in what ways they responded to it. So, after the clarifications related to the first interview were made, each child was asked to draw a picture showing something that happened at school that made them feel unhappy or sad. Discussions followed in relation to the specific incidents they drew.

These interviews were also tape recorded and transcribed. Apart from the transcripts the drawings of the children were also another source of information. All these data were then analysed. Open coding was used for the analysis of the data, and in particular descriptive coding was used. Certain categories were then developed. For example, one of the categories developed was 'Responses' under which the subcategories 'rather active' and 'rather passive' were placed (specific examples for these categories will be provided in the next section).

Findings

Taking into account the children's, the teacher's and my perspectives, four children were identified as possibly experiencing marginalisaton in this classroom. Specifically, these four children's experiences of marginalisation seemed to be related to different factors. However, there were some common themes in relation to the way children felt and the way they responded. It was noticeable, for example, that children's feelings and responses were closely related to the way that other children behaved towards them. This finding is in accordance with Allan's (1999) work, as well as the findings of Ainscow et al. (1999).

So, for example, three of the children when they were asked to draw something that happened at school and made them feel unhappy, drew an incident from the playground which involved other children. The fourth child also drew something which took place in the playground but did not involve any other children. In addition, the explanations they gave involved other children. For instance, one of the children expressed feelings of unhappiness because the other children called her names and made fun of her because of her appearance (they called her fat). Another boy, who had a hearing impairment, expressed feelings of unhappiness and marginalisation in relation to his religion. Particularly, he said that people at school are throwing his hat because they don't like him going to that school because his religion is different (he said that one boy told him that). It seems, therefore, that his experience of marginalisation did not have anything to do, at least in his own understanding, with the fact that he had a hearing impairment and had to spend time out of the classroom but with the fact that his religion was different. This was a belief which was created because of what other children did and said. Another boy, who had to spend time outside the classroom for individual support, said that he did not want to be outside the mainstream classroom because he wanted to be with the other children. Conversely, there was a boy who experienced difficulties with learning and said that he would prefer to receive special help in another setting so that he would be better in the classroom and not have to ask for help from other children. So again, it could be said that the way he was thinking and feeling was influenced by his peers' actions. It seems, therefore, that children give more emphasis to social aspects of school life, rather than its academic practices and the way that classrooms are organised.

In addition, these four children's responses ranged from rather active ones to rather passive ones, as I chose to name them, and again these were influenced by other children's behaviour. However, sometimes children used a combination of both responses. I will use an example from my observations in the classroom: The teacher has given each group a small white board and she has asked them to write one sentence each in the third person singular. She first asks them to give themselves numbers and then write the sentences accordingly. I sit next to Samantha's group and they have an argument on who is going to be which number. Samantha and Lian both want to be number one. The others do not seem to bother. Samantha tells her that she always wants to be first and this is unfair. While they are still discussing this the teacher says that they have run out of time, and she asks to see who is each number in each group. When she calls for all number ones to raise hands, Lian signals to Samantha to raise her hand. So, it seemed that she has accepted that Samantha will be number one. However, when Samantha picks up the white board and starts writing the day and the date on the top, Lian grasps the white board from Samantha's hands, rubs out what she wrote, starts writing the same things again and then starts writing the first sentence. Lian becomes number one in the end. Samantha just stares at her without saying or doing anything.

In the above incident Samantha's first kind of behaviour was a rather active one where she supported the fact that she wanted to be number one and that it was unfair that Lian always got it. However, within a short period of time she showed that she accepted the situation and behaved in a rather passive way. Why didn't she complain to defend herself? Why did she choose not to say anything and let Lian do what she wanted? These are two areas for further investigation.

Reflections on the methodology

I experienced many challenges in finding ways in which primary-aged children's views could be captured. At the same time I was left in no doubt that it was valuable in relation to the development of inclusive practices. In particular, the actual techniques used proved to be helpful in understanding more about what children think about school and how they feel about certain experiences. The 'Message in a bottle' idea worked very well for the purposes for which it was used, as did the children's drawings. The only technique I would question is the sociometric measures and the sociograms that were derived from them. I am in a position to say this since I also asked children to give me the reasons for the specific nominations they made. Interestingly enough, though they gave different names of children for the different prompts (who they would like to play with; who they would like to work with, etc.), they gave more or less the same reasons. How then did they choose different children?

It was also interesting that on the last day that I went to the school one girl said that she wanted to talk to me about something. She asked me to change her second nomination of who she would like to play with, since she had now changed her mind. This suggests that sociograms can only provide us with a rough indication of children's preferences and that we should not rely on them. More importantly, in terms of ethical issues, sociometric measures may not be appropriate since children are asked to think in negative ways about their classmates.

Reflecting on these techniques I would say that their potential lies in the fact that they enable adults to gain access into children's way of thinking in a rather playful and enjoyable way. Therefore, though the techniques described above were used for the purposes of this research they could be very easily used by teachers themselves in an effort to understand how children feel and think about the school, in order to modify their practices for the benefit of all children.

Conclusion

Having completed this study, I am left conscious of the individuality of each child. Clearly this has implications for teachers and their work. It would be, of course, rather naïve to claim that our practices can be tailored in such ways that each voice is always satisfied. It would also be naïve to claim that it is feasible to take into consideration each child's preferences and organise our practices accordingly. However, what I am claiming here is that if we are aware of such voices we might be able at least to be more sensitive to individual perspectives.

While I was carrying out this research I shared with the classroom teacher some of the data I was collecting, along with my initial thoughts that later provided the basis for data analysis. At one point she said: 'I am so sorry that these children won't be mine next year. Now that I know, I could do something about them.' Surely this is exactly what inclusion is about. It makes us think about new possibilities and, therefore, act in new ways that can improve the participation and learning of all children.

I am certain that there are as many issues uncovered and as many voices still unheard as the ones that I managed to bring to the surface. The four children were only four possible children in the particular classroom who were experiencing marginalisation. What is important is that through listening to their voices we were stimulated to think in different ways and look beyond the obvious.

Acknowledgements

I would like to thank the Overseas Research Students Awards Scheme and the University of Manchester for providing me with financial support to conduct this research, and especially my supervisor Professor Mel Ainscow for reading and commenting on an earlier draft of this chapter.

The study was partly funded by Award L139 25 1001 from the Economic and Social Research Council.

References

Ainscow, M., Booth, T. and Dyson, A. (1999) Inclusion and exclusion in schools: listening to some hidden voices. In K. Ballard (ed.) *Inclusive Education: International Voices on Disability and Justice*. London: Falmer Press.

Ainscow, M. (2000) Profile. In P. Clough and J. Corbett (eds) *Theories of Inclusive Education*. London: Paul Chapman.

Allan, J. (1999) *Actively Seeking Inclusion: Pupils with Special Needs in Mainstream Schools*. London: Falmer Press.

Ballard, K. (1995) Inclusion, paradigms, power and participation. In C. Clark, A. Dyson and A. Millward (eds) *Towards Inclusive Schools?* London: Fulton.

Booth, T. and Ainscow, M. (1998) (eds) *From Them to Us*. London: Routledge.

Davies, L. (2000) Researching democratic understanding in primary school. *Research in Education*, **61**, 39–48.

Farrell, P. (2000) The impact of research on developments in inclusive education. *International Journal of Inclusive Education*, **4**(2), 153–162.

Hall, L. J. and McGregor, J. A. (2000) A follow-up study of the peer relationship of children with disabilities in an inclusive school. *The Journal of Special Education*, **34**(3), 114–126.

Lewis, A. (1995) *Children's Understanding of Disability*. London: Routledge.

Maykut, P. and Morehouse, R. (1994) *Beginning Qualitative Research*. Bristol: Falmer Press.

Mordal, K. N. and Stromstad, M. (1998) Norway: adapted education for all? In T. Booth and M. Ainscow (eds) *From Them to Us*. London: Routledge.

Moreno, J. L. (1978) *Who Shall Survive?* New York: Beacon House.

Sebba, J. and Ainscow, M. (1996) International developments in inclusive schooling: mapping the issues. *Cambridge Journal of Education*, **26**(1), 5–18.

Udvari-Solner, A. and Thousand, J. (1995) Effective organizational, instructional and curricular practices in inclusive schools and classrooms. In C. Clark, A. Dyson and A. Millward (eds) *Towards Inclusive Schools?*. London: Fulton.

Vlachou, A. D. (1997) *Struggles for Inclusive Education*. Buckingham: Open University Press.

Chapter 4

Engaging with the views of disaffected students through 'Talking Stones'

Janice Wearmouth

Introduction

'Talking Stones' is an interview technique that is designed to support self advocacy particularly for groups of disaffected students whose views may be difficult to ascertain. It makes an assumption that, for the individual student, everything is perceived and mediated by what is salient, socially and personally. This chapter illustrates how the technique lends itself to practice in schools by laying bare problematic relationships between, commonly, students and teachers, and opening up dialogue between them.

Student self advocacy in schools

It seems obvious that behavioural interventions and learning programmes are likely to be more effective when students have some sense of ownership over them. Taking the young person's view seriously and attempting to understand his/her perspective is essential to any consideration of how we might reduce barriers to students' learning (Hart, 1995). In studying what teachers and students understand by 'effective teaching' Cooper and McIntyre (1996), for example, concluded that:

- effective learning outcomes in classrooms are often seen as arising out of interactions between teachers' concerns and perceptions and those of their students;

- students prefer active rather than passive involvement in lessons and that student involvement and participation in lessons is a vital component for effectiveness;
- some of the characteristics of effective teacher–student relationships are collaboration, co-operation and co-option rather than coercion;
- some of the conclusions reached in relation to effective teaching ad learning accord with established theories of learning proposed by Vygotsky and Bruner.

In England, Wales and Northern Ireland, the right of students to self advocacy during the process of assessing, and drawing up Statements of Special Educational Needs to address individual difficulties in learning, including those associated with behaviour, is an area of particular focus, exemplified by the guidance given in England in the *Special Educational Needs Code of Practice* (DfES, 2001, chapter 3, pp 27–31). International law also supports student self advocacy. For example, in the United Nations Convention on the Rights of the Child (1989), Article 12 states:

> Parties shall assure to the child who is capable of forming his or her own views the right to express those views freely in all matters affecting the child, the views of the child being given due weight in accordance with the age and maturity of the child.
>
> For this purpose the child shall in particular be provided the opportunity to be heard in any judicial or administrative proceedings affecting the child, either directly or through a representative or an appropriate body, in a manner consistent with the procedural rules of national law.

Article 13 (1) states:

> The child shall have the right to freedom of expression; this right shall include the freedom to seek, receive and impart information and ideas of all kinds, regardless of all frontiers, either orally or in print, in the form of art or any other media of the child's choice.

Over the past 20 years there has been progress in involving children more actively in their education. However, 'such progress as has occurred has been patchy, unsystematic and slow' (Gersch, 2001, p 228), leaving 'a wealth of untapped resource for teachers, schools and other professionals' (ibid).

Engaging with students' views 'may not always be easy' (DfES, 2001, 3:3), however. In many schools professionals will have encountered students with whom communication has been difficult:

> Many are socially isolated and, to judge by body language, feel appalled at their own loneliness yet just cannot do anything about it. I well remember the case of 'Peter', undernourished, dirty, smelly, and always alone, but hovering as close to the entrance of the school building as he could manage. Deliberation on the situation led me to try to get him involved in a lunchtime mutual-support group of students, but was told on the phone by his father: 'I'm not having my son associating with a load of drongos …

I don't want him labelled.' ... I could never find a way to communicate with 'Peter' to see if there was anything the school could do to support him better.

'Arnold' was another student about whom I had many concerns. Over the two years I worked with him in a comprehensive upper (13–18) school his written work showed just how little progress he seemed to have made in literacy skills. He just did not seem to care. He came to school in a shirt that was always dirty. He smelled of body odour and nicotine. I never knew what 'Arnold' was thinking. I never knew what he felt about his own lack of literacy. If we had known, it might have made a difference either to our approach or to the outcome educationally. 'Arnold' left school functionally illiterate.

(Wearmouth, 2003)

Some, like 'Larry', interviewed in a study of adults' recollections of school, may reject any approach from teachers:

I really didn't want teachers to know me ... They just did their job and no more. I got help when I wanted it – eventually. I didn't want teachers hanging around me.

(Wearmouth, 2000)

For a number of reasons it is particularly important to understand how students who are disaffected from school and disengaged with school learning feel about the learning environment and themselves as learners. Failure to address the 'problems' of non-engagement with their education of significant numbers of disaffected students costs society dearly 'both in terms of reduced economic contribution in adult life and, for some, of criminal activity and prison' (DfEE, 1997, p. 78). In addition, in recent years in the special educational needs field, there has been a move towards a view that the source of students' difficulties in learning, including those difficulties associated with challenging behaviour, may arise as a result of aspects of the learning environment (Clark et al, 1997; 1998; Cline, 1992; Cooper, 1993; Davies et al, 1998, Dyson, 1997). Sometimes the source of difficulties is described as stemming from the interaction between the characteristics of the learner and those of the context (Wedell, 2000; Mittler, 2000). Following this line of thinking requires a re-conceptualisation of the learner as active agent in his/her own learning, and of both learning and behaviour as dynamic between learner and context if students are to become active participants in schools' communities of learners (Lave and Wenger, 1991; 1999). Everyone both creates his/her own world and is created by it and by others around (Ravenette, 1984; 1997). If this is the case, schools need to take account of how students make sense of their own circumstances and what impression is conveyed of others' constructions of them.

'Talking Stones'

'Talking Stones' is a sensitive pedagogic tool which adopts a view of students as active agents in their own learning in addressing the challenge of working through what are often difficult situations in schools, and matching provision to real needs. This is a projective technique derived from techniques related to Personal Construct Psychology and developed from Crosby's therapeutic work with adults (unpublished report, 1993, Centre for Personal Construct Education). It is a very powerful tool and should not be used without due regard to ethical considerations, particularly as they relate to issues of confidentiality, regard for the sensitivities of individual students and, most importantly, the principle of 'non-maleficence', that is 'above all do no harm' (McLeod, 1998, p 289).

During an individual interview, students are given a pile of stones of varying shapes, sizes, colours and textures and asked to choose from the pile to represent themselves in school and discuss their choices. They are then asked to select more stones to represent significant others in school (or the subject or area about which there is current discussion). They talk about their choices, and place the stones on a rectangular cloth or large sheet of sugar paper whose edges set a boundary to the positioning of the stones and their distance from each other. As students project on to these stones their thoughts and feelings about school and themselves in relation to it, the stones, their attributes and their positions in relation to each other come to represent individually constructed meanings.

This technique is illustrated and discussed below with reference to part of an interview carried out with a 15-year-old school student, 'Darren'.

Context of the study

'Darren' was a student at an urban comprehensive secondary school in a socio-economically deprived area of an East Midlands county in England at a time when the school was developing an initiative to reduce student absence and exclusion. Records of high levels of school absence and reports of behaviour seen as the focus of disruption in class had revealed that a group of ten Year 10, 14–15 year old students, mostly boys, were particularly disaffected from school learning. An alternative curriculum which included group discussion and counselling was organised for them for part of the week. As part of this initiative, the students were encouraged to express their feelings about themselves and their experiences of schooling. 'Talking Stones' was one technique used in the process of eliciting the individual views of some of these students. Individual interviews were carried out in the privacy of the office of a Head of Year at times when the group was together for discussion and counselling sessions. 'Darren' was one of the group of students who were interviewed. His interview took place over two separate sessions.

'Darren's' story

'Darren' was described by teachers as surly and taciturn. He never acknowledged his name when the class register was called and never talked to staff about anything of personal interest to himself. At the beginning of the first session, he sorted through the pile of about twenty stones of various sorts, and chose a striking-looking piece of grey fossilized mud that was lumpy and full of holes to represent himself in school. He explained his choice as:

> It's rotten right through. I'm rotten right through ...

This highly pejorative description of himself came as a shock to the interviewer. She had expected reticence of him. He, however, had immediately volunteered a damning, negative self portrait. He went on to discuss his family background and, as he did so, establish a possible link between his reluctance to answer to his name in class and his feelings about his own 'rottenness' and membership of his family:

> I come from a very bad family. My family are all thieves – well, not actually my family, but my cousins are all thieves. They've all been in trouble for stealing. One of them's banged away now for stealing, and there's another one who's a drug pusher ...

He went on to support this pejorative self-view with a description of incidents outside school where he had been in trouble with the police for drunkenness on the street and for suspected vandalism to property.

The first session with 'Darren' was interrupted after a very short period in a most unfortunate way by the Head of Year, leaving no time for closure in the discussion.

The interview resumed one week later, this time with a request to 'Darren' to choose stones that related specifically to his experience in school. Asked to pick out a stone to show what he was like as a student he chose a small, grey, mottled stone with a very rough texture because:

> ... it's rough ... I've chosen it because it shows how I mess about in school.

As he talked, he began to use the same stone to represent not only himself as a disruptive influence on peers in class but the quality of his work which he also described as 'rough'. This time he referred to the colour of the stone:

> because it's dark grey and it's black –

In 'Darren's' view, teachers had a great deal of influence over the level of his academic achievement. He felt he was victimised:

> ... it's not really fair ... if you're brainy the teachers let you talk a bit and laugh a bit – not a lot, but they let you do it a bit if you're brainy, but they don't let me ...

He had a clear view of teachers 'giving up on' him in relation to homework:

> I don't think we ought to do homework. We spend six hours a day in school and then we're expected to do more work at home. I don't see why I should. Anyway, teachers realise that I'm never going to do it. They realised that I wasn't going to do it when I was in Year 9 so eventually they gave up.

Creeping into the dialogue at this point was a fear that, behind the scenes, there was an intention to exclude him from the school permanently:

> If you're late three times in a week you're meant to get a detention but I don't get it. You're supposed to, but they don't give it to me ... Actually they've said that now they're letting it all build up, and when it gets bad enough they're going to get rid of me altogether.

Not everything about 'Darren' in the interview was negative, however. He used the stones to talk about himself on the football field:

> The thing I'm best at is playing football for X (football team) ... one thing about me when I play football – I can get very angry on the pitch. ... If I start a move and someone misses it, for example ... I start the move and get it going and pass the ball, and someone messes it up and just misses it altogether and doesn't score the goal, I get ever so angry.

He picked out a medium-sized, smooth stone in vivid shades of red, purple, orange and brown to show how he felt as a footballer:

> It's got lots of different colours in it. ... The red and orange colours, show what I'm like when I'm playing football cos I have lots of different moods when I'm on the pitch, but it shows what I'm like when I'm angry. Sometimes I get angry when I get fouled on the football pitch as well.

Clearly this stone was very different in colour and texture from the one that represented him in school. Comparing the stone-as-footballer with the lumpy grey one that represented self-as-student he said:

> It hasn't got any colour. ... I haven't got any colour at school.

That had not always been the case, however. As a younger student, he was a more 'colourful' figure and a higher achiever in class:

> I think my work in school was quite good till I got to the second year in middle school and I started turning bad and messing about. Talk in class and throw things about. I used to throw rubbers about and bits of paper, and my work started getting bad –

As he had chosen to mention previous higher achievement it seemed important to investigate how well he would like to be doing with his work. When asked he replied:

> At the top for everything.

To be at the top he would:

> ... have to try harder and not mess about, but the problem is that to be at the top I'd have to do that – to try harder and not mess about.

He was not prepared to do that, however, because:

> It would be boring.

'Darren's' conceptualisation of 'top' and, by implication, of 'bottom' also enabled the interviewer to introduce the idea of an imaginary line on which both the quality of work and also standards of behaviour could be rated from 'very good' to 'very bad'. Asked to chose stones to represent the two ends he picked out a whitish and smooth stone for the top. This, he said, symbolised 'good work'. For the bottom he chose the same small, grey, rough, mottled stone that he had used to represent both himself as one who 'messes about' and his work as 'rough'. He then rated his work and his behaviour on the imaginary line between the two in a number of subject areas. In English he rated himself as:

> Probably just below halfway. ... For work and behaviour.

and indicated the appropriate place on the 'line'.
In mathematics lessons he said he was:

> Here. Near the top...

He felt his behaviour was:

> Near the top as well.

because:

> I like the new Maths teacher. ... Because he explains things to you. He's funnier as well. ... I used to be just under halfway for Maths as well, but I didn't like the teacher then and I asked to change sets, and I like the teacher that I've got now, and my work is much better...

To represent the new Mathematics teacher he chose:

> That bright orange stone.

There was a second orange stone in the pile, but 'Darren' had selected the first:

> Because it's smoother. This one is smoother than the others. ... he's a better teacher.

To represent the 'worst teacher', he picked up a small, mottled, grey and black stone:

> Well, the worst teacher ... I've chosen this little kind of lumpy stone 'cos she's really a bit thick. I mean, we have to correct her spellings. ... She's moody as well. ... She lets some people do things and not others. If some of the girls say: 'Can we go to the toilet?' she lets them go to the toilet, but she doesn't let us.

Much more could be quoted from the transcript to exemplify 'Darren's' use of the stones, but space precludes further description. However, in it, 'Darren' demonstrates how he was using the attributes of colour, shapes and texture of other stones in the pile to discuss his hopes and plans for the future.

Discussion

'Talking Stones' is a technique whose rationale is underpinned by Personal Construct Theory (PCT) (Kelly, 1955). PCT is a psychology of interpersonal, not merely common, understandings. Kelly (1955) stressed the importance of 'reflexivity' in PCT. What applies to students must also apply to those who teach them. Inclusion as membership of a community of learners in schools implies a model of the student as active agent in his/her learning. For teachers and other professionals, listening to students and taking serious note of what they say is not optional, but fundamental. As noted above, student self advocacy is also a matter of human rights.

Stones have texture, size, shape, colour and mobility. They enable students to articulate their feelings about themselves in relation to school in ways not previously open to them. Above all, they move students and meanings mediated by their own personal saliences to the centre of the learning process. 'Talking Stones' is a flexible pedagogic tool which enables individuals to invest meaning in concrete objects which have no intrinsic meaning themselves apart from their own stone-ness.

In commenting on the link between low self worth and student behaviour that challenges the school system, Bruner (1996) notes the crucial importance of self advocacy to the development of self esteem:

> ... the management of self-esteem is never settled, and its state is affected powerfully by the availability of supports provided from outside. They include above all the chance for discourse ...
>
> (Bruner, 1996, p 37)

One of the prime responsibilities of schools is to support the construction of a student's sense of Self and self efficacy, that is, confidence in the ability to act and achieve in social situations, through an acknowledgement of agency:

> if agency and esteem are central to the construction of a concept of Self, then the ordinary practices of school need to be examined with a view to what contribution they make to these two crucial ingredients of personhood. If school is an entry into the culture then we must constantly reassess what school does to the young student's conception of his *(sic)* own powers (his sense of agency) and his sensed chances of being able to cope with the world both in school and after (his self esteem)
>
> (Bruner, 1996, pp 38–9)

In facilitating students' self advocacy, 'Talking Stones' thus has the potential to contribute to the 'ordinary practices' of schools in developing students' sense of agency, self esteem and belonging in the world.

Students actively engage in learning about the Self and the world through social interaction which shapes the pattern of their thought processes. The use of 'Talking Stones' allows a way of understanding more of what the student's experience is from the student's own viewpoint. Every act of learning, every act that deviates from social expectation, every refusal to co-operate is a personal engagement. Interpreting behaviour in this way may not make disruptive acts any easier to tolerate in the mainstream class. However, it does mean that the behaviour can be understood in the same way as any other. Further, it implies that it is possible to hold dialogue and see the world more closely through learners' eyes.

The interview transcript provides powerful evidence of 'Darren's' 'spoiled' identity (Goffman, 1963). He had constructed a view of himself as 'rotten right through' empirically from his experiences at school where he perceived staff as waiting to rid themselves of him, from his membership of a family that he described as thieves and drug-pushers, and from his own treatment at the hands of the police. He had been described by teachers as a dour, uncommunicative, inarticulate boy who was:

- feared by many of his peers;
- 'at very high risk of exclusion' from his school as a result of open verbal defiance of staff in lessons and suspected theft of master keys to the school premises;
- disengaged in all school learning, except for sport;
- frequently under the influence of drugs;
- suspected of petty crime in the vicinity by the local police.

'Talking Stones' enabled him, for the first time, to articulate a perception of himself and of what was happening around, and to, himself.

Student self advocacy in schools

For a school to engage with the perspective of a boy such as 'Darren' it must recognise a number of philosophical and practical issues associated with conflict of values both within and between individuals and their roles in schools (Garner and Sandow, 1995, p 20). For example, student self advocacy may conflict with professionals' values and assumptions about students' rights and abilities to express their own views and about their own responsibilities for maintaining control and direction in the school. In addition, it can be intrusive. Asking personal questions may be construed as prying into a student's privacy.

Its use is also ethically questionable in practice unless there is a positive payoff for the interviewee. Those using this technique should be aware of ethical principles associated with counselling-type practices, for example those of 'non-maleficence' and 'beneficence'. As McLeod (1998, pp 272–3) notes, 'non-maleficence' refers to the principle of not doing any harm, and 'beneficence' to promoting human welfare. Furthermore, its practice raises the question: what should we do with sensitive information of this sort that is very important to an understanding of an individual, but may be used by some to damn or to reinforce the stereotype? There are many instances in schools where teachers find themselves in situations where students disclose very sensitive information about themselves. Before engaging in any activity where this is likely to happen, including using 'Talking Stones', teachers need to be well acquainted with any guidelines existing in their own schools in relation to information that may emerge from student self disclosure.

There are also a number of pragmatic aspects of 'Talking Stones' that need to be taken into account if it is to be embedded into the curriculum. For example, it:

- can only be carried out on an individual basis;
- is time-consuming;
- requires an understanding of counselling theory and practice. In terms of practice it is important to recognise that:

> True listening is an art; children will make decisions about people they can talk to and trust, and those they cannot. We know from the counselling literature that good listeners offer time, support, non directive questions, acknowledgement of feelings, reflecting back, and such non-verbal behaviour as eye contact, sitting next to (rather than opposite, behind a desk), and a basically trusting atmosphere which communicates that it is all right to speak honestly.
> These are not easy situations to create in school...

(Gersch, 1995, p. 48)

Once a student has begun to disclose personal information, it may be difficult for a teacher-interviewer to bring about closure in a way that leaves the student in a frame of mind sufficiently comfortable to return to regular classroom activities. The first interview with 'Darren' was interrupted very suddenly at a very sensitive moment, and it was not possible to reach closure on the discussion. 'Talking Stones' is a technique not to be used lightly, therefore.

Conclusion

'Talking Stones' may enable students to discuss themselves and their concerns in a way which enables a much greater understanding of their viewpoints than has been possible before. 'Darren', for example, appeared to be experiencing competing values and expectations which stemmed from his own individual internal processes or from family and sub-cultural values which differed from those of the school and were leading him to reject everything related to school learning (Ravenette, 1984). The social consequences of his view of himself as 'rotten right through' seem to be very damaging, enabling him to gain little positive from school. At the time of interview he was in danger of experiencing only further confirmation of his devalued status.

In laying bare the problematic relationships between 'Darren', peers and certain members of staff, 'Talking Stones' enabled him to be understood not as 'mad' and, therefore, threatening, but engaging with life in an alternative mode. This view of his behaviour did at least imply that it was possible to enter his reality and hold dialogue.

'Talking Stones' is a powerful technique. The ethics surrounding its use should therefore be taken into careful consideration. It should only be used where there is positive benefit to the student.

References

Bruner, J. (1996) *The Culture of Education*, Cambridge, Mass: Harvard

Clark, C., Dyson, A. and Millward, A. (1998) *Theorising Special Education*, London: Routledge

Clark, C., Dyson, A., Millward, A. and Skidmore, D. (1997) *New Directions in Special Needs*, London: Cassell

Cline, T. (ed) (1992) *The Assessment of Special Educational Needs*, London: Routledge

Cooper, P. (1993) *Effective Schools for Disaffected Students*, London: Routledge

Cooper, P. and McIntyre, D. (1996) 'The classroom expertise of year 7 teachers and pupils', *Education 3–13*, 24(1), 59–66

Crosby, S. (1993) Unpublished manuscript, London: Centre for Personal Construct Education

Davies, J., Garner, P. and Lee, J. (eds) (1998) *Managing Special Educational Needs: the role of the SENCO*, London: Fulton

Department for Education and Employment (1997) *Excellence for All Children: meeting special educational needs*, London: DfEE

Department for Education and Skills (DfES) (2001) *Special Educational Needs Code of Practice*, London: DfES

Dyson, A. (1997) 'Social and educational disadvantage: reconnecting special needs education', *British Journal of Special Education*, 24(4), 152–7

Garner, P. and Sandow, S. (1995) *Advocacy, Self Advocacy and Special Needs*, London: Fulton

Gersch, I. (1995) 'Involving the child', in *Schools' Special Educational Needs Policies Pack*, London: National Children's Bureau

Gersch, I. (2001) 'Listening to Children: an initiative to increase the active involvement of children in their education by an educational psychology service', in J. Wearmouth (ed) *Special Educational Provision in the Context of Inclusion*, London: Fulton

Goffman, E. (1963) *Stigma: notes on the management of spoiled identity*, London: Penguin

Hart, S. (1995) 'Down a different path', in *Schools' Special Educational Needs Policies Pack*, London: National Children's Bureau

Kelly, G. K. (1955) *The Psychology of Personal Constructs, Vols 1 and 2*, New York: W W Norton and Co Inc

Lave, J. and Wenger, E. (1991) *Situated Learning: legitimate peripheral participation*, Cambridge: Cambridge University Press

Lave, J. and Wenger, E. (1999) 'Learning and pedagogy in communities of practice', in J. Leach and B. Moon (eds) *Learners and Pedagogy*, London: Paul Chapman

McLeod, J. (1998) *Introduction to Counselling*, Buckingham: Open University Press

Mittler, P. (2000) *Working towards Inclusive Education: social contexts*, London: Fulton

Ravenette, A. T. (1984) 'The recycling of maladjustment', *A. E. P. Journal*, 6(3), 18–27

Ravenette, A. T. (1997) *Selected Papers, Personal Construct Psychology and the Practice of an Educational Psychologist*, Farnborough: European Personal Construct Association

UNICEF (1989) *United Nations Convention on the Rights of the Child*, New York: UNICEF

Wearmouth, J. (2000) *Special Educational Provision: meeting the challenges in schools*, London: Hodder

Wearmouth, J. (2003) Unpublished PhD manuscript

Wedell, K. (2000) Audiotape interview in *E831 Professional Development for Special Educational Needs Co-ordinators*, Milton Keynes: Open University

PART 2
Cultural issues

Chapter 5

Academic disidentification: unravelling underachievement among Black boys

Jason W. Osborne

Introduction

Educational and psychological research has long noted that students of African or Caribbean descent (collectively referred to here as Black) tend to experience poor academic outcomes relative to White majority students. This trend persists even after controlling for exogenous variables such as socioeconomic status, prior academic preparedness, and family structure (for a recent overview of this research, see Steele 1997). There are numerous explanations for these trends in the literature, including differences in cognitive style (e.g. Shade 1982), aversion to intellectual competition (Howard and Hammond 1985), language barriers and general cultural differences (e.g. Jacob and Jordan 1993) and even genetics (Herrnstein and Murray 1994). However, as authors such as Steele (1997) have pointed out, these theories tend not to be very satisfying. For example, if cultural differences are the culprit, why do children who emigrate from cultures drastically different from ours (e.g. Middle Eastern countries, Asian countries) often do better than Black children who come from families and communities with cultures that are arguably more similar to those of the majority White culture? Why do African immigrants (children not born into the majority White culture) do better in school than African-descended children born into the majority White culture? It is questions such as these that tend to make genetics and lingual/cultural theories unsatisfying. Other observations also raise interesting questions. For example, the Black–White gap is not static, nor is it present at the beginning of schooling. The gap between White and minority students widens by as much as two grade levels by sixth grade (e.g. Alexander and Entwhistle 1988; Valencia 1991, 1997).

Recently, theories focusing on social psychological factors have emerged in the literature to raise and attempt to answer some of these questions. Specifically, Claude Steele's stereotype threat theory, John Ogbu's cultural ecological theory, and Majors and Billson's cool pose theory all focus on social psychological and cultural factors that cause Black students to psychologically withdraw from (disidentify, selectively devalue) school. These three theories all examine the same problem from slightly different angles, yet all seem to come to similar conclusions – that it is difficult for students of color to view themselves as good students, to define the self through academics, to value academics while still maintaining the integrity of the self.

This is exceedingly important, as individuals who are unable to define themselves through academics, to identify with academics, are more likely to experience adverse academic outcomes (e.g. withdrawal from school, poor grades). This view is supported by a growing number of empirical studies. More importantly, this perspective on the academic disparity between White and Black students provides clear avenues for impacting and ameliorating this problem.

Theoretical perspectives on underachievement among Black boys

Stereotype threat

Steele (1992, 1997) has attempted to understand the chronic underperformance of disadvantaged minority students through examining the socio-cognitive dynamics of schooling and the academic environment, specifically the effects of negative group stereotypes. Steele argued that schooling and the school environment is aversive to members of groups for whom there are negative group stereotypes long before the achievement gap manifests because of negative stereotypes concerning the intellectual ability of group members. While most students experience some anxiety over being negatively evaluated, students who belong to groups with a negative intellectual stereotype not only risk personal embarrassment and failure but also risk confirming the negative group stereotype. This, he argued, leads to increased anxiety for these students, which depresses performance at every level of preparation.

Steele further argued that being continually immersed in an aversive environment can contribute to what he called 'disidentification', the selective devaluing of academics. There is a rich tradition in psychology, dating back to William James (1890/1950) of viewing humans as motivated to view themselves in a positive light. Many theories of self-esteem state that performance in a domain will affect the self-esteem only to the extent that that domain is valued, or central, to the self-concept. Domains that are devalued have little impact on the overall self-esteem, and domains that are highly valued have a great deal of impact on self-esteem. Further, individuals appear to be extremely facile in their ability to alter which domains they perceive as central in order to maintain a certain positivity of self-esteem. Several authors have argued that individuals are particularly likely to selectively devalue domains for which their group, or they personally, fare poorly and selectively value domains for which their group, or they personally, fare relatively well (e.g. Crocker and Major 1989; Major and Schmader 1998; Tesser 1988). For example, Taylor and Brown (1988) reported that individuals tend to value those domains which they fare well in, Tesser and Campbell (1980) reported experimental evidence for selective devaluing in response to relatively poor performance, and Tesser, Millar and Moore (1988) reported heightened negative affect in response to poor performance on a valued dimension compared to a devalued dimension (for a more thorough discussion, see Major and Schmader 1998).

Thus, according to this perspective, there are two good reasons why Black students should disidentify, or selectively devalue academics: to reduce anxiety and improve self-esteem by eliminating a source of negative evaluation – academics. Ironically, this self-protective strategy should increase the likelihood of disidentified students experiencing adverse academic outcomes. Students who are more identified with academics should be more motivated to succeed because their self-esteem is directly linked to academic performance. In contrast, students not identified with academics should be less motivated to succeed because there is no contingency between academic outcomes and self-esteem – good performance is not rewarding, and poor performance is not punishing, leaving those who have disidentified with no compelling incentives to expend effort in academic endeavors. These disidentified individuals may therefore be at higher risk for academic problems, especially poor grades and dropping out, but also absenteeism, truancy, and delinquency (see also Finn 1989; Hindelang 1973; Newmann 1981).

Steele further argued that disidentification is not a normal state of affairs for Black students, that they do not begin schooling disidentified (a point empirically supported by Osborne 1995, 1997a). On the contrary, he argued that all students begin schooling strongly identified with academics, and that there must be something in the educational environment (what he termed 'unwise schooling' in homage to Goffman) to cause students to become disidentified.

Ogbu's cultural-ecological perspective

While many authors tend to lump disadvantaged minority students together, Ogbu (e.g. 1997) has made an argument that not all minority groups are equal.

He separates minority groups into two groups: those in a country or society voluntarily (immigrant or voluntary minorities) and those that have been subjugated and/or brought into a society against their will (involuntary or non-immigrant minorities). In the United States, for example, Asian and some Latino (e.g. Cuban) populations are examples of the former, while Black, Native-American, and other Latino (e.g. Puerto Rican) populations are examples of the latter. Ogbu argued that the social realities for students from these two groups are very different and, as such, lead to different outcomes. Involuntary minorities tend to develop a social or collective identity that is in opposition to the social identity of the dominant group (Whites). Thus, while voluntary minority students are able to view education as a path to success in their newly adopted country, Black students tend to view education as a system controlled by the group that subjugated them, their oppressors. School is seen as an inappropriate aspect of 'proper' Black identity (see Fordham and Ogbu 1986). Black children are instead encouraged to value other aspects of society, usually whatever is in opposition to White values, as appropriate for themselves. Ogbu labels this 'cultural inversion'.

This cultural inversion arose initially, he argues, to serve boundary-maintaining and coping functions under subordination. Today, inversions remain because there are few incentives to give them up while members of these groups still feel subjugated and oppressed. In the specific example of school learning, members of involuntary minority groups might consciously or unconsciously interpret school learning as a displacement process detrimental to their social identity, sense of security, and self-worth. Furthermore, these minority groups have observed that even those who succeed in school are not fully accepted or rewarded in the same way that White students are. This, combined with peer pressure and cultural pressure not to 'act white' (e.g. Fordham and Ogbu 1986), may make a compelling force against identification with academics.

Conversely, Ogbu argues, voluntary minority students have a much easier time integrating academics into the self-concept and excelling at school. For these students, who have come to a culture willingly, education is generally seen as the route through which they are able to build a better future for themselves. While they tend to have greater lingual and cultural barriers to overcome than involuntary minority students, they tend to do better because they are able to identify with academics. There is no culture of opposition, no collective identity opposing excelling at school. In fact, in many of these communities there is significant peer and group pressure to excel, a situation in stark contrast to the group dynamics found in involuntary minority groups.

Thus, while voluntary minorities are able to identify with academics, involuntary minority students are less able to do so due to the social dynamics of their society.

Majors and Billson's cool pose

Ogbu's oppositional perspective is echoed by other authors, including Majors and Billson (1992). They argue that Black males adopt a 'cool pose', or a ritualized form of masculinity that allows that boy or man to cope and survive in an environment of social oppression and racism. According to Majors and Billson, cool pose allows the Black male to survive by projecting a front of emotionlessness, fearlessness, and aloofness that counters inner pain from damaged pride, poor self-confidence, and fragile social competence that comes from existing as a member of a subjugated group. Unfortunately, as with Steele's notion, cool pose depicts Black males as victims of their coping strategies. In terms of education, cool pose often leads to behaviors, such as flamboyant and non-conformist behavior, that often elicit punishment in school settings. Equally unfortunately, the development of a cool self-concept appears to be incompatible with a hard-driving, motivated, identified student. Thus, Black boys, according to this perspective, adopt a strategy for coping with group membership that appears to be incompatible with identification with academics.

Summary

While these theories seek to understand the problem of Black student under-achievement from different perspectives, all three seem to imply that Black students, as well as other students of color, are at high risk for academic disidentification. It may be that Black students are at disproportionately higher risk due to the extremely negative way society tends to view them. This increased level of disidentification, in turn, is likely to be a significant contributing factor to academic problems, including under-performance, withdrawal from school, delinquency, and other undesirable academic outcomes.

Empirical evidence

Recently, several studies have provided evidence supporting the notions that: (a) Black students (specifically Black boys) are more likely to experience academic disidentification, (b) disidentification is a developmental process, (c) identification with academics is related to academic outcomes, and (d) the social dynamics of the environment (e.g. salience of stigma vulnerability) can adversely affect academic performance.

Black boys are more likely to disidentify than other students

One of the central tenets of this chapter is that, for a variety of possible reasons delineated by Steele, Ogbu, Majors and Billson, Fordham, and others, Black students, especially Black males, are more likely to experience academic disidentification (detaching of self-esteem from academic outcomes) than Whites. Implicit in this statement is the assertion that students from other involuntary minority groups are also likely to experience this outcome. An important corollary to this is that academic disidentification is expected to be developmental in nature, increasing over time.

Osborne (1995, 1997a) tested this assertion within the context of a large database that is representative of the population of American students, the National Education Longitudinal Survey of 1988 (National Center for Educational Statistics 1992). In this study identification with academics was operationalized at the group level as the correlation between global self-esteem (the Rosenberg Self-View Inventory, Rosenberg 1965) and academic outcomes (achievement tests and cumulative grades). The results of these studies were striking. As presented in Figure 5.1, at the beginning of the study (eighth grade), all groups studied (White, Latino, and Black boys and girls) were significantly identified with academics (all correlations ranging from $r = .22$ to .27, all $p < .001$). However, by tenth grade the correlations for Black boys had dropped dramatically and significantly to $r = .07$, while all other groups remained substantially the same. By twelfth grade the correlations for Black boys had dropped to $r = -.02$, while the correlations for other groups again

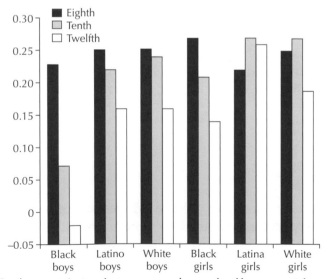

Figure 5.1 Trends in the correlation between grades and self-esteem: Identification with academics

remained highly significant. Note that socioeconomic status was partialled out of these correlations, and that controlling for locus of control did not substantially change the results.

Other studies also support this assertion. For example, Osborne, Major and Crocker (1992) found experimental support for Steele's hypothesis that the self-esteem and affect of Black college students is less reactive to academic feedback than that of Whites, even when that feedback is explicitly presented as diagnostic of a student's academic potential and ability. In other cross-sectional studies, there have been lower correlations between self-esteem and academic outcomes for Blacks than Whites (Demo and Parker 1987; Hansford and Hattie 1982; Jordan 1981; Lay and Wakstein 1985; Rosenberg and Simmons 1972). Thus, these findings lend strong support to the argument that Black males are particularly at risk for academic disidentification.

Disidentification is a developmental process

The results from Osborne (1995, 1997a) support the notion that most students begin schooling identified with academics and learning. Even as late as eighth grade there is no evidence of relative group-level disidentification among any group, especially Black boys. While a more sensitive measure might detect the beginnings of disidentification earlier, the good news from these data is that, while the seeds of disidentification are undoubtedly sown much earlier, there is a long grace period within which we can work to prevent disidentification.

Identification with academics is related to academic outcomes

Another crucial piece to this puzzle is the assertion that disidentification will adversely affect academic outcomes. As discussed above, there is excellent theoretical support for this notion. Clear empirical evidence is more elusive, but available in limited fashions at this point. First, Osborne (1997b) showed that identification with academics predicted several academic outcomes in the context of a two-year prospective longitudinal study, such as cumulative grades, withdrawal or dismissal from school, as well as receipt of academic honors. Second, Osborne and Rausch (2001) demonstrated that, within the NELS, a nationally representative sample of American students, withdrawal from school is related to identification with academics, especially for boys, and that even among the most at-risk students (students who are members of disadvantaged racial minority groups (Latino and Black), low in socioeconomic status, and poor academic outcomes), strong identification with academics was associated with remaining in school.

The social dynamics of the environment can influence academic outcomes

A final piece of this puzzle is why Black boys would be more likely to disidentify than other students. Steele (1992, 1997) argued that it is heightened anxiety associated with concern over confirming the stereotype of the group as intellectually inferior that drives this phenomenon. Osborne (in press) has found that state anxiety while testing explains up to 46 per cent of White–Black differences in test performance. Further, Steele and Aronson (1995) found that by experimentally reducing the perception of an academic task as diagnostic of ability (thus, in Steele's theoretical framework, reducing anxiety and stereotype threat), Black students expended more effort and performed at a higher level than their counterparts who were tested under 'normal' testing conditions. This study provides empirical support for a causal link to poorer academic outcomes (via reduced effort expenditure) because of disidentification. Thus, Steele and Aronson (1995, and other studies, summarised in Aronson, Quinn, and Spencer 1998) experimentally demonstrated that the social dynamics of the environment can drastically influence academic performance, and that Blacks are vulnerable to this effect, even in the absence of a task that is perceived to be diagnostic of ability.

Summary

While much work is left to be done, there appears to be very good initial support for the argument that Black boys underperform in academic arenas, relative to Whites, due at least in part to higher levels of academic disidentification. Specifically, there is evidence that Black males are particularly vulnerable to disidentification, that disidentification is linked to adverse academic outcomes including, but not limited to, poor grades and withdrawal from school, that disidentification is a developmental process that does not occur until exposure to years of schooling, and that concern over confirming the negative group stereotype is related to poor performance. Further, while the majority of these data come from studies done in the USA, it should be in no way limited to students within the USA. At the least, it should hold within Westernized, White-majority countries, and Gibson and Ogbu (1991) present evidence that caste-like minority groups around the world show poor academic outcomes relative to the majority population, including IQ scores, academic performance, withdrawal from school, and exhibition of behavioral problems. Examples of these groups include the Maoris of New Zealand, West Indians in the UK, the Baraku of Japan, and Oriental Jews in Israel. These findings make this line of inquiry all the more important.

Derailing disidentification

There appears to be convergence in these three theories discussed above. In all cases, there are social psychological forces turning Black boys away from being psychologically invested in educational achievement. All three authors present suggestions for reducing or reversing this effect, although they vary a great deal in terms of ease of implementation and scope of intervention necessary. One particularly hopeful sign is that research supports Steele's assertion that disidentification is a developmental process that occurs over years of schooling, thus giving a broad window of opportunity for derailing this process and allowing Black boys to remain identified. Another positive note is Osborne (2001) that shows students who remain identified with academics also tend to have better academic outcomes, regardless of race.

Derailing disidentification from a stereotype threat perspective

According to Steele's theory, there appear to be two things working together to cause disidentification in Black boys (aside from other, less remediable factors, such as low socioeconomic status, family expectations, and peer pressure): a salient negative group stereotype and anxiety over confirming the negative group stereotype on the part of the student (note that Steele and Aronson 1995 demonstrated that the student does not have to believe the stereotype in order for it to affect their performance). Steele (e.g. 1997) has argued that a true multicultural curriculum could help students of color find a place in education and reduce the stigma vulnerability that leads to disidentification. He argued that most so-called multicultural curricula are simply the traditional Eurocentric curricula with some ancillary information about people of color added on (a view supported by Grant and Sleeter 1985, who labelled this type of curriculum as ethnic studies). This approach to multicultural education separates and marginalizes members of these groups, often relegating them to special periods of time during which they are to be studied, but not at other times of the year (e.g. Black History Month). Steele (1992) argued that a true multicultural curriculum (where the contributions of people of colour are infused throughout the school curriculum, Grant and Sleeter 1985) would serve to diffuse stigma vulnerability and disidentification by making people of color less invisible in academia. Majors and Billson (1992) also explicitly support this intervention as a way to assist Black boys.

Steele (1997) also suggests changing remediation practices to improve identification with academics. In the US, at least, but I suspect in other countries as well, Black males are remediated at a rate much higher than whites. If one reflects on the message remediation sends a student, it is clear that, while well-meaning, it cannot help but exacerbate the problem of stigma vulnerability and disidentification. To students already fighting overt and subtle messages telling them they might be intellectually inferior, the authorities in the school send them the message that they are in dire peril, doomed to failure, unless they receive help. Theoretically, this should increase stigma vulnerability and the likelihood of disidentification.

Perhaps worse, one of the things that traditional remediation does is 'dumb down' the curriculum. Students are perceived as not being able to handle difficult 'mainstream' material, so the difficulty of schoolwork is reduced until it becomes unchallenging. From a self-esteem standpoint, this is a tragic turn – by eliminating the challenge to academics (and often, the possibility of failure), it eliminates the reward, the reason to stay ego-involved in schooling. An examination of what school-age students are engrossed in reveals a common theme of challenge and possible failure: sports, dating, peer relations, video games. These activities are difficult, and success is by no means certain. It seems that the potential for victory, the challenge, and the infrequent victories over long odds keep people hooked most effectively (a variable reinforcement schedule, for those Skinnerians reading this).

Accordingly, Steele (1997) suggests replacing the traditional model of remediation with a model of challenge, whereby students would be given challenging work in a supportive, collaborative environment. He argues that this conveys respect for their potential and shows that they are not 'regarded through the lens of an ability-demeaning stereotype' (p. 625). This makes sense, not only from the perspective of Stigma Vulnerability theory, but also from a motivational standpoint, discussed above. Challenging activities can be more ego-involving and rewarding than non-challenging activities. While these two aspects of schooling are most immediately obvious for intervention and attempts at preventing disidentification or facilitating re-identification, Steele (1997) discussed other strategies.

As many in Western countries view IQ and intelligence as genetic, stable, trait-like, and immalleable, belonging to a group with a stigma of intellectual inferiority is a daunting prospect. It becomes an intellectual caste system, especially if one buys into the genetic argument posited by Herrnstein and Murray (1994). Unfortunately, this may be closer to the layperson's view of intelligence than we would like to admit. Thus, promoting the idea of intelligence as malleable, expandable, and responsive to training (as in Jausovec 1994) could go a long way toward improving the motivation and optimism of students who belong to these groups, especially Black males.

One thing that multicultural curricula have been relatively successful at doing is providing role models. Black males need to see that Black males can be successful in academic domains, that they can become scientists, engineers, mathematicians, teachers, etc. The popular media are notoriously poor at allowing these role models to receive widespread attention. Here's an anecdotal example: when a recent article of mine (on this topic) was published (Osborne 1997a) there was a great deal of media attention in the US. One of the most widely-read newspapers in the US (*USA Today*) put a write-up of the findings on the front page of the Life section of their paper. It was not until I had shown it to many colleagues that one pointed out the irony of its presentation. Immediately above the story, in full color, was a picture of some professional basketball players, all Black males. Immediately below it was a picture, in full color, of a group of White doctors performing surgery. This reflects the messages prevalent in society. If you are White you have certain options and paths open to you. If you are Black, especially if you are a Black male, you have other options. More exposure to academic role models can help counteract the popular media's message, and it is something that individual teachers and administrators can do.

Derailing disidentification from a cultural-ecological perspective

From Ogbu's perspective, it is not the social-cognitive aspects of the school environment that are leading to disidentification, but rather the social stratification and continuing subjugation of Blacks in the US and, presumably, other Western European nations. Thus, Ogbu suggests more community-oriented interventions. For example, Ogbu (1992) cites the observation that, while almost all segments of society verbalize the importance of academic achievement, voluntary minority and majority students often feel the sting of stigma associated with poor grades. In contrast, he argues, there is less community and family pressure to achieve good grades among involuntary minorities, with little social rejection or stigma attached to being a poor student or a dropout. In fact, peer pressure probably attaches stigma to academic excellence, in marked contrast to other segments of society. Involuntary minority students who excel at academics often must adopt self-presentational strategies in order to remain accepted as part of their peer group. Thus, he highlights changing community and family norms to emphasize academic achievement, celebrate those who excel in academics, and place pressure on those not doing well.

Second, Ogbu (1992) discusses different strategies students tend to use. He identified one, in particular, that should allow students to identify with academics, and excel, without losing their peer group or self-concept. He labelled this strategy 'accommodation without assimilation'. This strategy involves students' recognizing that they can participate in two cultural frames for different purposes without losing their own cultural identity or undermining their loyalty to their minority community. It also happens to be the strategy most often adopted by successful voluntary minority students.

This essentially involves behaving according to school norms while at school and community norms while at home. These students are able to excel at school without paying the costs associated with completely adopting majority norms (for a thorough discussion of the costs associated with racelessness or 'acting White', see Fordham 1988).

To facilitate this process, Ogbu (1992) suggests that special counselling and related programs should help involuntary minority students to learn to separate attitudes and behaviors enhancing school success from those that lead to 'acting White', avoid interpreting the former as a threat to their social identity and group loyalty, and take responsibility for their own academic performance and school adjustment.

On the community level, Ogbu also suggests that community leaders and respected members need to model positive achievement behaviors and help children separate attitudes and behaviors that lead to academic success and behaviors that lead to loss of ethnic identity. Further, community members need to provide children with concrete evidence that academic achievement is valued and appreciated on the same level that other activities, such as sports and entertainment, are valued. On this note, Osborne (1997a) reported evidence that Black males tended to become increasingly identified with sports performance and peer popularity while they became disidentified with academics. This suggests that this particular argument and recommendation is a key component to reducing disidentification.

Finally, Ogbu (1992) suggests that the involuntary minority middle class need to remain active in their communities. The voluntary minority middle class retains strong ties with the communities they come from, in spite of often residing outside that community. These individuals tend to regard their accomplishments as community accomplishments, and vice-versa. In this community, the middle class provides concrete evidence that school success pays and is compatible with membership in the community. In contrast, members of involuntary minorities tend to view success as their ticket out of the community. In this case, success means leaving the community, which may make it a strong disincentive to strive for success. Perhaps more importantly, there are few examples of how academic success equates to personal and community success available to children in the involuntary minority communities. This may influence identification with academics as there is no perceived contingency between academic success and financial or personal outcomes.

Cool pose and derailing academic disidentification

Similar to Ogbu, Majors and Billson (1992) make a compelling argument that the self-protective 'cool pose' adopted by Black boys (and other involuntary minority males, probably) is responsible for academic disidentification. Many of the roots of cool pose seem to be similar to the social issues Ogbu discusses (perceived subjugation, etc.). In addition to recommendations discussed above (such as moving toward a true multicultural curriculum, and overhauling our notion of remediation), Majors and Billson (1992) focus on several other ideas for diffusing this need for self-protection that leads to disidentification. One of these suggestions is for Black students to receive more Afrocentric socialization (teaching values such as cooperation, mutual respect, commitment, and love of family, race, community, and nation). Majors and Billson argue that this is not an anti-White or oppositional ideology, but rather encourages a more collective focus that reflects the Black situation in Western European cultures more accurately than White values of individualism and competition. Majors and Billson also encourage closer linkages between high schools and postsecondary institutions to facilitate high school completion, such as the Upward Bound program has done.

Summary

This chapter reviewed three theoretical perspectives (Steele's stereotype threat, Ogbu's cultural-ecological framework, and Majors and Billson's Cool Pose) that all suggest that certain disadvantaged minority students, Black boys in particular, are at higher risk for academic disidentification. There is evidence to support this perspective, although this is a fairly recent topic of discussion. Finally, authors' suggestions for improving the academic lives of Black boys (and other students in similar situations) were discussed, with particular attention paid to proposals that would inhibit disidentification or facilitate re-identification. Initial evidence (presented by Steele 1997) indicates that at least some of the interventions discussed above can be implemented successfully on small scales – individual teachers, schools, and school districts. Research by Steele and Aronson (1995) reinforces the fact that even small changes to the school or classroom environment can have large effects for the students. While much work remains to be done, these findings leave this author, at least, hopeful that we are on the brink of a more profound understanding of the factors influencing academic underachievement in minority groups, especially Black boys, and possibly being able to do something meaningful about it.

References

Alexander, K. L. and Entwhistle, D. R. (1988) 'Achievement in the first two years of school: Patterns and processes', *Monographs of the Society for Research in Child Development*, **53**, 2.

Aronson, J., Quinn, D. M. and Spencer, S. J. (1998) 'Stereotype threat and the academic underperformance of minorities and women', in J. K. Swim and G. Stangor (eds) *Prejudice: The Target's Perspective*, New York: Academic Press.

Crocker, J. and Major, B. (1989) 'Social stigma and self-esteem: The self-protective properties of stigma', *Psychological Review*, **96**, 4, pp. 608–30.

Demo, D. H. and Parker, K. D. (1987) 'Academic achievement and self-esteem among African-American and White college students', *Journal of Social Psychology*, **127**, 4, pp. 345–55.

Finn, J. D. (1989) 'Withdrawing from school', *Review of Educational Research*, **59**, 2, pp. 117–42.

Fordham, S. (1988) 'Racelessness as a factor in Black students' school success: Pragmatic strategy or Pyrrhic victory?' *Harvard Educational Review*, **58**, pp. 54–84.

Fordham, S. and Ogbu, J. (1986) 'Black students' school success: Coping with the burden of "acting White" ', *The Urban Review*, **18**, pp. 176–206.

Ghouri, N. (1998) 'Race chief attacks training negligence', *TES*, July 3.

Gibson, M. A. and Ogbu, J. U. (1991) *Minority Status and Schooling: A Comparative Study of Immigrant and Involuntary Minorities*, New York: Garland Publishing.

Grant, C. A. and Sleeter, C. E. (1985) 'The literature on multicultural education: Review and analysis', *Educational Review*, **37**, pp. 97–118.

Hansford, B. C. and Hattie, J. A. (1982) 'The relationship between self and achievement/performance measures', *Review of Educational Research*, **52**, pp. 123–42.

Herrnstein, R. A. and Murray, C. (1994) *The Bell Curve*, New York: Grove Press.

Hindelang, M. J. (1973) 'Causes of delinquency: A partial replication and extension', *Social Problems*, **20**, pp. 471–87.

Howard, J. and Hammond, R. (1985) 'Rumors of inferiority', *The New Republic*, **193**, September 9, 17–21.

Jacob, E. and Jordan, C. (eds) (1993) *Minority Education: Anthropological Perspectives*, Norwood, NJ: Ablex.

James, W. (1890/1950) *The Principles of Psychology*, New York: Holt, Rinehart and Winston.

Jausovec, N. (1994) 'Can giftedness be taught?', *Roeper Review*, **16**, pp. 210–14.

Jordan, J. T. (1981) 'Self-concepts, motivation, and academic achievement of Black adolescents', *Journal of Educational Psychology*, **73**, pp. 509–17.

Lay, R. and Wakstein, J. (1985) 'Race, academic achievement, and self-concept of ability. 25th annual forum of the Association for Institutional Research', *Research in Higher Education*, **22**, 1, pp. 43–64.

Major, B. and Schmader, T. (1998) 'Coping with stigma through psychological disengagement', in J. K. Swim and C. Stangor (eds) *Prejudice: The Target's Perspective*, New York: Academic Press.

Majors, R. and Billson, J. M. (1992) *Cool Pose: The Dilemmas of Black Manhood in America*, New York: Lexington Books.

National Center for Educational Statistics (1992) *National Education Longitudinal Study of 1998 First Follow-up: Student Component Data File User's Manual*, US Department of Education, Office of Educational Research and Improvement.

Newmann, F. M. (1981) 'Reducing student alienation in high schools: Implications of theory', *Harvard Educational Review*, **51**, pp. 546–64.

Ogbu, J. U. (1992) 'Understanding cultural diversity and learning', *Educational Researcher*, **21**, pp. 5–14.

Ogbu, J. U. (1997) 'Understanding the school performance of urban blacks: Some essential background knowledge', in H. Walberg, O. Reyes and R. Weissberg (eds), *Children and Youth: Interdisciplinary Perspectives*, London: Sage Publications.

Osborne, J. W. (1995) 'Academics, self-esteem, and race: A look at the underlying assumptions of the disidentification hypothesis', *Personality and Social Psychology Bulletin*, **21**, 5, pp. 449–55.

Osborne, J. W. (1997a) 'Race and academic disidentification', *Journal of Educational Psychology*, **89**, pp. 728–35.

Osborne, J. W. (1997b) 'Identification with academics and academic success among community college students', *Community College Review*, **25**, pp. 59–67.

Osborne, J. W. and Rausch, J. (2001) Identification with academics and academic outcomes in secondary students. Paper presented at the national meeting of the American Education Research Association, Seattle, WA.

Osborne, J. W. (2001) 'Testing stereotype threat: Does anxiety explain race and sex differences in achievement?' *Contemporary Educational Psychology*, **26**, pp. 291–310.

Osborne, J. W., Major, B. and Crocker, J. (1992) 'Social stigma and reactions to academic feedback'. Poster presented at the annual meeting of the Eastern Psychological Association, Boston, March.

Rosenberg, M. (1965) *Society and the Adolescent Self-image*, Princeton, NJ: Princeton University Press.

Rosenberg, M. and Simmons, R. (1972) 'African-American and White self-esteem: The urban school child', Rose Monograph Series, Washington, DC: American Sociological Association.

Shade, B. (1982) 'Afro-American cognitive style: A variable in school success', *Review of Educational Research*, **52**, pp. 219–44.

Steele, C. (1992) 'Race and the schooling of African-American Americans', *The Atlantic Monthly*, April, pp. 68–78.

Steele, C. (1997) 'A threat in the air: How stereotypes shape intellectual identity and performance', *American Psychologist*, **52**, pp. 613–29.

Steele, C. M. and Aronson, J. (1995) 'Stereotype threat and the intellectual test performance of African-Americans', *Journal of Personality and Social Psychology*, **69**, 5, pp. 797–811.

Taylor, S. E. and Brown, J. D. (1988) 'Illusion and well-being: A social psychological perspective on mental health', *Psychological Bulletin*, **103**, pp. 193–210.

Tesser, A. (1988) 'Toward a self-evaluation maintenance model of social behavior', in L. L. Berkowitz (ed.) *Advances in Experimental Social Psychology*, **21**, pp. 181–228, San Diego, CA: Academic Press.

Tesser, A. and Campbell, J. (1980) 'Self-definition: The impact of the relative performance and similarity of others', *Social Psychology Quarterly*, **43**, pp. 341–47.

Tesser, A., Millar, M. and Moore, J. (1988) 'Some affective consequences of social comparison and reflection processes: The pain and the pleasure of being close', *Journal of Personality and Social Psychology*, **54**, pp. 49–61.

Valencia, R. R. (1991) 'The plight of Chicano students: An overview of schooling conditions and outcomes', in R. R. Valencia (ed.) *Chicano School Failure and Success: Research and Policy Agendas for the 1990s* (pp. 3–26). The Stanford Series on Education and Public Policy, London: Falmer Press.

Valencia, R. R. (1997) 'Latinos and education: An overview of sociodemographic characteristics and schooling conditions and outcomes', in M. Barrera-Yepes (ed.) *Latino Education Issues: Conference Proceedings*, Princeton, NJ: Educational Testing Service.

Chapter 6

Teachers and pupils – relationships of power and resistance

Cecile Wright, Debbie Weekes and Alex McGlaughlin

The material in this chapter relates to an ethnographic research study which examined issues of race, class and gender in exclusions from four inner-city secondary schools in England in the late 1990s.

Introduction

The concept of 'resistance' in relation to schooling has been employed by a number of writers keen to explore how specific groups of pupils negotiate and respond to their marginal positions in schools, whilst avoiding a determinist analysis of schools' ability to reproduce these social and cultural inequalities. The seminal work of Paul Willis (1977) attempted to interrogate the division between structure and agency that earlier social reproduction accounts had introduced. Through suggesting that the resistance of the working-class males in his study acted to reinforce their social class positions, Willis argued that this was a choice his participants actively made. In this way he attempted to engage debate on the issue of structure and agency. However, Willis's work has been criticized as dualistic and determinist (Walker 1986). It has been suggested that though Willis wished to avoid a determinist analysis through giving the 'lads' agency, he posited an image of working-class culture as oppressive. Though feminists attacked Willis's work for its over-romanticized view of working-class masculinity (McRobbie 1991), their own work on female resistance also acted to cement the lives of their respondents in working-class culture, albeit through their respondents' own choosing (McRobbie 1978; Anyon 1983; Davies 1983). The term 'resistance within accommodation' has been used by feminist researchers to suggest that young women strategically employ aspects of exaggerated femininity in schools, such as blushing and giggling with (male) teachers, in order to avoid work. In this way it is argued, young women effect forms of resistance within the context of the classroom and the teacher–pupil relationship. However, often the issue of what is specifically being resisted by pupils becomes more complex, where theorists' assume that the exaggeration of femininity described above can be seen as a rejection of the norms of femininity (Gewirz 1991). The problems relating to structure and agency within resistance theories were therefore closely related to their emphasis on social reproduction. Critics suggested that though resistance theories were ideally placed to explore pupils' responses to schooling (Sultana 1989), they continued to focus on students' rejection of social structures. As McFadden (1995) has argued:

> disadvantage and inequality of achievement at school is related more to the rejection of the curriculum and pedagogy encountered by students than to a conscious resistance to the dominant ideology of society.
>
> (McFadden 1995: 297)

Therefore research on resistance has led to alternative interpretations of pupil responses to schooling. Some writers have argued that resistance to schooling is not restricted to that of working-class pupils (Aggleton 1987; Watson 1993) and indeed that some resistance may not be particularly class based (Meyenn 1980). Other research, particularly in the area of 'race', has shown that African-Caribbean pupils, particularly males, exhibit pro-school as well as anti-school attitudes (Gillborn 1990; Sewell 1997). This is particularly important as much educational research conducted on Black pupils in British schools has focused on disaffection (Mac an Ghaill 1988; Cashmore and Troyna 1982). Another important aspect not restricted to 'race', but which has certain 'race'-specific connotations, is that contrary to the basis of earlier resistance theories, many pupils do not reject the concept of education itself, but rather the authoritarian function of teachers (Mac an Ghaill 1994) and the form and content of the curriculum. Research has also indicated that many Black pupils do recognize the value of education but reject the wider racialized and gendered discrimination which filters through into perceptions of their behaviour by peers and teachers (Fuller 1982). Therefore McFadden (1995) argues that resistance theory needs to account for the variety in pupil responses to schooling which may be mediated through class, gender and 'race' and the importance of the intersection between pupil and teacher perceptions. It is also important to view the resistances of pupils as a response to the nature of knowledge which they receive in schools. He suggests that

> students from certain kinds of backgrounds have experiences of schooling which restrict their opportunity to extend their knowledge. The response to this form of

schooling for many students is to resist it. What students are constantly rejecting, or sometimes at best, merely complying with regardless of class, gender, race and ethnicity, is schooling which depowers them.

(McFadden 1995: 297)

Research on 'race' and resistance within schooling has been subject to criticism which suggests that it is difficult both to distinguish between pupil resistance and simple 'messing about' (Brittan and Maynard 1984; Gewirz 1991), and to 'prove' empirically that the teacher racism against which the majority of anti-school Black pupils resist, actually exists (Foster 1990, 1991; Hammersley and Gomm 1993). In a similar form to the criticism levelled at feminist theorizing of 'resistance within accommodation', the nature of the criticism directed at much research on 'race' has suggested that Black pupils merely reinforce dominant racialized stereotypes (Gewirz 1991; Foster et al. 1996). For example, theorists on race and educational inequality have suggested that Black pupils exhibit particular forms of speech (Mac an Ghaill 1988), ways of walking (Gillborn 1990), and more recently types of dress (Sewell 1997), which are indicative of pupil resistance. As will be shown in the accounts of the young people interviewed in the study and presented below, resistances were often located in pupils' wider racialized and gendered positions. Forms of speech, dress and ways of walking are often indicative of displaced contestations or resistances (Aggleton 1987) and these expressions hold greater cultural currency when used in an area (school) where Black pupils are in a numerical and power-related minority.

Resistance, contestation or challenge?

Though it remains important for a study of pupils' schooling experiences to explore whether they respond in resistant ways, there are certain issues which must be addressed in order to theorize these responses effectively. Resistance theorists have been criticized for 'launching too readily into optimism without sufficiently articulating the constraints which limit and subvert the transformative potential of resistance' (Sultana 1989: 289). The debate is ongoing as to whether or not resistance to schooling embedded within anti-school attitudes can actually effect change. However, if indeed pupils do resist the practice of knowledge production which takes place in schools, particularly where they feel this knowledge does not reflect them culturally or experientially, the transformative nature of their resistance is problematized when they cut themselves off from gaining any form of knowledge.

The work of Aggleton (1987) has been important in differentiating between intent and outcome in relation to pupil responses to schooling. Aggleton argues that it is necessary to differentiate between challenges against wider societal power relations and more localized principles of control, such as those occurring within schools. In this way it is possible to identify behaviours as resistant or contestual. Additionally, in differentiating between intent and outcome it becomes possible to view the contestations of Black pupils against specific processes within schools as having more resistant outcomes, in that often their responses are located within wider racialized discourses. Clearly, the added focus on school exclusion, and the power embedded within it as one of an educational institution's most important sanctions, will provide an additional emphasis on the nature of the power struggle between pupils and teachers within schools. With these theoretical considerations in mind, it is now possible to explore the resistant possibilities within pupil responses to schooling.

The effect of sanctions on teacher–pupil relationships

An important aspect of the experience of school sanctions, and one which is important to an analysis of pupil resistance and contestation, relates to the issue of power. Within the school environment relationships between pupils and teachers are structured on a basis of power and powerlessness. Resistance theories have often been criticized for assuming these relationships are unidirectional through placing students and teachers within predictable power positions (Mac an Ghaill 1994). The following accounts will show that pupils use forms of resistance/contestation to negotiate the form that their relationship with teachers will take. Much resistance was used to subvert the traditional teacher as powerful, student as powerless relationship. However, the power which teachers have to impose various school sanctions on pupils, culminating in school exclusion, adds a further dimension to the pupils' resistance. Contrary to the teacher's perceptions, these pupils did not exhibit anti-education sentiments. Rather, the pupils' responses were situated in their wider racial and gendered positions. Additionally, in similar ways to the 'macho lads' in Mac an Ghaill's (1994) study, the pupils' resistance was a response to the 'domination, alienation and infantilism' (1994: 57) they experienced. This was not always as a result of being situated in lower sets, as Mac an Ghaill suggests of his respondents, but in relation to the threat of school sanction and permanent exclusion which, under present education policy conditions, is continuously reinforced in schools (Blyth and Milner 1996).

The extent to which the responses of some pupils to school could be read as resistant was quite school-context dependent. Thus the school ethos, and the extent to which particular pupils felt that they had a stake in it, depended on the use of school sanctions/exclusions, the place of rewards within pastoral policy and the explanations drawn on by staff to account for pupil behaviour.

In School D for example, many pupils interviewed had either experienced particular traumas outside school, including assault, discord between parents and partners and degrees of family poverty, or had developed particular roles within their local communities which were played out within their school peer groups. Others had learning difficulties which they attempted to mask in particular behavioural forms, the majority of which were conflictual. These circumstances were not 'race' specific. In a large number of cases where pupils were seen by staff to be behaving inappropriately, explanations were drawn from pupil circumstance. However, in other schools the extent to which staff would draw on alternative explanations for pupil behaviour did not often help to mediate in situations of conflict. In School A, the focus on academic standards meant that often despite other factors which may have also been contributing, badly behaved pupils were seen simply as badly behaved. In Schools B and E, where many pupils also experienced various social problems outside the school environment, both schools responded with numerous exclusions and other sanctions. In School B this left very little room for staff to draw on whatever background information might have been available about the child. Similarly, in School E sanctions were increasingly used because it was felt that many parents had either lost or abdicated responsibility for the control of their children.

In respect of this, the pupils who had experienced school exclusion in School D did not talk in terms of *resisting* particular aspects of school. There was much low level disruption present in many of the lessons observed and teachers readily pointed to the persistently difficult pupils in the school. On their part, pupils talked about not liking particular lessons or teachers and some of the older pupils spoke of school as though it were an irritating interruption to their lives in their communities. The Head also commented that though many pupils caused disruption in classrooms, at a recent school inspection all pupils had been well behaved including those who were persistently disruptive. She commented that pupils had been *intentionally* punctual and attentive for the inspectors illustrating a degree of loyalty to the school which many of the staff had found pleasantly surprising. Therefore, rather than finding many pupils who wished to react against the control of their teachers at this school, there were instead groups of teachers, including those in senior positions reacting against the powerless positions they had been placed in both professionally and in terms of the poor reputation the school had developed over the years. This provides an interesting point of departure for theorizing resistance in schools and will be explored later in this chapter.

However it is necessary at the outset to note that pupil resistance must always be viewed in relation to what, if any, effects it can have on the position of the pupil. Although pupils may complain of differential treatment, the unfairness of particular policies or their inability to be heard by staff, it is the extent to which pupils respond, either verbally or behaviourally, to these circumstances that can lead to a discussion as to whether or not such resistances exist.

In School B, a number of pupils interviewed had gradually become aware of the changing focus on discipline. Mr Mills, the Headteacher, had made announcements in assemblies, in the school magazine and to the governors, about the changing discipline policy. Shahid, a Pakistani pupil in Year 10, commented on the changing policy in view of the restrictions it would place on him academically. He had a wide network of older friends outside school, and felt that should he not achieve well, he would become drawn into criminal activity.

> 'Since Mr Mills came back if a teacher says something to you and you don't even answer back, you just talk to them, they think you're answering back and then they go and tell Mr Mills and Mr Mills will exclude you like that. That's what's bad about him. He's too strict. I want to get my marks and get out of this school one time. When I get them now I'll [probably] end up in a hotel washing dishes. Because that's what you have to do nowadays. Cabbying, drug dealing. There is money in them things. Drug dealing, there's a lot of money in that. [But] the risk of getting caught, that's your life. Your life's unbearable. I'd rather be a normal guy that's got a job, who gets good pay.'
>
> (Shahid, Pakistani pupil, Year 10, School B)

Unlike the rebels in Sewell's (1997) study of Black male resistance, Shahid does not place a greater value on the forms of knowledge gained within local communities than that gained in school. Shahid talks of the knowledge he has accrued about ways to be successful from spending time with his peers in his neighbourhood. But he does not want to be precipitated into this alternative means of achieving financial success through an experience of exclusion, and recognizes that the new policy in place at school may indeed put him in such a position. Shahid was involved in very low level classroom disruption, but only when a certain other pupil was present in his lessons. This pupil was often out of school on exclusions or spending time in the on-site unit and thus Shahid could avoid trouble. He had also experienced school sanctions for smoking, but did not pose a serious threat to the overall order of the school. However, the new discipline policy could make a potential casualty of a pupil such as Shahid and it is within this context that Shahid spoke about the inevitability of his educational career. Even with qualifications, he jokes that he may only achieve the status of washing dishes in hotels. Shahid therefore did not rebel against the function of education, but did have particular problems relating to Mr Mills the Headteacher. The extent of Shahid's resistance to Mr Mills was as low level in nature as his disruption and lay somewhat in the shadows of the responses of some of his African-Caribbean male peers. As he commented, in the light of the changing climate around discipline that the Headteacher had fostered:

Shahid: They [African-Caribbean Year 11 boys] all wear hats. You know
when Mr Mills sees them he says 'yeah take your hat off'. Like me
for example, if I'm wearing a hat if he sees me, he's like take it off
there and then. But most of the time they argue back with him.

Researcher: But he's not scared of you seeing as he's always telling you to take
off your hat?

Shahid: I'm not worried about him, I won't say nothing to that teacher. But if
he done something serious to me, I'd wait for him outside the school
premises. He would never ever walk in them areas especially in [his
local area]. I'm not really scared to walk into anywhere, because I've
got enemies and I can walk into their areas. If you get beat up, you
get beat up. But him now, he's a bad teacher, I don't think anyone
would let him walk into their area. All the people he's been bad to.

Shahid spoke almost as if he was in awe of the way that Nehemiah and many
of the older African-Caribbean pupils in his school-based peer group (two of
whom had since been excluded) had responded to Mr Mills. Theirs was a level
of resistance which challenged the authority of Mr Mills to remove simple items
of clothing from them. Such low level examples of indiscipline were clearly very
difficult for Mr Mills to react against through the use of sanctions, although it
was not impossible for him to do so. Rather, there was a certain fear of some of
the older African-Caribbean boys that Shahid was certainly aware of and which
appeared to prevent Mr Mills from using his authority in those immediate
circumstances. Instead he was more likely to rely on the fast track procedure
which would no doubt bring Nehemiah and his friends to his office, where he
could issue them with an exclusion in relative safety.

Shahid's level of resistance was that he intended fully to remain within the
school and achieve the qualifications that he needed in order to to avoid the
otherwise inevitability of criminal behaviour that he spoke of. Thus he did not
directly challenge Mr Mills on the occasions when he was asked to remove his
hat. This in itself is not low level, but a quite well-developed way of resisting
the threat of school exclusion.

Shahid presents an example of a pupil aware of what he needed to do in order
to resist what he saw as Mr Mills' intentional attempts to remove him from the
school. He was part of a peer group of boys who were seen as the serious
disrupters to the order of the school and thus could derive a certain sense of
safety from his position within this group. He was also aware of the wider issues
at stake should he not succeed in his attempt at resistance. But whereas the
activities of some of his peers acted as forms of resisting the authority of the new
discipline policy, when Shahid took part in them it meant that his own resistant
activity, achieving the grades necessary to leave school and do well outside was

not being nurtured. It is also possible that such a long-term goal – Shahid was in Year 10 at the time of interview – was not having immediate effects for Shahid and its validity as a means of resisting the harshness of the new policy was limited.

Racializing resistance

At School C, there was no similar ethos of harshness surrounding discipline as evident by the Head's views on the unhelpful concept of punishment. This second exploration of resistance draws upon the work of 'race' and education theorists (Gillborn 1990; Mac an Ghaill 1988; Wright 1985, 1987; Sewell 1997) in looking at young Black pupil definitions of teacher racism and their resistance to it.

School C had developed a complex pastoral system which involved the Deputy Head, two senior teachers responsible for pastoral issues across the school, a specific room in which these teachers were housed, followed by the hierarchies of Heads of Year, Heads of Departments and form tutors. The Headteacher, as with School A, did not have to necessarily become involved in disciplinary matters but would do so occasionally. One African-Caribbean Year 9 pupil was quite certain that the Deputy Headteacher, Ms Gotham, awarded sanctions differentially between Black and White students. She based this not only on her own experience of the teacher, but also on that of older pupils who had friends excluded by her in the past.

> 'Some of the teachers are racist. They've got favouritism. I don't get on with [Ms Gotham] because, well me personally, she's always picking on Black people. I'm not the only one that has said that. Even students in the upper years if you ask them. I know a couple of people in Year 10 and 11 and we asked them because we thought it was just us saying that. We asked them and they said, she is always picking on us as well.'
>
> (Nicola, African-Caribbean pupil, Year 9, School C)

Nicola qualifies her perception of the racism of Ms Gotham by commenting that 'she's always trying to think of a way to get to us lot'. She notes that when being told off by other teachers for what she recognizes as 'messing about' on the stairs and corridors, that Ms Gotham will always appear to transform low level childish behaviour into an activity which warrants more serious sanction.

> 'One day in assembly someone had let off some gas and me and my friends, we always sit together and we was all moving up. Ms Gotham asked to see us all after assembly and she said "I'm keeping my eye on you lot because in lessons you are always getting in trouble". But when we ask our teachers if we are all right, they say "yes". We don't understand why she is always saying that.'
>
> (Nicola, African-Caribbean pupil, Year 9, School C)

Like Shahid above, Nicola did not take part in serious disruptive activities. She had experienced a fixed-term exclusion for hitting a girl who had barged into her after she had experienced an accident. She had recognized that she had been wrong and her parents had also been disappointed in her, but she felt that for some reason Ms Gotham simply did not *like* her and that she made a point of finding out whether or not Nicola had been in any trouble at the classroom level.

> 'Since I've come to this school, she's never liked me or my friends. My mum wanted to move me out of the school. I didn't want to leave because I'd made all my friends. [The first time] we was in the canteen and my friend Shanelle nicked some grits from the canteen. And [Ms Gotham] wanted, oh she really wanted me to be in it and I didn't do anything. And [Ms Gotham] went "oh did you do anything?" Shanelle said "no it was just me on my own". I thought why couldn't she just accept that. But she wants it to be me really badly so I get into trouble. The other day I found out this boy had a fight with another Year 10. They were investigating because they wanted to get to the bottom of it. I was at a funeral and my friend Shanelle got pulled out of a lesson by Ms Gotham. And [Ms Gotham] said "where's Nicola?" Shanelle said "she's gone to a funeral". [Ms Gotham] said "you know what I want to talk to you about, it's about the fight". She said "if anyone asks you, just say we are speaking about Nicola". Why does she have to use my name? Couldn't she use anyone else's name?'
>
> (Nicola, African-Caribbean pupil, Year 9, School C)

Nicola therefore is rejecting a form of teacher dislike. She is aware that she, and many of her friends, are being sought out by a particular teacher. She also recognizes that even in her absence she is being associated with, and in a sense implicated in, a negative incident, simply because she knows what may have happened. Though there is no immediate threat of school exclusion here, none the less, Nicola is aware from her conversations with other pupils that Ms Gotham seeks out particular groups of young people for her attention. It is the approach taken by Ms Gotham, trying to ensure that there is very little chance for Nicola to misbehave and Nicola's attendant perception that Ms Gotham does not like her as an individual, that is causing Nicola the most trouble. Nicola responds to Ms Gotham in a similar way to Shahid, above:

> 'My mum just said "ignore her". I can do it because I can stare Ms Gotham out. Like she will look at all my friends in assembly and they will all just look back at her. Just look at her. Me, I'm not making her ruin my chances of being what I want to be in life. I will just stick it out because I haven't got that long left in school.'
>
> (Nicola, African-Caribbean pupil, Year 9, School C)

Like the young Black women who 'resist within accommodation' (Mirza 1992; Fuller 1982), Nicola feels the best way to outwit and hence show a greater resistance to Ms Gotham is to achieve longer term educational goals. Nicola commented that she would like to go to university and recognizes what she would need to achieve in order to do so.

The fraught relationship which existed between Nicola and Ms Gotham is situated within a climate towards discipline which was changing within the school. The school was moving away from the image it had gained of being a high excluder of Black pupils. The Head had introduced new forms of classroom management for teachers, and they had been involved in much in-service training. However, the relationship of the staff to their Black pupils remained ambivalent, and Nicola's situation becomes quite interesting within this context. Though many teachers avoided talking directly about the racial differences of the pupils, they clearly perceived certain differences to exist between pupils. The new approach to discipline was balanced on the side of leniency, particularly for some of the pupils who may have required some work from pastoral staff. However, teachers in other schools had commented that the pastoral structure at School C was undeveloped, that the staff had received little training in defusing situations and that those defusing were more comfortable with confrontational approaches. Regardless of this the exclusion figures were gradually reducing, helped as pointed out by Nicola above, by some parents who were asked to withdraw their children, or indeed by others who *made the decision to withdraw themselves*. The circumstances under which these decisions were made varied, for example as with Nicola's mother, who was aware of the negative relationship developing between Ms Gotham and her daughter.

The shape of racism within schools

Rather than introducing a climate in which Black pupils were increasingly sought out, as Nicola felt, one African teacher thought that the teachers were damaging the educational chances of Black children first by being too lenient with them, and then by resorting to exclusion once their behaviour had grown out of control.

> '[Black children] live in a society where people just think if they say something they will be accused of racism. So they allow this to wear away. Children are not being dealt with at the initial stage. You don't allow it to get to that instance before dealing with it. People don't speak to most of the minorities because they are afraid to because of racism. Personally I believe the teachers are not doing their job. I see my black students roaming about and nobody says anything to them. We know there's racism but they shouldn't use it as an excuse of doing nothing.'
>
> (Mr Ogbu, Teacher, School C)

Mr Ogbu is speaking about those pupils who are left to their own devices until it becomes possible to exclude them permanently and thus is talking about a different group of Black pupils. However, this contrasts with the experience of Nicola and her group of Black female friends. She does not fit into the category of the pupils left alone by staff. Perhaps her involvement in the educational programme supported by the Black voluntary organization sets her apart from the pupils that Mr Ogbu despairs of. There may indeed be a multitude of other explanations, but it is clear that Nicola has sought a more immediate strategy to her schooling experience. Both of her strategies must, however, be situated within the climate of racialization which exists within her school.

However, Mr Ogbu makes an important point surrounding the responses of staff to ethnic minority pupils, which he perceives to be one of initial avoidance with almost intentional outcomes, and Nicola sees as one of confrontation and differentiation. Pupils who responded to the existence of racism in their interactions with staff did so because of a real perception of differential treatment. All of the young women in Nicola's 'gang' were of African-Caribbean and mixed parentage. The group of young men who Mr Mills wanted to 'weed out' of his school described earlier by Shahid, were African-Caribbean and, as will be highlighted in the chapter to follow, many other pupils at this school felt differential experiences of school sanction existed between Black and White pupils. There were occasions, however, which Mr Ogbu may be alluding to, where racism was seen by pupils who would then admit later on that it had not actually existed. However, this behaviour was rare among the pupils. It was often the case that they would interpret particular responses of staff as racist or believe certain comments to be racist. Even where in some cases it was doubtful that a racist incident had taken place, what is important is that the pupils' experience of that incident was that it *had* been racist and that it was a real perception.

> 'I do think sometimes, this might sound awful, it might come out wrongly, but sometimes they can use racism to exclude their behaviour. Their behaviour, if it's wrong doesn't matter what race you are it's still wrong. It's got to be dealt with.'
>
> (Mrs Frank, Head of Year 10, School A)

Mrs Frank is of course quite correct that where behaviour has been wrong it should be treated as such and that teachers should respond to all indications of misbehaviour equitably. However, many pupils saw that others were being allowed to continue misbehaviour whilst they would receive a sanction. Where the pupils allowed to continue misbehaving were White, ethnic minority pupils came to what they saw as a logical conclusion, thus placing all of their strategies to resist the authority of that teacher within a racial context.

> 'You get different kinds of racism, you get undercover racism as well. They react in different ways, treat us different from Whites.'
>
> (Chantel, mixed parentage, Year 10 pupil, School B)

Each school had developed equal opportunities policies and whereas in School D, this and the anti-racist philosophy of the school was discussed with all pupils by all teachers when they arrived in Year 7, in School C for example,

Black professionals were brought in to add the necessary 'multicultural' focus to the school. Gillborn (1990) warns against developing anti-racist policies which are 'merely an empty exercise by which yet another document is produced to be debated, adopted and ultimately forgotten by the majority of teachers' (Gillborn 1990: 119). In the majority of schools equal opportunities statements prohibited racial harassment and name calling among peers in school. Very rarely do such documents look at the possibility of racism occurring between staff and pupils where staff, rather than pupils, are the perpetrators. Within this context, therefore, staff were not willing to accept the accusations of racism levelled by some of the pupils above, and were more inclined to see them as excuse making, or simply malicious.

> 'He thinks that everything that anybody ever tells him off for is to do with the colour of his skin. He doesn't think that it's to do with his behaviour. It's like some women think that everything that goes wrong in their life is because they are a woman. Whereas it might be because of their personality. I don't get promotion because I'm a woman. In fact they don't get promotion because they are not good enough. I wish I felt happier to deal with it. But I'm concerned that if I once go down that road, I might get labelled as being racist.'
>
> (Mrs Keys, Assistant Head of Department, School B)

Mrs Keys sees herself as a victim of her attempts to challenge what a particular pupil has said. Teachers are seen as non-racist individuals because of their status within the school and the likelihood that a child has used the accusation in order to get him/herself away from a troubled situation (Gillborn 1990). For other Black members of staff however, the experience of being seen as racist by Black pupils was particularly worrying.

> 'Worst I've ever been called was by an Afro-Caribbean kid that had been excluded. It was about coconuts. I found that in many ways quite wounding, insulting. It wasn't because it was from another Black person to another Black person. But by the nature of it. You condemn [their] behaviour and that therefore somehow you are negating the colour of your skin you know. I find that quite offensive. Apart from the fact when he first said anything I couldn't understand what it was. I asked somebody and I think one of the parents told me. You know black on the outside, white on the inside. I hadn't got a clue.'
>
> (Mr Cheatle, Deputy Head, School A)

Understandings of racism for Black staff were quite similar to those expressed by pupils. In School C, where the issue of school exclusion had become increasingly racialized, the focus on Black children in staff discussions was worrying.

> 'I think every school has [racism]. I think there is racism at School B. Whenever I'm sitting in the staffroom, sometimes you'll be sitting in the[re] and you'll hear the staff going on about this list of kids. And 8 times out of 10 it will be a list of Black kids.

No I'm not saying … some of them are bad. Nehemiah, he's just completely barmy, and the only way to cope with Nehemiah is to laugh at him and laugh with him. Once you start being heavy, you get into a confrontation situation and you've lost it. I feel sad that [another African-Caribbean boy] was permanently excluded, he's another statistic. You've got to learn how to survive in the system. You know you see so many of them [Black pupils] wearing the headphones and big baggy coats. And I think "I know what my view of you is but what are White teachers' views of these Black pupils?". And you can't get an honest answer to that because if you ask white teachers they will say "I've got no problems with Black pupils, I treat everyone the same". This is the standard answer. So you can't really get to the root of it and the causes of the problem. Some of the teachers cannot cope with the Black kids, just in terms of talking to them. And that's where the problems stem from, if they could talk to them in a different manner.'

(Mr Shotter, Subject teacher, School B)

However, he felt that pupils talking about racism among staff was not the way to move beyond the potential of becoming another statistic. He did feel that racism was present, but he felt it essential for Black pupils to use responses more effectively to achieve change, rather than simply reacting to what they perceived to be racist comments.

Teacher understandings of resistance

The case studies presented above are only a few of the indications of pupils' resistance to various forms of authority from among those interviewed. Pupils resisted in a variety of other ways to their schools. Other pupils in School B, who were disappointed with the buildings in which the majority of their learning took place, developed a lack of respect for them. Litter was found everywhere, and some children had even begun to spit in corridors. The rules which had been promoted in the school at the beginning of the year in tandem with the new discipline policy were rejected by many pupils, primarily because they felt they had not had a say in their development.

'[School rules] are important but nobody does them. They put them how a teacher would look at it.'

(Chantel, mixed parentage, Year 10 pupil, School D)

Another pupil in School A, who felt alienated from the school ethos around high academic standards due to his learning difficulties, also disagreed with the rules at his school

'Nobody goes by them [rules]. When people ask us to do something, when someone puts a rule up saying don't do this, they [pupils] think "I'll go against it". It's like everyone has got to prove something.'

(Richard, White Year 9 pupil, School A)

An Indian pupil at School C felt that the boundaries were constantly being changed by his teachers, which is reflective of the changing climate around discipline within which Nicola's experiences were situated.

> '[You're] messing around with the teacher, the teacher laughs and then when you say something else and the teacher sends you out because they don't like what you're saying, I think "what did I do? You were laughing and I get sent out".'
>
> (Deep, Indian, Year 10 pupil, School C)

Deep responded by verbally challenging his teachers when he felt that they were in the wrong. Many teachers comment on this behaviour by pupils which is seen as indicative of insolence. For the pupils, it is often the only opportunity they have to 'save face' when they have had a confrontation with a teacher which has taken them completely by surprise. Pupils require extraordinary levels of sophistication to be able to cope with individual teachers, particularly in view of the speed at which teachers can respond to them differently in a variety of different situations (Reid 1987). It is therefore necessary for teachers to engage in consistent behaviour wherever possible as pupils can be particularly sensitive to a teacher who laughs and jokes with them at one stage and then decides the jokes are no longer funny the next.

The extent to which a pupil's negative response to particular aspects of school are recognized by their teachers can illustrate whether or not that pupil's behaviour is resistant. The resistant activities of Black pupils who wear specific items of clothing, or use particular ways of responding to teachers that are culturally specific (i.e. kissing their teeth, talking to each other in patois), were not always interpreted by staff as forms of behaviour which meant anything other than insolence (Wright 1985; Gillborn 1990; Mac an Ghaill 1988). The extent to which these practices can therefore effect change for the pupils concerned is questionable (Sultana 1989), although the use of these practices as a means of regaining personal dignity and as a coping strategy cannot be disregarded (Gillborn 1990). However, in certain cases teachers are aware of the strategies used by pupils and of the reasons behind them and where pupils have been successful in transmitting their anger and frustrations to staff, the transformative possibilities of their contestual behaviours are increased. Thus for example, although it is unlikely that any member of staff at School C could prevent the disadvantage present in the community in which Shahid lived, introducing a more tolerant conception of discipline may have gone some way towards enabling him to remain in school and sit the examinations that would find him employment.

However, though teachers may recognize why pupils resist their control, unless they are in a position to assist them, the knowledge is of no use. One White male technology teacher in School C was the form tutor for an African-Caribbean girl who was badly behaved with almost all of her teachers.

His comment, however, was that the majority of teenage girls are disaffected, and that there is very little a school can do to prevent that. Keys and Fernandes (1993) found that pupils' attitudes to school tend to deteriorate between the ages of 11 and 14 and it has been suggested that 'deviant behaviour is a normal part of growing up and a part of becoming a person in one's own right' (McManus 1989: 76). The behaviour of young people therefore can be unpredictable and the technology teacher has suggested an awareness and acceptance of his tutee's behaviour. However, in this respect, the tutor's response to the pupil's behaviour, and the frustration with schooling that it demonstrates, will not enable that young woman to move beyond whatever has created her disaffection. School C, in moving from a fairly harsh response to the pupils on its roll it considered undesirable, has adopted a *laissez-faire* approach to discipline. Whereas other schools with similar pupils may attempt to look at the reasons behind the behaviour of pupils and work with pupils to resolve difficulties as far as possible, the positive teaching approach adopted by staff at School C does not enable them to use their evaluations of pupils to any great effect.

At School B there was a very clear division between senior management staff and the rest of the school. It is likely that children's perceptions of the huge distinctions between themselves and senior members of staff were well formed by the time the school decided to change to a more relaxed approach to teaching. In this climate, therefore, no change would have been successful, and pupils interviewed commented on their opinion of the state of the school buildings and increasing antagonism between them and the senior staff who gave them sanctions for poor behaviour. However, in understanding the behaviour of the pupils who are disruptive in school, Miss Bean places the blame of the ills of her pupils at the door of society generally.

> 'There are an awful lot of pupils we are seeing going through school who know, or who anticipate that they are never going to work. And therefore what is the point? We can't offer them that carrot any more of "work hard in school and you'll do OK", because some of them won't regardless of their ability in some cases. Society is shaped in such a way that we can no longer offer full-time employment to everybody. We haven't got to a stage where we can offer them an alternative. How many are going home seeing parents who don't work? Where there is no hope of work in communities, where a lot of people have no hope of work? 10 years ago you could say to a child, if you work hard at school this will happen. Although we may still say that, for an awful lot of people it's not true.'
>
> (Miss Bean, Head of Department, School B)

This teacher is aware of the difficulties which may inform the behaviour of some of the children in the school and many of her opinions were shared by other members of teaching staff at the school. There was an increasing level of cynicism by some of the non-senior teachers, which not only reflected the sense of hopelessness they felt for many of their pupils, but also the fact that particular processes within the school itself either aggravated or failed to respond to these pupil needs. As Docking (1987) suggests:

> '[T]he behaviour of any human being at any particular time is materially affected by the context in which she or he is placed ... The main factors which predispose many children to behave unacceptably may lie outside the immediate control of the school, but the extent to which a child realizes any tendency to behave badly will depend upon the quality of life experienced at school. Children who experience a high level of stress due to disharmony in the home, for instance, may or may not use the school to vent their frustration, depending upon their perception of what is expected of them at school and how they believe they are valued in the school community.'

(Docking 1987: 16)

Understanding racialized resistances

Resistances against situations seen as unfair were not restricted to pupils in schools. Teachers, who feel powerless against policy changes made by senior members of staff, who are not consulted on major school decisions, who teach in schools which are seen as 'sin bins' and, most importantly for the issue under present discussion, reject the use of school exclusion, are likely to attempt to use their positions as teachers to assist their pupils as far as possible within these restricted contexts. Often teachers are presented as an undifferentiated category by pupils within schools, as indeed are pupils by their teachers. However, where particular school approaches to the issue of exclusion have not worked effectively, this is usually because they are resisted by both pupils and some members of staff. In addition to this, the fatalistic attitude to the situations of some pupils described above, will not be shared by all staff, and as one teacher pointed out in relation to the underachievement of Black male pupils 'you shouldn't just say look at this awful statistic, you say what can we do about it, who can we work with?'. It is unlikely that these members of staff can affect forms of resistance to particular school-based or wider educational policies. In the same way despite the resistance of many pupils to their negative relations with some staff, it was not enough to alter them. However, the contesting of unfair practices can challenge, however temporarily, the powerless position within which unhappy individuals have been placed.

When speaking of differentiating the category of teachers, an immediate starting point relates to that of 'race'. Though there were very few Black teachers in the schools visited, many of them saw their roles as teachers extending beyond the ordinary teacher–pupil relationship. Much work has pointed out the complex positions that Black teachers find themselves placed in

(Callender 1998; Sewell 1997), particularly where they find themselves teaching in a minority, or in schools where Black children are experiencing educational problems.

The pupil population in School E was almost entirely made up of White children. There was one African-Caribbean female pupil in Year 9, and three mixed parentage pupils. Interestingly all were selected by senior staff as pupils who gave teachers cause for concern. Within this environment there were only two ethnic minority members of staff. One, an African-Caribbean male, was the site manager for the school and thus had no teaching responsibilities at all, and the other was an African-Caribbean science teacher.

> 'I think you have to establish yourself with the staff because I think when I first started teaching people were very suspicious, because I was the only Black teacher on the staff. Also the relationship with the kids can be a strain at times. I've had one incident of racial abuse, I've had two since I've been here, so I suppose that's not bad. They still have latent ideas about Black people, and it's not until you start talking to them, and they make an off-the-cuff remark, that you realize that it's just underneath the surface. A classic one was when they were collecting for charity, and one of the kids in my form said "I hope it's not going to them Black people in Africa." So I said "what's wrong with that?" He said "we should be spending it here."'
>
> (Mrs Lewis, Science Teacher, School E)

Unlike some of the other Black teachers interviewed who felt that they could support Black pupils or at least assist their colleagues when responding to ethnic minority pupils, Mrs Lewis felt that the Black pupils at School E were looked after by other pupils, despite the racial antagonism that existed in the local community.

Other Black teachers were critical of their colleagues who refused to take racial differences of the pupils into account.

> 'In an inner city school I'm surprised by the lack of knowledge some of my colleagues have about others who come from Black African-Caribbean and Asian backgrounds. I think it's appalling. Your view is different and your perception of the world you live in is different. I think if you are a Black teacher and you have got some political awareness of the issues, then you bring those views to the school and you can see things in a way that I don't think White teachers ever see because I don't think they understand. I don't think White teachers understand contemporary Black youth culture, they don't understand how it affects young people. Some of the things that Black kids have said to teachers, I don't think they mean it in the way that the teachers have taken it. They're just rapping and the teachers say "who do you think you are talking to me like that?" When all they need to say is "yeah and you too".'
>
> (Mr Shorter, African-Caribbean, Subject teacher, School B)

And in view of the difficulties colleagues may experience in understanding particular cultural aspects, Black teachers were faced with a lot of responsibilities both to their colleagues and to other Black pupils.

'I think it's very lonely and very hard being a Black teacher which White teachers don't understand and don't appreciate because you work in a real sense of isolation. And you have to compromise yourself. Because you've got to fit into a White working environment. You can't say the things you want to say, you can't do the things you want to do because you've got to fit in with the context of the other people. Kids judge you straight away and they judge you as a Black teacher. It's even harder as a Black teacher because if I fail in my job, I'm letting down the Black kids in this school and further Black teachers. Whereas if I do a good job as a Black teacher then firstly, hopefully I'll get the respect of the kids and secondly the respect of my fellow members of staff and thirdly any other Black teachers who apply for jobs here.'
                              (Mr Shotter, African-Caribbean Subject Teacher, School B)

Thus the cultural misunderstandings which arose between some of the Black pupils in School B and the White members of staff often escalated into conflict which Mr Shotter clearly felt was avoidable. However, although he had the knowledge which could assist some Black pupils in confrontations that may develop with staff, this teacher clearly could not always be available to interpret for his colleagues what particular pupils may have meant, or alternatively to prevent the type of responses Black pupils would give to staff whom they perceived to be crossing particular cultural boundaries. There were clearly some things that he as an African-Caribbean teacher could say to pupils, but which would not be received in a similar way if said by a teacher who did not share that cultural background. Mr Shotter felt that staff needed to come to their own understanding of cultural differences rather than rely on him.

Understanding why particular ethnic minority pupils were resistant to aspects of school was not welcomed as readily by all ethnic minority teachers. And whereas Mr Shotter would engage in specific forms of banter, which interestingly he could only do with the majority of the African-Caribbean *male* pupils that he taught, others felt that to do so would cross the professional, and power-related boundaries between themselves and pupils. For one of these teachers there were specific situations when the sharing of a cultural background in a way that was not accessible by other White members of staff/pupils, was not acceptable. In an environment where Black teachers are in more of a minority that the pupils themselves, it is often necessary for professional boundaries to be maintained in order that respect be gained from staff.

Others who did not feel particularly marginalized within their schools were likely to approach the issue of 'race' more confidently with Black pupils. Some felt it their duty to do so whereas others did not mind that pupils from a similar background felt comfortable talking to them about particular issues.

'There will be an extra sensitivity on my part to the progress and behaviour of Asian and Afro-Caribbean people. I'm not stressing *better*. I'm not saying its nice, I'm just saying there's an extra sensitivity there. I can say things to both those groups that maybe some of my White colleagues would shy away from. I can more easily bring to the attention of Afro-Caribbean and Asians, that I found it can sometimes be hard and prejudiced and that having a good education is one of the ways in which you can break down some of those barriers.'

(Mr Cheatle, African-Caribbean, Deputy Head, School A)

'There are some students who will say something in one of the languages and try and be a bit more pally with me, asking me questions about my background and I will answer it quite truthfully. I don't mind at all. They'll ask me things like do you wear a sari? Or do you do this, do you like Indian music. Well that's my culture so I'll say yes, no, whatever. We relate more because they know they've got someone in a position of authority who is one of them.'

(Miss Kular, Indian, Subject teacher, School C)

For another, trying to help Black children proved to be difficult, but he still felt that helping them to succeed was important, regardless of their opinion.

'The caring is different. You care more. The value is different. They [Black pupils] can hate me provided I think I am doing the right thing. You want them to like you when you are destroying them, then you are not helping them. Because these are people who really need education in order to go forward. They don't want to be told off, they don't want to be corrected. If you allow them to do whatever they're doing they'll be your best friend. Because you don't allow [it] they say who are you to challenge me when no other person challenges me?'

(Mr Ogbu, African, Subject teacher, School C)

Conclusion

There are clearly many instances where the behaviour/attitudes of individuals within schools may be read or interpreted as resistant. However, as has been suggested here, the possibilities of deeming behaviour resistant can rely on the extent to which such behaviour effects change for the resisting individual. The oppositional acts and attitudes highlighted within this chapter by Shahid, for example, demonstrated that there is not a simple relationship between opposition and resistance. Even where the use of 'attitude' by Nicola to respond to a classroom situation may have had more immediate resistant effects, the likelihood that her 'attitude' could solve longer term problems would be more difficult to achieve. Much pupil 'oppositionality' involves 'face-saving' where they have felt embarrassed by teacher action or the experience of sanction. But it is rare that such action can achieve the longer term objectives of theorized resistance. Rather it is important that an understanding of racialized pupil resistance within schools takes into account that often resistant actions on the part of Black pupils are a response to a relationship with the school that has built up negatively over time. The outcome of the resistance is only ever temporal – Nehemiah and his friends can refuse to remove their hats for their Headteacher to the extent that he will move away from the situation and the relations of power are temporarily reversed until, of course, their actions result in exclusion or other sanction.

It is also important to look at the place of 'race' within the resistance debate. Actions, attitudes and other signifiers can become imbued with racial meaning, but this can be interpreted differently by the various parties involved in the education process. Teachers considered references to 'racism' which can be employed by some students as indicative of excuse, whereas pupils may read racism in teacher actions, and perceive teacher indifference to their concerns as further evidence that racism has taken place. It is important that discussions around racism be held openly, as it is at the basis of much Black pupil resistance within school. However, racism itself is also undercut by the gendered discourses which place Black boys and girls in different levels of conflict and hence varying rates of exclusion within schools.

References

Aggleton, P. (1987) *Rebels Without a Cause: Middle-class Youth and the Transition from School to Work*, London: Falmer Press.

Anyon, J. (1983) 'Intersections of gender and class: accommodation and resistance by working class and affluent females to contradictory sex-role ideologies', in S. Walker and L. Burton (eds) *Gender, Class and Education*, Lewes: Falmer Press.

Blyth, E. and Milner, J. (1996) *Exclusion from School: Inter-professional Issues for Policy and Practice*, London: Routledge.

Brittan, A. and Maynard, M. (1984) *Sexism, Racism and Oppression*, Oxford: Basil Blackwell.

Callender, C. (1998) *Education For Empowerment*, Stoke-on-Trent: Trentham Books.

Cashmore, E. and Troyna, B. (eds) (1982) *Black Youth in Crisis*, London: Allen & Unwin.

Davies, L. (1983) 'Gender, resistance and power' in S. Walker and L. Barton (eds) *Gender, Class and Education*, Lewes: Falmer Press.

Docking, J. W. (1987) Control and Discipline in School: Perspectives and Approaches (2nd edn), London: Harper and Row.

Foster, P. (1990) *Policy and Practice in Multicultural and Anti-racist Education*, London: Routledge.

Foster, P. (1991) 'Case still not proven: a reply to Cecile Wright', *British Educational Research Journal*, 12(2): 165–70.

Foster, P., Gomm, R. and Hammersley, M. (1996) *Constructing Educational Inequality*, London: Falmer Press.

Fuller, M. (1982) 'Young, female and black', in E. Cashmore and B. Troyna (eds) *Black Youth in Crisis*, London: Allen & Unwin.

Gewirz, D. (1991) 'Analyses of racism and sexism in education and strategies for change', *British Journal of Sociology of Education*, 12(2): 183–201.

Gillborn, D. (1990) *'Race', Ethnicity and Education: Teaching and Learning in Multi-ethnic Schools*, London: Unwin Hyman.

Hammersley, M. and Gomm, R. (1993) 'A response to Gillborn and Drew on "race", class and school effects', *New Community*, 19(2): 348–53.

Keys, W. and Fernandes, C. (1993) 'What do students think about school?', A report for the National Commission on Education, Slough: National Foundation for Educational Research.

Mac an Ghaill, M. (1988) *Young, Gifted and Black*, Milton Keynes: Open University Press.

Mac an Ghaill, M. (1994) *The Making of Men: Masculinities, Sexualities and Schooling*, Milton Keynes: Open University Press.

McFadden, M. (1995) 'Resistance to schooling and educational outcomes: questions of structure and agency', *British Journal of Sociology of Education*, 16(3): 293–308.

McManus, M. (1989) *Troublesome Behaviour in the Classroom: A Teacher's Survival Guide*, London: Routledge.

McRobbie, A. (1978) 'Working class girls and the culture of femininity' in Women's Studies Group (eds) *Women Take Issue: Aspects of Women's Subordination*, London: Hutchinson, for University of Birmingham Centre for Contemporary Cultural Studies.

McRobbie, A. (1991) *Feminism and Youth Culture from 'Jackie' to 'Just Seventeen'*, London: Macmillan.

Meyenn, R. (1980) 'Schoolgirls' peer groups' in P. Woods (ed.) *Pupil Strategies: Explorations in the Sociology of the School*, London: Croom Helm.

Mirza, H. (1992) *Young, Female and Black I*, London: Routledge.

Reid, J. (1987) 'A problem in the family: explanations under strain', in T. Booth and D. Coulby (eds) *Producing and Reducing Disaffection*, Milton Keynes: Open University Press.

Sewell, T. (1997) *Black Masculinities and Schooling: How Black Boys Survive Modern Schooling*, Stoke-on-Trent: Trentham Books.

Sultana, R. (1989) 'Transition education, student contestation and the production of meaning: possibilities and limitations of resistance theories', *British Journal of Sociology of Education*, 10(3): 287–309.

Walker, J. (1986) 'Romanticising resistance, romanticising culture: problems in Willis' theory of cultural production', *British Journal of Sociology of Education*, 7: 59–80.

Watson, I. (1993) 'Education, class and culture: the Birmingham ethnographic tradition and the problem of the new middle class', *British Journal of Sociology of Education*, 14: 179–97.

Willis, P. (1977) *Learning to Labour: How Working Class Kids Get Working Class Jobs*, Aldershot: Saxon House.

Wright, C. (1985) 'School processes – an ethnographic study', in J. Eggleston et al. (eds) *Education for Some: The Educational and Vocational Experiences of 15–18-Year-Old Members of Minority Ethnic Groups*, Stoke-on-Trent: Trentham Books.

Wright, C. (1987) 'The relations between teachers and Afro-Caribbean pupils: observing multi-racial classrooms', in G. Weinger and M. Arnot, *Gender Under Scrutiny: New Inquiries in Education*, London: Hutchinson.

Chapter 7

Youth development circles

John Braithwaite

Introduction

Restorative justice circles or conferences have shown considerable promise in the criminal justice system as a more decent and effective way of dealing with youthful law breaking than punishment. The social movement for restorative justice has a distinctive analysis of the crisis of community and the possibility of community in late modernity. This chapter raises the question of whether this approach might fruitfully be applied to the holistic development of the learning potential of the young and the whole range of problems young people encounters – drug abuse, unemployment, homelessness, suicide, among others – in the transition from school to work.

The late modern structural dilemma of human and social capital

In the new information economy, it is clear that human capital (the skills of people) and social capital (social skills for interacting with others including dispositions such as trust and trustworthiness) are becoming progressively more important to economic development than physical capital (Dowrick, 1993; Fukuyama, 1995; Latham, 1998). Young people whose human and social capital remains undeveloped are destined for unemployment. Mostly families with high endowments of human and social capital pass those on to their children. There is a strong correlation between parental involvement in the education of their children and academic performance (Finn Report, 1991, p. 151). For children whose families lack endowments of human and social capital, we rely on state-funded education systems to compensate.

Yet we quickly run up against the limits of the capabilities of formal education bureaucracies to make up for deficits which are profoundly informal (especially on the social capital side) [1]. Our objective in this essay is to come up with a new policy solution to this limitation [2]. At the same time, we want to help solve the problem of children from families with high endowments, but where human and social capital development is interrupted by problems like drug addiction, bullying by peers, sexual abuse, depression and suicide.

Our hypothesis is that both the low family endowments problem and the interrupted transmission problem need a more informal yet more systematic solution than the formal education system can provide. Mentoring programmes like 'Big Brothers' and 'Big Sisters' head in the right direction (reducing drug abuse and violence in one eight-site evaluation (Elliott, 1998, p. xviii)). But they are insufficiently social, communal and plural to deal with the kinds of deficits at issue with reducing youth unemployment, drug addiction, delinquency and suicide.

In terms of social structure, we see the problem as one of a late modernity where:

(a) nuclear families are isolated from extended families which used to compensate for deficits of nuclear families; and

(b) formal education bureaucracies are too formal to compensate for the social aspects of the deficits that thereby arise – for example, in teaching trust, love, respectfulness.

This structural dilemma of late modernity has crept up on us over the past century. Social historians have shown that early in the 20th century parents much more commonly than today shared child-rearing obligations with extended families, churches and other community networks (Lasch, 1977; Zelizer, 1985). Single parents, who in Western societies are more likely to be black and poor (LaFree, 1998, pp. 147–148), are particularly likely to become 'solo practitioners' of child rearing. Mothers struggling alone to educate their children without support from the village therefore worsen inequalities of race and sex. Remedial policies to spread burdens of informal education and support for children are thus imperative to tackling the inequalities arising from our dual structural dilemma of modernity.

How the education system can learn from the criminal justice system

The direction for a solution to this dual structural problem is captured by the African proverb that it takes a whole village to raise a child. But this of course begs the question raised by the structural problem; we do not live in villages in the West. Recent experience with restorative justice innovation in the criminal justice system has come up with an interesting solution to a similar structural dilemma of crime control. Criminologists know that crime is a result of failures of informal community ordering (Sampson & Laub, 1993; Sampson & Raudenbush, 1999) and of social support for young people (Cullen, 1994). Unfortunately, however, most remedial programmes fail because of the structural impossibility of building village solutions in the city or suburb. Neighbourhood Watch seems like a good idea, but the evidence is that it is not very effective in reducing crime (Sherman *et al.*, 1997). One reason is that most of us do not care enough about our community or are just too busy to turn up to Neighbourhood Watch meetings. They work somewhat better in highly organised middle-class communities – where they are least needed in terms of crime.

A recent innovation that has been quite successful in solving this problem has been the restorative justice or family group conference (as they are called in the Southern hemisphere) or healing circle (as they are more often called in North America). Actually, it is an innovation that picks up ancient village traditions of justice and adapts them to the metropolis. When a young person is arrested, they are asked who are the people they most respect, trust, love. The most common answers are mum and dad, brothers and sisters and grandparents. But often with children who are homeless because they have been sexually abused by parents, parents will not be on the list. Members of a 'street family' (Hagan & McCarthy, 1997) may be on the list here. But there still may be an aunt, brother, or grandparent who is loved by the homeless child. That child may have been stigmatised by most of the teachers at his or her school, but there may be just one staff member who he or she believes has treated her decently. That member of the school staff, the street family and the few members of the extended family who are still respected are then brought together in a conference. The conference sits in a circle with victims of the crime (and supporters of the victim) to discuss the consequences of the crime and what needs to be done to right the wrongs that have been done and to get the young offender's and the victim's lives back on track. With a homeless child, it might be agreed that the young offender will go and live in the home of his uncle or his older brother, who will undertake to help him get back into school.

The diversity of supporters for young people in conferences or circles is considerable. There can be elders from an indigenous community, football coaches, ballet teachers, neighbours, or friends who share a hobby. It is this diversity which makes the circle modern and urban. Human beings are social animals. There are almost always other human beings they enjoy interacting with. It is simply not true that most homeless children are alone in the world; they have 'street families' whose company they enjoy. Hagan and McCarthy (1997) found that a majority of their youth living on the streets of Toronto and Vancouver actually referred to their intimates as their 'street family'. Second, human beings find meaning from social identity; there always exist people we identify with or respect. We train circle coordinators who report back that a young offender who is totally isolated should try again, to work harder to discover people she likes or respects, even if it means bringing in the one sibling or uncle who is respected from another city. The late modern sense of community is fragmented across space, but it exists. What the restorative justice circle does is bring that community of care together for the first time in one room. In the quintessentially late modern case, one of the participants may be a friend from cyberspace who the young offender physically meets for the first time. It is wrong to say that these faceless friendships are always artificial and meaningless. Community in the metropolis is in some ways more meaningful than community in the village because it can be based on casting a wide net among a very large group of people to find a few who have very similar interests to our own, such as an interest in the history of Reggae music which would be hard to share in a small English village.

Early evidence is only preliminary, but it is encouraging that these conferences mostly work well in various ways, though we still have much to learn about contexts where they backfire (Braithwaite, 1999). The fact from this literature we want to emphasise here is that when supporters are invited to attend these conferences, they generally come. I do not go to Neighbourhood Watch Meetings, even though I think that would be a public spirited thing to do. But if a young neighbour singled me out as someone they would like to be their supporter at a conference after they had got into trouble with the police, I would attend. Why? The answer is that in the conference case I am honoured to have been nominated by a human being as someone they respect. Second, I am personally touched by their predicament. They are in trouble and they have made a personal appeal to me, so I feel it would be callous to be unwilling to give up my evening for the conference. In short, community fails with Neighbourhood Watch but works with the restorative justice conference because it is an individual-centred communitarianism. This individual-centred communitarianism tugs at the sense of obligation that works in the late modern world of community based on geographically dispersed ties of respect and identification.

To date, the evaluation research evidence is consistent with this conclusion. More than a dozen studies have found participant satisfaction (among offenders, victims and their families) running at over 90% (Braithwaite, 1999, pp. 20–27). Both participant satisfaction and participant perceptions of procedural fairness, effectiveness, respect for rights and equality before the law are higher in conference than in court (Braithwaite, 1999, p. 26). It is premature to conclude whether restorative justice conferences are in fact effective in reducing crime. A number of studies show markedly lower reoffending rates among young offenders who go to conferences compared to those who go to court (Forsythe, 1995; Chan, 1996). Large parts of such differences are likely to be selection effects – less serious cases going to conferences – in studies with inadequate controls. Burford and Pennell's (1998) study of adult family violence conferences has more impressive controls and found substantial reductions for conference compared to control families in 31 problem behaviours ranging from alcohol abuse to violence against wives or children. Most notably, abuse/neglect incidents halved in the year after the family group decision making conference. Other early studies of victim–offender mediation with more adequate controls (or randomisation) and with positive effects on reoffending were conducted by Schneider (1986), Pate (1990), Nugent & Paddock (1995) and Wynne (1996). Umbreit *et al.* (1994) found results that favoured victim–offender mediation, but which did not reach statistical significance. McCold & Wachtel's (1998) findings were mixed at best, discouraging at worst, findings that are hard to interpret because of unsatisfactory assurance that the randomly assigned treatment was delivered. The Restorative Justice Group at the Australian National University is finalising the largest randomised controlled trial of conferences compared to court for juvenile and adult offenders under the leadership of Lawrence Sherman and Heather Strang. An update of the Braithwaite (1999) review has been completed as this article goes to press (Braithwaite, forthcoming). It reports a surge of new studies suggesting that restorative justice does contribute to crime reduction.

Now we will seek to translate to education as an institution our analysis from the sociology of crime about what mobilises community. In doing so, we will also attempt to solve one of the problems of restorative justice circles – that the very act of assembling the community of care on the occasion of a youth being in trouble can stigmatise a young person as a troublemaker.

Youth development circles – the idea

The basic idea is to translate the conference/circle from criminal justice into the arena of educational development. Unlike conferencing in the criminal justice system, the idea presented now has not been subjected to any piloting. The main difference is that the circle would be a permanent feature of the young person's life rather than an ad hoc group assembled to deal with a criminal offence. Initially, the circle would be constituted to replace parent–teacher interviews in high schools.

Twice a year from entry to high school at age 12 through to successful placement in a tertiary course or a job (modal age 18), the Youth Development Facilitator (operating from an office in a high school) would convene a meeting of the young person's community of care. This meeting would be called a Youth Development Circle.

The circle would have Core and Casual Members. Core Members would be asked up front to commit, as an obligation of citizenship and care, to try to attend all circles *until the young person is successfully placed in a tertiary course or a job* and to continue to be there for him/her should the young person subsequently request a Circle or get in trouble with the police or the courts. Core members would actually sign a contract to keep meeting and helping the young person until that tertiary or job placement was accomplished.

Core Members would normally include:

- Parents or guardians
- Brothers and sisters
- One grandparent selected by the young person
- One aunt, uncle or cousin selected by the young person
- A 'buddy', an older child from the school selected by the young person
- A pastoral adult carer from the school selected by the young person (normally, but not necessarily, a teacher)
- A neighbour, sporting coach, parent of a friend or any other adult member of the community selected by the young person as a mentor

Casual Members could include:

- Current teachers of the young person
- Current girlfriend or boyfriend
- Closest mates nominated by the young person
- Professionals brought in by the facilitator or parents (e.g. drug counsellor, employer from an industry in which the young person would eventually like to work)
- The victim of an act of bullying or delinquency and victim supporters

The Circle would commence with the facilitator introducing new members and reading the young person's six-month and long-term life goals as defined by him or her at the last meeting (six months ago). The young person would then be invited to summarise how he/she had got on with the six-month objectives and in what ways his/her life goals had changed in that period. In good circles, this would be followed by a series of celebratory speeches around the circle about what had been accomplished and the efforts that had been made. The crucial skill of the facilitator would be to elicit affirmation for accomplishment and offers of help (as opposed to criticism) when there was a failure of accomplishment. Gathering together for the ritual is all the communal signalling needed to show that accomplishment matters; personal criticism on top of this is only likely to foster rejection of the value of accomplishment. Indeed, through the ritual interpretation of poor accomplishment as a communal failure to give a young person the help they need, young people are less likely to interpret poor performance as reason for rejection by those they initially identify with. Rejection of the rejectors and devaluing accomplishment is less likely when there is a community of care who share the burden to build accomplishment come what may – unconditional support.

Normally, expert adults relevant to the six-month life goals would then be invited to comment (the mathematics teacher on a mathematics improvement goal; the school counsellor on improving relationships). Members of the Circle who had undertaken to provide agreed help towards those goals would be asked to report on whether they had managed to deliver it (Auntie Pat reporting whether they had managed to get together for an hour a week to help with maths homework).

In light of this discussion, the young person would be asked his/her thoughts on goals for the next six months and others would be invited to comment on this topic.

The facilitator would then ask the young person first, then all other participants, if they saw any other challenges in the young person's life where care and support might be needed. Whether new goals were needed to respond to these challenges would be discussed.

If no one else raised it, the facilitator would ask the young person and then his/her peers: 'Do your friends and other kids at school help you to achieve your goals or do they sometimes tempt you to do the wrong thing?' Responses to this are discussed by everyone and suggestions for action might be raised.

The facilitator then announces a tea break during which relevant sub-groups (e.g. the nuclear family, the young person's mates) might meet together informally to discuss a plan of action to propose to the Circle. Everyone is asked to think during the break about whether any new objectives or plans should be considered after the break.

The Circle reconvenes to discuss these issues and ends with the young person reading out his/her new goals and the names of members who have agreed in some way to provide help or support towards them. An adult member should be nominated as responsible for ensuring specific and important things be done on time. The facilitator checks that these adult members are happy to take on these obligations. The meeting is closed with thanks to the participants for their care and citizenship.

Over the years, the emphasis on the Circle would shift from educational and relationship challenges to the challenge of securing employment. With young people who were not doing well at school, special efforts would be made by the Core Members of the Circle to bring in Casual Members who might be able to offer work experience, advice on skill training and networking for job search.

A ritual of love

The foregoing makes the Circle seem a dry affair – rather like an expanded parent–teacher interview. For it to change lives, however, it would have to break out of this formal bureaucratic mould to become a ritual of caring in the way good restorative justice circles work. The literature on restorative justice conferences shows that love is central to understanding what makes them succeed. Nathan Harris's (1999) research on Canberra conferences concludes that reintegration (as opposed to stigmatisation) of offenders is critical to success. The attitude item with the highest loading on the reintegration factor in a factor analysis of offender attitudes toward the conference was 'During the conference did people suggest they loved you regardless of what you did?' In court cases, this item had the lowest loading on the reintegration factor of all the reintegration items. In short, the feeling by the offender that they were in receipt of unconditional love seems a crucial ingredient for the success of circles. And so, we hypothesise, with the Youth Development Circle.

The key ingredient for social capital formation that neither good education systems nor dysfunctional families can adequately supply is love. In conditions of modernity, even functional families lack sufficient ritual occasions to communicate how deeply they care about the child and how much they admire her efforts to develop her capacities. The rituals we do have – weddings, funerals, graduation, bar mitzvahs – are too few in the life of moderns. Village life had various low-key rituals around the campfire to compensate for this. Moderns must create new rituals of love and care that are meaningful in a modern setting and that can transmit modern endowments for success in life. This is the idea of holistic Youth Development Circles.

Theory of why youth development circles might succeed

There is a lot of failure in existing programmes to deal with youth problems such as poor school performance, hatred of the school as an institution, truancy, bullying, drop-out, drug abuse, delinquency, suicide, homelessness and unemployment. They fail because they approach young people as isolated individuals. Youth development circles would not aspire to treat isolated individuals targeted because of their problems (and thereby stigmatising them as individuals). They would seek to *help young people develop* in the context of their communities of care. The help would not stigmatise as it would be provided universally to young people in a school, not just to the problem students. The young people themselves would be empowered with a lot of say over who those supporters would be. Circles would be a move to find something better than seeking to solve educational problems by one-on-one encounters with the school counsellor, drug problems by individual encounters with rehabilitation services, employment by one-on-one interviews at job placement services, youth suicide by public funding of psychiatrists. Certainly, one of the aspirations of circles would be to embed choices to opt for such rehabilitative services in networks of support that build commitment to make them work. But the aspiration is bigger than that.

Cultures of disadvantage are grounded in failures of families and peers with whom young people are most strongly bonded to value and nurture learning. Regular out-of-school help with things as simple as reading stories improves literacy. The accumulated evidence of the discipline of criminology is that social support is one of the strongest predictors of crime prevention (Cullen, 1994). The research on bullying in schools shows that it can be halved by restorative whole-school approaches grounded in utilising the social bonds that operate across a school (Olweus, 1993). The evidence from studies of successful job searches is that one-on-one job placement services are less important than access to personal networks of knowledgeable people who care enough about the unemployed person to help them with leads, contacts and introductions (Granovetter, 1974). Informal networking seem to be no less the stuff of getting professional, technical and managerial jobs than of blue collar jobs (Granovetter, 1973, p. 1371). Crucial elements of social capital, such as trust and trustworthiness, are learnt in trusting relationships. Yamagishi and Yamagishi's wonderful Japanese programme of trust research shows that trust builds social intelligence, that you have to learn to take the risk of trusting others to learn how to make wise judgements about who is trustworthy (Yamagishi, 2000). It is this kind of social intelligence that makes young people employable. Human and social capital, in short, are constituted by informal circles of social support. The theory of Youth Development Circles is that an institutional infrastructure would be created to foster the emergence of this informal support, that this institutionalisation would also build a citizenship obligation to participate in circles and that the circles would lend ritual power to informal support. Gathering in the Circle creates a sense of an occasion where it is appropriate to raise certain things, to articulate certain emotions of concern or admiration. Heimer and Straffen (1995) have shown that in contexts where those with power are dependent on people who are normally stigmatised, social regulation of those people is in fact highly reintegrative. In their study, hospital staff from intensive care wards treated young black single mothers highly reintegratively – because they were dependent on those young mothers to hang in with their unhealthy babies and take them off the hospital's hands. The Australian convict colony treated convicts in a highly reintegrative rather than stigmatising way because there was a labour shortage which meant the colony was dependent on convict labour (Braithwaite, 2001). As a result of this reintegration, the convict colony became a low-crime society in the 19th century. The Youth Development Circle is an attempt to lock people into a similarly reintegrative institutional dynamic. The only way for the citizens in the circle to end the obligations to attend meetings and offer practical help to the young person is to get them into a steady job or a tertiary institution.

Stigmatising them, giving up on them, will be seen in the circle as likely to delay that release.

Enriching civil society

Circles might help educate all of our children for democracy itself. Democratic deliberation is learnt, but our society does not teach it to the young. Being a beneficiary of care, of cooperative problem-solving when one is young, may be the best way to learn to become caring, dutiful democratic citizens as adults. Such citizens who are creative in co-operative deliberation not only build strong democracies but are also able workforces which attract investment (see Putnam, 1993). The hidden curriculum of Youth Development Circles would therefore be giving the young the literacy to live in civil society, learning to listen, to accommodate the perspectives of others in setting their own goals. Democracy cannot flourish without citizens who are educated for excellence in governing their own lives (Barber, 1992). Youth Development Circles are in sum an idea for deliberative education that democratises education as it serves as an education for democracy.

If a programme of Research and Development of the idea showed that Youth Development Circles did meet some of its aspirations in a major way, it would create a case for a new tripartite view of obligations of citizenship:

1. A citizenship obligation to be the primary supporter of the education and development of any child one parents.
2. A citizenship obligation to be a secondary supporter of more than one child beyond one's own children until infirmity excuses us.
3. An obligation of the state to assign a facilitator to ensure that no child misses the benefits of the obligations in 1 and 2.

These are different from the mostly disrespected obligations to attend Parents and Citizens' Association meetings and bake cakes for them. They are obligations to come along to help a particular child whom they love, to whom they have a professional obligation or who has nominated them as someone the child respects. The citizenship obligation to be a supporter of at least one child should not expire with retirement, only with infirmity. The special wisdom that comes with age incurs a special obligation to spend time with the young for passing on that wisdom to a new generation. As elders have lost their seat at the informal rituals of the campfire, respect for elders has been one of the most unfortunate casualties of modernity. Respect for the elders is the missing cement of modern civil society. Old people feel it and for this reason have enormous untapped reserves of willingness to serve the young.

At the other end of the age spectrum, older buddies of the child are especially important. Buddy selection should be driven by a combination of the child's preference for another she identifies with and by the objective of matching children with weak endowments with buddies having the strongest endowments. This is a strength of weak ties argument (Granovetter, 1973). The child with a network low in human and social capital is given a bridge into the social capital of the network of the buddy with wonderful endowments. For the highly endowed buddy, who has few problems at school, a central issue in her own circle becomes setting objectives about helping her younger buddy to succeed – learning to lead, learning to be a builder of civil society. Endowed children would be taught in the circle how to mobilise their own networks to help less endowed buddies – partly through observing how adult leaders mobilise-networks to help *them*. The key idea of the circle is that generational help begets help as a dynamic in civil society.

Thinking about R & D on youth development circles

In a sense R & D has already been under way since 1991 as restorative justice circles rather like these have been operating in Queensland schools to deal more narrowly with delinquency and behaviour problems (Cameron & Thornborne, 2000). The preliminary evidence is most encouraging (Braithwaite, 1999).

The first priority with R&D more specifically focused on Youth Development Circles would be disadvantaged high schools. Success there could lead on to pilots in primary schools and high schools that are not disadvantaged. Preliminary trials should be qualitative and process oriented. Experimentation would be needed with different ways of running Circles, different invitation lists, different kinds of follow-up, different kinds of training for facilitators. Evaluation measures would have to be piloted.

Then perhaps 10–20 volunteer pilot schools might learn how to manage Youth Development Circles for at least 50 students. An independent review committee might then report to government on whether the preliminary R & D to that point was sufficiently encouraging to proceed with random assignment of say 2000 Year 8 students, 1000 to Youth Development Circles, 1000 to traditional parent-teacher interviews. Each school would then be able to compare at least 50 Circle students with 50 students who continue with traditional parent-teacher interviews. Randomisation would ensure that the two groups were identical in all respects except the Circle intervention.

Data would be collected from these 2000 students (with informed consent from students and parents) annually on:

- School marks
- Self-reported enjoyment of school and learning
- Truancy
- Bullying and victimisation by bullies
- School-reported behaviour problems
- Drop-out
- Employment after drop-out
- Strength of family bonds
- Homelessness
- Self-reported drug use
- Self-reported suicide proneness and depression that predicts actual suicide and attempted suicide (though statistical power may not be sufficient in the latter case even over 10 years for 2000 cases)
- Self-reported delinquency
- Police-recorded delinquency.

The process of monitoring these outcomes should continue until evidence of failure or success is clear. Clear failure can be revealed quite quickly under this methodology. Clear success on unemployment reduction would require a decade of follow-up for 12-year-olds.

At any point during this decade, it might be decided that the accumulated weight of the evidence was sufficient to resource the program beyond the experimental schools. In the first instance, these might be volunteer schools invited to innovate on improving the successful experimental protocol.

Why the cost of youth development circles might be self-liquidating

Youth Development Circles would be costly. The biggest costs would be borne privately by the citizens who gave time to the Circles, to being mentors to young people, to helping them find jobs, to helping them with their science experiments. A cadre of Youth Development Facilitators would also be a substantial burden on the public purse. The offsetting saving on both fronts from replacing parent-teacher interviews would be modest.

However, the offsetting economic benefits of having a more employable workforce, a more socially skilled and committed workforce, might be massive in comparison. The most obvious benefits are with those children who have cost the criminal justice and youth welfare system over a million pounds by the time they are teenagers by virtue of their delinquency and drug abuse. As a universal programme Circles would seek to give problem-free children the social support to set themselves ever-higher goals for excellence, to discover that it might not be uncool after all to be a 'try-hard'. The hope is for enhanced economic performance by nurturing innovation and accomplishment at the top of the curve as well.

The intangible benefits of job creation through acquiring more innovative business leaders with enhanced social intelligence and educational accomplishment acquired as a result of Circles would be impossible to measure, except through the crude proxy of how wealthy these individuals are ten years on. However, the reduced levels of crime, drug abuse and unemployment among 1000 experimental children compared to 1000 control children over 10 years of follow-up could be readily costed and measured against the cost of running the Circles for those 1000 children.

Cultural pluralism in implementation

Obviously there would be great cultural variation in the appropriate ways of implementing Youth Development Circles. One of the depressing things about working on new approaches to tackling unemployment through education or nurturing capital investment in some other way is that they invariably seem more feasible in rich nations than in the poorest nations where investment is most needed. The institutional innovation therefore becomes another way the gap is widened between rich and poor nations. Youth Development Circles are a rare case where the reverse may be true. We have assumed the worst in our analysis – that there exists no village that can be mobilised as a resource to raise a child. But of course in the poorest of nations there are still villages. Creative institutional design might link human and social capital development to persisting extra-familial networks. These networks might be harnessed as an underexploited comparative advantage of pre-modern societies in modern conditions of capital formation.

I will use Bali as a brief case study for two reasons. First, some readers will be familiar with the culture because it is a tourist destination. Second, it is an extreme case of the comparative advantage I have in mind since modernisation came so late to Bali. Due to its lack of good ports, the Dutch did not bother colonising the southern half of the island until 1906. In Bali *every* citizen is a member of a banjar, the traditional social hub of village life. This has been true since at least AD 914 (Eiseman, 1990, p. 72). The banjar is both a physical meeting place and a social organisation for cooperative work groups, education, Hindu religious instruction[3], family and community health planning, management and conservation of the environment and various other cooperative efforts in a village. But even in the large city of Denpasar everyone belongs to a banjar. Indeed Eiseman (1990, p. 88) reports that banjars do such a good job of both adult and child literacy training that there are some banjars in Denpasar without a single illiterate member.

That said, things are far from rosy in Bali, especially with the collapse of the tourist industry in the wake of the Indonesian instability since 1997. While banjar-level commitment to basic education in literacy and Hindu teaching is high, motivating high levels of formal education, constant innovation to find more efficient practices to traditional economic activities (in agriculture for example) often is not the stuff of banjar enthusiasm. Yet surely if the Indonesian state wants to enthuse the populace of Bali about encouraging their children into higher levels of educational accomplishment, into a learning-innovation culture, then the banjar stands ready as the vehicle for accomplishing that. In the Bali context, banjars could graft Youth Development Circles as a banjar institution, and this might give them more clout in human and social capital formation than could ever be hoped for in Western cities.

Conclusion

Youth Development Circles are a policy idea to address the dual structural problem of human/social capital formation in late modernity. This is that (a) intergenerational ties that compensated for human and social capital deficits of the nuclear family have unravelled and that (b) formal education bureaucracies cannot compensate for such deficits when they are informal, when they are about love and dependent on intimate circuits of endowment-building beyond the school. This is best accomplished by bringing into a circle around the young person a combination of those she most loves and those she most identifies with – in the hope that the latter will in time come to count among those she loves and those who most encourage her to strive for her goals. It is a hope for a world where funerals become rituals that honour us not only for the care we have extended to our children, but also for the love and help we have granted to children in circles, children we have embraced into our own family, friendship and economic networks, particularly during old age. The idea is to multiply the meaning of care and intimacy in a life through better institutional sharing of the burden of parents during their period of peak load by asking peers and older citizens to work harder at passing on their wisdom during the periods when their burdens of care are lowest. In turn, if Circles succeed in extending ripples of love, we might hope that when children blossom into young adults some might share some of the burdens of care for the old folk who have shown love to them. At both ends, this might help relieve the inequitable burdens of care currently born by post-motherhood women.

The programme we are proposing would not be cheap. Problems such as youth crime and drug abuse involve a staggering cost to the community and there is encouraging evidence now from meta-analyses that educational development may have a significant impact on these problems (Pearson & Lipton, 1999). Moreover, Youth Development Circles are a type of programme that is amenable to random assignment of a sufficiently large number of cases to assess readily measurable costs (such as salaries) and benefits (such as crime reduction) with impressive statistical power. Hence, a government bold enough to spend an eight-figure sum on a decade of R&D would be in a position to ascertain with a high degree of confidence whether my hypothesis that benefits would far exceed costs is wrong. The magnitude of the policy objective of upgrading human and social capital might justify the boldness of the experimentation proposed.

Acknowledgements

My thanks to Brenda Morrison for helpful comments on this chapter.

Notes

1. One alternative kind of program that seeks to confront this challenge is the Responsible Citizenship Program in Canberra schools. It invites parents and supporters of children to participate in a process that makes conflict resolution an explicit part of the school curriculum. The program's hidden curriculum is building responsible citizenship (see Morrison, forthcoming). Another is the Lewisham Primary School connect project in Sydney (Blood, 1999).
2. And in doing so we do not seek to devalue existing approaches to building school-community, professional-public partnerships for problem solving, such as those mentioned in the last footnote.
3. Non-Hindu banjar members are excused from these aspects of banjar obligations.

References

Barber, B. R. (1992) *An Aristocracy of Everyone: the politics of education and future of America* (New York, Oxford University Press).

Blood, P. (1999) *Good Beginnings: Lewisham Primary School Connect Project* (Sydney, Lewisham Primary School).

Braithwaite, J. (1999) Restorative justice: assessing optimistic and pessimistic accounts, in: M. Tonry (Ed.) *Crime and Justice: a review of research*, Vol. 25, pp. 1–127.

Braithwaite, J. (2001) Crime in a convict republic, *The Modern Law Review*, 64, 1, pp. 11–50.

Braithwaite, J. (forthcoming) *Restorative Justice and Responsive Regulation* (New York, Oxford University Press).

Burford, G. & Pennell, J. (1998) *Family Group Decision Making Project: outcome report, Volume I* (Newfoundland, St. John's; Memorial University).

Cameron, R. & Thornborne, M. (2000) Restorative justice and school discipline – mutually exclusive?, in: H. Strang & J. Braithwaite (eds) *Restorative Justice and Civil Society* (Cambridge, Cambridge University Press).

Chan, Wai Yin (1996) Family conferences in the juvenile justice process: survey on the impact of family conferencing on juvenile offenders and their families, *Subordinate Courts Statistics and Planning Unit Research Bulletin*, February (Singapore).

Cullen, F. T. (1994) Social support as an organizing concept for criminology: Presidential address to the Academy of Criminal Justice Sciences, *Justice Quarterly*, 11, 4, pp. 527–59.

Dowrick, S. (1993) New theory and evidence on economic growth and their implications for Australian policy, *Economic Analysis and Policy*, 23, 2, pp. 105–121.

Eiseman, F. B. (1990) *Bali: Sekala and Niskala, Volume II* (Singapore, Periplus Editions).

Elliott, D. S. (1998) *Blueprints for Violence Prevention* (Boulder, Institute of Behavioral Science, University of Colorado).

Finn Report (1991) *Young People's Participation in Post-compulsory Education and Training* (Canberra, Australian Government Publication Service) p. 151.

Forsythe, L. (1995) An analysis of juvenile apprehension characteristics and reapprehension rates, in: *A New Approach to Juvenile Justice: An Evaluation of Family Conferencing in Wagga Wagga*, edited by David Moore, with Lubica Forsythe and Terry O'Connell, A Report to the Criminology Research Council (Wagga Wagga, Charles Sturt University).

Fukuyama, Francis (1995) *Trust: the social virtues and the creation of prosperity* (New York, Free Press).

Granovetter, M. S. (1973) The strength of weak ties, *American Journal of Sociology*, 78, pp. 1360–1380.

Granovetter, M. S. (1974) *Getting a Job: a study of contacts and careers* Cambridge, Mass.; Harvard University Press).

Hagan, J. & McCarthy, B. (1997) *Mean Streets: youth crime and homelessness* (Cambridge, Cambridge University Press).

Harris, N. (1999) Shame and Shaming: An Empirical Analysis. PhD dissertation, Law Program, Australian National University, Canberra.

Heimer, C. A. & Straffen, L. R. (1995) Interdependence and reintegrative social control: labeling and reforming 'inappropriate' parents in neonatal intensive care units, *American Sociological Review*, 60, pp. 635–54.

LaFree, G. (1998) *Losing Legitimacy: street crime and the decline of social institutions in America* (Boulder, Co., Westview Press).

Lasch, C. (1977) *Haven in a Heartless World* (New York, Basic Books).

Latham, M. (1998) *Civilising Global Capital: new thinking for Australian labor* (St. Leonards, Australia, Allen and Unwin).

McCold, P. & Wachtel, B. (1998) *Restorative Policing Experiment: the Bethlehem Pennsylvania Police Family Group Conferencing Project* (Pipersville, PA, Community Service Foundation).

Morrison, B. E. (forthcoming) *From Bullying to Responsible Citizenship: a restorative approach to building safe school communities* (Melbourne, Australian Council for Educational Research).

Nugent, W. R. & Paddock, J. B. (1995) The effect of victim-offender mediation on severity of reoffense, *Mediation Quarterly*, 12, 4, pp. 353–67.

Olweus, D. (1993) Annotation: bullying at school: basic facts and effects of a school based intervention program, *Journal of Child Psychology and Psychiatry*, 35, pp. 1171–90.

Pate, K. (1990) Victim-offender restitution programs in Canada, in: B. Galaway & J. Hudson (Eds), *Criminal Justice Restitution and Reconciliation* (New York, Willow Tree Press).

Pearson, F. S. & Lipton, D. S. (1999) 'The Effectiveness of Educational and Vocational programs: CDATE Meta-Analyses', Presentation to the American Society of Criminology Meeting, New York.

Putnam, R. D. (1993) *Making Democracy Work: civic traditions in modern Italy* (Princeton, NJ, Princeton University Press).

Sampson, R. J. & Laub, J. H. (1993) *Crime in the Making: pathways and turning points through life* (Cambridge, Ma., Harvard University Press).

Sampson, R. & Raudenbush, S. W. (1999) Systematic social observation of public spaces: a new look at disorder in urban neighbourhoods, *American Journal of Sociology*, 105, pp. 603–651.

Schneider, A. (1996) Restitution and recidivism rates of juvenile offenders: results from four experimental studies, *Criminology*, 24, pp. 533–52.

Sherman, L., Gottfredson, D., MacKenzie, D., Eck, J., Reuter, P. & Bushway, S. (1997) *Preventing Crime: what works, what doesn't, what's promising: a report to the United States Congress*, (Washington, D.C., National Institute of Justice).

Umbreit, M., with Coates, R. & Kalanj, B. (1994) *Victim Meets Offender: the impact of restorative justice and mediation*, (Monsey, New York, Criminal Justice Press).

Wynne, J. (1996) Leeds Mediation and Reparation Service: ten years experience with victim-offender mediation, in: B. Galaway & J. Hudson (Eds), *Restorative Justice: International Perspectives*, (Monsey, NY, Criminal Justice Press).

Yamagishi, T. (2000) Trust as a form of social intelligence, in: K. Cook (ed.),
  Trust in Society, (New York, Russel Sage).
Zelizer, V. (1993) *Pricing the Priceless Child*, (New York, Basic Books).

Chapter 8

Achieving cultural integrity in education in Aotearoa/New Zealand

Russell Bishop and Ted Glynn

The context of New Zealand

The historical pattern of cultural superiority and subordination established between the European migrants and the indigenous peoples of New Zealand has set the pattern for subsequent relationships with new migrants. Some attempts have been made to rectify this pattern by introducing the philosophies and practices of multiculturalism and biculturalism. However, such policies largely have not been successful. These policies have ignored the importance of the need to address the relationship between the dominant Pakeha (people of European origin) and the indigenous population because the aspirations of the indigenous people are subsumed within the majority culture's designs for the future of New Zealand. Unless this relationship can be changed, the dominant-subordinate pattern of intercultural relationships will remain.

Development of the pattern of intercultural relationships

Two peoples created the nation of New Zealand when, in 1840, lieutenant-Governor Hobson and the chiefs of New Zealand signed the Treaty of Waitangi on behalf of the British Crown, the Maori people, and their descendants. Maori people have long seen the Treaty as a charter for power sharing in the decision making processes of this country, for Maori determination of their own destiny as the indigenous people of New Zealand, and as the guide to future development of New Zealand. Posttreaty government policy in New Zealand has moved from one at first opposed totally to these aspirations to one only recently attempting to come to terms with Maori and non-Maori aspirations for equity and social justice through self-determination.

Despite the promises of the Treaty of Waitangi, the history of Maori and Pakeha relationships in New Zealand since the signing of the Treaty has not been one of partnership, of two peoples developing a nation, but one of political, social, and economic domination by the Pakeha majority, and marginalization of the Maori people through armed struggle, biased legislation, and educational initiatives and policies that promoted Pakeha knowledge codes at the expense of the Maori (Bishop, 1991; Simon, 1990; Walker, 1990; Ward, 1974). Despite the created myth that the New Zealanders are 'one people' with equal opportunities (Hohepa, 1975; Simon, 1990; Walker, 1990), results of Pakeha domination are evident today in the lack of equitable participation by Maori people in all positive and beneficial aspects of life in New Zealand, and by their overrepresentation in the negative aspects (Pomare, 1987; Simon, 1990).

In education, for example, the central government's sequential policies of assimilation, integration, multiculturalism, and biculturalism (Irwin, 1989; Jones, McCulloch, Marshall, Smith, & Tuhiwai-Smith, 1990) along with programs such as Taha Maori (Holmes, Bishop, & Glynn, 1992; Smith, 1990), while ostensibly showing concern for the welfare of the Maori people, effectively maintains pressure on Maori people to subjugate their destiny to the needs of the nation state, the goals of which remain largely determined by the Pakeha majority.

In short, the development of New Zealand since the signing of the Treaty of Waitangi in 1840, despite continual armed and passive resistance by the Maori people, has been one in which the Pakeha majority has benefited enormously and in which the Maori have been politically marginalized, culturally and racially attacked, and economically impoverished within their own country.[1] These claims hold as true for education as for all areas of economic and social policy.

The implications of this historical pattern for peoples of other cultures who migrate to New Zealand is profound. The dominance of monoculturalism and monolingualism is so pervasive in New Zealand that the majority culture appears to be unable to accept cultural diversity as a positive feature that new immigrants bring to the nation state. As a result, new migrants (as opposed to those who arrived here in the 19th century) are seen by the majority Pakeha culture as having deficiencies that need remedial action. Furthermore, since the reforms promoted by the Education Act of 1989, the new market-driven approach to education means that Asian students for example are being seen as economic commodities who bring money to educational institutions. Little is heard of pedagogic assets and opportunities for cultural diversity in the classroom.

Dominant–subordinate intercultural relationships have a profound effect on language maintenance with consequent impact on cultural retention and identity. A 1995 study by the Maori Language Commission on the current use of Maori language by Maori 16 years of age and older showed the effects of the dominant–subordinate relationship pattern on language retention and maintenance. The study showed that the majority (60%) of the adult Maori population speak some Maori, although the range of language ability varies considerably. Of those who speak some Maori, only 6% were in the high/very-high fluency category, with a further 8% identified at the medium-high level. This indicates a drop in the number of fluent adult Maori speakers since the last Maori language survey in the mid-1970s. At that time, 18% of the total Maori population were estimated to be fluent speakers of Maori.

Furthermore, the survey results suggest that fluency among adult speakers of Maori remains greatest in the older age groups with consequent implications as aging proceeds. It is estimated that 44% of speakers in the high/very high fluency category are age 60 years and older, whereas a mere 3% are between 16 and 24 years of age. In addition, levels of fluency are higher in rural areas than in urban areas. Regional differences also exist. A higher proportion of the total number of adult Maori speakers in Waikato/Bay of Plenty/Gisborne (8%) are of high/very-high fluency. This is the region served by the university with the greatest focus on delivering tertiary education through the medium of the Maori language. In Northland/Auckland the equivalent proportion is 5%, and in the remainder of New Zealand it is 6%. The situations in which Maori is most used are the marae (meeting place; 37%), school (34%), and church (27%) (Education Gazette, Feb, 1996).

These statistics clearly demonstrate how the majority culture has treated the indigenous population in New Zealand. Because the pattern of dominant–subordinate relationships is pervasive, it is suggested that this is the likely model for relationships with new immigrants that may produce similar outcomes.

Assimilation as policy

Article two of the Treaty of Waitangi guaranteed the Maori people chieftainly control (tino Rangatiratanga, that is, self-determination) over all that they treasured (taonga katoa), particularly the power to define what constitutes a treasure and the power to protect, promote, prefer, and proscribe treasures (Jackson, 1993). Despite this guarantee, Pakeha political control over decision-making processes in education within the context of an assimilationist agenda has marginalized the Maori language, cultural aspirations, and Maori-preferred knowledge-gathering and information-processing methods and contexts. These things are all treasures (taonga) as defined by the Maori themselves.

The education system developed in New Zealand after colonization attempted to replace a preexisting and complex system,[2] and subsequently attempted to deny or belittle its existence. Furthermore, the introduced system considered the Maori language and culture a prime obstacle to the educational progress of Maori children and instigated practices to eradicate them. Colonization within education has been further promoted by the belief that the Maori do not have a full literature, rather only arts and crafts, and that they therefore are a simple culture not worthy of serious concern within the mainstream school curriculum. In the wider context today, this assimilationist agenda remains pervasive, and when applied to relationships with other cultural groups, this agenda denies that ethnic minorities bring anything of intrinsic or educational value to the nation state beyond superficial celebrations of feasts and holy days.

The outcome of the dominance of non-Maori knowledge codes coupled with the economic and political marginalization of the Maori has meant that there is currently a crisis in Maori education: underrepresentation of Maori in the 'success' indices and overoccupation of the 'failure' indices (Davies & Nicholl, 1993; Jones, *et al.*, 1990). The crisis is well summarized by the Waitangi tribunal in its conclusion:

> The education system in New Zealand is operating unsuccessfully because too many Maori children are not reaching an acceptable level of education. For some reason they do not or cannot take full advantage of it. Their language is not protected and their scholastic achievements fall far short of what they should be. The promises of the Treaty of Waitangi of equality of education as in all other human rights are undeniable. Judged by the system's own standards, Maori children are not being successfully taught, and for that reason alone, quite apart from the duty to protect the Maori language, the education system is being operated in breach of the Treaty.
>
> (Hirsch, 1990, p. 24)

Impact of research

Research into Maori people's lives and activities has promoted the assimilationist agenda through a process of reification, that is, the removal of cultural elements from their sense-making context. This not only has had belittling effects, but also has helped to destroy the historical memory for Maori people. Giroux and Friere in Livingstone (1987) concluded thus:

> Forgetting instances of human suffering and the dynamics of human struggle not only rendered existing forms of domination 'natural' and 'acceptable,' but also made it more difficult for those who were victimized by such oppression to develop an

ontological basis for challenging the ideological and political conditions that produced such suffering.

(p. xv)

Such circumstances led many Maori people to forget the contemporaneous elements that contributed to making total sense of their lives and their history. Furthermore, myths created as part of the dominant discourse are taken up by many Maori as truths, this creating many social, psychologic, and human development problems for Maori people.

This process over time is very powerful. For example, non-Maori and Maori educators commonly suggest that Maori children 'do well with their hands', preferring not to deal with abstract concepts. This is a myth created in the 19th century that can be directly sourced in the rationalization for the limited curriculum created for Maori children in the 'native schools' (Simon, 1990). This myth is exploded when Maori children learn effectively in Maori cultural contexts within the contemporary Maori educational system, for example, in Kaupapa Maori education institutions or through immersion in hui (gatherings) at marae. In these contexts, teaching is constantly conducted within and through abstract concepts, metaphors, allusions, and imagery.

The large body of knowledge created about Maori, essentially by non-Maori for non-Maori purposes over generations, has become very powerful and oppressive. This created knowledge permeates the domain of everyday life through school texts, popular literature, and mass media, which engage in their own particular and peculiar selection processes of storytelling and sensationalism. The remnants of the 19th-century evolutionary theories of monogenetic and polygenetic sources of racial differentiation (Belich, 1987; Bishop, 1991; Simon, 1990), together with deficit or cultural deprivation theories common in the 20th century, have created a legacy of cumulative discourse about racism that over time has become a self-fulfilling prophecy for many Maori and non-Maori peoples alike and affects relationships between all cultural groups in New Zealand today.

The native schools

The adaptability and flexibility of Maori culture was suppressed during the late 19th and early 20th centuries when education for Maori children was subsumed within the needs of the new nation state, which were defined by the settler-controlled General Assembly. The Education Act of 1867 developed the first part of what was to become a two-tier education system. The part developed for Maori children was controlled by the central government's Department of Education, which oversaw the development of native schools in rural Maori communities. In 1877, the second-tier provincial board controlling education for the children of the settlers was introduced. Due to the dominance of the settlers in all aspects of New Zealand life, this second tier eventually became the mainstream educational provider for all New Zealanders. However, the native schools were very influential among the mainly rural Maori people, especially until World War II.

In contrast to the full national curriculum taught in the board schools, the native schools operated a limited public school curriculum, emphasizing health and hygiene and manual dexterity, all of which were taught in the English language. Teachers were to use Maori only as a means of introducing English. Furthermore, by the turn of the century, Maori language had been banned from the school grounds (Edwards, 1990), a prohibition often enforced by corporal punishment. This practice was to continue into the 1950s. In 1930, for example, a survey of Maori children attending native schools estimated that 96.6% spoke Maori at home. By 1960 this percentage had dropped to only 26%.

These native schools served to limit the ability of Maori people to compete with the rapidly expanding commercial farming sector, the beneficiaries of which dominated the politics of the country (Simon, 1990; Simpson, 1984) by emphasizing training for manual work. Maori were considered to be unsuitable for 'mental work'. The native schools promoted this goal by limiting the curriculum that was taught, subsequently suppressing Maori language and culture, then limiting the avenues of higher education for Maori children. Such policies effectively marginalized the mainly rural Maori population from equal participation in the economic and political mainstream.

The war years, 1939 to 1945, and the following years were to affect Maori people profoundly. Many Maori families lost young men during World War II. Maori people entered the postwar reconstruction period bereft of many who would have been leaders and participants in the new world opening up as a result of the postwar prosperity. After World War II, Maori people moved to the cities in one of the most rapid urbanizations undergone by any people in the world. Coupled with the decimation of young Maori men during the war, the migration triggered a breakdown of tribal and extended family units as young people moved to the cities, leaving behind older family and tribal sources of language, customs, and culture. The effects of the earlier education policies on language retention along with the rapid urbanization of Maori people was profound. Although the Maori language had been excluded from schools for nearly a century, rural Maori communities had maintained the discourse of Maori. Urbanization into a totally unsympathetic environment provided such a 'body blow' to the Maori language that in 1979 its death was predicted (Benton, 1979).

Integration as policy: effects of urbanization

During the period of mass urbanization after World War II, Maori children entered mainstream schools organized within the developing New Zealand traditions of free, secular, and compulsory education. However, these altruistic values also embraced numerous covert values, attitudes, and assumptions that further promoted success for the children of the dominant group. These included values (Metge, 1976) such as individual competition, individual achievement, and self-discipline, in which abstract analysis and compartmentalized thinking emphasized the removal of spirituality from culture. The educational system promoted achievement based on mastery of abstract concepts, from written texts that were alien to New Zealand, in the context of self-development and individual betterment. Such values stood in sharp contrast to the experiences of many Maori children who had been socialized into family, community and peer groups that valued both group competition, and cooperation, that was dominated by both group achievement and peer solidarity, and that emphasized complementarity of abstract and concrete thought, physical and social achievements, and religion and culture. Such socialization emphasized the interdependence of the group and the individual.

Such conflicts created cultural and psychologic tensions for children, tensions that were further exacerbated by the manner in which the values of the dominant group were expressed in school organization, the selection and training of teachers, the behavior of teachers, the choice of subjects, the curriculum within the subjects,[3] the relative emphasis and resourcing allocated to particular areas of interest, and the stated and unstated agendas of priorities and goals (Metge, 1990). Because the schools were organized monoculturally, Maori students often found that their cultural knowledge was unaccepted, their intentions and motivations misinterpreted, and their language and names mispronounced. This amounted to a systematic assault on their identity as Maori people. Their resulting confusion was often manifested as frustration, inadequacy, and failure, which in turn was confusing to well-meaning but poorly trained teachers.

However, it was not until 1960 that statistics and data identifying Maori disadvantage on a number of indices, including education, were published (Hunn, 1960). As a result of this new analysis by a committee organized by and for the majority culture, a new solution to the challenge of cultural diversity was suggested. According to this new solution called 'integration', instead of the minority culture and language being destroyed, the minority groups were to be integrated with the culture of the dominant group. In effect, the best of both cultures would be integrated into one culture. Those elements of Maori culture that had 'stood the test of time' would become part of a New Zealand culture while the Maori maintained their own identity. This approach never questioned administrative and control structures being dominated by one culture nor the reasons why ethnic minorities were invisible in decision-making processes. It also did not encourage the maintenance of ethnic minority languages and cultures.

In effect, the new policy was no real improvement for the Maori over the earlier notion of assimilation because as Hunn (1960) suggested, compared with living a 'backward life in primitive conditions', Maori people would be much better off conforming to the Pakeha way of life. Hunn equated this way of life with modernity and progress. No reference was made to the cause of Maori impoverishment other than indications that it was the result of rural or desultory living. In effect, the proposed solution was a further denial of Maori culture and language as a means of addressing life's problems. Such an approach reinforced the notion that living as Maori remained a problem, a deficiency.

Empirical researchers sought to explain how such situations occurred. Much educational research was inspired by the currently fashionable approach in the United States that focused on 'cultural deficiencies'. Research conducted in the early 1960s by Lovegrove (1966) was of this type. He undertook a comprehensive study designed to investigate whether or not there were significant differences between Maori and European school children on tests of scholastic achievement and certain selected determiners (i.e., intelligence, home background, attitude toward school, speed of performance and listening comprehension). He sought also to assess the relative importance of these variables in determining the scholastic achievement of Maori and European children.

As a result of his study, Lovegrove (1966) claimed that Maori and European children from almost comparable home backgrounds performed similarly on tests of scholastic achievement. From this he concluded that 'it should be remembered that reasons for Maori retardation (in the education system) are more probably attributable to the generally deprived nature of the Maori home conditions than to inherent intellectual inferiority' (p. 31). In other words, the Maori child was able to compete with the European child, 'providing home conditions have some degree of similarity' (p. 33).

As a result, Lovegrove (1966) suggested that there might be cultural 'retardants' creating the disparity. He identified in particular that the reality of the Maori rural home was perhaps different from the type of upbringing a child needs to ensure progress at school. However, he further suggested that because intellectual differences (as measured by intelligence tests) existed between the races, even if Maori homes were able to provide enough support for the child in the primary years, it would appear that the 'environments they [Maori parents] provide are not conducive to the development of the complex intellectual processes assessed by tests of intelligence' (p. 34). For example, Lovegrove observed that the Maori child's home compared with the home of a European child is less visually and verbally complex as well as less consciously organized to provide a variety of experiences, which are essential to broaden children's intellectual understanding.

Maori children were therefore 'suffering a pathology' that manifested itself in inadequate language and intellectual development. Such pathologies were thought to be the result of a deficient cultural background. The solutions projected for Maori children's underachievement were catch-up programs, additional remedial assistance, and the like. In other words, an attempt would be made to accelerate and emphasize the implementation of the previous policy of assimilation (now termed *integration* by Hunn, 1960).

Attempts to critique the foundations of such ideas were made by other researchers (Harker & George, 1980; see Watson, 1967, 1972, cited in Metge, 1990), but the ideas of Maori culture being deficient remained so entrenched in the common knowledge of the dominant culture that these ideas of deficiency continued to be dominant in education department publications, school organization, and teachers' attitudes and behaviors for many decades (Metge, 1990; Simon, 1984).

The idea that Maori home conditions constituted the prime contributor to academic underachievement was a major step forward in scholastic reasoning about Maori children. Before this, it was thought that Maori people were intellectually (genetically) inferior, a belief rooted in the social Darwinism and polygenesist racism of the 19th century (Belich, 1987; Bishop, 1991; Simon, 1990). Research such as that by Lovegrove in the 1960s at least gave hope that something could be done for the children, in the way of compensatory programs similar to the Headstart programs developed in The United States. Nevertheless, this focus on cultural differences (rather than racial inferiority) itself engendered some depressing conclusions about the state of Maori education more than a decade later.

Harker (1979) recognized that cultural differences and different value systems between those who developed the educational institution and cultural minorities will have an impact on the educational achievement of minority culture children. He suggested that such realizations will create pressure either to 'attempt to restructure the value system of Maori children in order to bring it into line with the requirements for success in the school environment,' or to 'make adjustment to the school environment [such as curriculum reform] in order to provide greater continuity with the Maori value system' (p. 49), or some combination of these. However, Harker concluded that the former solution had been tried without success for over a century, and the second was hopeless because no matter what changes were made to the criteria for success at school, 'those groups with high cultural motivation to succeed will adapt and continue to succeed under the new criteria. … Hence achievement differences cannot be ameliorated by changes to the educational system' (p. 49).

This may sound depressing, but what is more depressing is Harker's conclusion that the problem may not be one of searching for ways of catering to ethnic diversity, but rather one of questioning the wisdom of insisting on equalizing performance for all ethnic groups. Harker's (1979) conclusion is grim; 'If New Zealanders are genuine about their society as a multicultural one, in which all cultures are accorded equal status, *then perhaps we have to learn to live with some measure of achievement differences between ethnic groups*' (p. 50; italics added).

Multiculturalism and biculturalism

Gradually during the 1970s and the 1980s ideas of multiculturalism as a means of addressing and catering to ethnic diversity replaced integration as the dominant educational policy foundation. Notions of multiculturalism were expressed in school curricula, (e.g., social studies), in which notions of exploring cultural diversity, celebrating differences, and promoting cultural identification were advocated. Furthermore, these programs sought to involve the cultural and language practices of all ethnic groups represented in schools, and in so doing enhance the self-esteem and cultural identity of all students.

Despite these good intentions, these pedagogic values and practices, while embracing a range of different ethnic groups internationally, were not readily applied to Maori students or their language and culture. Contemporary Maori culture remained invisible in the majority of mainstream classrooms. Furthermore, when other cultures were studied, the majority culture remained the major referent in mainstream schools. Children were encouraged to compare those other cultures with their own, a strategy that is developmentally sound in that children began by understanding their own culture first, then learned to define their own culture through a process of comparison with a different culture. However, because monocultural Pakeha teachers continued to dominate the education system, and because these teachers, being part of the dominant majority, did not perceive that they themselves had a culture and promoted the nonculture phenomenon, children of different cultures were forced in their learning to see others through the eyes of the majority culture. In effect, it was actually the culture of the teacher that became the yardstick for comparison (see Alton-Lee, Nuthall, & Patrick, 1987). As a result, children of that culture continued to take for granted that theirs was the main reference point, a process that reinforced the ever-present and persistent notions of cultural superiority and reinforced for Maori children that in these classrooms their culture was treated as an 'other'.

Gradually, during this period, the Department of Education began responding to pressure from Maori people (Awatere, 1981) and started to promote a philosophy of biculturalism as a preferred approach to understanding multiculturalism (Irwin, 1989). It was suggested that the majority culture needed to address the Maori–Pakeha relationship first before a multicultural approach could be developed in New Zealand. Such arguments were based on the need to recognize the Treaty of Waitangi as the founding document of New Zealand. Maori people were seeking visibility in their own country and inclusion in the mainstream education system on equal terms. The Maori argued that the relationship between Maori and Pakeha must be addressed in such a way as to remove the dominant–submissive pattern and to develop the partnership pattern envisaged in the Treaty of Waitangi. Relationships with other peoples could then be developed from this bicultural basis.

One practical implementation of the biculturalism policy has been the development of Taha Maori (literally the Maori side) program in schools. This program was an initiative of the former Department of Education in the early 1980s in response to the growing call among Maori and non-Maori educators for some recognition of the place of Maori as tangata whenua (indigenous people) in Aotearoa (the Maori name for New Zealand). To clarify this voice in education, former race relations conciliator, Walter Hirsch, in 1989, interviewed a number of Maori and non-Maori educators about the achievement of Maori children in schools. One of the subjects covered in these interviews was taha Maori, defined as 'Maori perspectives being developed in all aspects of school organization and curriculum' (Hirsch, 1990, p. 37). In his report to the Ministry of Education in 1990, Hirsch stated that the people he spoke to during the preparation of the report had at least two expectations of taha Maori.

The first expectation was that taha Maori programs would have the potential for validating Maori culture and language in the minds of Pakeha New Zealanders. In a research study of the impact of taha Maori in the schools of Southern New Zealand, Holmes, Bishop, and Glynn (1992) identified that this potential is being realized. The study indicated that a generally positive attitude now exists among the communities sampled toward the validity of Maori culture and language. Maori initiatives such as kohanga reo, kura kaupapa Maori, bilingual units, enrichment studies, and immersion classes are receiving positive support also from an increasing number of Pakeha New Zealanders. Such an outcome is important, because, as Ritchie (1991) pointed out, there is a tremendous need in New Zealand for 'attitude modification techniques' to reduce Pakeha prejudice. The provision of simple factual information about Maori educational aspirations and initiatives may be all that is required to begin this process of attitude change. Taha Maori programs in southern schools are helping to meet this need.

The second expectation that Hirsch (1990) identified was that 'taha Maori [would have] the potential to help Maori students feel a greater sense of identity and self-worth on the one hand and may enhance their educational achievements as well' (p. 38). The results of the study by Holmes, Bishop and Glynn (1992) suggest that goal is being met only to a very limited degree because the curriculum remains geared to the needs and aspirations of majority culture members. Furthermore, data showed clearly that there is widespread lack of understanding by schools and their boards of trustees about which Maori perspectives should be developed in all aspects of school organization and curriculum. This lack of understanding is seen in the almost exclusively monocultural school 'mission statements'. Only one in the study explicitly acknowledged the need for a Maori perspective.

Taha Maori sought to add a Maori perspective to a curriculum, the central core of which was decided by the majority culture, rather than include Maori worldviews as any substantial component in the curriculum-planning process. Maori people are seen as resources to be drawn upon, rather than partners to be included in the process of education. This research identified (within southern New Zealand at least) numerous examples of Maori resources being used to implement mainstream curriculum initiatives without any recognition to the financial, cultural, and spiritual costs involved. The intention may have been benign, but the effects have been the belittlement of the partnership principles embodied in the Treaty.

It is significant that at the same time as mainstream educators were attempting to introduce a Maori perspective into the (structurally unaltered) curriculum, Maori people were developing and privately funding preschool 'language nests' for the preservation of the Maori language. In effect, even if taha Maori was originally intended to address issues of Maori achievement in schools, it is most unlikely that it could address the underlying issue of retrieving a colonized language and culture because taha Maori (as an implementation of biculturalism) was designed to meet the aspirations of the Pakeha majority and not those of the Maori people.

In effect, attempts to promote biculturalism within the educational mainstream has meant that the focus of change has been on the Pakeha society. This focus on teaching Pakeha people about Maori culture has often consumed resources at the expense of Maori language and cultural aspirations. Such a situation is exacerbated by existence of little change in the monocultural status and approach of those in control of teacher education. Preservice teacher training programs still attempt to teach all trainees a smattering of Maori language (days of the week, colors, simple greetings, etc.) rather than meet the aspirations of Maori people for in-depth training in the use of Maori as the medium of instruction. The vast majority of teachers in the schools are still monocultural Pakeha, which means that changing the mainstream education system to meet the aspirations of Maori as well as Pakeha people is an enormous task.

The clear message from these studies into attempts by the mainstream to address cultural diversity is that when mainstream educators and politicians attempt to see the ethnic diversity as a challenge they must respond to alone on their own terms, they inevitably fail to address the aspirations and needs of the other parties. The next section details how Maori initiatives have begun to address Maori aspirations and how mainstream policymakers in response are understanding how a pattern of partnership can be fostered within the country.

Kaupapa Maori: Maori educational initiatives

During the period when attempts to address the challenge of ethnic diversity continued to be defined by members of the majority culture, Maori critique of these mainstream initiatives saw the development of a proactive, Maori political discourse termed Kaupapa (agenda) Maori[4] (Awatere, 1981; Irwin, 1989; Smith, 1990, 1992a, 1992b; Smith, 1991; Walker, 1990). Kaupapa Maori emerged from within the wider ethnic revitalization movement (Banks, 1988) that grew in New Zealand after the rapid Maori urbanization of the post-World War II period. This movement blossomed in the 1970s and 1980s with the intensification of a political consciousness among Maori communities (Awatere, 1981; Walker, 1990). More recently, in the late 1980s and the early 1990s, this consciousness has figured in the revitalization of Maori cultural aspirations, preferences, and practices as a philosophical and productive educational stance and resistance to the hegemony[5] of the dominant discourse.

Kaupapa Maori responded to the dual challenge of imminent language death and consequent cultural demise, together with the failed succession of government policy initiatives such as assimilation, integration, multiculturalism and biculturalism to sustain Maori cultural and language aspirations (Jones *et al.*, 1990). Maori educator Graham Smith (1992b) explained that this development occurred among Maori groups across all educational sectors, such as Te Kohanga Reo, Kura Kaupapa Maori, and Waananga Maori and included other groups such as the NZ Maori Council, The Maori Congress, Maori health and welfare bodies, and Iwi authorities. For Maori, the specific intention was to achieve 'increased autonomy over their own lives and cultural welfare' (Smith, 1992b, p. 12). In education, this call for autonomy was in response to the lack of programs and processes within existing educational institutions that were designed to 'reinforce, support or proactively coopt Maori cultural aspirations in ways which are desired by Maori themselves' (p. 12). Smith further suggested that the wish for autonomy also challenged the 'increasing abdication by the State of its 1840 contractual obligation to protect Maori cultural interests' (p. 10).

Maori demands for autonomy in this context is generally articulated as tino Rangatiratanga (literally 'chiefly control', metaphorically 'Maori self-determination'). This call is often misunderstood by non-Maori people. It is not a call for separatism, nor is it a call for non-Maori people to stand back and leave Maori alone, in effect to relinquish all responsibility. It is a call for all those involved in education in New Zealand to reposition themselves in relation to these emerging aspirations of Maori people for an autonomous voice (Bishop, 1994, 1996).

The early post-Treaty education system that developed in New Zealand, the mission schools (Bishop, 1991), the native schools (Simon 1990), and the present mainstream schools (Irwin, 1992) have all been unable to 'successfully validate matauranga [knowledge] Maori, leaving it marginalized and in a precarious state' (p. 10). Furthermore, whereas mainstream schooling still does not serve Maori people well (Davies & Nicholl, 1993), the Maori schooling initiatives of Te Kohanga reo (Maori medium preschools), Kura Kaupapa Maori (Maori medium primary schools), Whare Kura (Maori medium secondary schools), and Whare Waananga (Maori tertiary institutions), 'which have developed from within Maori communities to intervene in Maori language, cultural, educational, social and economic crises …, *are successful in the eyes of the Maori people*' (Smith, 1992b, p. 1, italics added).

Te Kohanga Reo

Ironically, the first major Maori educational initiative, Te Kohanga Reo (Maori medium preschools), resulted from pressures outside of the education sector. It was during a review of the department of Maori Affairs in 1977, in response to the concern that the Department was 'culturally removed from Maori people' (Irwin, 1990, p. 113), that a working party was sent throughout the country speaking and listening to local Maori communities. They received an unequivocal message. Maori people wanted an education that 'maintained their own lifestyles, language and culture whilst also enhancing life chances, access to power, and equality of opportunity' (p. 111).

A series of hui held in the early 1980s followed soon after, and these meetings focused on the concern about language loss and urged the establishment of 'language nests', places where the language could be nurtured. There was much scepticism voiced in the wider community about the potential of such initiatives and much discussion of Maori problems as seen by outsiders, such as Maori having an impoverished community base, limited traditional cultural resources, few capital resources, and alienation from the traditional cultural base. Nevertheless, outsiders were not aware of the power to be released when these new educational initiatives tapped into the cultural aspirations of Maori people to revitalize the language and culture. The success of the language nests (TKR) has been phenomenal.

Since the opening of the first center in 1982, there has been rapid growth. By 1987 there were 513 centers operating. By 1993 the number had grown to 809, surpassing both kindergartens (582) and play centers (577; Bishop, Boulton, & Martin, 1994). In 1982, only 30% of Maori children age 2 to 4 years, compared with 41% of non-Maori children, participated in early childhood contexts. By 1991, the Maori participation rate had risen to 53% largely as a result of Kohanga Reo fostering increased Maori participation in early childhood education (Davies & Nicholl, 1993). By 1993, 14,027 Maori children (96.6% of students) were enrolled at Kohanga Reo that had proliferated around the country, representing 49.2% of Maori children in early childhood education. However, despite this growth, the participation rate for non-Maori children in early childhood education has increased at a faster rate than for Maori children. In 1985, Maori children made up 22% of all children in early childhood education. In 1992, this percentage, despite a large numeric increase, had fallen to 17%, a further indicator of the continued socioeconomic impoverishment of Maori families.

That the language nests do foster the language is confirmed in research reported in Hohepa, Smith, and McNaughton (1992). Early research in 1968 by Dame Marie Clay (cited in Hohepa *et al.*, 1992) had identified that a sample of 77 urban Maori children were unable to understand or follow instructions in Maori. In contrast, the Samoan children she studied were found to be predominantly bilingual, understanding both Samoan and English.

In 1989, Clay's assessment tool was used by Smith et al. (1989, cited in Hohepa *et al.*, 1992) to examine the language competencies of a Maori group of children ages 5 to 7 years in a Maori immersion school (kura kaupapa Maori). These children were graduates of Te Kohanga Reo, and they were found to have bilingual competencies similar to those of the bilingual Samoan children in Clay's original study. Furthermore, these are children whose parents are not necessarily strong in Maori language and culture. Indeed, these were the children of the generation studied by Clay in 1968.

The kaupapa (philosophy/agenda) of Kohanga Reo is that (a) children will learn the Maori language and culture including spiritual values through immersion; (b) language and cultural learning will be fostered for all members of Te Kohanga Reo whanau (this includes adults as well as children); (c) members of TKR whanau will learn a range of other skills such as administration and financial control; (d) collective responsibility will be fostered; (e) all involved will feel the sense of belonging and acceptance; and (f) the content, context and control of learning will be Maori (Irwin, 1990, p. 117).

The involvement of whanau (extended family principle: literally all ages being represented) has meant that Maori parents have been able to exert a significant degree of local control over the education of their children despite changes in government. The whanau approach is characterized by a collective decision-making approach, and each whanau has its own autonomy within the wider philosophy of the movement (Irwin, 1990, p. 118). Hence, control over what children should learn, how they should learn it, and who should be involved in the learning are in the hands of the controlling whanau.

Some outcomes of TKR are that young children leave TKR-speaking Maori feeling positive about their language and culture. The language and cultural practices of native speakers have also been affirmed. Parents have been stimulated to learn Maori. There has been a socioeconomic intervention through activation of whanau, and participation by parents in the education of their children has been stimulated. TKR has arrested the fragmentation of the traditional language and cultural base.

'By far the most significant message to come out of Kohanga Reo is that Maori are able to run big enterprises just as well as anyone else and that they can do this in a mix of languages and cultures and amid much criticism and scepticism' (Brell, 1995, p. 11). This has occurred despite the fact that funding for TKR came entirely from the community until 1990, when the national TKR trust was able to gain state funding. The government review of TKR concludes that 'TKR is a vigorous, lively movement, has arrested the fragmentation of the traditional cultural base, has revitalized the use of marae, and is helping preserve the Maori language. All this had come about through the autonomy of the Kohanga Reo within the kaupapa' (Irwin, 1990, p. 119). In other words, Maori people control the decision making over how, when, where, and why for the education of their children.

Such a dramatic turnabout has important implications for language acquisition and classroom processes. Kaupapa Maori educational initiatives are based on the notion that language is the key to the culture, and that language and culture together are keys to sociopolitical interventions. In other words 'acquiring linguistic knowledge and acquiring sociocultural knowledge are interdependent' (Hohepa et al., 1992, p. 334). Such sociocultural approaches to language acquisition stand in contrast to previous dominant assimilationist ideologies in that children are socialized through learning, and language learning is organized by sociocultural processes. In this way, language learners are active, not passive. Drawing on Leontiev's theory of activity, Hohepa et al. (1992) suggested that it is 'through participation in structured social activities that language learners acquire linguistics and sociocultural knowledge. These social actions are, in turn, socioculturally and linguistically structural and organized' (p. 334). Furthermore, as sociocultural and linguistics knowledge structures activity, so does activity create and recreate knowledge in both domains.

The research undertaken by Hohepa et al. (1992) suggested that TKR acts as an enculturating context by providing a culturally structured environment within which children develop. Language development plays a vital role in this process. In their study, 'culturally preferred contexts and beliefs as well as activities were found to provide contexts or to act as setting events for specific language mechanisms such as language routines and language focusing strategies in this Kohanga Reo. Furthermore, these resulting language mechanisms in turn set up contexts for the passing on or teaching ways of thinking and acting which are culturally valued' (Hohepa *et al.*, 1992, p. 343).

As a further outcome of the study, routines after repetition of language with immediate social reinforcement were capable of being modified in order for roles to shift and language flexibility to progress. The language focusing strategies identified in the study can be linked to Maori preferred pedagogies; looking, listening, and imitating, that is modeling (Metge, 1983). Metge (1983) observed that traditionally Maori place great emphasis on memorization and rote learning and teaching by demonstration so that people are able to participate appropriately in Maori sociocultural contexts in which oral participation and presentation are crucial.

Educational restructuring: Maori autonomy

The success of Te Kohanga Reo, the development of the first Maori immersion primary schools, and a growing voice for self-determination in educational matters by Maori people coincided with New Zealand's fourth Labor government's (1984–1990) radical restructuring of school administration according to recommendations made by the Taskforce to Review Educational Administration (Picot, 1988). The main thrust of the restructuring was for policymaking to remain the domain of a new Ministry of Education, whereas responsibility for many administrative decisions was to be in the hands of locally constituted boards of trustees.

Under the new provisions, all schools were to ensure that their 'policies and practices seek to achieve equitable educational outcomes for both sexes; for rural and urban students; for students from all religions, ethnic, cultural, social, family, and class backgrounds; and for all students irrespective of their ability or disability' (New Zealand Ministry of Education, 1988, p. 8). Each board of trustees was required to accept 'an obligation to develop policies and practices which value our dual cultural heritage' (New Zealand Ministry of Education, 1988, p. 6).

However, many Maori parent groups remained unconvinced that such reforms were likely to meet their cultural aspirations. They preferred for their children to continue with the Maori medium education that had been started in the Kohanga Reo. Initially, the government was reluctant to allow the development of new Maori medium primary schools within the new provisions for state schools. That is to have their own autonomy while following very serious representation by Maori leaders and educationalists, Kura Kaupapa Maori were incorporated into the reform (The Education Act, 1989) legislation as a fully recognized and state funded schooling alternative within the New Zealand state education system (Graham Smith, personal communication, 1994).

Subsequently, the Ministry of Education has undergone considerable policy shifts in response to the growth of Kaupapa Maori educational initiatives. Learning the Maori language as a subject in its own right was a traditional approach fostered by the Ministry and the previous Department of Education, but now in the mid-1990s, policy direction is toward 'making the language the center of the learning process within whole educational institutions and their communities. Kura kaupapa Maori, Maori immersion education, and using Maori as a medium for implementing new curricula are the key components of developing te reo (Maori language) in Aotearoa' (Ministry of Education, 1995, p. 12).

The Ministry of Education is committed to supporting the establishment and administration of Kura Kaupapa Maori, to providing suitable accommodation, and to identifying resources needed. The first kura was established at Hoane Waititi marae in 1984, and 12 others were established by 1989, mostly without state support. However, provisions have been made for the establishment and state funding of kura on the same basis as that for other state funded schools. A total of 38 kura had been approved by June 30, 1995, and approval has been given for 15 new Kura Kaupapa Maori to be established over the next 3 years.

In contrast to the 1960s, the current focus of Ministry policy is much closer to the Maori's aspirations for education. Instead of blaming the children and their homes and condemning Maori language as an impediment to development, current policies focus on te reo Maori (Maori language) as an essential cornerstone of Maori development. Policy is underwritten by the need to address Maori achievement rates, which in mainstream educational contexts still fall behind those of non-Maori. Perhaps the most dramatic shift in policy has been from a paternalistic approach to one that argues for 'increasing the opportunities for Maori to take more responsibility for the control of Education' (Brell, 1995, p. 7).

It is now seen by the Ministry of Education that 'Maori language, Maori education, and Maori development are inextricably linked. Maori see education as a key component of a wider strategy for greater self-determination' (Brell, 1995, p. 7). One outcome of this approach has been the 1992 decision by the Ministry of Education to introduce a Maori medium curriculum that would have outcomes identical to those of the mainstream curriculum but would follow different pedagogies, knowledge, and information systems to achieve those outcomes. Within this curriculum, structures and procedures have been developed to give the Maori control over decision-making protocols on language use and pedagogical developments as they relate to the Maori language. In this way the policymakers are attempting to facilitate Maori parents in having a greater say and more responsibility in the education of their children. This is seen as a key to improving Maori achievement in education.

This model of self-determination has become a burning issue for an increasingly large proportion of the Maori population. They see language as absolutely essential to their essence, their being, and their identity as Maori. The Maori people want to maintain their integrity, which comprises te reo (language) tikanga Maori (Maori customs) and a matauranga (knowledge) base, the foundation from which Maori people are able to express themselves and participate in the world.

There remains, however, a serious constraint on the provision of Maori medium education, and that is the availability of teachers fluent in te reo Maori. Spolsky (1987) estimated 'a need for at least 1,000 qualified Maori bilingual teachers over the next decade' (p. 21). He suggested a number of ways to address this problem: training fluent Maori speakers as qualified teachers, developing Maori fluency in qualified teachers, and training Maori bilingual teachers (Waite, 1992). However, despite the obvious need, teacher training institutions have been slow to respond. Pem Bird, head of Maori studies at the Auckland College of Education, maintained that the revitalization of the Maori language remains in jeopardy because of the continued shortage of Maori teachers. He, along with Waite and others, called for a national languages policy, and more particularly, a national strategic plan that would unite all providers of teacher education in a common purpose, 'producing teachers with the ability to deliver education in the Maori language, within a Maori context and derived from a Maori language base, in satisfactorily large numbers to ensure that all parents who choose to have their children educated through Maori can, in fact, realistically exercise that option' (Pem Bird, personal communication, 1996).

Past education policies removed Maori as a community language from the homes of most Maori families. Now schools are seen as the catalyst for revitalization, and as identified in a study of language transference from Te Kohanga Reo to the home (Tangaere, 1992), often leading to revitalization of the language in the home as well. However, despite recent policy shifts, the residual effects of 150 years of marginalization and monolingualism are profound.

Implications for the development of new policies

Language implications

A major outcome of the political and economic colonization of New Zealand by English-speaking Europeans is that contrary to practice in many other parts of the world, the level of bilingualism in the total New Zealand population is extremely low. When bilingualism occurs, it is found mainly in minority language groups, among Maori speakers, and in minority ethnic communities including new settler language speakers. Bilingualism is rare among the majority of the population, which consists primarily of New Zealanders (82%) of European descent. No language other than English features in the top 10 most popular subjects at secondary school (Waite, 1992, p. 19).

The monolingualism that has marked education and New Zealand society for some decades has an inertial effect on student desires to undertake study of a language, especially at senior levels. Evidence of this effect is that the limited number of students learning te reo Maori are in the senior secondary schools (15% of Maori who learn Maori language in schools). This limits the pool of students able to take up tertiary study in the language and thus to undertake training in Maori educational contexts.

The low incidence of bilingualism among first-language speakers of English is derived from historical ideas of cultural superiority. Although such ideologies nowadays are being widely challenged, monolingualism is still being fostered by the somewhat erroneous impression that English is the international language. As a result, it is felt that New Zealanders on the whole have little need to learn other languages for other than purely utilitarian (economic and trade) reasons. Hence, much is made over the benefits for trade and tourism of learning the languages of, for example, trading partners such as the Japanese, the Koreans, and the Malaysians. Increasingly, within the New Zealand business community, bilingualism is seen as a benefit for the entrepreneur desirous of entering the largely competitive international marketplace by ensuring that market research, contracting, and personal contacts can be made on the client's terms. This is seen as an essential ingredient in promoting and developing economic and trade relationships. Similarly, on the rapidly diversifying domestic scene, bilingualism with English alongside economic and trade languages increasingly is a skill sought after in teaching, tourism, journalism, interpreting, translation, and social work.

However, although monolingualism and monoculturalism remain dominant, opportunities for promoting bilingualism are denied people unable to maintain their own language or unable to acquire an adequate knowledge of English. It is sharply ironic in New Zealand today that there is an increasing demand for bilingual Maori–English speakers in education (Education Gazette, 1996), but that this demand cannot yet be fully met by adult Maori people because of their loss of language and culture created by the past emphasis in the education system on monolingualism.

Policymakers in New Zealand have been from the majority monolingual culture, and thus are essentially unaware of the aspirations of Maori people for the revitalization of their language as an integral element of the culture and cannot appreciate the extent to which the language and culture have been eroded by the education system. Maori people, however, have recently developed their own educational initiatives and are focusing educational practice on their language as a means of transmitting their culture through the curriculum. They have contested and won a share of state education funding to support these initiatives. This model is one that policymakers for new settler migrants could well emulate. Unless they do, community languages used in New Zealand will continue to decline.

Despite attempts to develop language maintenance programs for languages other than English, such provision has to contend with the continued dominance of English as a medium of instruction, a dominance reinforced by primary school level preservice teacher training that does not make available training in language teaching.

The continuing dominance of monolingualism is seen in the newly drafted National Curriculum of New Zealand (Ministry of Education, 1991). This document specifies the seven 'essential learning areas' – mathematics, science and environment, technology, social sciences, the arts, physical and personal development, and language.

The learning area of 'language' includes English (which is a required study) and may optionally include Maori, community languages, and international languages. That is, for first language speakers of English, the learning of another language is not proposed as a required part of the common curriculum. As a result, the pervasiveness of monolingualism is unlikely to change in the foreseeable future.

Conclusion

The need to establish a coherent and comprehensive New Zealand language policy has been highlighted for the last 20 years. Although there is currently no such policy available, a major report, *Aoteareo*: Speaking for Ourselves was produced by the Ministry of Education in 1992 (Waite, 1992). This report acknowledged the need for all New Zealanders to have a sound knowledge of standard New Zealand English, but strongly advocated the benefits of bilingualism. An attempt was made in the report to balance social justice issues with the government's trade- and economic-based desires and visions as outlined in the draft document, Education for the 21st Century (Ministry of Education, 1993). The Waite (1992) report proposed six ranked priorities for public policy: revitalization of the Maori language, second-chance adult literacy, children's ESL and first-language maintenance, adult ESL, national capabilities in international languages, and provision of services in languages other than English (McPherson 1994, pp. 18–22). The need for such a policy has never been more pressing, but processes of dominance and subordination must not drive its development. Partnership as promised in the Treaty of Waitangi is a more preferable and enduring course.

Notes

1. Research has contributed to and continues to contribute to the persistent attacks on Maori cultural integrity, and as a result has promoted Maori political and economic marginalization and the subsequent impoverishment of Maori people in Aotearoa/New Zealand today. Despite Maori people being one of the most researched people in the world, in the domain of knowledge definition there is a great deal of evidence that much research into Maori people's lives and experiences, conducted by educational and other researchers, has been parasitic, that is of benefit to the researchers more than to those who have been the objects of study. It has been the researchers, rather than the people being researched, who have determined the research agendas, controlled the research processes, and reported the research outcomes in terms defined to suit their worldviews. Consequently this has contributed to the marginalization and impoverishment of the Maori people. In short, this process of research has maintained the power to define what constitutes research and the criteria for evaluation and presentation of research finding in the hands of those people doing the observing, gathering, and processing of data as well as the construction of meaning from/about the research experiences.

2. As King (1978), Metge (1983), and Salmond (1975) reported, these learning processes continue today in the Maori world, exemplified in the oral art forms of whaikorero (oratory), karanga (ceremonial call) and pakiwaitara (storytelling). The records of the hearings of the current Waitangi Tribunal are today in accessible Maori. Learning processes emphasize the importance of many Maori concepts and their contextual relationships. These include whakapapa and the nature of humans in relation to creation stories, the birth of Te Ao Marama (the world of light that was revealed when Tane separated his parents, Rangi, the Sky Father, and Papa, the Earth Mother), the search for the kits of knowledge and the subsequent messages contained in these kits for humankind, an awareness of the importance of Mauri-Mana-Tapu-Noa,

and the complementarity of these concepts (Irwin, 1984; King, 1978; Marsden, 1975; Metge, 1976, 1983; Pere, 1982, 1988; Rangihau, 1975; Walker, 1978).

3. One example of the effect of outsider selection of curriculum material on the identity of indigenous peoples is seen in the way in which Maori culture was studied in the schools of this period. Maori culture was presented in the curriculum as it was supposed to have been in Pre-European times. Contemporary Maori culture was ignored.

4. Smith (1992b) described Kaupapa Maori as 'the philosophy and practice of "being and acting Maori" ' (p. 1). It assumes the taken for granted social, political, historical, intellectual, and cultural legitimacy of Maori people in that it is a position in which 'Maori language, culture, knowledge, and values are accepted in their own right' (p. 13). Furthermore, Kaupapa Maori presupposes positions committed to a critical analysis of the existing unequal power relationships within our society. These include rejection of hegemonic belittling, 'Maori can't cope' stances, simplification and commodification of Maori intellectual property, and the development of a social pathology analysis of Maori underachievement (Bishop, 1995) together with a commitment to the power of conscientization and politicization through struggle for wider community and social freedoms (Smith, 1992a).

5. The concept of hegemony is used here in the sense defined by Foucault (Smart, 1986), who suggested that hegemony is an insidious process gained most effectively through 'practices, techniques, and methods which infiltrate minds and bodies, cultural practices which cultivate behaviors and beliefs, tastes, desires and needs as seemingly naturally occurring qualities and properties embodied in the psychic and physical reality of the human subject' (p. 159).

References

Alton-Lee, A., Nuthall, G., & Patrick, J. (1987). *Take your brown hand off my book: Racism, in the classroom* (Set 1, Item 8). Wellington, New Zealand: New Zealand Council for Educational Research.

Awatere, D. (1981). *Maori sovereignty*. Auckland: Broadsheet.

Banks, J. (1988). *Multi-ethnic education: Theory and practice*. Boston: Allyn & Bacon.

Belich, J. (1987). *The New Zealand wars and the Victorian interpretation of racial conflict*. Auckland: Penguin Books.

Benton, R. (1979). *Who speaks Maori in New Zealand*. Wellington: New Zealand Council for Educational Research.

Bishop, R. (1991). *He whakawhanaungatanga tikanga rua: Establishing links: A bicultural experience*. Unpublished master's thesis, Department of Education, University of Otago. Dunedin, New Zealand.

Bishop, R. (1994). Initiating empowering research. *New Zealand Journal of Educational Studies*, 29(1), 1–14.

Bishop, R. (1996). *Collaborative research stories: Whakawhanaungatanga.* Palmerston North: Dunmore Press.

Bishop, D., Boulton, A., & Martin, S. (1994). *Education trends report* (Vol. 6[1]) Wellington: Ministry of Education.

Brell, R. (1995). *Managing education realities in Asia and the Pacific.* Seapreams 14th Regional Symposium December 4–8, 1995, University of Auckland. Auckland, New Zealand.

Davies, L., & Nicholl, K. (1993). *Te Maori i roto i nga mahi whakaakoranga: Maori in education.* Wellington: Ministry of Education.

Edwards, M. (1990). *Mihipeka: Early years.* Auckland: Penguin.

Glynn, T. (1985). Contexts for independent learning. *Educational Psychology*, 5(1), 5–15.

Glynn, T., Fairweather, R., & Donald, S. (1992). Involving parents in improving children's learning at school: Policy issues for behavioural research. *Behaviour Change* (Special issue on behavioural family intervention), 9(3) 178–185.

Harker, R. (1979). *Research on the education of Maori children: The state of the art.* Paper presented to the first National Conference of the New Zealand Association for Research in Education. Victoria University, Wellington.

Harker, R., & George, R. (1980). *Conclusions and consequences: Some aspects of M.N. Lovegrove's study of Maori and European educational achievement reconsidered.* Paper presented to Priorities in Multi-Cultural Education conference, Department of Education, Wellington.

Hirsch, W. (1990). *A report on issues and factors relating to Maori achievement in the education system.* Auckland: Ministry of Education.

Hohepa, M., Smith, G. H., Smith, L. T., & McNaughton, S. (1992). *Te kohanga reo hei tikanga ako i te reo Maori: Te kohanga reo as a context for language learning* (Educational Psychology, Vol. 12, numbers 3 & 4, pp. 333–346). Auckland.

Hohepa, P. (1975). The one people myth. In M. King (Ed.), *Te Ao Hurihuri: The world moves on* (pp. 98–111). Auckland: Hicks Smith.

Holmes, J. (1990). Community languages: Researchers as catalysts. *New Settlers and Multicultural Education Issues*, 7(3), 19–26.

Holmes, H., Bishop, R., & Glynn, T. (1992). *Tu mai kia tu ake: Impact of taha maori in Otago and southland schools* (Te Ropu Rangahau Tikanga Rua Monograph No. 4). Department of Education, University of Otago.

Hunn, J. K. (1960). *Report on the department of Maori affairs.* Wellington: Government Print.

Irwin, J. (1984). *An introduction to Maori religion.* Bedford Park: Australian Association for the Study of Religions.

Irwin, K. (1989). Multicultural education: The New Zealand response, 1974–84. *New Zealand Educational Journal of Education*, 24(1), 3–18.

Irwin, K. (1990). *The Politics of kohanga reo*. In S. Middleton, J. Codd and A. Jones. (Eds.), *New Zealand educational policy today: Critical perspectives*. Wellington: Allen & Unwin/Port Nicholson Press.

Irwin, K. (1992). *Maori research methods and processes: An exploration and discussion*. Paper presented to the joint New Zealand Association for Research in Education/Australian Association for Research in Education Conference. Geelong, Australia.

Jackson, M. (1993). *The Treaty of Waitangi*. Seminar presented to Community and Family Studies Department, University of Otago.

Jones, A., McCulloch, G., Marshall, J., Smith, G. H., & Tuhiwai-Smith, L. (1990). *Myths and realities: Schooling in New Zealand*. Palmerston North: Dunmore.

King, M. (1978). Some Maori attacks to documents. In M. King (Ed.), *Tihei Mauriora: Aspects of Maoritanga* (pp. 9–18). Auckland: Longman Paul.

Livingstone, D. W. (1987). *Cultural pedagogy and cultural power*. Massachusetts: Bergin & Garvay.

Lovegrove, M. N. (1966). The scholastic achievement of European and Maori children. *New Zealand Journal of Educational Studies*, 1(1) 16–39.

Maori Language in Education (1996, February). *Education Gazette*, 75(2) pp. 1–2. Wellington: Ministry of Education.

Marsden, M. (1975). God, man and the universe: A Maori view. In M. King (Ed.), *Te Ao Hurihuri: The world moves on* (pp. 143–164). Auckland: Longman Paul.

McPherson, J. (1994). Key issues in language education in Aotearoa/New Zealand. In J. McPherson, *Making changes: Action research for developing Maori language policies in mainstream schools* (pp. 5–20). Chapter 1. Wellington: NZCER.

Metge, J. (1976). *The Maoris of New Zealand: Rautahi*. London: Routledge & Kegan Paul.

Metge, J. (1983). *Learning and teaching: He tikanga Maori*. Wellington: Department of Education.

Metge, J. (1990). *Te Kohao o te ngira: Culture and learning*. Wellington: Learning Media, Ministry of Education.

Ministry of Education. (1988). *Tomorrow's Schools: The reform of educational administration in New Zealand*. Wellington: Government Printer.

Ministry of Education. (1991). *The national curriculum of New Zealand: A discussion document*. Wellington: Learning Media.

Ministry of Education. (1993). *Education for the 21st Century: A discussion document*. Wellington: Ministry of Education.

Ministry of Education. (1994). *Trends Report*, 6(1), October 1994.

Ministry of Education. (1995). *Nga Haeata Matauranga: Annual Report 1993/94 and Strategic Direction 1994/95*. Wellington: Ministry of Education.

New Zealand Official Yearbook. (1995). Wellington: Statistics in New Zealand.

Pere, R. (1982). *Ako: Concepts and learning in the Maori tradition*. Hamilton: Department of Sociology, University of Waikato.

Pere, R. (1988). Te wheke: Whaia te maramatanga me te aroha. In S. Middleton (Ed.), *Women and girls in education* (pp. 6–19). Wellington: Allen & Unwin.

Picot, B. (1988). *Administering for excellence: Effective administration in education: Report of the taskforce to review education administration*. Wellington: The Taskforce.

Pomare, E. (1987). *Hauora: Maori standards of health*. Wellington: Department of Health.

Pongudom, W. (1995). *Acculturation at a cost: Language and educational difficulties experienced by Cambodian refugees in Dunedin*. Unpublished doctoral thesis. University of Otago.

Rangihau, J. (1975). Being Maori. In M. King (Ed.), *Te ao hurihuri, the world moves on: Aspects of Maoritanga* (pp. 165–175). Auckland: Hicks Smith.

Ritchie, J. (1991). *Becoming bicultural*. Wellington: Hui Publications.

Salmond, A. (1975). *Hui: A study of Maori ceremonial greetings*. Auckland: Reed & Methuen.

Simon, J. (1984). 'Good intentions, but ...' *National Education* 66(4), 61–65.

Simon, J. A. (1990). *The role of schooling in Maori-Pakeha relations*. Unpublished doctoral thesis. Auckland University.

Simpson, T. (1984). *A vision betrayed: The decline of democracy in New Zealand*. Auckland: Hodder & Stoughton.

Smart, B. (1986). The politics of truth and the problems of hegemony. In D. C. Hoy, (Ed.), *Foucault: A critical reader* (pp. 157–173). Oxford: Basil Blackwell.

Smith, G. H. (1990). Taha Maori: Pakeha capture. In J. Codd, R. Harker, & R. Nash (Eds.), *Political issues in New Zealand education* (pp. 183–197). Palmerston North: Dunmore.

Smith, G. H. (1992a). *Research issues related to Maori education* (The Issue of Research and Maori Monograph No. 9). Department of Education, University of Auckland.

Smith, G. H. (1992b). *Tane-nui-a-rangi's legacy ... propping up the sky: Kaupapa Maori as resistance and intervention*. A paper presented at the New Zealand Association for Research in Education/Australia Association for Research in Education joint conference. Deakin University, Australia.

Smith, L. T. (1991). Te rapuna i te ao marama: Maori perspectives on research in education. In J. R. Morss, & T. J. Linzey (Eds.), *The politics of human learning: Human development and educational research* (pp. 46–55). Dunedin: University of Otago Press.

Spolsky, B. (1987). *Report of Maori-English bilingual education*. Wellington, Department of Education.

Tangaere, J. (1992). *Language transference from Te Kohanga Reo to home: The roles of the child and family*. Unpublished master's thesis, University of Auckland.

The Education Act 1989 in Statutes of New Zealand. Wellington, New Zealand Government Printer.

Waite, J. (1992). *Aoteareo: Speaking for ourselves*. Wellington: Ministry of Education, Learning Media, Wellington.

Walker, R. (1978). The relevance of Maori myth and tradition. In M. King (Ed.), *Tihe Mauriora: Aspects of Maoritanga …* (pp. 19–33). Auckland: Methuen.

Walker, R. (1990). *Ka whawhai tonu matou: Struggle without end*. Auckland: Penguin.

Ward, A. (1974). *A show of justice*. Auckland: Auckland University Press/Oxford University Press.

Wong Fillmore, Lilly. (1991). When learning a second language means losing the first. *Early Childhood Research Quarterly*, 323–346.

Chapter 9

Sweet As: a collaborative, culturally responsive school-wide behaviour intervention

Mere Berryman and Ted Glynn

Introduction

This case study has been taken from a report on five sites of effective special education practice for Māori (Berryman, Glynn, Walker, Reweti, O'Brien, Boasa-Dean, Langdon & Weiss, 2002). It describes an intervention that took place in a small decile 1 (low socioeconomic status) school in Hastings, New Zealand in 2001. The report includes comments from some of those most closely associated with the intervention that were recorded by the researchers as the research progressed. This school used the 'Eliminating Violence' (EV) programme developed by the Specialist Education Services (now known as Group Special Education within the Ministry of Education) as a means of reducing the incidence of undesirable student behaviours.

At the time, the primary school in which this intervention took place had 97% Māori students, a non-Māori principal and non-Māori teaching staff. Māori whānau (families) were strongly represented on the Board of Trustees (BOT), which was led by a Māori woman who had long been associated with the school and with the community. The Specialist Education Services (SES) EV co-ordinator was non-Māori. These participants and some of the students themselves shared the changes that took place in this school as a result of a change in principal and the implementation of the EV programme. One of these outcomes was the collaborative renaming of their school to SWEET AS!

The intervention

'Eliminating Violence' is a programme that was developed to address school-wide behavioural issues through the collaborative actions of staff, student and community members (Adair, Moore & Lysaght, 1996). Important first stages of implementing EV are the defining of violent behaviours, the acceptance that such acts are extremely problematic and the commitment of the staff and community to eliminate such behaviours from the school environment. The definition of violence that is used covers a wide range of behaviours from the purposeful ignoring or rejection of others, to verbal abuse such as name-calling, put downs and coercion, to physical abuse where harm to others is occurring. Observations by trained co-ordinators and co-workers are gathered to identify where these behaviours are occurring and the extent to which they are occurring. The observation data is then shared with the school and community and action plans are collaboratively set to manage the reduction and eventual elimination of such behaviours from the school. Once the school has reached this stage the 'elimination violence' intervention is then renamed and a special day of celebration is held to welcome the behaviour change programme into the school. After on-going support, and at a pre-determined time in the future (usually one year), the observations are repeated and further feedback is given.

From the outset of the researchers' visit it was clear that the school had recently come through a challenging period of experiencing community dissatisfaction as a result of its long-standing history of student behaviour issues. One outcome of this dissatisfaction had been a drop in student roll. An opportunity to refocus the direction of the school was provided by the appointment of a new principal. The BOT were strongly involved in the selection of the new principal. The Chairperson commented:

> I knew she was the right person (for the principal's job) because when her and I went round the school to have a look at the classroom, as we went into the younger kids classroom, she wouldn't have put one foot in the door and she just said to me 'Oh I can feel these babies in here now.'

At about the same time the local Special Education Services (SES) office sent faxes out to all of the local schools signalling the availability of the EV programme in the area:

> A fax came through from SES, inviting schools to give them expressions of interest to eliminating violence. A fax from SES talking about eliminating violence as a possibility for some schools in this region. I guess, my advantage here is having worked in SES previously. At one time when I was in South Auckland I went to a training about EV.
> I talked to my staff and said look I know about this programme.

(Principal)

The fact that the implementation of the programme would involve one year of on-going support and feedback from professionals had immediate appeal.

> What would be good about it is that they would have to be with us for a year. They couldn't just drop the baby like a lot of other training programmes deliver and it's kind of like, well there you are, you've been to the course of such and such, now go and make it work. They are actually contracted to work with us and stand and walk with us really for the whole year.
>
> (Principal)

The SES EV co-ordinator also talked about the initiation of EV in this school:

> We distributed a letter in the format of a flyer giving a little bit of information about the EV programme and that went out to all the primary and intermediate schools in Hawkes Bay. With C's (the principal from this school) case, she was very proactive in approaching us. On her fax back sheet, which was how those 13 schools responded back to us, I think she had written in great big letters along the bottom, 'Please we want this urgently. We need this!'
>
> We also were very aware that the first school we took on was going to be essentially my first school so it was important that it be a manageable school. It is difficult to work with schools in crisis as they need surplus energy (and resources) to be able to implement the programme. It was seen that the School was a manageable school, a school which had needs because we had a number of SES behaviour clients there, but also a school with a very positive principal and supportive staff, so it came through. We were made aware it was a very good choice.
>
> At the staff presentation, there were about seven people there, they did include as always some of the wider community, there were some BOT members there, and it was 100% go for it.

The Principal identified that two of the aims within her new rôle as principal of this school were appropriate school-wide behaviour management and increased collaborative relationships between the school and the community.

> At the time the staff and I had been working hard here on behaviour. We had senior boys, five in my room, who were very difficult and we had been talking a lot about behaviour in the school. When I was interviewed for the job they said, 'can you control difficult behaviour kids?' I went, 'Oh yes, I think so.'

The Principal had some very clear expectations about the services that she expected from SES:

> It wasn't just like, oh we've got a problem. They (SES) would actually come in and gather data. But they would work hard at enrolling everyone on staff to participate and they wouldn't go ahead until that had been achieved. So I already knew some things about it and I was really quick to fax back. I said, 'Our school, we are really keen to look at this.' Then L (the EV co-ordinator) came and talked about it with us and talked about the cost. I thought it was worth it because we were subsidised because we were decile 1. I thought it's $1600 well spent really. I knew it would go for a year and I knew or had a sense that changing the culture in a school takes a long time.

Part of this initiative involved whānau (the extended family) contributing to decision-making about participation in EV. The Principal recalled:

> I said to L that we were improving, that we had been working hard with our kids, not using confrontational styles, and we were already developing relationships, supporting the parents and we were really trying to change it around here and so this would just really add to it. They (parents and other family members) were keen. We booked in the training for the first two days before school started this year.

The EV co-ordinator realised that if the programme was going to work for the school, commitment of the people was an essential ingredient:

> Yes you do want your programme to be successful, but you also want it to make a difference. So you want to take it on at a school where they have significant needs and where you know its going to make a difference. But there has to be enough commitment from the staff to know that it's going to be worthwhile and just to support that. You could have a very, very high needs school but in order to put EV in place you have to do a one hour presentation for all the staff. When you present to the staff, at the end they have a ballot on whether or not they are prepared to take it on board. If you don't get 90% agreement from the staff, then it doesn't go ahead. So it is about ensuring success. You might have a very needy school but if you've got only 60–70% of the staff prepared to take it on board then it doesn't run. Because basically you know that the values of the staff will be in conflict and you won't be able to deliver the programme to the school. You could change some of those staff around in the process, which would actually be really good and to that extent you'd have to question that high ballot rate because it doesn't allow for growth and during the two-day workshop I think there is a big opportunity for growth. People seem changed.
>
> Successful implementation of the EV programme or any programme that facilitates change relies on the potential of a school or community to adapt and accommodate change. My criteria, for measuring the success of the programme, are reflected in a happier and more successful school, students and community.

Talking with the BOT Chairperson it was clear that collaborative consultation amongst school staff and BOT members was part of the process of defining what EV would become in this school. It was also clear that the Principal and BOT Chairperson collaborated right from the beginning.

> Well first of all her (Principal) and I talked about it, the staff talked about it, then the board talked about it, then we called a community meeting letting them all know about it.

An example of this collaborative consultation can be seen in the process of renaming the initiative and in planning for the continued implementation of EV. The Chairperson of the Board of Trustees comments:

> But knowing this community as well as I do, we didn't want to hit this community with EV so we tagged it under another name. Each of the kids had to come up with a new name. C and the staff did it in their classrooms.

The Principal recalled:

> There was a democratic way of getting the name even though I was naughty and influenced it. I knew that one of my staff members didn't like it, it reminded her of misbehaviour, so she found it really difficult. But we set it up so that the children would choose and we already knew they would choose the name, 'Sweet As', because we knew they liked that anyway. But it was like, making them own it by having them choose and then vote for their name.

Members of this school community were already well on the way to defining how they were going to achieve the standards of behaviour that they wanted within their school when they decided to take EV on board. The collaborative problem-solving adopted by those involved in the project reflected more traditional Māori family practices. This is reflected in the way the new principal and BOT chairperson had also begun to participate by having the whole community's views included in the setting of group goals. Already they had a good idea about what they needed in this respect and how it should be implemented.

The Principal shared with the researchers practical examples of the benefits to her school community:

> The children have a framework upon which to hang skills. We wanted to teach pro social skills to children. We wanted to see a big reduction in first physical, but by the time they did the data we had really got on top of that using our own methods, so the benefits were to really close down on physical contact, physical inappropriate behaviour. Then we knew we had a big job with verbal and putdowns. We started to teach these skills, but we could hang it on this 'Sweet As' programme which the kids had begun to own because they had named it. And in the naming of it, you know you name a concept for children they can hang everything on it, so could staff. Staff could hang on it. Why are we giving out stickers? Because we are, what are we? Sweet As! So it's like the benefits are a happier school. Way more secure staff because they are on a plan. It's just a happier place and I feel, as a principal, I think I feel supported by my staff because it kind of works. Like the staff get to really enjoy school, way more secure staff because they are on a plan, it's just a happier place and I feel as a principal, I think I feel supported by my staff because it kind of works. Like the staff here get to really enjoy it. The other day the fair play man came to give us our certificates, and there are some of the fair play things like this, (indicating thumbs up). We had already had that, so when he put the thumbs up, well his poster up to show the kids, which is something about thumbs up, well that's their slogan (already). All of our kids saw this thing and went like, 'Sweet As!' He was blown away but we were blown away. We were blown away because we could see, I don't know what you would call it. It's like, how can you get this stuff right, like hitting gold, like finding gold.

Recognising the symbol, and generalising the use of it back into their experiences in a practical and meaningful way had positive implications for this school community. Also of benefit were the specific data, collected in the school as part of SES training to staff. These data were able to provide evidence of improvement as a result of the school's own drive to improve behaviour in the school. These data would also provide evidence of behaviour change over the duration of the implementation of the 'Sweet As!' intervention with SES. They also highlighted the behaviour areas for priority targeting. The Principal commented:

> The children know that we are hitting the name calling and bullying. That if they come and tell us we do something. Because that was in the data, a huge amount that went unreported. They didn't tell anyone, didn't tell mum and dad, didn't tell us. So now there is a lot more telling and there is action. Like I would say they would know if the data was done again, I would have a sense that staff are responding to children's complaint. I had a couple of students say, I told him (the student teacher) but he didn't do anything. Now he was in on the training, but he hasn't been here enough to pick up on the modelling that we're all doing in front of each other, about responding to child complaints. So what I did is I got him with the child and I said to the girl … and this little girl came from Ruatahuna, total immersion (that is a school where the only language spoken is Māori) … so we were talking really quiet and I had to model with her how to be assertive with Mike, 'Oh no you have to say excuse me, Matua,' you know, and in a really loud voice I said, 'You complain, because when you complain, he'll do something,' and Mike's nodding away to her. So I know that the only complaints from children that something wasn't happening were only coming from him … and he hadn't been here enough to hear the modelling. So when I modelled to her that she needed to lift her voice … and I felt that maybe she was manipulating both of us a bit too, but she got to see what we were demanding of her in order to make a complaint.

The Principal felt that a part of the strength of the intervention came from this consistent and powerful modelling that had started to take place between staff and students:

> And they modelled all the time. I say to staff even before the programme, 'We don't let anything go, everything is important.' So the benefits for the children are that they come and tell us, and they know what's not okay. The other huge benefit is that they are far more supportive, like we use the WIT thing, walk away, ignore, tell somebody, making an 'I' statement and they get reinforced for using the WIT. They come and say, 'So and so needs to be in the "caught being good" books, because I saw them walk away.' So the children also are getting benefits from using their skills that we are teaching.

The Principal noticed that children learned to use praise statements from seeing them modelled by staff.

> That little boy that came up to me out there, you saw him come up to me, and say, 'Can I tell you something now?' I walked him away. The benefit for him is that we listen. In another situation I might have said, 'No, no sit down, it's assembly.' He wants to tell me something and it's so valuable. He wanted to get a sticker for the other boy who had helped him do something. Now that's getting pretty sophisticated student support for each other. That young boy who was doing that, would have what we call behaviour difficulties, has trouble with his peers all the time, and there he is, wow gold, you know!

It is evident from the Principal's contributions that everyone associated with the EV programme received benefits. The learning that occurred was substantial and exciting. From the children's point of view they took ownership of the programme. By utilising 'Sweet As', not only within the school but also in their homes with family members and in their neighbourhood, they extended the programme so that their whole community was safe and 'Sweet As'.

The BOT Chairperson and some of the mothers talked about their experiences with 'Sweet As'. One mother said, for example:

> But this 'Sweet As' programme is I believe a good thing for the kids. A fine example is my daughter. A young boy came into the school just recently and my daughter was given the job, she was asked if she could look after this boy. He knew nothing of 'Sweet As' and he got a little bit pushy, just shoved her about a bit. My girl is seven, and she said, 'Hey, don't do that, it's wrong, it's naughty, it hurts.' He went and growled at her, and she went 'Sweet As'. He looked and looked and the teacher explained. Like she (the daughter) knew what she had to put in place in order to correct him, or to calm him down, but she continues to look after him, wasn't a problem.

Another commented:

> Like at home, I've got five teenagers at home and there's a lot going on in the house especially when its first up best dressed, the young ones are walking around, come on and you hear 'Sweet As'. So it's all, it's being put in place by the little ones. It's not the adults or the teenagers putting it in place the kids are saying 'Sweet As'.

According to the BOT Chairperson, the school:

> Used to have a chronic 'lunches going missing' a real problem, well the kids all know now, if you are hungry come to me, or go to somebody and they'll get something to eat, under Tu Tangata (a programme in which Māori adults attend school and participate in classes when children are experiencing learning and/or behaviour difficulties) we hope to do breakfasts here, that's in our plan. Lots of things are happening. You only have to look at our school roll. The school roll has exceeded 50% in two years. And this community every third or fourth home would have kōhanga kids in it, so we want to rope them in here now, we want to focus on them, bring them in.
>
> There are heaps of Māori in the school now, heaps, and still room for more. Parents are not whakamā to come down here now and say I can't pay for my kid's book. Can I pay $5 a week? Nobody is frightened now anymore, which is really good.

Especially noticeable had been the introduction of a sports programme:

> We had a school that didn't have sports. The chief things around here now are kapahaka, Māori and sport. It's awesome!
>
> My son is doing his last year here, he went from pre school, right through here, he's doing his last year and it's the first time he's ever played sport and he's loving it.
>
> My girl's playing rugby.
>
> 'I'm playing rugby today Dad!' And the child is going on to 11 years old and it's the first time he's ever had interest in any sport because there was nothing here.

> Back in the days when my boys were small they had to go to a club. There was no rugby here so the kids had to go to a club. My kids now play sport for the school, they represent the school and so it should be.

The BOT Chairperson felt that much of the change and development in the school had resulted from the leadership style of the Principal:

> Different leadership as well. C (the Principal) is just a breath of fresh air around here, very much so. She empowers everybody, she's the leader of the school, but she empowers everybody to walk alongside her, rather than behind her you know. She's empowered the Board, and when C came in she said, 'No, you're running right, you just do what you want to do, and we work together as a team.'

The result of her style of leadership was a noticeable increase in parental involvement at the school. One mother noted:

> The amount of parents in the school it's amazing, I was amazed at everyone. They came out of their hole for the Sweet As and Tu Tangata programme. It's made a huge difference to our school.
> The kids are allowed to play here after school and they have someone here and that person whoever, is here.

The BOT Chairperson agreed with this observation:

> It's everybody, the doors open, they are coming in.
> They are just not coming down to the school, they're getting involved. They're asking questions, they are voicing their concerns, in saying that it might work for that kid but it won't work for mine and they are giving their suggestions. They are saying 'Oh well if you are going to do that here at school, we'll take it home and carry it through.' So yeah, they are taking ownership

These mothers talked also about pursuing opportunities that will result in others benefiting from improved relationships between the school and home community.

> There's a lot of new people in our area and it's just getting to know them, encourage them to come to the school. I see them come to the hockey games on Saturday morning but I haven't seen them at the school yet. I try and worm my way around them and try to encourage them.

As well as developing and increasing relationships between family members this community was also seeking to co-ordinate better the support of other agencies. As the BOT Chairperson commented:

> We're actually going out there. It's not just focused here in the school, we go out into the community. I have very good liaison with Housing NZ and when houses are empty we can hear everybody telling me about them. And fair enough, but what I do is I write a letter and leave it on the door introducing myself, telling them where we are and what school, what we've got to offer down here. And that makes them feel so

welcome they come down here. I mean even if they decide they don't want to send their kids here, they still come down.

Researchers asked the EV co-ordinator to consider how she may also have benefited from the implementation of EV in this school:

At this school I've benefited through having contact with positive people and seeing a good model of a school that's working well. They have children who have difficulties behaviourally, and watching one lunch time, just watching the way that C was able to, in a very positive way, to respond to children in need and redirect activities. That's been really positive for me to see her in action. But also just the neat spirit of the children and to see them come on board with us and pick something up and run with it, so that's been really positive. We had a feeling that the change was going to be really positive anyway, and to actually see that come to fruition was really great. And I think working with some really neat people and seeing the team really pull together.

It is evident from her contribution that the team of whom she speaks extends beyond the principal, students and SES:

At our core group meetings, which we've been having once a fortnight while the programme was getting under way, and seeing the way that everybody has pulled together. The RTLB (resource teacher for learning and behaviour who worked in a support rôle at the school) has been fantastic in terms of the creation of social skill packages, which have been delivered to the children. The social worker has been involved and she has been a little bit more behind the scenes I guess but she has been involved with the families. Seeing the way that R, the BOT person who is also a parent, has made contact with the other parents, and given us that understanding of the needs of the whānau in terms of the need to organise our parents' workshop, that sort of thing. Just the atmosphere in the school, it's lovely. A lovely school to be involved in.

The successful implementation of the programme within the school, by a community, of committed and dedicated people such as this, means that EV is talked about positively by all who are aware of it in a very positive light. The benefits to the community are reflected in the comments made by the BOT chairperson and a group of mothers:

I love it, it's really more of an education. We have a lot of young parents that still need educating, we can't make a perfect world but at least we can make our area more friendly.

(Mother)

The kids are definitely being re-educated. I have parents acknowledging that fact. The big brother will go and hit the little girl or the little brother and you hear, 'oh we don't do that at this school, we've got Sweet As.' So it's good. Even our local shopkeeper knows about the Sweet As programme. So it's good. You have got to start somewhere, because I've lived that road of violence, it's got to start somewhere.

(BOT Chairperson)

The extent to which community-driven intervention is now embedded in the school can be illustrated by comments from parents and the BOT chairperson in relation to a school initiation the Tu Tangata (People Standing Tall) programme runs simultaneously with 'Sweet As' in order to raise students' self esteem and pride in their own ethnic origin:

We have a Tu Tangata programme here now which is a programme that is owned by the community. The whānau will come down and support the programme, kids all know we're here.

(BOT Chairperson)

The good thing about it is it gives us the opportunity to go in the classroom, because you know how teachers, anybody, doesn't matter what profession they come from, they can jargon on you. Well that's not at a child's level. Whereas you go into the classroom, a lot of the teachers, I went through high school last year and all I got is students talking to the teachers telling them, 'Talk on our level' because they (the teachers) forget.

(Mother)

The teachers that we have in place now are brilliant, but we have had teachers in the past that have taken for granted that the Māori kid next door to the non Māori kid can understand what's being said. But it's not the case, it's not the case at all. It's a fact that Māori are more visual than anything else, and the ESPs (Education Support Person) that work under the Tu Tangata programme go into the classroom. That one child or two children may need to be given that explanation once or twice more. The knowing, it boosts them up with self-esteem.

(BOT Chairperson)

Trying to bring them all up, you really do succeed in those programmes (EV and Tu Tangata), as parents we're volunteering our services to build that child up. Really it's that self-esteem you are trying to build up, encouraging them.

(Mother)

And we've seen that here, you know the kids are so good now in the playground as you saw today. They feel safe, they've been given the materials to play with to keep their mind active, like the rugby ball, the badminton. When the last principal was here her attitude was when they all came back, there would be one ball missing so the kids wouldn't get another game for a week. I could sit here and tell you quite a few things that went on here and sometimes it's unbelievable.

(BOT Chairperson)

The researchers were interested to hear from this group, what it was in their opinion that made it happen for Māori students:

I believe it's because the teachers here are caring.

(BOT Chairperson)

They are willing to learn. I think just listening to the children and wanting to know their whakapapa, like Julie came up to me one day and said Mrs T wants to know where my granddad came from. I've had seven kids attend this school, first teacher ever to ask any of my children.

(Mother)

Yes they actually want to know the people behind the child, not just the pupil. I think the teachers have a willingness to learn the culture. They are actually putting that extra step forward out of their teaching box to learn the culture.

(BOT Chairperson)

I came to school one day and the kids were having kapahaka out on the tennis courts, and teachers were out there singing away, singing the songs, helping with the actions, and I think it's good every teacher is out there learning with the children. It doesn't belong to us.

(Mother)

There is an acceptance (of the Māori culture) from the children, from the staff.

(BOT Chairperson)

For these people there was evidence of beneficial changes occurring in the home and in the school. These changes included improved social skills, improved relationships and connections between home and school and evidence of parents who were now willing to communicate and participate within the school. The Principal understood the issues related to the cultural needs of these Māori students and parents and had considered this from both the teachers and families' perspective.

We've got non Māori teachers here, a non Māori principal, three others and myself teaching as well, and we're all non Māori teachers. But there's one really important thing about us that I know in my heart, that's not a problem for them, the non Māori teachers, to be in this school, and that's crucial. In my heart I know that they don't have a problem with Māori, they're not coming with that block. Often the most well intentioned pākehā people, you know how hard they try, they've got that thing, they've still got that block and that's absolutely crucial too.

R would say about some past staff members here, she'd have to tell them to leave their middle class values at the gate, and she'd tell them. At the moment she hasn't had the need to do that.

You can't really screen schools for that I know but that's actually why it works here too. When I came to this school there had been violence in the school. I knew that when I took on the job. So when I came to this school I brought this pounamu (greenstone) because I just sensed that there was a lot of healing that needed to be done in the school. So I gave this to the children and I say to them, when you are feeling unhappy the pounamu is in the office and you can go and hold it and have awhi (support) with the pounamu. So that's probably why there is pounamu on that sticker.

You know we had such angry children here, girls and boys. They had been hurt, and they had been hurt by an adult. So that's how I came into the school, knowing that there really needed to be a change in the culture. There was a spiritual atmosphere here that needed addressing as well. The concept that the children are sacred I value a lot. Also the social worker here thinks along those lines as well, the chairperson, so we have a strong, I suppose you could say, without speaking religiously, there is a very strong spiritual feeling here. A depth and presence in the people here, that's really helped too.

R has been on the Board here since forever and was the person who gave me the background of the school before I took the job on. Effectively she is my kuia, I'm accountable for this programme having some benefits for working, and I'm accountable to her. She would also tell me that we collectively are accountable to our parents. I'm accountable though I suppose for me, I'm accountable to the children and that's where my stand is. I'm accountable to these children. But they'll never know that, those words like accountability don't quite say it.

Yeah, so I know that when I'm writing our draft curriculum thing here, that will be an introduction to where the school heads next, that it will start aligning with their values. Like valuing students individually for their talents, which fits the Māori thing anyway, and working in a more collective way. When I first came here the behaviour of my senior boys' room was just horrific. I couldn't get them to work in groups they were just totally destructive. I knew that working in groups was where we should be going with it, but we just started buddy reading the other day and the whole school was out there with their buddies, with the Aspergers boy climbing the fence, roaring like a caged lion. I just looked out and there were all the kids on the grass with their buddies and the Aspergers boy climbing the fence and roaring, and all the kids ignoring him, just amazing. I'm going, 'please come down from the fence.' I'm trying to get Mum here, 'please don't fall off the fence and cut your head open.' You know.

The Principal's accountability is focused on the children of the school and she bases the school's programme upon that. She acknowledges her accountability to the BOT Chairperson, who she sees as her kuia (respected elder). Through her kuia she ensures her accountability back to the parent community. Her sense of accountability is embedded within her in terms of her understandings of Māori physicality and spirituality.

> We all share, we live in each other's homes, we share kai (food). We wanted the community to take ownership of the school, as it should be. We wanted to bring back the people, the established whānau of this community, we wanted to bring them back into the school grounds, to the life of this school, because that was lost, everybody was cheated of that. And that's what we've done.
>
> (BOT Chairperson)

Conclusion

The involvement of the entire community is the factor that makes this intervention effective for Māori. The changes that have ensued within the school environment have emanated from and then back into the community. It has been carried there by the commitment of the children, the commitment of the school staff and the commitment of the parents and families who have all embraced the programme. In turn the EV programme has been facilitated by a co-ordinator who understands the power of this community and who recognises her place in it. She has been responsive to the requests of this community and has supported the tailoring of the programme to meet the needs of the school.

This collaborative story is a rich source of Māori lived experiences and demonstrates that by being able to bring their experiences to the intervention families were able to make valid and worthwhile contributions. Further, the story provides evidence of professionals working within an ecological-educational behavioural model. From this inclusive paradigm professionals are working collaboratively with Māori families in order to take into careful account all factors within the child's environment. A consequence of this strategy is that data collection is used to inform and more effective intervention strategies have resulted. Māori voices are able to maintain authority.

This story also demonstrates the development of effective working partnerships between Māori and non-Māori. Researchers saw evidence of non-Māori professionals, learning three important lessons about how to work more effectively with their Māori partners. These general characteristics of effective partnerships were:

1. acknowledging the mana and expertise of each partner
2. working collaboratively with their partner, from within the partner's worldview
3. learning from their partner and changing their own behaviour accordingly.

The demonstration of collaborative and culturally competent approaches to understanding and resolving problems requires being able to understand the cultural dimensions of the problem. In this intervention this meant allowing Māori to define what the problem was in the first place. When this occurs, one is more likely to be heading for an appropriate and acceptable solution for the Māori client.

In the story of the 'Sweet As!' school, there is clear evidence of a close, collaborative working partnership between the non-Māori principal and her kuia. This collaboration stems from their mutual recognition of the power in the role that the other plays in the school and community, and of the expertise of the other in 'getting things done'. The strong contribution of the kuia, including that of being BOT Chairperson, is predicated on her recognition of the efforts of the Principal. These efforts include the Principal constantly striving to pronounce and understand Māori words correctly, and to use Māori images, concepts and icons in talking about the school community, and to practise the values of manaaki (caring), aroha (love), wairua (spirituality) and whanaungatanga (mutual connections). They also include the Principal's willingness to encourage the community to have input into the school, and not to cling to a one-way relationship where the school tries to impose change on the community, without being willing to change itself. This collaborative working partnership has resulted in the entire Māori community being fully committed to improving the quality and safety of teaching and learning in this school. Benefits from their commitment to change can be seen both in classrooms and on the playground. Further, the parents have taken these practices back into their homes and out into their community. The strong collaborative partnership within this school has ensured that the Eliminating Violence programme has been delivered in ways that were defined and legitimated by the Māori community. The voices within this effective intervention illustrate what can happen when this process of cultural and linguistic colonisation is replaced with collaborative partnerships that are developed and understood from within a strong Māori worldview.

References

Adair, V., Moore, D. and Lysaght, K. (1996). *Elimination of violence in schools evaluation*. Project Progress Report No. 2. Wellington: Ministry of Education.

Berryman, M., Glynn, T., Walker, R., Reweti, M., O'Brien, K., Boasa-Dean, T., Glynn, V., Langdon, Y. and Weiss, S. (2002). *SES sites of effective practice for Māori 2001*. Draft report to the SES Board and Executive Team. Wellington: Specialist Education Services.

PART 3
Psychological perspectives

Chapter 10

Emotional growth and learning

Paul Greenhalgh

Introduction

In order to develop a structure of personal meanings which sustain development we need an environment of emotional safety and trust. In particular, in order for learning to proceed effectively, we need to feel safe and accepted, to develop internal strength and the capacity to symbolise, to feel secure and be able to explore, and to have a sense of individual identity. In this chapter each of these is discussed in turn.

First, what sort of general developments might be expected at various stages in childhood? A Kleinian-influenced view of the construction of experience and the development of emotional life and learning is summarised in Figure 10.1.

Figure 10.1 gives an overview of expectations about development. Yet development is highly individual, and it does not always proceed in line with general expectations. The following discussion selects some key areas of emotional experience, without which it is difficult for development to proceed. The more schools are able to provide these emotional experiences, the more learning will be facilitated. To experience these qualities in school is particularly important for troubled children, who may have only limited experience of them elsewhere in their lives. Whatever the external reality of each child's life, we must remember that each individual will subjectively make his/her own meanings. However we have constructed our own meanings, the following experiences are vital for further development. Development is able to proceed naturally when we have had sufficient of these sorts of experience to have internalised their helpful qualities.

Infancy, 0–6 months:

The stage of infancy is characterised by the split between love and hate, the former being associated with joy and pleasure and the latter with anger, destructiveness, fear of annihilation or disintegration, and envy.

6 months to 1 year:

At this time the capacity to love and hate the same person, associated with the depressive position, potentially begins. Transitional objects begin to have a role, providing a place to play, think, reflect, have fun. The wish to make reparation emerges, along with separation anxiety. The core of the self begins to develop, along with the beginnings of psychological separation and individuation.

1–3 years:

Between the ages of 1 and 3 years, continuing individuation and separation provide further developments in autonomy. During this time there are intense sexual feelings for both parents. Girls feel rivalrous of the mother: at this stage girls are said to feel the mother's envy. There is a danger of omnipotent fantasies and behaviour, flight into 'I can do it all myself.' This is associated with temper tantrums and fear of abandonment.

4–6 years:

This is said to be the age when differences, for example of race and gender, can be acknowledged with awareness and acceptance. Sibling rivalry intensifies. Thinking is concrete, magical, timeless, animistic. Feelings are related to concrete thoughts through symbols.

6–10 years:

The 6–10 age-group has traditionally been termed the latency phase. Here there is increasing autonomy and socialisation, a rapid acquisition of skills, the relinquishment of omnipotence, opening to vulnerability and a sense of inferiority. Thinking remains concrete. Potential problems associated with this stage include isolation, depression, and a retreat into a fantasy world.

10–14/15 years:

Early adolescence is said to be characterised by a re-emergence of the qualities of early sexuality and of the love/hate phenomenon. There is alternating rivalry and identification with both parents. Omnipotence re-emerges and oscillates with despair. There is experimentation in relationships and activities, but confusion over identity, particularly sexual identity.

15 years onwards:

The late adolescent phase is characterised by a movement towards physical separation and independence. Identity consolidates and real intimacy and a sense of responsibility emerge. There is an increase in energy. The capacity to think in abstract terms relates to the growing capacity to develop creative ideas.

Figure 10.1 A Kleinian-influenced view of the developmental stages of childhood (adapted from Trowell 1990)

Feeling safe and accepted

To experience the feeling of safety and acceptance, we have to allow ourselves to feel in some ways dependent upon significant other people in our lives. We cannot risk trust if we cannot risk some form of dependence on another person. At first the child is in almost absolute dependence on the support of the mother-figure, followed by her careful and incremental actions to withdraw her support for the infant's total dependency (Winnicott 1984). The way in which the adult manages the child's conflicting needs for dependency and independence has an impact on the child's ego development. The ego is the conscious part of the personality, relating and mediating between inner and outer realities. Having a weak ego might be compared to being like a learner driver; a strong ego to being like a strong, competent driver.

Dependency is the pre-condition for independence, but too much dependence is emotionally depleting. From a state of absolute dependence, the person moves towards independence through a stage which Winnicott (1984) describes as relative dependency. This is significant for the teacher, since there are times when it is necessary to support relative dependency, in order to help a child to feel safe and accepted, but not to do so at the expense of the child's need to move towards independence. A measure of relative dependency can thus be helpful for learning. This is particularly the case in relation to children whose ego strength is limited or fragile.

Hirschhorn (1988) explains the function which relative dependency fulfils for the process of learning. Discussing a company training programme in which adult trainees adopted a dependent role, Hirschhorn comments that the trainees liked the programme, since they could sit in awe of the experts who protected them, and so did not feel frustrated at their own incompetencies. However, the trainees felt that they had to grab all they could get so that they could walk away with at least some of the expertise displayed before them: greedy people feel empty and angry at those who deny them 'food'. '[I]nsofar as they become dependent on the instructors and on the program, they believed that they had no inner resources' (Hirschhorn 1988: 128). Generalising from such evidence, Hirschhorn describes two models of a training situation, and shows how some degree of dependency for a learner is appropriate. In learning, one experiences one's ignorance, one's lack of skills. If learners develop a secure relationship with their teacher, they may feel protected from the consequences of their own ignorance. The trainer stands between them and the inner, judgemental voices that admonish them for their stupidity. In short, they regress, and an appropriate relationship of dependency emerges between the two. However, if for some reason they fail to develop this relationship, they can be overwhelmed by the experience of their own helplessness and consequently transform their self-punishing impulse into attacks on the teacher. The relationship between the teacher and the learner is thus central to the learner's experience.

Developing internal strengths and the capacity to symbolise

Much of our capacity for internal strength derives from the ego's mediation of inner and outer realities. The ego's mediation helps us to manage difficult feelings such as loss, frustration, greed and envy. The ego also defines the boundary between 'me' and 'not me'. Winnicott's work has aided understanding of how the emotionally available adult can help mediate forces in the child's experience – those psychologically unintegrated affects – which may hamper the development of the ego, and thus help the psychic negotiation required for ego development. These processes are dependent upon trust. In the context of a trusting relationship, the child feels safe enough to 'let in' – to feel and to think about – a greater range of experience, which in turn facilitates the child's growing capacities for differentiation of both affect and thought. In contrast, where the child experiences a lack of empathetic 'holding' by the adult, feelings of disintegration can be produced. In such situations the personality 'closes in' to protect itself, and there is little capacity to undertake the risks involved in learning. The level of a child's ego functioning can be assessed (Dockar-Drysdale 1990) in relation to such factors as the child's dependency, his/her management of difficult feelings, the capacity for empathy, stress, aggression, communication, and modelling upon those admired (where the last of these is accompanied by a retention of individual identity).

How does the development proceed of the capacity to understand 'me/not me', to perceive oneself as a separate person, and to develop and make use of ego strength? A key feature of these developments was identified by Winnicott as the young child's capacity to make use of what he termed 'transitional objects'. Transitional objects refer to the soft toys or rags to which the young child becomes attached. The child's use of a transitional object represents the first indication of symbolisation, and belongs to the stage in a child's development when s/he is beginning to separate from the mother. The transitional object bridges the gap between mother and child. 'The object represents the infant's transition from a state of being merged with the mother to a state of being in relation to the mother as something outside and separate' (Winnicott 1974: 17). The transitional object is also symptomatic of the beginnings of the child's ego development. For Winnicott the transitional object was one indication that a relationship to the outside world, acceptable to the self, had begun (Davies and Wallbridge 1990). Transitional objects act as a sort of bridge to the handling of 'not me' objects, forming the first possession recognised as 'not me'.

Through the infant's affectionate fondling activity with the transitional object, this object may become very important to the infant. There is a sense in which this is the first possession which affectively belongs to the infant, and yet which is not part of the infant, like the thumb or fingers. The infant needs this object to be available, needs it to be returned when thrown away, over and over again. 'From the infant's point of view this first object was indeed created out of his or her imagination. It was the beginning of the infant's creation of the world' (Winnicott 1964: 167).

Winnicott argued that an object such as a child's teddy-bear actively helps the child separate from his/her mother. The object stands both *for* the mother and *between* the child and the mother. The child projects onto the teddy-bear the good relationship s/he has with mother and so feels protected by the teddy-bear in his/her mother's absence. As the child develops, s/he then takes back inside those images and good feelings associated with the mother. S/he no longer places them in the teddy-bear but rather contains them wholly in her/his own mind. The teddy-bear thus helps the child make the transition from dependency to independence.

Rollinson (1992) describes the field of the transitional object as a 'neutral area of illusion' which will not be challenged:

> Once experienced sufficiently mothers can introduce disillusionment, the introduction of object reality as part of the gradual change to independence which is operating naturally in the infant, vital to prevent illusion from becoming disillusion. However, the experience of the areas of overlap enables continued use of objects to help with the development of 'me' and its differentiation from 'not me'. Now this intermediate area between subjective inner reality and objective external reality, where both can interplay, protects the child from serious trauma of disillusionment. It provides a safe place for it to continue in a way that need not negatively affect functioning in the shared world. With trust in the environment established, playing occurs which helps develop a whole human being, who can experience intensely, be creative, act spontaneously and enrich the self while discovering 'meaning in the world of seen things'.
>
> (Rollinson 1992: 9)

Once trust in the environment happens there can be what Winnicott refers to as a psychological 'potential space', a third area beyond the I/thou dichotomy, a space in which creativity can take place.

> A baby can be *fed* without love, but loveless and impersonal *management* cannot succeed in producing a new autonomous human child ... Here where there is trust and reliability is potential space, one that can become an infinite area of separation, which the baby, child, adolescent, adult may creatively fill with playing, which in time becomes the enjoyment of the cultural heritage.
>
> (Winnicott 1974: 127)

Through cultural experiences 'each human being as a unique individual can form a bridge leading from the past to the future' (Davies and Wallbridge 1990: 170).

How do learners need transitional objects to secure their potential for learning? Hirschhorn (1988) suggests that if the learner were to be totally dependent on the teacher, s/he would not learn, and if the learner were to have no experience of psychological support, s/he would be overwhelmed. Teachers have the task of incorporating psychologically acceptable forms of transitional objects into their practice for those children who have need of them, whatever their age. Hirschhorn argues that techniques themselves can function as transitional objects: they help learners make the transition from feelings of incompetence to feelings of competence. As learners feel competent, they depend less on the technique and more on their own situational judgements and intuitions. Also, Hirschhorn maintains, a working alliance between the teacher and the learner can create a transitional relationship: learners can depend on the teacher to protect and help them as they develop their competence. But learners can learn and teachers can facilitate their learning only if the teachers develop a working alliance with the learners in which teachers become, in terms of psychoanalytic theory, an 'object' onto which learners can assign complex feelings.

Learners experience the teacher as a source of frustration, but also as someone who can stand to one side of their experience and understand it. The learners feel dependent and look to the teacher for guidance, but the teacher can also become their collaborator, as learners pass through a stage of frustration and discover their own expertise and capacity to learn. Learners must identify with the teacher's observing and interpreting stance so that they can learn to deploy their own 'observing ego', i.e. their capacity to observe themselves and use these observations to make judgements about managing themselves in relation to other people or a task.

Feeling secure and able to explore

Bowlby's work on attachment made a major contribution to our understanding of the issues involved in feeling secure, and being able to undertake the exploring which is necessary for learning. 'All of us, from the cradle to the grave, are happiest when life is organised as a series of excursions, long or short, from the secure base provided by our attachment figure(s)' (Bowlby 1988: 62). Bowlby argues that human infants are programmed to develop in a socially co-operative way, and that whether they do so or not depends largely on how they are treated. 'Children who have not participated in a "good enough" relationship with an "attachment figure" are less likely to learn effectively in school' (Barrett and Trevitt 1991: 4). Attachment is the condition from which emotions and purposes arise.

> The organisation of meaning depends on a maturing power to conceptualise the relationship between feelings, purposes and actions. Attachment influences this development, not only as our first and for a long time most crucial experience of security and danger, order and predictability, but as the guarantor of all other learning. … growth rests on the durability of the expectations we have already learned to trust.
>
> (Marris 1986: ix, 104)

The more secure we feel, the more open we are to experience, so long as we believe it will enlarge rather than undermine our sense of self.

Ainsworth's (1967) study of mothers and infants in Uganda showed how infants, once mobile, commonly use their mother as a base from which to explore. When conditions are favourable an infant moves away from mother on exploratory excursions and returns to her again from time to time. By 8 months of age almost every infant observed who had had a stable mother-figure to whom to become attached showed this behaviour, but when the mother was absent, such organised excursions became much less evident or ceased. Similarly, according to a study conducted in a London park, a healthy 2 year old child whose mother is resting on a garden seat will make a series of excursions away from her, each time returning to her before making the next excursion. On some occasions, when returning, the child simply smiles; on others s/he leans against the parent's knee; on yet others s/he wants to climb on the parent's lap. In this situation the child stays for a long period only when s/he is frightened or tired or thinks the parent is about to leave.

Bowlby (1988: 26–7) defines attachment behaviour as 'any form of behaviour that results in a person attaining or maintaining proximity to some other clearly identified individual who is conceived as better able to cope with the world'. He formulated three patterns of attachment. The first he terms *secure attachment*. This pattern develops where the individual is confident that the parent figure will be available, responsive and helpful should s/he encounter adverse or frightening situations. With this assurance, s/he feels bold in explorations of the world. When there is assurance that primitive wants will be satisfied, confidence to confront the uncertainties of growth is renewed (Marris 1986).

> those [children] who are most stable emotionally and make the most of their opportunities are those who have [parent figures] who, whilst always encouraging their children's autonomy, are none the less available and responsive when called upon. ... for a person to know that an attachment figure is available and responsive gives him a strong and pervasive feeling of security, and so encourages him to value and continue the relationship.
>
> (Bowlby 1988: 12, 27)

This sense of security is related to the development of confidence, because of the qualities of relationship which the child internalises. 'The confident child becomes increasingly adventurous and can tolerate brief separations, because he can carry a picture of himself interacting with his mother [or significant parental figure] inside his head' (Barrett and Trevitt 1991: 9). Barrett and Trevitt speak of how the child builds up a picture of him/herself as a worthwhile individual interacting with a preferred attachment figure by being validated through numerous gestures, tone of voice, and eye contact, as well as concrete provision.

> It is unlikely that these feelings are consciously recognised by an infant until later in his first year of life, but these two important aspects of an internal working model – the infant's active seeking of attention from his mother and mother's active response to this – affirm a secure base. Then, if all goes well, the infant can extend his

goal-seeking beyond the immediate presence of his mother; he has built up an internal picture or memory of his attachment figure, which he can retain even when she is not close-by. This is a gradual process; in the early months eye contact will suffice as re-assurance, but later it becomes possible to tolerate actual short separations, safe in the knowlege that this figure will return.

(Barrett and Trevitt 1991: 29–30)

So, as long as the attachment figure remains accessible and responsive, the attachment behaviour – which confirms the internal memory of attachment – may consist of little more than checking by eye or ear on the whereabouts of the figure and exchanging occasional glances and greetings.

So long as the attachment bond endures, the various forms of attachment behaviour which contribute to it are active only when required. The systems mediating attachment are triggered by a sense of strangeness or fear, and come to an end if a familiar environment or the ready availability and responsiveness of an attachment figure is lost (Bowlby 1980).

Bowlby termed his second mode of attachment *anxious resistant attachment*. This occurs when the child is uncertain whether the adult will be available or responsive when called upon. The child becomes prone to separation anxiety, tends to be clingy, and is anxious about exploring the world. 'When an individual (of any age) is feeling secure he is likely to explore away from his attachment figure. When alarmed, anxious, tired, or unwell he feels an urge towards proximity' (Bowlby 1988: 121).

Bowlby's third mode of attachment is *anxious avoidant attachment*. With this type of attachment the individual expects to be rebuffed when seeking care, and tries to become emotionally self-sufficient, developing a narcissistic, or, in Winnicott's terms, a false, self.

Who better to summarise the concept of attachment than Bowlby:

it seems clear that sensitive loving care results in a child developing confidence that others will be helpful when appealed to, becoming increasingly self-reliant and bold in his explorations of the world, co-operative with others, and also ... sympathetic and helpful to others in distress. Conversely, when a child's attachment behaviour is responded to tardily and unwillingly and is regarded as a nuisance, he is likely to become anxiously attached, that is, apprehensive lest his caregiver be missing or unhelpful when he needs her and therefore reluctant to leave her side, unwillingly and anxiously obedient, and unconcerned about the troubles of others. Should his caregivers, in addition, actively reject him, he is likely to develop a pattern of behaviour in which avoidance of them competes with his desire for proximity and care, and in which angry behaviour is apt to become prominent.

(Bowlby 1988: 82)

One of the key questions for people working with children is 'How can we help the children to feel safe?' Bowlby's work has helped the recognition that, to feel safe, pupils need to feel secure in their attachment to the teacher, and to feel that their autonomy is respected and appropriately encouraged. Where an adult displays the qualities of sensitivity, responsiveness and emotional involvement, the child is encouraged to make an emotional attachment to the relationship (Schaffer, 1977). The significance of attachment and separation in education was also recognised by Winnicott (1964: 203): 'The more we look, the more we see that if teachers and pupils are living healthily they are engaged in a mutual sacrifice of spontaneity and independence, and that is almost as important a part of education as teaching and learning in the set subjects.'

Individual identity

An emerging ego strength and a sense of inner security facilitate the risk-taking necessary for learning. A sense of personal identity, as it relates to purpose in the world, is necessary to enable a person to learn in relation to wider contexts of meaning. Learning, and its meaning, become related to the wider social and cultural sphere.

Winnicott argues that it is first through the development of inner reality that the infant becomes recognisable as an individual. 'Of every individual who has reached the state of being a unit with a limited membrane and an outside and an inside, it can be said that there is an inner reality to that individual, an inner world which can be rich or poor and can be at peace or in a state of war' (Winnicott 1975, quoted in Davies and Wallbridge 1990: 29–30). The concept of 'personal psychic reality' comes into being, according to Winnicott, as part of the self, as soon as the infant has reached:

> the state of being a unit with a limiting membrane and an inside and outside. ... The establishment of this state of affairs roughly corresponds to, or is soon followed by, the beginnings of self-consciousness, so that it becomes possible to talk about an individual with the connotation of personal identity.
>
> (Davies and Wallbridge 1990: 54)

Jung's concept of the self is helpful in thinking about the process of finding one's own meaning in relation to the wider world. Jung (1971: 460–1) defined the self as expressing 'the unity of the personality as a whole. ... it encompasses both the experienceable and the inexperienceable (or the not yet experienced)'. Jung extended psychological work beyond the confines of work with ego consciousness. He viewed the ego and the self as being in dynamic relation to each other. Relatedness between ego and self brings balance, and the capacity for emotional regeneration – psychological homeostasis. Where ego development is inhibited, the self of the child is unable to manifest as an independent entity. For a time after birth, the self is preserved within the self of the mother. Following Jung's work, analytical psychologists such as

Neumann (1973) and Kalff (1980) have postulated that, after approximately one year, the self of the child separates from that of the mother, and most often between the second and third years of life establishes itself in the unconscious of the child. Once this has happened, the child can begin the process of individuation, that is, a person's becoming himself or herself. The process of individuation in children was first recognised and identified by Fordham (1969).

As one gains identity in relation to inner and outer worlds, one is increasingly able to engage in open-ended learning explorations, with the complexity of potential connections these entail. The development of identity is closely linked with the development of autonomy.

> In our plural society, personal autonomy is an avowed educational aim … When the behaviour is autonomous the agent feels that he is acting on his own, not as the agent of another who is primarily responsible. … personal autonomy implies a coming to terms with oneself, one's society, the cosmos. It is a settlement, not a posture. Mere rebellion, willful self-assertion, the rejection or usurpation of authority, defiant doing of one's own thing, does not amount to autonomy, although it may be a necessary negative moment in the achievement of autonomy.
>
> (Blackham 1978: 27–9)

Summary

- Feelings have a vital role in the development of learning, since it is through our subjective, emotional world that we develop our personal constructs and meanings of outer reality, and make sense of our relationships and, eventually, of our place in the wider world.
- To be open to learning and to be able to learn effectively we need:
  - to feel safe and accepted – which requires a measure of 'relative dependency' upon the teacher or other key adult. We can allow some form of dependency to take place in relationships and settings where we experience trust. Dependency is a pre-condition for independence.
  - to be able to symbolise.
  - to have a well-enough functioning ego to mediate the experiences of our inner world and outer experience.
- Transitional objects are an aid to establishing our psychological separation as an individual person, and to symbol formation and ego development.
- In order to be able to make the explorations involved in autonomous learning, we need to feel secure in our attachment to significant adults.
- The development of personal identity is necessary for learning to develop in relation to the wider world of meaning.

References

Ainsworth, M. D. S. (1967) *Infancy in Uganda: Infant Care and the Growth of Attachment*, Baltimore: Johns Hopkins University Press.

Barrett, M. and Trevitt, J. (1991) *Attachment Behaviour and the Schoolchild: An Introduction to Educational Therapy*, London: Routledge.

Blackham, H. J. (1978) 'The Concept of Autonomy', in Blackham, H. J. (ed.), *Education for Personal Autonomy: An Enquiry into the School's Resources for Furthering the Personal Development of Pupils*, London: Bedford Square Press.

Bowlby, J. (1980) *Attachment and Loss*, London: Hogarth.

Bowlby, J. (1988) *A Secure Base: Clinical Applications of Attachment Theory*, London: Routledge.

Davies, M. and Wallbridge, D. (1990) *Boundary and Space: An Introduction to the Work of D. W. Winnicott*, London: Karnac; New York: Brunner/Mazel.

Dockar-Drysdale, B. (1990) *The Provision of Primary Experience: Winnicottian Work with Children and Adolescents*, London: Free Assocation.

Fordham, M. (1969) *Children as Individuals*, New York: G. P. Putnam's Sons.

Hirschhorn, L. (1988) *The Workplace Within: Psychodynamics of Organizational Life*, Cambridge, Massachusetts, and London: MIT Press.

Jung, C. G. (1971) *Psychological Types*, Collected Works, Vol. 6, London: Routledge and Kegan Paul.

Kalff, D. M. (1980) *Sandplay: A Psychotherapeutic Approach to Psyche*, Santa Monica: Sigo.

Marris, P. (1986) *Loss and Change*, London: Routledge and Kegan Paul.

Neumann, E. (1973) *The Child: Structure and Dynamics of the Nascent Personality*, London: Karnac.

Rollinson, R. (1992) 'Myths We Work by', *Therapeutic Care and Education*, 10, 1: 3–22.

Schaffer, R. (1977) *Mothering*, Glasgow: Fontana.

Trowell, J. (1990) 'The Development Perspective', presentation to the Advanced Course in Consultation to Individuals, Groups and Organisations, The Tavistock Clinic, October.

Winnicott, D. W. (1964) *The Child, the Family and the Outside World*, London and Harmondsworth: Penguin.

Winnicott, D. W. (1974) *Playing and Reality*, London: Pelican.

Winnicott, D. W. (1984) *The Maturational Processes and the Facilitating Environment*, London: Hogarth.

Chapter 11

Self-esteems and emotional differentiation

Tim O'Brien and Dennis Guiney

Introduction

This chapter considers the emotional context for learning and its relationship to differentiation. For reasons that will become clear we are particularly interested in issues that surround the concept of self-esteem as well as commenting upon teaching and learning experience, the nature of self and our personal susceptibilities. We open this chapter with what might appear to be a large claim – *self-esteem does not exist*.

By making this claim we are not intending to devalue emotional factors relating to personality or self-concept, for example; we are simply pointing out that self-esteem itself is not 'real', it is a construct, a descriptive and explanatory construct. It does not exist in the form in which we constantly hear it applied and used in teacher-learner systems. It is used to describe and explain a combination of factors with multiple variables and outcomes that are relative and contextual. Definitions and explanations of self-esteem do not seem to help us to become more analytical and sophisticated in planning for emotional differentiation. We find it difficult to make substantial progress in defining or measuring it because it does not exist. We may want it to exist and therefore we talk about it as if it is real. We create and adopt tools to measure it, when these tools often highlight a relationship between thinking, feeling and behaviour. However, the identification of such a relationship does not explain causation and nor does it prove that self-esteem exists as a singular characteristic of an individual.

At times, we have tried to engage in discussion with teachers about self-esteem and asked challenging questions of each other. In many situations it is like trying to discuss the concept of a persons soul or spirit. What is it? Where is it? What influences it? How do we know about it? How can we alter it? One general outcome of such discussions and debates is that many people see self-esteem as a concrete concept – there is a belief that all people have a self-esteem that is high or low depending on how we feel about our'self', especially in relation to how others perceive us. Self-esteem appears to be located on a linear scale ranging from high to low. Clearly we do not dismiss the importance of emotions in relation to learning and we are not saying that emotional factors do not exist.

For example, we would accept that a learner aged seven who wishes that they were dead does have a devastatingly negative image of their self and worth. In this example, if the teacher believes that the seven year old has low self-esteem, perhaps at rock-bottom level and as a singularly defining characteristic, then what routes can they design to offer learning for that child? Herein lies a serious difficulty. If you buy into the 'low self-esteem culture' then it is most likely that your teaching routes will only be defined within the parameters of the child's negativity and despair. This may distort your thinking and planning and will impact upon your operations within the zone of proximal development (ZPD). As detailed elsewhere, you are always seeking to act in the most open, creative and positive manner on behalf of learners within the ZPD, not to enter into their negativity, no matter how bleak this may appear. If in this situation we do not seek positive support and solutions, we are in danger of becoming as emotionally paralysed as the learner. What value would you bet upon in such a relationship?

We are proposing that self-esteem is a weak construct and should be defined in terms that demonstrate that it is responsive to different persons and contexts. This is another situation where differentiation is necessary – in this case we need to differentiate the construct. This allows us to explore it in relation to concepts that are concurrent throughout this book, value, flexibility and scale being especially relevant. Thus, if we are looking at emotional responses to teaching and learning we need a fluid rather than a concrete construct. This can be achieved by a minimum alteration to the word that makes an optimal alteration to the construct. Consequently, this chapter deals with a debate around *self-esteems* as against *self-esteem*.

We select self-esteems as we feel that differentiation in this area needs to begin with a workable proposition that can operate above the level of what has become almost a cliché. A term that is used so often that its meaning is rarely called into question. This follows the ethos underpinning this book in asking you to question and requestion your own practice and the practice within your teaching and learning system. Not in the form of negative questions but in a positive manner to sustain, create and engender a respectful teaching and learning environment for all.

When working with schools, learners and parents or carers we often see planning that speaks of the learner's self-esteem – it is always the learner's self-esteem that is under the spotlight. When self-esteem is raised as a difficulty it is low self-esteem that needs to improve. It is rarely high self-esteem which needs to move higher. The focus is usually on repairing brittle, broken and fragile self-esteem. This poses the question as to what self-esteem is, how and where it becomes so vulnerable to collapse, and whether it is possible or perhaps worthwhile to define it as a whole. To become analytical and for teachers and learner to benefit, it is more helpful to eyeball the concept in a different way. Redefining it as self-esteems offers the learner and the teacher a more meaningful insight into a complex constellation of factors that are fluid and changeable. Self-esteem has become a catch-phrase involving the casting of a wide net that trawls everything into it, resulting in a sometimes chaotic and often ill-defined mass. It is a concrete, solid and problematic construct, unlike self-esteems, which are holistic. Our task is to try and break down the self-esteem monolith in order to bring a fully differentiated focus to bear on the reality lying beneath the label. To do this we need to look closer at self-esteem so that we can understand why a more fluid concept is required – a concept that enables us to gain more data about learners and their emotions.

Self-esteem – what is it?

Clear and succinct definitions are not that easy to come by. Often people turn to dictionaries for precise definitions but interestingly it is difficult to find a single entry for the hyphenated term in many dictionaries. Therefore we are reduced to looking at them individually. Common definitions are as follows:

> *Self*: individuality, essence, oneself.
> *Esteem*: think favourably of, regard as valuable, positive opinion, respect.

Definitions of self-esteem involve combinations of these notions, along with other self-centred associations such as self-concept, self-confidence, self-worth and self-respect. The notion of self-esteem is linked to these, there is a correlation between them, but it also appears to be different from them too. This is particularly evident in its usage and application. In our view it has become a shorthand form of interchangeable 'common speak' for a watery set of indistinct notions which are not useful to the process of differentiation. In fact, at some levels, differentiation is fundamentally hindered by the concept of self-esteem. We see self-concept as a clearer notion and most definitely one that supports the thinking that is associated with differentiation. Certainly there are espoused psychological theories around self-concept. In this chapter, self-concept is used to describe how a person sees her or himself.

Let us begin by thinking about the self. Here we are inviting you to think for yourself about what the notion of 'self' means to you. How does this relate to your 'selves' as teachers thinking about the other 'selves' with whom you regularly interact – that is, learners?

Three views of self

The concept of self is confronted and investigated in many sacred and philosophical writings from diverse cultures and traditions. Some traditions identify a conscious self that is often described in physical terms. Others see the concept of self as an illusion. There are religious doctrines that assert that there is only one permanent and everlasting true self, often described as God. Self is also a concept that is considered beyond philosophy and religion. We are interested in presenting what psychologists have said about self. The earliest concept of 'psyche', from which the word psychology derives, contained a notion of the self or soul that continued beyond death. We shall consider three psychological views of self. All that we offer are the very briefest of tastes of these different forms of thinking about self. Their outline is presented to orient your thinking. Each area has a wealth of material and literature associated with it that certain readers might wish to explore further. Our purpose is not to produce a textbook explanation of such theories and thinking but to highlight rich areas to provoke and stimulate your questioning. For this reason we have chosen the work of three well-known psychologists who offer differing perspectives. We present them in a non-judgemental fashion. We must emphasize, however, that they are all male views of self.

Carl Rogers: self and organism

Rogers divided the person into *self* and *organism*. The self is the 'I' or 'me'. He postulated that everyone has an ideal self. The ideal of what they would like to be.

The organism is the real world as seen and experienced by the 'I' or 'me'. Differences between these two can create deep-seated anxieties and result in conflict and a lack of congruency. For example, a learner may believe that they are the best linguist in the group. This is how they construct their self in relation to the speaking of foreign languages. However, when the teacher assesses written and spoken language, the learner might be in the lower 50 per cent of the group. This is the information gained from the real world. There is a gap or discrepancy between how the learner perceives their 'self' and the feedback from the 'organism'. Such a difference can move, through learning, to congruence and accommodation over time. In more serious situations than the example given, therapy may be required to enable the discrepancy to be dealt with. Given the right situation and support everyone can be led to resolve these personal crises *for themselves*. They can be seen to regard themselves positively. Rogerian therapy is known as Client Centred Therapy. It has also been used as a model for mutual support therapy groups.

John Bowlby: attachment theory

Bowlby developed attachment theory which he saw as social, emotional and behavioural characteristics resulting from an individual being in close proximity to their main caregivers. From this we construct working models based upon our experience of these absolutely critical relationships. This happens from the moment of birth and recent research would suggest it could happen before birth. Our early experiences provide powerful underpinnings to our sense of self and the way we operate within and upon the world. There are different types of attachment, such as secure attachment. There are also attachment behaviours, for example a baby crying to gain the care and attention of a main caregiver or to express anxiety about the unavailability of a main caregiver. These attachments facilitate us in playing, learning, socializing and in growing and developing emotionally. He thought that early patterns of attachment persisted throughout life. In positive situations attachment could result in an individual feeling a profound sense of self-worth and becoming confident in developing relationships with others. Bowlby proposed that secure attachment can result in a higher level of curiosity, risk-taking and determination in learning – being able to deal with perceived failure through persistence to get things right. In negative situations, such as insecure attachment, phobias and self-doubt could develop. Attachment is developmentally represented inside the head of the learner.

Sigmund Freud: id, ego and superego

Freud described the self as being made up of three component parts: *id, ego* and *superego*. The id is unconscious. It is present from birth and provides us with instinctual, impatient and impulsive urges to receive gratification. The ego is preconscious. It acts as an intermediary between the instinctive urges of the id and the outside world. The superego forms an internalized inhibiting force of control. This is an internal representation, for example, of parents or caregivers or teachers who may wish to impose cultural and societal morals. It is similar to the concept of a constraining conscience that can create feelings of guilt. It negotiates, mediates and differentiates. Freud proposes that there is a constant tension between the primitive forces of the id and the inhibiting control exerted by the superego, with the ego seeking to mediate between the two. Freud asserts that everyone develops coping mechanisms to help deal with their own concept of self not being gratified. These he refers to as defence mechanisms. For example, painful memories and experiences can be repressed or denied completely – as if they never happened or are not happening. At times, the feelings associated with one person or event can be projected onto another person or event.

Whatever self is, you will have your own ideas and views about it. Whichever factors mould, make, inhibit, enable or facilitate development of the self exist among the development of the selves of the learners you work with. Of course they were, and some would argue that they still are, continually around in the development of all of us as teachers.

After this brief consideration of self we now turn to esteem. The esteem part of the equation is probably easier to understand, dealing as it does with self-respect and a sense of inner confidence, value and worth.

Some characteristics of self-esteem

We have asserted that the construct or concept of self-esteems encompasses a holistic view of self. Self-esteem asserts the opposite – a monistic or one-sided view. It implies a singular characteristic that changes in a linear manner from low to high. It is a singular notion, as are self-confidence and self-respect. It has an evident hierarchical aspect to it.

Maslow (1954) proposed a hierarchy of human needs. At the lowest level are physiological needs, such as hunger, thirst, sex and sleep. One level above this is the need for safety – avoidance of pain, fear, illness, cold and wet, for example. At the next level is the need for belongingness and love. Above this is esteem – meaning self-confidence, worth, strength, capability, feeling useful and necessary in the world. Finally, at the top of the hierarchy is self-actualization. It can be seen in this structure that as human beings we cannot move up to the next level unless and until lower level needs have been satisfied. Therefore someone cannot have their higher-level needs met unless their basic human needs, such as eating, drinking and sleeping, are being met.

In this hierarchy of our needs, esteem is second from the top. We can see that notions, definitions and the sheer scope the term esteem covers are getting larger and larger as progress is made from one level to another. In this view there can appear to be a developmental element to thinking about self-esteem which in turn is often associated with behavioural and emotional disturbance. We hear this most commonly expressed with regard to learners who present with challenging behaviour, where planning to address their needs seeks to improve or build their self-esteem. Certainly it is felt that self-esteem as a singular entity can be measured, for example through self-esteem inventories, which in turn may enable a degree of labelling to occur.

Some characteristics of self-esteems

It seems evident to us that if we are to be more accurate in differentiating and bringing about grounded learning, then we need a term that represents what takes place in the real world. One of the authors recalls a learner that he recently taught (O'Brien, 2000). This learner was labelled as having 'low self-esteem'. He describes the learner as having low self-esteem in one area, reading, and high self-esteem in another, burglary. Whilst his self-concept was poor in relation to literacy, it was high in relation to illegal activity because he received peer group adulation for it, and his peers were important to him. This is provided as an example of considering self-esteems – looking at how learners feel in different contexts – rather than making assumptions based upon one universal, constant and concrete concept of self-esteem. The point being that the casually applied label that 'this learner has low self-esteem' may restrict opportunities to see what it is that makes someone feel good about what they do in certain contexts. If we transfer this concept to the curriculum then we can see the benefits of viewing a learner in terms of their self-esteems.

Consider the teacher planning which seeks to improve self-esteem. How can a teacher know when self-esteem has been improved? What evidence can they seek? How will a teacher conceive indicators of the totality of a vague and ill-defined notion of self-esteem when the learner somehow demonstrates it? It could be proposed that vague planning and lack of clarity in goal setting do not enable a teacher to raise a learner's self-esteem. The problem is seen as being located with the teacher and their practice rather than with an understanding of self-esteem: it is the teacher's fault. We see the problem as broader than this – self-esteem is a phrase and an explanatory construct that, although it feels intuitively right, promotes fixed rather than fluid and holistic thinking. Worse than this, because it is such a global term it can be a constant negative theme in a learner's career.

The curriculum is multidimensional and therefore a learner's experience of it is not flat. In this context we define the curriculum as all learning that takes place in and through the school. A learner's experience and emotions undulate according to their own perception of their ability in relation to achievement and attainment in different curriculum areas. Even within one specific subject area a learner can have multiple esteems.

Consider this example. A teacher comments or writes that Suki encounters various learning problems, sometimes she acts out, especially in practical lessons in science, and she can be emotionally fragile. With this type of behaviour and her family difficulties, a link is made and the judgement is that she has low self-esteem. The next learning plan includes broad targets to improve her self-esteem. A support professional fills in a self-esteem inventory in interview with her. Suki objects to this interview taking place and the outcome is that she *has* got low self-esteem. The plan from now on has to be to build and improve her self-esteem.

> How can this be done?
> *By?* Making her feel good about herself.
> *How?* By making her feel good about herself.
> This is not the most analytical or helpful starting point for planning.

At the planning meeting there are two nonplussed members. The drama teacher sits scratching her head as, in the last lesson, Suki once again took the lead in choreographing a dance, which will be performed at an open evening to be held in three weeks time. The other teacher who is bemused, the learning support assistant, has been working with Suki on a collage in art lessons, where she has been able positively and creatively to express feelings about some of her family relationships, though this remains a tender and fragile area. Suki's brother died two years ago. Her father left the family. Suki feels the loss. However, she has even discussed with her teacher the possibility of displaying her collage in the school entrance area.

Has Suki got low self-esteem or has she got variable self-esteems, in changing and different contexts? In this example it would appear that she presents with a range of self-esteems according to the differing facets of her personality, individuality and sense of self. Doubtless these have arisen from a complex combination of past experiences, learning and development and current susceptibilities. She evidently has high and robust self-esteem in the context of dance, extending to creative leadership and group management. She has growing self-esteem in the area of her artistic expression and representation. She may have low self-esteem in science but we cannot assume that she has low self-esteem in every aspect of the science curriculum.

This has pinned down the actual work that needs to be done in understanding the experience of learners within and beyond the curriculum and differentiated the original casually applied label. Yet ideally we would suggest a further progressive focusing on the actual esteems themselves within these areas which need developing and working on. How can they be scrutinized and targeted? What has to be done, how can it be planned for, taught and evaluated, to show that a focus has been placed upon Suki's esteems?

This is why we must take another look at self-esteem and recast it as a complementary and more inclusive concept. This will encourage a more holistic view and one that matches the complexity of individuals and the processes of teaching and learning. Self-esteems is a circular concept which describes a continuous and multidimensional approach. If it was linear there is a temptation to leave it alone once it is high. If it is cyclical then high or low it can always be developed further. It can add to definition and understanding of needs and help to identify areas that require further support and differentiation. These factors or facets of the self exist and coexist in a complex manner and it is better to think of them in terms of interaction and inter-relationships rather than overidentifying a block of self-esteem with certain behavioural presentations. Lastly, this more qualitative approach to the complexity of esteems can address and combat the negativity and stereotypes that are the outcomes of a process of bulk labelling. The difference between the two concepts is summarized below.

Self-esteems	Self-esteem
Holistic	Monistic
Circular	Linear
Complex	Singular
Flexible	Fixed
Insights	Labels
Multiple focus	Single focus
Positive power	Negative power
Destination	Navigation

Mapping self-esteems: lost in space?

What we are proposing here is a conceptual shift from self-esteem to the complementary and inclusive notion of self-esteems. This is in fact really a mapping exercise. Just as the curriculum has its own topography, an undulating landscape, so do esteems. The notion of self-esteem feels rather like the description of a small-scale map of a region. It can be likened to a space journey where you are in one part of the galaxy and wish to travel to another part. Given the vast scale of the universe, the first task in finding the planet you seek would be to arrive at the right portion of the galaxy. For this purpose you want a general map rather than a detailed one. You would not need a map of downtown Manhattan, even if arriving in this part of New York was your ultimate goal.

Instead you would want a map with sufficient detail only to locate you in the correct sector of the solar system. This map must deal in an easy to manage form with vast detail and scales. Therefore information has to be prioritized and fine detail, which causes confusion to the bigger picture, is discarded. Once you arrive in the correct corner of the universe then the map that helped to get you there is no longer useful. At this point, you still do not want a plan of individual streets and blocks within a city. You scale down again and use a map that has selected data that can help you locate one particular planet.

So the process goes on, you continually select and reject data at different levels of detail in order to home in on the target area. When you arrive in the city of your choice you are no longer using a map of the solar system to help you navigate. Using this image, let us call that original map 'self-esteem' and consider that it was useful for a given purpose. It is no longer useful for the fine detail of differentiated teaching and learning. It was useful to navigate with initially, to get you moving in the right direction. It worked well to help you in the process of arriving but it operates at a macro level and is no longer employable at the scale at which you are now seeking to work. In fact to use it still would be negligent. Now we need a map that can deliver much more exact locations in fine detail. These are the maps of 'self-esteems'.

They describe the detail and interrelations of the emotional ecosystems of individuals. A self-esteems map lays out all those factors that contribute to a sense of self, all with a sense of topography. It provides the shape, feel and flow of the surface in relation to the underlying structures. This is what we need to have an understanding of when seeking to provide emotional differentiation. We cannot hope to do this successfully if we are not aware of the question and impact of scale.

We believe that the notion of self-esteem is not useful because it predisposes us to look at the wrong scale. In fact, it causes us to look only at one scale. Although the purpose may be right, the map is wrong. This can leave us seeking to address subtle and powerful issues almost from a position of remote control. This maximizes the space between teacher and learner and is unlikely to bring about intimate learning. In its place we propose using the right tools for the job by dealing with self-esteems, a map to help locate the heart of the issue. Let us be clear – self-esteems will get you to your precise destination, whereas self-esteem will only offer navigation.

Positive and negative power

In this section we are using power in the sense of political and physical power. We consider negative power rather than positive power, as this is a regular concern of teachers that we have worked with. We remind you that teachers have self-esteems as well as learners, though we tend to hear more about those of the learners than we do of the teachers.

Negative power seems to be an orientation arising from low self-esteems in individuals, whether they are teachers or learners. This presents itself in a variety of forms within teaching and learning systems. In younger learners it may present as overt acting out behaviours. In older learners it can be a motivational presentation, in which they want teachers to know that they are disaffected and to experience their disaffection. Having access to some control and predictability is something that we have seen, through considering personal constructs, as being very important to us as individuals. The power underlying these acts of control or attempts to gain, regain or retain control can be perceived as either positive or negative. Not only do individuals exert positive and negative power but so do groups and systems.

Negative power in teachers as well as learners is likely to arise as the result of some key areas of esteems that require further development, attention, resourcing or differentiation. Adults tend to present with different forms of negative power within teaching and learning systems. Obviously, on a societal level, adults may fight, riot and engage in war, and these may be seen as the more extreme forms of negative power. We are referring to more subtle signs and indicators than this that we can learn to recognize and address through emotional differentiation.

Throughout this chapter we have spoken of open questioning being the basis underpinning inclusive and fully differentiated teaching and learning systems. We have to recognize that teachers and learners may employ questioning in a negative manner. Where this happens occasionally and in a balanced manner it is a natural by-product of human interactions. Where it happens routinely it is a sign that things are not as they seem. One linguistic indicator of this that we see a lot is in the polite use of the word 'but'.

I like it ... but

Imagine that one teacher has an idea or a plan. A plan to which they have given much consideration. They take it to another person, possibly a more senior person in the teaching and learning system, for consideration. The other person replies, 'I like it ... *but*'. The other person may register the 'but' in various ways, another common phrase being 'I hear what you are saying ... *but*'. Sometimes the 'but' is signalled and inferred by the pause only. How will this make the teacher with the new idea feel – about their 'self', their value, and about their idea? We are conscious that in drawing attention to this practice we are not aiming to prevent the term from being used from a positive basis. We are concerned with the power and status issues that might be inherent in the use of the word or the negative feelings it raises in relation to how it might affect a person's self-esteems. It is difficult to say to another adult that you do not like their ideas about teaching and learning, so the message can be sweetened with 'I like it … but'. If the idea or plan as a whole is not applicable, achievable or realistic then what is really needed is a conversation about aspects of their idea that might be useful within the teaching and learning system that they have responsibility for. This will impact upon their sense of worth and represents emotional differentiation in action. Of course, the same principle applies to learners, especially where the 'I like it' is subsumed by the message associated with the ensuing use of the word 'but'. Inevitably some teachers and learners will process 'I like it … but' as 'I do not like it at all'. We all exercise negative and positive power at times and the joint aim of teaching and learning systems is to minimize the destructive force that this can represent and maximize the creative force that positive applications can unleash.

Why should teaching and learning systems be particularly prone to variability in self-esteems on the part of teachers and learners? Of course they are not. All systems suffer from this, but the act of teaching and learning is very closely linked to basic life experience and evokes profound reactions in all concerned with the process. Teaching and learning is above all an emotional activity and this is why we need to plan for emotional differentiation. We fool ourselves if we ignore, deny or remain unclear about the degree of raw emotion that runs deep and strong in every learner teacher interaction. Some teachers have said to us that they are subject teachers and subject teachers only; it is as simple as that. Nothing could be further from the truth or from the reality of their professional work. The following are learner's views of the emotional hothouse that is their classroom or school. They know who is 'in' and who is 'out'. They can identify who is good and who is bad. They regularly reassess who is top and who is bottom in the pecking order. They know who is friendly with whom; who is not friendly with whom; and who should never be allowed to get friendly with whom. They can tell who likes what and who does not like what, who is trustworthy and who is untrustworthy, who can survive and who cannot survive – and this just describes their view of teachers!

The power within teacher–learner interactions is based upon the teacher having an agenda, knowing something and having the responsibility to impart this to the learners. We have written about the basic human predisposition to learn in other places previously but we are not naive enough to suppose that learners always want to learn what is being taught at the time that it is being taught. Therefore teaching and learning also involve power issues. As well as this, in most teacher–learner systems there are usually more learners than there are teachers at any given time. Often, a single teacher has a group to teach and is responsible for every individual's learning. The learners may not share the teacher's agenda and individually, or communally, through their internal group dynamic, may have other agendas to attend to instead and to learn from.

Therefore there are fundamental management and responsibility issues that fall upon the teacher rather than the learners.

Having set up a scenario of more negative learner interaction, we are keen to point out that we feel there are strong emotional factors at play in all teaching and learning systems and in fact in all human interactions, whether they be efficient or inefficient, positive or negative. What differentiates them is the outcomes for the learners and teachers.

Even where the teacher–learner energy transformation is high we propose that the same emotions are and have been present, but they have been harnessed and held in a different, more positive manner. They are differentiated in a way that sustains and develops personal esteems rather than attacking, degrading or demolishing them.

This emotional management task is felt very keenly by teachers but is just as relevant for learners. What adds further power to teacher–learner interactions is the potential at the outset for some form of conflict to be the result. We are not saying that teacher–learner interactions are typified by conflict. We are highlighting that when emotional management and differentiation issues are raised and tested, especially at the initial stages of interaction, the emotional stance of both parties becomes challenged and success may hinge on reactions to the possibility of conflict.

We have to investigate this further in order to understand what is taking place now that our mapping has located us at the very core of self and esteems.

Emotional management and differentiation

If, as we assert, there is a flow of emotional power in every single teacher–learner interaction this can produce stresses in each person. Stresses in the sense used here are seen as both positive and negative, whereas stress, another example of a monistic and broadly applied term, has become more clearly associated with negatives. These stresses arise from the conflict potential inherent in one person exerting teaching and learning responsibilities over a group of others.

When you, as a teacher of varying experience, next teach a group of learners of varying experience nobody knows exactly what will happen next. Think about it. You have an idea or a plan, and they have an idea or a plan too. Nobody knows what will happen or is happening until interactions unfold in real time, in front of you and them. From one perspective this could be seen as offering the potential for existential terror as everyone prepares for 'take-off'.

The experience is potentially stressful. The ways in which we cope with these stresses are complex and interesting. The following is one description of what you may experience in the act of teaching, and what learners may experience in the act of learning. When combinations of stresses are present what might be seen as negative reactions are most likely to be experienced. This is especially true when self-esteems are under threat. We need to be aware of how we react to such stresses because it is at this time that we are most likely to be the recipient, or the user, of negative power.

Physiological reactions

The liver produces glucose to fuel muscles so that energy is readily on tap. Hormones are released to aid conversion of fats and protein into sugar to fuel the muscles. One of the most powerful of these is adrenaline. This increases heart and breathing rates and blood pressure, and muscles become noticeably more tense. Saliva and mucus in the mouth may dry up (note that people addressing groups often have a cup of water to hand). Endorphins, natural painkillers, are then released. Surface blood vessels expand and contract. The spleen releases more red blood cells in order to carry and convert increasing amounts of oxygen. What we have described here, as many readers will have realized, is what is typically known as the *fight-flight response*: this is an innate or automatic response.

We cannot help this from happening to ourselves if we feel under threat. We are not suggesting that it follows that all teachers will feel these reactions all the time but the potential is always there. The potential stresses of teaching are not only associated with these types of interactions. We have had many teachers admit that they never sleep very well at the end of vacations when the start of a new term looms. Many of us will also admit to the stresses of teaching even causing us to experience worst-case scenarios in our dreams.

Psychological reactions

These can be many and varied. One key factor is decision paralysis. This is a difficulty in making key decisions at a time when, owing to stresses, a person needs to be able to make very clear and rapid decisions. The type of difficulty that would be problematic if you were, for example, employed as an air traffic controller. This is a serious point and highlights why people who work in situations where there is potential for multiple stresses practice and simulate their decision-making processes under extreme conditions: the armed forces, the police, and airline pilots are examples. This paralysis is linked to difficulties in retrieving relevant information from memory and the consequence can be thinking that becomes fixed and fixated. A person's ability to prioritize becomes impaired and choice-making about possible alternatives becomes stuck. Thus, we need to remain alert to what is going on under the surface for individual teachers and learners, groups and systems that will affect learning and behaviour. We are then in a better position to support each other through differentiation.

Emotional responses

Once again the 'health warning' needed here is to underline that these are also variable and that different individuals react differently to different stresses. But for those whose emotional reactions evoke negative responses and lowered esteems in key areas, there is an increased potential for experiencing feelings of guilt, apprehension, tension, fear, anger, aggression and displacement.

Teaching and learning systems, and the individuals and groups who are part of them, develop ways of 'holding' these emotions. This can be positive and can operate at informal and formal levels. Emotions can be held and differentiated through all of the usual aspects of collegiality that we find within all systems. These would include socializing, celebrations, cliques and factions, which can be representative of positive and negative power flows. A typical method that is common to many teaching systems is what amounts to 'coffee-cup-counselling'.

Coffee-cup-counselling

This is a well-developed system for dealing with teacher negative feelings and lowered self-esteems and for enabling emotional differentiation. It maintains the concept of 'group' but without adult fear of being seen to need direct support or counselling. It is useful and has purpose because it is provided in-house, at very regular intervals, in a non-threatening manner. It thrives upon informal and non-judgemental peer-support systems rather than external experts and so, from the perspective of the users, it remains relatively safe. Also, it is free.

It carries its own signals, language, personnel and counselling space and typically operates as follows. It is break time in teaching and learning systems all over the country. A teacher arrives in a staff room looking a little exasperated, takes a cup and proceeds to make some coffee. At the same time they open a conversation towards other colleagues by saying something like 'I have just been teaching Jimmy ... do you know what happened?' They proceed to sit down with the coffee and this is a signal to their colleagues that they wish to talk about a negative interaction with Jimmy. Colleagues may have their own cup of coffee, signalling that they are available to be engaged as peer counsellors. They will make a choice as to whether they wish to be part of the discussion. If they do, they can join in the exchange, offering sympathy, advice, commiseration and at times lightening the load by offering humour. They can also offer helpful and practical advice. The benefit of this occupational counselling is that it is easily available and the signals are so widely recognized. So much so, that it is rarely recognized, in the form we present it here, for what it really is. A problem will not be overly analysed and self-esteems are not called into question as such; it is not turned into an issue, a 'teacher danger' situation, as the teacher is not the focus of debate. It is usually dealt with in a manner which is understandable and which adds to the collegiate bond and group perceptions. This bond is often strengthened by the mutual exchange of problems. One negative outcome of such counselling could be that, given the fact that there is no time for critical analysis, it can become a forum for the labelling of learners and the transmission of assumptions.

Conclusion

In conclusion, we have dealt at some length with self-esteems as an important factor in aiding your analysis and understanding of emotional differentiation. We have sought to place this, unusually, within a context of looking at the self-esteems of both teachers and learners when dealing with issues of emotional differentiation. For too long it has been a one-way street with low self-esteem solely accorded to learners, almost to the point of becoming another negative and self-determining label.

References

Maslow, A. H. (1954) *Motivation and Personality*. New York: Harper and Row.
O'Brien, T. (2000) 'Providing inclusive differentiation', in P. Benton, and T. O'Brien (eds) *Special Needs and the Beginning Teacher*. London: Continuum.

Chapter 12

Cultural and historical origins of counselling

John McLeod

Introduction

To understand the diversity of contemporary counselling, and to appreciate the significance of current patterns of practice, it is necessary to look at the ways in which counselling has developed and evolved over the past 200 years. The differences and contradictions that exist within present-day counselling have their origins in the social and historical forces that have shaped modern culture as a whole.

People in all societies, at all times, have experienced emotional or psychological distress and behavioural problems. In each culture there have been well established indigenous ways of helping people to deal with these difficulties. The Iroquois Indians, for example, believed that one of the causes of ill-health was the existence of unfulfilled wishes, some of which were only revealed in dreams (Wallace 1958). When someone became ill and no other cause could be determined, diviners would discover what his or her unconscious wishes were, and arrange a 'festival of dreams' at which other members of the community would give these objects to the sick person. There seems little reason to suppose that modern-day counselling is any more valid, or effective, than the Iroquois festival of dreams. The most that can be said is that it is seen as valid, relevant or effective by people in this culture at this time.

The emergence of the 'trade in lunacy'

Although counselling and psychotherapy have only become widely available to people during the second half of the twentieth century, their origins can be traced back to the beginning of the eighteenth century, which represents a turning point in the social construction of madness. Before this, the problems in living which people encountered were primarily dealt with from a religious perspective, implemented at the level of the local community (McNeill 1951; Neugebauer 1978, 1979). In Europe, the vast majority of people lived in small rural communities and were employed on the land. Within this way of life, anyone who was seriously disturbed or insane was tolerated as part of the community. Less extreme forms of emotional or interpersonal problems were dealt with by the local priest; for example, through the Catholic confessional. McNeill (1951) refers to this ancient tradition of religious healing as 'the cure of souls'. An important element in the cure of souls was confession of sins, followed by repentance. McNeill (1951) points out that in earlier times confession of sins took place in public, and was often accompanied by communal admonishment, prayer and even excommunication. The earlier Christian rituals for helping troubled souls were, like the Iroquois festival of dreams, communal affairs. Only later did individual private confession become established. McNeill (1951) gives many examples of clergy in the sixteenth and seventeenth centuries acting in a counselling role to their parishioners.

As writers such as Foucault (1967), Rothman (1971), Scull (1979, 1981b, 1989) and Porter (1985) have pointed out, all this began to change as the Industrial Revolution took effect, as capitalism began to dominate economic and political life and as the values of science began to replace those of religion. The fundamental changes in social structure and in social and economic life which took place at this point in history were accompanied by basic changes in relationships and in the ways people defined and dealt with emotional and psychological needs. Albee (1977) has written that

> Capitalism required the development of a high level of rationality accompanied by repression and control of pleasure seeking. This meant the strict control of impulses and the development of a work ethic in which a majority of persons derived a high degree of satisfaction from hard work. Capitalism also demanded personal efforts to achieve long-range goals, an increase in personal autonomy and independence ... The system depended on a heavy emphasis on thrift and ingenuity and, above all else, on the strong control and repression of sexuality.

The key psychological shift that occurred, according to Albee (1977), was from a 'tradition-centred' (Riesman *et al.* 1950) society to one in which 'inner direction' was emphasized. In traditional cultures, people live in relatively small communities in which everyone knows everyone else, and behaviour is monitored and controlled by others. There is direct observation of what people do, and direct action taken to deal with social deviance through scorn or exclusion. The basis for social control is the induction of feelings of shame. In urban, industrial societies, on the other hand, life is much more anonymous, and social control must be implemented through internalized norms and regulations, which result in guilt if defied. From this analysis, it is possible to see how the central elements of urban, industrial, capitalist culture create the conditions for the development of a means of help, guidance and support which addresses confusions and dilemmas experienced in the personal, individual, inner life of the person. The form which that help took, however, was shaped by other events and processes.

The historical account pieced together by Scull (1979) indicates that during the years 1800 to 1890 the proportion of the population of England and Wales living in towns larger than 20,000 inhabitants increased from 17 to 54 per cent. People were leaving the land to move to the city to work in the new factories. Even on the land, the work became more mechanized and profit-oriented. These large-scale economic and social changes had profound implications for all disadvantaged or handicapped members of society. Previously there had been the slow pace of rural life, the availability of family members working at home and the existence of tasks that could be performed by even the least able. Now there was the discipline of the machine, long hours in the factory and the fragmentation of the communities and family networks that had taken care of the old, sick, poor and insane. There very quickly grew up, from necessity, a system of state provision for these non-productive members of the population, known as the workhouse system. Inmates of workhouses were made to work, under conditions of strict discipline. It soon became apparent that the insane were difficult to control and disruptive of the workhouse regime. As one workhouse report from 1750 put it,

> The law has made no particular provision for lunaticks and it must be allowed that the common parish workhouse (the inhabitants of which are mostly aged and infirm people) are very unfit places for the reception of such ungovernable and mischievous persons, who necessarily require separate apartments.
>
> (Cited in Scull 1979: 41)

Gradually these separate apartments, the asylums, began to be built, beginning slowly in the middle of the eighteenth century and given further encouragement by the 1845 Asylums Act, which compelled local justices to set up publicly run asylums. This development marked the first systematic involvement of the state in the care and control of the insane in European society.

At first, the asylums were seen as places where lunatics could be contained, and attempts at therapeutic intervention were rare. In a few asylums run by Quakers (for example, Tuke at the York Asylums), there evolved what was known as 'moral treatment' (Scull 1981a). In most institutions, however, lunatics were treated like animals and kept in appalling conditions. The Bethlem Hospital in London, for instance, was open to the public, who could enter to watch the lunatics for a penny a time. During this early period of the growth of the asylums movement, at the beginning of the nineteenth century, the medical profession had relatively little interest in the insane. From the historical investigations carried out by Scull (1975), it can be seen that the medical profession gradually came to recognize that there were profits to be made from the 'trade in lunacy', not only from having control of the state asylums which were publicly funded, but also from running asylums for the insane members of the upper classes. The political power of the medical profession allowed it, in Britain, to influence the contents of Acts of Parliament which gave the medical profession control over asylums. The defeat of moral treatment can be seen as a key moment in the history of psychotherapy: science replaced religion as the dominant ideology underlying the treatment of the insane.

During the remainder of the nineteenth century, the medical profession consolidated its control over the 'trade in lunacy'. Part of the process of consolidation involved rewriting the history of madness. Religious forms of care of the insane were characterized as 'demonology', and the persecution of witches was portrayed, erroneously, as a major strand in the pre-scientific or pre-medical approach to madness (Szasz 1971; Kirsch 1978; Spanos 1978). Medical and biological explanations for insanity were formulated, such as phrenology (Cooter 1981) and sexual indulgence or masturbation (Hare 1962). Different types of physical treatment were experimented with:

> hypodermic injections of morphia, the administration of the bromides, chloral hydrate, hypocymine, physotigma, cannabis indicta, amyl nitrate, conium, digitalis, ergot, pilocarpine, the application of electricity, the use of the Turkish bath and the wet pack, and other remedies too numerous to mention, have had their strenuous advocates.
> (Tuke, *History of the Insane*, 1882, cited in Scull 1979)

An important theme throughout this era was the use of the asylum to oppress women, who constituted the majority of inmates (Showalter 1985). Towards the end of the century, the medical specialism of psychiatry had taken its place alongside other areas of medicine, backed by the system of classification of psychiatric disorders devised by Kraepelin, Bleuler and others. Many of these developments were controversial at the time. For example, there was considerable debate over the wisdom of locking up lunatics in institutions, since contact with other disturbed people was unlikely to aid their rehabilitation. Several critics of psychiatry during the nineteenth century argued that care in the community was much better than institutionalization. There was also a certain amount of public outcry over the cruelty with which inmates were treated, and scepticism over the efficacy of medical approaches.

The issues and debates over the care of the insane in the nineteenth century may seem very familiar to us from our vantage point a century later. We are still arguing about the same things. But an appreciation of how these issues originally came into being can help us by bringing into focus a number of very clear conclusions about the nature of care offered to emotionally troubled people in modern industrial society. When we look at the birth of the psychiatric profession, and compare it with what was happening before the beginning of the nineteenth century, we can see that:

1 Emotional and behavioural 'problems in living' became medicalized.
2 There emerged a 'trade in lunacy', an involvement of market forces in the development of services.
3 There was an increased amount of rejection and cruelty in the way the insane were treated, and much greater social control.
4 The services that were available were controlled by men and used to oppress women.
5 Science replaced religion as the main framework for understanding madness.

None of these factors was evident to any extent before the Industrial Revolution, and all are still with us today. They can be seen as fundamental to the way that any industrialized, urbanized, secularized society responds to the question of madness. The French social philosopher Foucault (1967) has pointed out that one of the central values of the new social order which emerged in the nineteenth century was reason or rationality. For a society in which a rational, scientific perspective on life was all-important, the irrational lunatic, who had lost his or her reason, would readily become a scapegoat, a source of threat to be banished to an asylum somewhere outside the city. Foucault (1967) describes this era as an age of 'confinement', in which society developed means of repressing or imprisoning representatives of unreason or sexuality.

The invention of psychotherapy

By the end of the nineteenth century, psychiatry had achieved a dominant position in the care of the insane, now recategorized as 'mentally ill'. From within medicine and psychiatry, there evolved a new specialism of psychotherapy. The earliest physicians to call themselves psychotherapists had been Van Renterghem and Van Eeden, who opened a Clinic of Suggestive Psychotherapy in Amsterdam in 1887 (Ellenberger 1970). Van Eeden defined psychotherapy as 'the cure of the body by the mind, aided by the impulse of one mind to another' (Ellenberger 1970: 765). Hypnosis was a phenomenon of great interest to the European medical profession in the nineteenth century. Originally discovered by the pioneers of 'animal magnetism', Johann Joseph Gassner (1727–79) and Franz Anton Mesmer (1734–1815), hypnotism came to be widely used as an anaesthetic in surgical operations before the invention of chemical anaesthetics. During the 1880s, the influential French psychiatrists Charcot and

Janet began to experiment with hypnosis as a means of treating 'hysterical' patients. There were two aspects of their hypnotic technique that have persisted to this day as key concepts in contemporary counselling and psychotherapy. First, they emphasized the importance of the relationship between doctor and patient. They knew that hypnosis would not be effective in the absence of what they called 'rapport'. Second, they argued that the reason why hypnosis was helpful to patients was that it gave access to an area of the mind that was not accessible during normal waking consciousness. In other words, the notion of the 'unconscious' mind was part of the apparatus of nineteenth-century hypnotism just as much as it is part of twentieth-century psychotherapy.

The part played by hypnosis in the emergence of psychotherapy is of great significance. Bourguignon (1979), Prince (1980) and many others have observed that primitive cultures employ healing rituals which rely on trance states or altered states of consciousness. The appearance of mesmerism and hypnosis through the eighteenth and nineteenth centuries in Europe, and their transformation into psychotherapy, can be viewed as representing the assimilation of a traditional cultural form into modern scientific medicine. Cushman (1995: 119) has written about the huge popularity of mesmerism in the USA in the mid-nineteenth century: 'in certain ways, mesmerism was the first secular psychotherapy in America, a way of ministering psychologically to the great American unchurched.'

The key figure in the process of transition from hypnosis to psychotherapy was, of course, Sigmund Freud. Having spent four months with Charcot in Paris during 1886–7, Freud went back to Vienna to set up in private practice as a psychiatrist. He soon turned his back on the specific techniques of hypnosis, choosing instead to develop his own technique of psychoanalysis based on free association and the interpretation of dreams. Freud became, eventually, an enormously powerful figure not only in medicine and psychotherapy, but in European cultural history as a whole. Without denying the genius and creativity of Freud, it is valuable to reflect on some of the ways in which his approach reflected the intellectual fashions and social practices of his time. For example:

1 Individual sessions with an analyst were an extension of the normal practice of one-to-one doctor-patient consultations prevalent at that time.
2 Freud's idea of a unitary life-force (libido) was derived from nineteenth-century biological theories.
3 The idea that emotional problems had a sexual cause was widely accepted in the nineteenth century.
4 The idea of the unconscious had been employed not only by the hypnotists, but also by other nineteenth-century writers and philosophers.

The distinctive contribution of Freud can probably be regarded as his capacity to assimilate all of these ideas into a coherent theoretical model which has proved of great value in many fields of work. The cultural significance of Freudian ideas can be seen to lie in the implicit assumption that we are all neurotic, that behind the façade of even the most apparently rational and successful person there lie inner conflicts and instinctual drives. The message of Freud was that psychiatry is relevant not just for the mad man or woman in the asylum, but for everyone. The set of ideas contained in psychoanalysis also reflected the challenges faced by members of the European middle classes making the transition from traditional to modern forms of relationship. Sollod (1982: 51–2) writes that, in Victorian society,

> it was quite appropriate to view elders as father figures and experience oneself as a respectful child in relationship to them. In the (modern) secular world, impersonal economic and employment arrangements rather than traditional ties bind one to authority, so such transferential relationships to authority figures could be inappropriate and maladaptive rather than functional.

Freudian ideas had a somewhat limited impact in Britain and Europe during his lifetime, and until quite recently psychoanalysis was acceptable and accessible only to middle-class intellectuals and artists. In Britain, for example, the early development of psychoanalysis was associated with the literary elite of the 'Bloomsbury group' (Kohon 1986). It was not until psychoanalysis emigrated to the USA that psychotherapy, and then counselling, became more widely available.

The growth of psychotherapy in the USA

Freud had a great loathing of American society. He visited there in 1909 with Jung and Ferenczi, to give some lectures and receive an honorary degree at Clark University, and was later to write that America was a 'gigantic mistake' (Gay 1988). But American culture resonated to the ideas of psychoanalysis, and when the rise of fascism in Europe led to prominent analysts like Ferenczi, Rank and Erikson moving to New York and Boston, they found a willing clientele. Compared to Europe, American society demonstrated a much greater degree of social mobility, with people being very likely to live, work and marry outside their original neighbourhood, town, social class or ethnic group. There were therefore many individuals who had problems in forming satisfactory relationships, or having a secure sense of personal identity. Moreover, the 'American Dream' insisted that all people could better themselves, and emphasized the pursuit of happiness of the individual as a legitimate aim in life. Psychotherapy offered a fundamental, radical method of self-improvement. The psychoanalysts arriving in the USA in the 1930s found that there was already a strong popular interest in psychology, as indicated by the self-help books of Samuel Smiles and the writings of the behaviourist J. B. Watson. There was also a strong tradition of applied psychology, which had been given impetus by the involvement of academic psychologists in the US Army in the First World War. Psychological tests were widely used in education, job selection and vocational guidance, which meant that the notion of using psychology to help ordinary people was generally taken for granted.

The idea of psychoanalysis held a great attraction for Americans, but for it to become assimilated into the culture required an Americanization of Freud's thinking. Freud had lived in a hierarchically organized, class-dominated society, and had written from a world view immersed in classical scholarship and biological science, informed by a pessimism arising from being a Jew at a time of violent anti-Semitism. There were, therefore, themes in his writing that did not sit well with the experience of people in the USA. As a result, there emerged in the 1950s a series of writers who reinterpreted Freud in terms of their own cultural values. Foremost among these were Carl Rogers, Eric Berne, Albert Ellis, Aaron Beck and Abraham Maslow. Many of the European analysts who went to the USA, such as Erikson and Fromm, were also prominent in reframing psychoanalysis from a wider social and cultural perspective, thus making it more acceptable to an American clientele.

One of the strongest sources of resistance to psychoanalysis in American culture lay in academic psychology. Although William James (1890), who had been one of the first scholars to make psychology academically respectable in American universities, had given close attention to Freudian ideas, American academic psychologists had become deeply committed to a behaviourist approach from about 1918. The behaviourist perspective emphasized the use of scientific methods such as measurement and laboratory experiments, and was primarily oriented to the study of observable behaviour rather than obscure internal processes, such as dreams, fantasies and impulses. The behaviourist academic establishment was consequently fiercely opposed to psychoanalysis, and refused to acknowledge it as worthy of serious study. Although some academic departments of psychiatry did show some limited interest in psychoanalysis, most practitioners and writers were forced to work in private practice or within the hospital system, rather than having an academic base. When Rogers, Berne and Ellis developed distinctive American brands of therapy in the 1950s and 1960s, there was initially only very limited academic discussion of their work and ideas. One of the distinctive contributions of Rogers was to invent systematic methods of carrying out research into the processes and outcomes of therapy. The effect of this innovation was to reinforce the legitimacy of therapy as a socially acceptable enterprise by giving it the respectability and status of an applied science. In 1947, Rogers became the first therapist to be made President of the American Psychological Association (Whiteley 1984). The confirmation of therapy as an applied science was given further impetus by the entry into the therapy arena of cognitive-behavioural approaches in the 1960s, bringing with them the language and assumptions of behavioural psychology, and the image of the 'scientist-practitioner'.

The development of psychotherapy in the USA represented an enormous expansion of the 'trade in lunacy'. The weakness of the public health system in that country meant that most counselling and therapy was dominated by theories and approaches developed in private practice. The influence and prestige of the private practice model has been such that even counselling agencies which emerged in the voluntary sector, or in educational settings, have followed its lead. In the field of social work, the casework approach has been heavily influenced by psychotherapeutic practice.

The expansion of counselling in the late twentieth century

Why has counselling grown so rapidly in the final quarter of the twentieth century? Certainly in Britain and the USA, the number of counsellors, and the general availability of counselling, has shown a significant increase since the 1970s. There would appear to be a number of converging factors responsible for this growth:

- In a postmodern world, individuals are reflexively aware of choices open to them around identity; the self is a 'project'; counselling is a way of reflexively choosing an identity (Giddens 1991).
- Caring and 'people' professions, such as nursing, medicine, teaching and social work, which had previously performed a quasi-counselling role, were financially and managerially squeezed during the 1970s and 1980s. Members of these professions no longer have time to listen to their clients. Many of them have sought training as counsellors, and have created specialist counselling roles within their organizations, as a way of preserving their quality of contact with clients.
- There is an entrepreneurial spirit in many counsellors, who will actively sell their services to new groups of consumers. For example, any personnel director of a large company must have a filing cabinet full of brochures from counsellors and counselling agencies eager to provide employee counselling services.
- Counselling regularly receives publicity in the media, most of which is positive.
- We still live in a fragmented and alienated society, in which there are many people who lack emotional and social support systems. For example, in any major city there may be large groups of refugees. Increasing numbers of people live alone.

There is, therefore, a multiplicity of factors that would appear to be associated with the expansion of counselling. What seems clear is that counselling has grown in response to social demands and pressures, rather than because research or other evidence has proved that it is effective. But what does it mean that counselling can be seen to be socially contructed in this way? What is the social meaning of counselling?

The social meaning of counselling

The historical account given here is inevitably incomplete and partial. Not enough research and scholarly attention has been devoted to the task of understanding the emergence of counselling and psychotherapy in twentieth-century society. For example, much of the historical literature on the expansion of psychotherapy in the twentieth century focuses exclusively on what happened in the USA. There are undoubtedly different themes and factors to be discovered through studies of the history of therapy in European countries. However, from even this limited discussion of historical factors it can be seen that the form and shape of contemporary theory and practice has been strongly influenced by cultural forces (Woolfe 1983; Pilgrim 1990; Salmon 1991; Cushman 1995). In particular, it becomes evident that the key figures in the history of counselling, such as Freud or Rogers, were not inventors of new theories so much as people who were able to articulate and give words to a way of thinking or working which was beginning to crystallize in the culture around them. A historical account also brings to the surface and illuminates some of the underlying fundamental issues that cut across all theoretical orientations and all forms of counselling practice. These basic issues concern, first, our understanding of the *social meaning* of counselling and, second, the *image of the person* being promoted by counselling theories.

It was clear from the discussion of the origins of psychiatry that, certainly in the early years, the emphasis in psychiatric care was on the control of individuals who were seen as disruptive to the smooth running of society. Although much has changed in psychiatry, even now in most places psychiatrists have the power to enforce compulsory hospitalization. At the other extreme, humanistic counsellors aim for 'self-actualization' and assume that their clients have responsibility for their own lives and actions. There is a strong tendency for counsellors and counselling organizations to place themselves explicitly at the personal freedom and liberation end of this continuum. In practice, however, there are pressures in the direction of social conformity and control in all counselling situations. Most immediate and concrete are the values and beliefs of the counsellor regarding what behaviour is or is not socially acceptable in a client. Less tangible is the influence of who is paying for the counselling, particularly in counselling settings such as colleges, business organizations or voluntary agencies, where it is not the client who pays. Finally, in extreme cases, where clients threaten to harm themselves or others, there are powerful social pressures and sanctions that urge the counsellor to take control and do something.

Some writers have regarded their approach to counselling or psychotherapy as providing a critique of existing social norms, or even as a means of bringing about social change. The radical psychoanalyst Kovel (1981), for example, has argued that classical Freudian theory represented a powerful tool for political change, and regrets the ways in which second-generation, post-Freudian theorists adapted Freudian ideas, particularly in the USA:

> what was great in Freud – his critical ability to see beneath, if not beyond, the established order – was necessarily jettisoned; while what was compatible with advanced capitalist relations – the release of a little desire, along with its technical control and perversion – was as necessarily reinforced.

The argument that the radical edge of Freudian theory has been lost is also made by Holland (1977), and the idea of counselling or therapy as a vehicle for social change has been evoked by Rogers (1978). Within contemporary practice, the alliance between therapy and social action has been made most effectively by feminist and gay counsellors, and practitioners from ethnic minority groups. However, these attempts to radicalize counselling all necessarily confront the same contradiction: that of seeking social change through a medium which individualizes and 'psychologizes' social problems (Conrad 1981).

Another critical aspect of the social nature of counselling concerns the division of power between client and counsellor. Historically, the counsellor–client relationship has modelled itself on the doctor–patient and priest–parishioner relationships. Traditionally, doctors and priests have been seen as experts and authority figures, and the people who consulted them expected to be told what to do. In the counselling world, by contrast, many practioners would espouse the ideal of 'empowering' clients and would agree to a greater or lesser extent with the statement by Carl Rogers that 'it is the client who knows what is right'. Nevertheless, the circumstances of most counselling interviews reproduce aspects of the doctor–patient power relationship. The meeting takes place on the territory of the counsellor, who has the power to begin and end the session. The counsellor knows everything about the client; the client knows little about the counsellor. Some counsellors have been so convinced of the unhelpfulness of the counsellor–client power imbalance that they have advocated self-help counselling networks, where people take it in turns to counsel each other. It is also relevant to note here that numerically by far the greatest number of counselling contacts are made through telephone counselling agencies, in situations where the client has much more control over how much he or she is known and how long the session will last.

Many writers in recent years have drawn attention to the ways in which power can be abused in the counselling relationship; for example, through sexual exploitation of clients. One of these writers, Masson (1988, 1992), has compiled a substantial dossier of instances of abuse of clients. He argues that this kind of abuse does not merely consist of an occasional lapse in ethical standards, but is in fact an intrinsic and inevitable consequence of any therapeutic contract. Masson (1988: 296) has written that 'the profession itself is corrupt … The very mainspring of psychotherapy is profit from another person's suffering', and suggests that the abolition of psychotherapy is desirable. While few would agree with this position of absolute condemnation, it is nevertheless impossible to deny, in the face of the massive evidence he presents, that his arguments deserve serious consideration. The fact that so many of the examples of abuse which Masson (1988, 1992) has uncovered relate to situations of men abusing women invites comparison with the more general social phenomenon of male violence against women, expressed through physical violence, rape and pornography.

The social nature of counselling permeates the work of the counsellor in three ways. First, the act of going to see a counsellor, and the process of change arising from counselling, will always have some effect on the social world of the client. Second, the power and status of the counsellor derive from the fact that he or she occupies a socially sanctioned role of 'healer' or 'helper'. The specific healing or helping role that the counsellor adopts will depend on the cultural context. For example, therapists in hospital settings use the language of science to describe their work, while those employed in holistic or alternative health clinics use the language of growth and spirituality. Third, client and counsellor re-enact in their relationship the various modes of social interaction they use in the everyday world.

These three dimensions to the social or cultural basis of counselling interlock and interact in practice. An example of how these ideas can be brought together to construct an understanding of the way that counselling operates within a social context is provided by the 'status accreditation' model of Bergner and Staggs (1987). They suggest that therapists are viewed as members in good standing of the community. To be a therapist is to have received endorsement that one is rational, significant, honest and credible. Any attributes or characteristics that the therapist assigns to the client are therefore likely to be believed and accepted. Bergner and Staggs (1987) point out that in a positive therapeutic relationship the therapist will behave towards the client as if he or she is someone who makes sense, who is worthy of attention, who has the power to choose and who has strengths. The attribution or assignment of these characteristics from a high-status person (such as a counsellor or therapist) has the effect on clients of 'confirming them in new positions or "statuses" that carry with them expanded eligibility for full participation in society' (Bergner and Staggs 1987: 315). Frank (1974: 272) presents the same point of view in writing that, 'since the therapist represents the larger society, all therapies help to combat the patient's isolation and reestablish his sense of connectedness with his group; thereby helping to restore meaningfulness to life.' From this perspective, therapy can be viewed as a social process which offers people accreditation of their status as sane, worthy members of society. The process can be seen as the opposite of the 'labelling' by which people deemed to be 'mentally ill' are stigmatized as dangerous, irrational outsiders (Scheff 1974).

The image of the person

At a practical level, an approach to counselling such as psychoanalysis or behaviour therapy may be seen to consist merely of a set of strategies for helping. Underneath that set of practical procedures, however, each approach represents a way of seeing people, an image of what it is to be a person, a 'moral vision' (Christopher 1996). Back in the days of the asylums, lunatics were seen as being like animals: irrational, unable to communicate, out of control. Some of these meanings were still present in the Freudian image of the person, except that in psychoanalysis the animal/id was merely one, usually hidden, part of the personality. The behaviourist image of the person has often been described as 'mechanistic': clients are seen as like machines that have broken down but can be fixed. The image of the counselling client in cognitive approaches is also mechanistic, but uses the metaphor of the modern machine, the computer: the client is seen as similar to an inappropriately programmed computer, and can be sorted out if rational commands replace irrational ones. The humanistic image is more botanical. Rogers, for example, uses many metaphors relating to the growth of plants and the conditions which either facilitate or inhibit that growth.

Each of these images of self has a history. In the main, counselling has emerged from a long historical journey in the direction of self-contained *individualism* (Baumeister 1987; Logan 1987; Cushman 1990, 1995). The profoundly individualistic nature of most (if not all) counselling limits its applicability with clients who identify with collectivist cultural traditions.

The question of the kind of world that is represented by various approaches to counselling goes beyond the mere identification of the different 'root metaphors' or images of self that lie at the heart of the different theoretical systems. There is also the question of whether the counselling model reflects the reality of the world as we experience it. For example, psychoanalytic theory was the product of an acutely male-dominated society, and many women writers and practitioners have asserted that they see in it little that they can recognize as a woman's reality. Humanistic approaches represent a positive, optimistic vision of the world, which some critics would see as denying the reality of tragedy, loss and death. It could also be said that virtually all counselling theories embody a middle-class, white, Judaeo-Christian perspective on life.

The importance for counselling of the image of the person or world view represented by a particular approach or theory lies in the realization that we do not live in a social world that is dominated by a unitary, all-encompassing set of ideas. An essential part of the process of becoming a counsellor is to choose a version of reality that makes sense, that can be lived in. But no matter which version is selected, it needs to be understood that it is only one among several possibilities. The client, for example, may view the world in a fundamentally different way, and it may be that this kind of philosophical incompatibility is crucial. Van Deurzen (1988: 1) has suggested that

> every approach to counselling is founded on a set of ideas and beliefs about life, about the world, and about people ... Clients can only benefit from an approach in so far as they feel able to go along with its basic assumptions.

The different root metaphors, images or basic assumptions about reality which underlie different approaches to counselling can make it difficult or impossible to reconcile or combine certain approaches, as illustrated by the debate between Rogers and Skinner on the nature of choice (Kirschenbaum and Henderson 1990). Historically, the development of counselling theory can be seen as being driven at least in part by the tensions between competing ideologies or images of the person. The contrast between a biological conception of the person and a social/existential one is, for example, apparent in many theoretical debates in the field. Bakan (1966) has argued that psychological theories, and the therapies derived from them, can be separated into two groups. The first group encompasses those theories which are fundamentally concerned with the task of understanding the mystery of life. The second group includes theories that aim to achieve a mastery of life. Bakan (1966) views the 'mystery-mastery complex' as underlying many debates and issues in psychology and therapy.

Finally, there is the question of the way the image of the person is used in the therapeutic relationship, whether the image held by the counsellor is imposed on the client, as a rigid structure into which the client's life is forced, or, as Friedman (1982) would prefer, the 'revelation of the human image ... takes place *between* the therapist and his or her client or *among* the members of a group.'

Conclusions

This chapter began by noting the diversity of counselling theory and practice. To understand this diversity requires an appreciation of the history of counselling and its role in contemporary society. Members of the public, or clients arriving for their first appointment, generally have very little idea of what to expect. Few people can tell the difference between a psychiatrist, psychologist, counsellor and psychotherapist, never mind differentiate between alternative approaches to counselling that might be on offer. But behind that lack of specific information, there resonates a set of cultural images which may include a fear of insanity, shame at asking for help, the ritual of the confessional and the image of doctor as healer. In a multicultural society, the range of images may be very wide indeed. The counsellor is also immersed in these cultural images, as well as being socialized into the language and ideology of a particular counselling approach or into the implicit norms and values of a counselling agency. To understand counselling requires moving the horizon beyond the walls of the interview room, to take in the wider social environment within which the interview room has its own special place.

References

Albee, G. W. (1977) The Protestant ethic, sex and psychotherapy. *American Psychologist*, 32, 150–61.

Bakan, D. (1966) *Against Method*. New York: Basic Books.

Baumeister, R. F. (1987) How the self became a problem: a psychological review of historical research. *Journal of Personality and Social Psychology*, 52(1), 163–76.

Bergner, R. M. and Staggs, J. (1987) The positive therapeutic relationship as accreditation. *Psychotherapy*, 24, 315–20.

Bourguignon, E. (1979) *Psychological Anthropology: an Introduction to Human Nature and Cultural Differences*. New York: Holt, Rinehart and Winston.

Christopher, J. C. (1996) Counseling's inescapable moral visions. *Journal of Counseling and Development*, 75, 17–25.

Conrad, P. (1981) On the medicalization of deviance and social control. In D. Ingleby (ed.) *Critical Psychiatry: the Politics of Mental Health*. Harmondsworth: Penguin.

Cooter, R. (1981) Phrenology and the British alienists: 1825–1845. In A. Scull (ed.) *Mad-houses, Mad-doctors and Madmen*. Philadelphia: University of Pennsylvania Press.

Cushman, P. (1990) Why the self is empty: toward a historically-situated psychology. *American Psychologist*, 45, 599–611.

Cushman, P. (1995) *Constructing the Self, Constructing America: a Cultural History cf Psychotherapy*. New York: Addison-Wesley.

de Shazer, S. (1985) *Keys to Solution in Brief Therapy*. New York: Norton.

Ellenberger, H. F. (1970) *The Discovery of the Unconscious: the History and Evolution of Dynamic Psychiatry*. London: Allen Lane.

Foucault, M. (1967) *Madness and Civilization: a History of Insanity in the Age of Reason*. London: Tavistock.

Frank, J. D. (1974) Psychotherapy: the restoration of morale. *American Journal of Psychiatry*, 131, 272–4.

Friedman, M. (1982) Psychotherapy and the human image. In P. W. Sharkey (ed.) *Philosophy, Religion and Psychotherapy: Essays in the Philosophical Foundations of Psychotherapy*. Washington, DC: University Press of America.

Gay, P. (1988) *Freud. A Life for Our Times*. London: Dent.

Giddens, A. (1991) *Modernity and Self-Identity: Self and Society in the Late Modern Age*. Cambridge: Polity Press.

Hare, E. (1962) Masturbatory insanity: the history of an idea. *Journal of Mental Science*, 108, 1–25.

Holland, R. (1977) *Self and Social Context*. London: Macmillan.

James, W. (1890) *Principles of Psychology*. New York: Holt.

Kirsch, I. (1978) Demonology and the rise of science: an example of the misperception of historical data. *Journal of the History of the Behavioral Sciences*, 14, 149–57.

Kirschenbaum, H. and Henderson, V. L. (eds) (1990) *Carl Rogers: Dialogues*. London: Constable.

Kohon, G. (ed.) (1986) *The British School of Psychoanalysis: the Independent Tradition*. London: Free Association Books.

Kovel, J. (1981) The American mental health industry. In D. Ingleby (ed.) *Critical Psychiatry: the Politics of Mental Health*. Harmondsworth: Penguin.

Logan, R. D. (1987) Historical change in prevailing sense of self. In K. Yardley and T. Honess (eds) *Self and Identity: Psychosocial Perspectives*. Chichester: Wiley.

McNeill, J. T. (1951) *A History of the Cure of Souls*. New York: Harper and Row.

Mahrer, A. (1989) *The Integration of Psychotherapies: a Guide for Practicing Therapists*. New York: Human Sciences Press.

Masson, J. (1988) *Against Therapy: Emotional Tyranny and the Myth of Psychological Healing*. Glasgow: Collins.

Masson, J. (1992) The tyranny of psychotherapy. In W. Dryden and C. Feltham (eds) *Psychotherapy and Its Discontents*. Buckingham: Open University Press.

Neugebauer, R. (1978) Treatment of the mentally ill in medieval and early modern England: a reappraisal. *Journal of the History of the Behavioral Sciences*, 14, 158–69.

Neugebauer, R. (1979) Early and modern theories of mental illness. *Archives of General Psychiatry*, 36, 477–83.

Pilgrim, D. (1990) British psychotherapy in context. In W. Dryden (ed.) *Individual Therapy: a Handbook*. Milton Keynes: Open University Press.

Porter, R. (ed.) (1985) *The Anatomy of Madness, Volumes 1 and 2*. London: Tavistock.

Prince, R. (1980) Variations in psychotherapeutic procedures. In H. C. Triandis and J. G. Draguns (eds) *Handbook of Cross-cultural Psychopathology, Volume 6*. Boston: Allyn and Bacon.

Riesman, D., Glazer, N. and Denny, R. (1950) *The Lonely Crowd*. New Haven, CT: Yale University Press.

Rogers, C. R. (1942) *Counseling and Psychotherapy*. Boston: Houghton Mifflin.

Rogers, C. R. (1957) The necessary and sufficient conditions of therapeutic personality change. *Journal of Consulting Psychology*, 21, 95–103.

Rogers, C. R. (1978) *Carl Rogers on Personal Power: Inner Strength and Its Revolutionary Impact*. London: Constable.

Rothman, D. (1971) *The Discovery of the Asylum: Social Order and Disorder in the New Republic*. Boston: Little Brown.

Salmon, P. (1991) Psychotherapy and the wider world. *The Psychologist*, 2, 50–1.

Scheff, T. (1974) The labeling theory of mental illness. *American Sociological Review*, 39, 444–52.

Scull, A. (1975) From madness to mental illness: medical men as moral entrepreneurs. *European Journal of Sociology*, 16, 218–61.

Scull, A. (1979) *Museums of Madness: the Social Organization of Insanity in Nineteenth Century England*. London: Allen Lane.

Scull, A. (1981a) Moral treatment reconsidered: some sociological comments on an episode in the history of British psychiatry. In A. Scull (ed.) *Mad-houses, Mad-doctors and Madmen*. Pennsylvania: University of Pennsylvania Press.

Scull, A. (ed.) (1981b) *Mad-houses, Mad-doctors and Madmen*. Pennsylvania: University of Pennsylvania Press.

Scull, A. (1989) *Social Order/Disorder: Anglo-American Psychiatry in Historical Perspective*. London: Routledge.

Showalter, E. (1985) *The Female Malady: Women, Madness and English Culture, 1830–1980*. New York: Pantheon Books.

Sollod, R. N. (1982) Non-scientific sources of psychotherapeutic approaches. In P. W. Sharkey (ed.) *Philosophy, Religion and Psychotherapy: Essays in the Philosophical Foundations of Psychotherapy*. Washington, DC: University Press of America.

Spanos, I. (1978) Witchcraft in histories of psychiatry: a critical analysis and alternative conceptualisation. *Psychological Bulletin*, 85, 417–39.

Szasz, T. S. (1971) *The Manufacture of Madness: a Comparative Study of the Inquisition and the Mental Health Movement*. London: Routledge and Kegan Paul.

Van Deurzen, E. (1988) *Existential Counselling in Practice*. London: Sage.

Wallace, A. F. C. (1958) Dreams and the wishes of the soul: a type of psychoanalytic theory among the seventeenth century Iroquois. *American Anthropologist*, 60, 234–48.

Whiteley, J. M. (1984) A historical perspective on the development of counseling psychology as a profession. In S. D. Brown and R. W. Lent (eds) *Handbook of Counseling Psychology*. New York: Wiley.

Woolfe, R. (1983) Counselling in a world of crisis: towards a sociology of counselling. *International Journal for the Advancement of Counselling*, 6, 167–76.

Chapter 13

The nurture group in the primary school

Marjorie Boxall

Introduction

School, whether infant or nursery, is based on the assumption that the children are essentially biddable, will be willing to entrust themselves to the teacher and will have some understanding of her expectations. It presupposes that they have an awareness of how the world about them functions, are sufficiently well organized to attend and follow through what is required without being constantly reminded, and that they already have some sense of time through the comfort and security of routines established at home. Furthermore, the children are now in a large group situation and must therefore be able to wait when this is necessary, to give and take with the others, and to have some tolerance for frustration. School thus continues a learning process which began years before in the home.

These assumptions are not necessarily true for severely deprived and disadvantaged children. They do not always accept the teacher as a trustworthy and reliable person, and do not attach themselves with confidence; they cannot engage with the situation and they do not learn. The problems may well worsen as the child grows older, for they are cumulative as the gap widens. Many teachers intuitively recognize that the children lack the foundations that are essential for further learning and try to help them at an earlier level. The strain of meeting such a wide range of social, emotional and intellectual needs is, however, sometimes too great for the teacher who becomes like the children, eroded and fragmented, and even sometimes resistive and hostile.

The rationale of the nurture group

The problems of such children are assumed to stem from the erosion of early care and support in families suffering severe social fragmentation and stress. Crucially, constructive forward-moving interaction with the child is lost. He does not therefore experience the reliable sequences of events that would develop in him an expectant attentiveness and through which he would gain an understanding of the world about him, and trust is weakened because the level of help and support he gets does not sufficiently or reliably meet his needs.

In the nurture group the teacher and helper attempt to relive with the child the missed nurturing experience of the early years. They take as their model the mother and her young child and the method is correspondingly intuitive: teacher and helper 'feel into' the early years and interact with the child as a mother would within a relationship of continuing care and support, in an environment that is carefully managed and protective.

The setting is a domestic one, and there is scope for unhurried experiences at a baby and toddler level. The nurture teacher and helper allow the child to be and help him to do; they keep him close emotionally and gradually let him go as he becomes increasingly able to manage on his own. The general guideline to which the teacher and helper return whenever in doubt is: 'this child is 3, 2, 1 year old, in some cases even younger. I will be for him and do or him as I would for my own child at that age'.

This guideline is reassuring; it yields insights into the needs of the children, and from it flows a wide range of stratagems. But an essential prerequisite for these adult-centred experiences is a school day that is planned and structured appropriately for this early developmental level and in which experiences are controlled and are basic and focused. Protected from the overwhelming stimulation and complexity of the ordinary class, the child is free within the constraints imposed by the nurture group to function at his 'true' developmental level. The teacher and helper respond accordingly and early level experiences and relationships follow. The first and essential consideration, therefore, when setting up a nurture group is structure. This is loosened as the child develops, but without the initial tight structure the process will fail.

Recreating the processes of adequate parenting in the nurture group

Satisfactory emotional, social and cognitive development in the earliest years is the product of adequate and attentive early nurturing care. It is a many-stranded, intermeshing, forward-moving, unitary learning process that centres on attachment and trust and has its foundations in the close identification of parent and child, and the interaction and participation in shared experiences that stem from this. It is the first stage of a developmental process through which the child builds up adequate concepts and skills, learns to interact and share with others and feel concern for them. Through this process he becomes increasingly self-supporting and self-directing and able to profit from the learning experiences offered at school.

But the child who has not experienced satisfactorily this early nurture-based stage of learning will not be able to engage with normal, age-appropriate school provision and will fail if the loss is not quickly made good. The task of the nurture group is to give the child the opportunity to go through these missed early experiences by creating a setting conducive to early developmental learning. Understanding the determinants of this process is of primary importance: the content then follows.

The determinants of early developmental learning

The constraints of early childhood

The nurturing context of early childhood is set by the child's physical status at birth, by his physical dependence and need for protection, by his motor and sensory development and the rhythm of his physical needs. These factors, and the intuitive involvement of his mother at the appropriate level, determine the things that interest him and to which he gives his attention, and lead to experiences that are restricted and highly focused at first. The constraints that determine these experiences are intrinsic to the early stages of childhood. They have to be deliberately built into the nurture group and in this way the situation is made appropriate for an earlier developmental level: simpler, more immediate, more protected. The child engages at this level, their attention is held, they experience pleasure and approval and basic experiences are consolidated. Rhythm and routines give security and a sense of order and they learn to anticipate events with confidence and interest.

In the home, there is emotional and physical attachment and proximity from the beginning. The waking day is short and slow moving, broken up by rests and simple, repetitive routines; management of the child's needs is consistent. Within this structure, the parents intuitively provide manageable learning experiences through appropriate play material and developmentally relevant interaction.

In the nurture group, close proximity in the home area of the classroom facilitates emotional and physical attachment. Early basic experiences are made available and are controlled by the teacher and helper, who direct the child's attention to features that are developmentally relevant. Everything is taken slowly and the day is broken up by slow-moving routines and interludes. There is a clear time structure; order and routine are emphasized, management of behaviour is consistent.

In these ways the growth-promoting patterns which the child missed in the early years in the home are established.

Attachment: earliest learning

In the earliest years the foundations of trust and security, positive mood and identity are built in through continuing support and shared basic satisfactions in the context of emotional attachment and physical proximity of the child and the adult. Feelings are communicated and shared, there is an understanding of subtle non-verbal signals and close identification and empathy, the one with the other. Developing with this is a shared experience, registered in language, of the basic attributes of objects, and simple cause and effect, leading to an understanding of objects and their relationships. These are the first and crucial stages of learning.

In both the home and the nurture group there is food, comfort, consistent care and support, and close physical contact seen in cradling, rocking, sensory exploration and communication by touch. Eye contact is central to the parent–child dyad and has to be purposefully established in the group. Mood and feelings are communicated through expression in face and in voice, with a spontaneous exaggeration of response. There is closeness, intimate interplay, shared feelings and satisfactions, with verbal accompaniment and the expression of mutual pleasure. Expectations are limited and infantile behaviour is accepted but the situation is kept safe and under adult control.

The first stages of learning are being consolidated.

Letting go and bringing back: developing autonomy

The child has already internalized the security that comes from attachment to a reliable, attentive, comforting parent and this security is reinforced through the continuing repetition of the simple routines of his daily life. These become a familiar and meaningful sequence of events and through these the child gains a sense that the world about him is stable, orderly and predictable. In the course of maturation and the appropriate opportunities provided he has acquired basic competencies. He has also experienced adequately consistent management of his behaviour, achieved and conveyed by explicit setting of boundaries.

From this secure base, the parents help the child to personal autonomy through a complex process of 'letting go' and 'bringing back'. He is 'let go' into experiences that the parents control and ensure are manageable and where support is provided when needed, and he is 'brought back' to the security of close contact with the parents when the situation is overwhelming and he can no longer cope. Because the parent is sensitively involved and intervenes when necessary, new experiences are manageable and the child is able to assimilate and consolidate them. He becomes personally better organized and learns to give and take and control his own behaviour; he explores with purpose and confidence, makes constructive relationships and realizes that he has some control over his environment.

In the home, the child does things with mother or with mother nearby. In the nurture group it is the teacher or helper who is with the child or nearby. In both there is frequent contact and reassurance, and expression of pleasure and approval, with the children in the group being collected together frequently, calmly, with eye contact re-established. In the home there is a spontaneously arising need for 'transitional objects' (to use Winnicott's term for the battered toy or piece of blanket from which so many young children are inseparable) to provide comfort, support and control. In the group the teacher or helper satisfy this need by making these available and encouraging their use.

Young children at home engage in simple experiment and repetitive play and of their own accord persist at this level and so, in the group, early play is introduced and if necessary is demonstrated; the experiment and repetition characteristic of this stage is given support and children are encouraged and helped to persist. In the home, children do not experience unnecessary frustration because their level of physical development and the mother's intervention determine the nature of their investigation and exploration. However, because children in the group are older their physical development is ahead of their experience and organization and they can therefore get into situations that are beyond their competence and overwhelm them.

The adult, therefore, selects activities for children's investigation and exploration; experiences are basic, controlled and directed; unmanageable situations are anticipated and avoided. And just as the mother responds with pleasure to each new achievement, the teacher or helper gives immediate praise for each small gain. The mother helps or intervenes when necessary and often plays with her child for mutual enjoyment; they share experiences and learn together and this is important in the nurture group too. In the home children are related to individually; the child, the object and the task are intuitively identified by name and the adults provide a running commentary. Similarly, early in the group, requests and instructions are always individual, never general; each child, object and task is deliberately named and there is continuing verbalization.

Normal early development is gradual, and in the course of physical maturation simple experiences come before complex ones and so, in the group, everything is provided in incremental stages with basic experiences coming first; situations are structured, essentials are highlighted and complex instructions are broken down. Sharing and choosing in the pre-school years similarly come in manageable stages and there is little need to cooperate with other children. There is space to play and the mother anticipates problems. Correspondingly, in the group the need to share and choose is at first limited. There is always enough for everyone; sharing and choosing are built in manageable stages; grabbing is controlled; play space is respected. Cooperative work and play is not expected at this stage but it is encouraged, introduced and controlled and, as in the home, the teacher and helper anticipate problems.

The young child in the home needs and demands order and the mother meets her own and the child's need for order. In the group, therefore, as in the home, there is simple, consistent and unremitting basic training; the child is involved in orderly routines, tidying up, sorting out and putting away, with the adult giving help and reminders as they are needed. Expectations are made clear and constantly stressed; what is required is demonstrated. Approval and disapproval are immediate and evident; there is verbal commentary and reinforcement appropriate to an early level.

Children can now manage on their own for limited periods in a familiar environment. They are beginning to take responsibility for their own behaviour and will soon be able to take part without direct help in a bigger group. The foundations of their autonomy are becoming established.

Selection of children for the nurture group: pre-nursery needs

Selection of the children is made by the school. The criterion is the children's inability to engage themselves constructively in the day-to-day life of the class because of difficulties which seem crucially linked with impoverished experiences in the early years. These difficulties cover a wide range and include children who are unresponsive and never speak, those who are violently aggressive and disruptive and in the extreme case are markedly anti-social; others again who are unhappy, unventuring children, sometimes severely disturbed.

The problems are many and varied and we suppose, from the nature of the difficulties and the needs shown by the children, supported by case histories when we have these, that early nurture has been impaired in one or many of the ways outlined already. But although the ensuing problems vary with the nature and extent of the stress and with age, the children have in common a need for help at a pre-nursery level. Broadly based opportunities at an early stage are therefore made available in the nurture group; the children take from these the experiences they need, and the teacher and helper respond accordingly.

Organization within the school

Nurture groups have on average 12 children at any one time, but it is usual for many more children than this to go through the group in a year. A classroom preferably, or, failing this, a hut in the playground, is provided with comfortable domestic furnishings as well as work and play space. The relaxed setting is particularly important.

The nurture concept is implemented in different ways. Most schools have children in the group full-time, always with some interaction with the mainstream of the school from the beginning. Some have modified the basic pattern and admit some of the children part-time, while in others virtually all the children are part-time. One practice is to use the nurture facilities for new entrants felt to be 'at risk'. These variations reflect the nature and distribution of problems in the school as a whole and the range of competent functioning in the ordinary class. Whatever the approach, it is generally felt that some children need a full-time nurturing experience, while others actively benefit from greater contact with the ordinary class. The difference between full- and part-time nurture groups is thus largely one of emphasis.

The aim of the nurture teacher is to get the child back into an ordinary class. The child must therefore not feel, nor be felt by others to be, separate and different from the other children in the school. Indeed, he or she is not a special category of child; merely in one way or another at the extreme end of a continuum of disadvantage, often multiple, and in the ordinary class there are other children who are not very different. For these reasons the nurture group is fully part of the school, a resource with flexible boundaries for both teachers and children. This is fostered in different ways. In some schools the nurture children register with their class and are helped to feel part of that class, while in many schools extra children regularly go into the nurture room to play, often before school begins. In some schools the class teacher has 'breakfast' with the nurture group from time to time, or joins them for a birthday party. The nurture teacher or helper might go into the ordinary class to help the children settle in or, when a group runs only in the mornings, might work alongside the class teacher to give support to children in need.

Sympathetic rapport and good communication between the nurture teacher and class teacher is clearly important, each sharing an interest in the children's progress, and reinforcing what the other one does. Logically this implies a nurture orientation throughout the school, with all the teachers and ancillary staff in sympathy with the approach. The head teacher is the key person in fostering a good working partnership with the nurture group teacher, and the good relationships throughout the school as a whole on which the work depends.

In general the trend in schools with established nurture groups is towards nurture provision at the earliest possible age. Where the need is widespread, the more intensive work is done within the nurture group on a part- or full-time basis, but the other classes are modified accordingly and have an increasing and supportive involvement with the parents.

The activities and management of the nurture group

The brief account which follows is taken from the collated material from infant and junior groups where a high proportion of the children were impulse-dominated and had serious problems of aggression. It attempts to bring out the pre-school principles involved but the emphasis varies from one group of children to another, and in some schools is more explicit than in others. The detailed planning and structuring of the child's experience is not always apparent, as is the case in a well-functioning ordinary class where the organization of the teacher does not obtrude. Similarly, the baby behaviour of the children, so vivid in description, takes its place as a transient, though intense and necessary, developmental need. This need might suddenly change, and a child who has been wearing a pretend nappy one moment might be absorbed in a constructional game the next. To a visitor the most striking feature might well be the easy physical contact between adult and child, the warmth and intimacy of the family atmosphere, and the good-humoured acceptance, with control, of infantile and resistive behaviour.

General approach

The relaxed setting facilitates close physical proximity and eye contact, and the children become aware, often for the first time, of the adult's face, her expression, her gestures, the tone in her voice and what all these mean. Eye contact is of crucial importance and for most of the children can be established many times during the day when they are collected together in the 'home' area, for here they are able to settle and wait and attend.

In many different ways a close tie with the teacher and helper is established and maintained, and individual supports are built in because the children are too inexperienced to manage on their own. In the early days toys and work would be handed to the children individually, and instructions and requests would be specific to each child, spoken quietly in close physical proximity, with eye contact and touch where necessary. Teacher and helper settle the children down individually, giving simple reminders with much repetition. The complexity for the child of every task, however simple, is anticipated; it is broken down into stages and structured accordingly. Similarly there would be little or no choice at first because the children have no experience from which to exercise it; the biscuits offered at the breakfast table would be all the same and their toys would be chosen for them.

There is stress on tidying up and putting away in a particular place, because this basic training helps to build organization into the child; it gives him or her security, confident anticipation and prediction, and a sense of time. A slow pace is important, for the children need time to assimilate each stage; if taken on too quickly they become confused. Formal work, too, is structured, and for most of the children is at a very early level with much repetition. Children who are distractible in an ordinary class can give sustained attention to simple activities. The language of the teacher, as with the mother, instinctively matches the level of activity of the child and a running commentary, where appropriate, is a help in internalizing the experience and the expectations.

At this stage various braking techniques are built in, familiar and reassuring routines that control children's unchannelled energy, so that they attend and take in and feel satisfied. In ways such as these children's experiences and behaviour are monitored as by a mother. They are 'held' by the teacher. She controls the situation so that they are not bombarded, and gradually lets them go as they become better able to manage on their own. Stress in this situation is reduced and the problems are considerably relieved, particularly temper tantrums.

Children whose difficulties arise from inadequate and ill-organized experiences respond well in this secure setting. Others, however, have been managed erratically or punitively at home and present more serious behaviour problems. Control of their behaviour is an urgent priority and the strict and unremitting attention given to this in the groups is crucial. Desirable behaviour is constantly stressed and gets a positive response; undesirable behaviour like fighting is as far as possible ignored. The teacher's expectations are made absolutely clear and the only pressures in the group at this stage are those concerned with personal control. This is straightforward training: 'I see, I grab, I don't get.' Their teacher is always fair and gives a reason and the children quickly accept her requirements, adopt her standards for themselves, and support her in relation to the other children.

Food

Food is fundamental in the mother–child relationship and has special symbolic value. With few exceptions the children appear to experience the family-food occasions, or the giving of even a tiny sweet, as the expression of the teacher's and helper's attachment to them in a loving and caring relationship. It is part of their fabric of support, reassures them of their worth, and contributes to a sense of comfort and well-being. Some children, particularly the timid tearful ones, form this attachment from the beginning. Others do not, and food becomes part of a satisfying relationship only later when they acknowledge the teacher and attach themselves with trust. For these children, among whom are the particularly aggressive ones, food is not initially the expression of a relationship. Food is something they want; it may be at first the only thing to which they attend, and in attending to the food they attend to the teacher.

This may be the first time that eye contact is established, the first time they wait, and in waiting see themselves in relation to the teacher. At this stage food for these children, who may be virtually unmanageable, provides a powerful 'holding' situation affording maximum control. It is particularly important in the early days. In this situation, as in all others, the primitive behaviour which immediately becomes apparent in many of the children is not aggression but greed; if this is not anticipated, the children will grab at anything, and push and fight. This greed is controlled, as it is with toys and other experiences, by exposing the children to the situation in tolerable stages and not giving a surfeit; and praise is lavish, for the children are greedy also to be the best and get the most praise.

The timid inhibited children are reassured by the firm control, and the teacher–child equilibrium they see established helps them to be more assertive. In the more open situation of the ordinary class they hold back and get left out, and anything they have they keep to themselves. In the nurture group as they become less fearful they begin to eat and gradually they, too, learn to share. For all the children, 'family' food occasions provide an important opportunity to build in vital learning experiences: holding back, waiting, sharing, choosing, taking turns, giving up for others, anticipating their needs, and tolerating frustration. As one of the helpers put it, 'We have a tremendous palaver for a tiny piece of toast'. Food may be 'breakfast', perhaps no more than half a slice of toast and a choice of jam, or biscuits with their milk. Food for all the children becomes less important as time goes on; they take their security for granted and are free within themselves to become interested in other things.

Infantile needs and interests

All the children, whatever their difficulties, have available to them early infantile experiences. In both infant and junior groups a general need, in some cases intense, is for close physical contact with the teacher and helper. In some this seems primarily a need for reassurance and affection. In others there seems to be a need for attachment at the baby stage, and repeatedly a teacher or a helper describes the baby-like curl of the feet and the aimless baby-like movements. They lie on her lap and are cradled and rocked, stroke her hair and ruffle it; they play with her hands and her feet and her jewellery, and love to comb her hair. Some slip into baby sounds and crawl on the floor. They babble and jabber and want to be picked up, or they move in an uncoordinated way, fingers in their mouths. They pick things up and give them to their teacher, or bang them noisily on the table.

An interest in their bodies and its functions is shown by many of the children. For some of them this is absorbing and all-consuming and they describe their experiences in uninhibited detail. They readily identify with each other at this level and live each other's anecdotes with avid pleasure. With the older children this is more than an interested monologue; it is the stuff of their conversation. They have uninhibited sexual interests too; for most of the children these interests are childish and ephemeral and lively involvement one week has disappeared without trace by the next. In a few cases these interests seem likely to be reality-based and inappropriate sexual experiences may have been a major factor in the child's anxiety and disturbed behaviour.

Play

These early developmental stages link with the initial lack of interest shown by the children in small dolls and cuddly toys. They seem to move on to doll play, and caring for the dolls, only after their own need for affection has been met; in the early days it is they who wear the nappy and suck from the bottle, and play babies together and comb each other's hair and feed each other. But big stuffed dolls and animals are important to them at an early stage and are the object of fierce love and hate. Later they become members of the peer group, and a monkey in a junior school sits at the table, pencil in hand, wearing an anorak and doing his sums, while in another junior school a bear is given a book to read.

Many of the children have a special need to mess with paints, clay, water and sand and enjoy this at a sensuous level. Even junior children spend hours with the sand; they enjoy scooping it, and like to feel it and let it run through their fingers. They enjoy the water trough, too, blowing bubbles and experimenting for long periods of time. Many of them spend days in repetitive play, perhaps doing a simple jigsaw over and over again, or crashing the cars, or pushing and pulling heavy toys in the playground. For many children play is at first solitary, but they get used to playing alongside each other, and then gradually parallel and then cooperative play develops, becoming more elaborate as they act out their feelings and take on roles. Occasionally the solitary and repetitive play seems a defence, a retreat from the world when it is all too much.

Whatever the level and nature of their play, the teacher and helper are available to share the experience, guide, put in ideas, or participate in the role demanded by the child and so contribute to the development of the play. At other times it may be more important for the children to play quietly at their feet as they talk.

Behaviour management: learning self-control

Most of the children in the nurture groups have serious behaviour problems; others, who at first barely function or are baby-like in their behaviour, go through a phase of fights and tantrums. Many of these outbursts have the quality of infantile fury and, as with a very young child, the incidents which provoke them are trivial, but they can be difficult to manage because the children are big and strong. The orderliness and organization of the day help to reduce the problems; they give shape to the children's behaviour and the manageable experiences provided engage their attention and direct their energy. This makes it easy after an upset to re-engage the child in a known and comfortable routine.

It is usually possible to avoid an escalation of trouble by intervening at the first sign of niggly interference; and if the group gets 'high' the children can generally be calmed by drawing them into the 'home' area and waiting until everyone is quiet and still. Many fights and tantrums can be averted because the children are dominated by immediate perceptions and it is easy, therefore, to attract their attention to something else. All these are stratagems that a mother would instinctively use with her very young child. Talking about the situations that provoke trouble, and the angry feelings the children have, is important. They are taught not to hit out when they have these feelings, but to keep them inside and show their annoyance in a more grown-up way; and they talk about other people's feelings and the sort of things that hurt.

Verbalizing in this way slows the children down; they are able to reflect on what they would otherwise do impulsively and in this way begin to internalize the teacher's expectations and controls. Games centring on facial expression and feelings also help, as does looking at themselves in a mirror because it makes them more aware of feelings that they have not recognized and helps to develop self-control.

In the early days of a difficult group a high-risk period is first thing in the morning, especially on Mondays, and 'breakfast', usually provided at about 10 o'clock, has a markedly stabilizing effect. If a fight does break out the children move away from the disturbance and carry on with their activities as they have been trained to do, for they are then less likely to suck in the anxiety and become inflamed by the aggression. The fight itself is, as far as possible, ignored. A child in a temper tantrum would be held until it was all over, or left to pummel the cushions; the teacher would talk about what had happened and when it was all over would explain about the sort of behaviour she likes, and would then give reassurance and support. Difficult groups seem to reach a crescendo of bad behaviour, fights and tantrums and then calm down and consolidate.

Becoming independent

The children in the groups are closely identified with the teacher and helper and this attachment is seen in the use of their belongings as 'transitional objects'. These provide a tangible link with the teacher and helper and seem to act as a symbol both of the child's attachment to the adult and of the adult's support and control. The children wear her jewellery, her poncho, and the more immature children particularly love to wear her scarf. Sometimes the adult leaves them with something to help them manage their feelings when she is not there. This might be a ribbon, tied on the child's wrist when they go on an outing, or the comment when she leaves him alone, 'Keep my seat warm, I won't be long.'

Sometimes the children give a clear indication of their need for the adult's comfort, support and control to be expressed in a tangible form. Thus a girl, running from the play centre when she saw her teacher leaving at the end of the day, asked for a kiss. Her teacher kissed her lightly because she had just put on her lipstick and didn't want to leave this on the child's face. 'No, kiss me properly,' said the child, 'I want your lipstick'.

Some of the children, typically the more aggressive ones, are excessively dependent on their teacher and in these cases separation might be initiated by the teacher. A nine-year-old boy would lie for long periods on his teacher's lap and followed her everywhere. She brought in a large 'gonk' which she cuddled on her knee during story time and the child cuddled up by her side. After a few days, if his teacher did not have the 'gonk' he would go looking for it and would sit with it and plait its hair and tie its arms round his wrist. It became important to him, satisfied his need for his teacher, and he did not go on her lap again.

These early needs and infantile protests are only a stage in the children's development, and as they become less dependent they move out into wider and more complex experiences. Choice is extended, frustrations are built-in in ways which are tolerable, and satisfactions are delayed. Group activities in the form of games with enjoyable rules and rituals are introduced. The content of the games centres on basic sensory and cognitive skills, personal identity and social awareness. The rules and rituals that are built into these games are an acceptable discipline when in the context of 'fun' and the sequence of satisfying events leading to the anticipated goal helps the children to delay gratification. Basic cognitive skills are also more readily built up in the non-threatening ambience of the games and these achievements contribute to the development of self-confidence and a feeling of personal worth.

Visits out are planned, but the children are always carefully prepared, are told what to expect and how to behave, and may practise in school beforehand. A favourite visit, when this is feasible, is to the helper's or teacher's home for a drink and cake and chat. Their interest in the teacher and helper is insatiable; they love hearing about their children and ask for the same anecdotes over and over again. Talking, too, is very important, when baking with the helper or sitting round the ironing board while she irons, or as a 'family' occasion over their drinks.

The children play a great deal in the group but need input from the teacher and helper in the form of suitable material and ideas, and comments that take the play forward. The teacher and helper also set up play projects which they exploit at every level. Games, too, carry learning experiences and are devised to meet needs of all kinds. 'Mother's lap', 'mother's knee' and 'mother's day' activities provide opportunities for the introduction of basic language, mathematics and science, and lend themselves quite naturally to explicit educational input from the teacher. All the children also attempt some kind of directed formal work, and although in some cases this is at a very early level, it is always linked with, or relevant to, the work of the ordinary class. This formal (now National Curriculum-oriented) work may quickly take up a substantial part of the day.

Adult relationships as a model

The relationship between the teacher and helper is of great importance, for this is often the only opportunity the children have of seeing constructive interaction between adults. For this reason the teacher and helper talk together, share views, demonstrate concern for each other, acknowledge courtesies, and have fun and laugh. The head teacher is also important, representing the wider world of school, and being seen to support and value the teacher and helper. It is usual and helpful for a man to be involved if only peripherally, perhaps the caretaker, or the husband of the helper or teacher. He is seen to support and value the helper or teacher; he might romp with the children or tell them a story, or join them for a game in the park.

Parental involvement

Parental involvement is encouraged but varies widely. Some parents are never seen, others are known only through home visits, others again call in at school from time to time, while others take part in the school day and may become very dependent on the relationship. The policy adopted varies from school to school, some using opportunities as they arise, while others have parents' evenings from time to time and make considerable efforts to encourage the parents to attend. Parents' evenings are informal social occasions affording an opportunity for teachers and parents to share views and air differences on such important themes as play, discipline and happiness in relation to learning. The parents, many of whom have previously been difficult to reach, feel valued for themselves, not just because they are parents of the children, and in some cases their response is overwhelming.

On these occasions it is useful to provide a variety of quickly accomplished tasks that have a pleasing outcome. This gives the parents some understanding of what is being done in school. It is also a relaxing and enjoyable experience which they share with the others, and this may be particularly important for parents who are socially isolated or new to this country. A few of the parents need as much help and support as their children, not only in understanding how to organize their materials, but in coping with frustration when things go wrong. Where possible, everyone in the family is invited to these evenings, and it is usual then for the children to prepare the food and hand it round. The importance for the children is that home and school visibly become one, for they see parent and teacher talking together on equal and friendly terms. With few exceptions the parents are content with the shared nurturing between home and school, and many have remarked with relief and pleasure on the children's improved behaviour at home and greater progress in school.

Measuring progress

We know that the children are making progress when they get satisfaction from pleasing the teacher and helper and from meeting their expectations. Clear standards of behaviour have been set and they now identify with these and show unease when they transgress the limits. Some of the children, however, are so ridden with fear that they dare not assert themselves or take what is legitimately theirs, and the first stage in their progress might be deliberately provocative and defiant behaviour, a phase of naughtiness through which they test out their new-found selves before they, too, begin to function constructively in the group. Others, again, are so disorganized and lacking in confidence that they are over-concerned to please and the first stage in their progress would be a lessening of this concern to please.

Consolidated progress is shown when the children begin to be concerned for and take pleasure in each other. They relate more constructively, share spontaneously, and can accept disappointments and tolerate frustration. They develop a sense of humour and can laugh at themselves. Their concentration and attention span improve and they become more friendly, more confident, and much, much happier. It is of interest that the children seem to experience the steps they take towards social maturity as lessons. They seem aware that the teacher is providing a learning experience and get a sense of satisfaction and achievement when they succeed. This is perhaps best expressed in the words of a particularly aggressive six-year-old girl, who remarked to the helper one day: 'Miss, it's a nice feeling, being good.' Not surprisingly, with this developing maturity comes a marked improvement in their academic work.

Getting back into the ordinary class

This more mature behaviour is built in through a close interaction with the teacher and helper; it becomes part of the child and is not imposed from without. The children become better able to participate in the group without direct help and as soon as they seem ready to manage are tried out in the ordinary class for short, carefully planned periods. This may be before they are quite ready, because there comes a critical point when greater progress is made in the ordinary class even though there may be difficulties at first. Boredom is a good indication that they are ready to move on. The situation, however, has to be carefully watched by everyone because the children's experience is still shaky and inadequate, their personal control is flimsy, and anxiety and panic may quickly surface.

Although some children settle in their ordinary classes with very little direct support, and in some cases may take the initiative to go, others need more help if they are not to be put into a situation where they will fail. The teacher or helper would assist children in preparing their things and might go with them to their class to settle them in. If another child is being 'weaned' at the same time, the two children might well go off together. A less secure child might take something from the teacher, perhaps a special pencil or her bracelet, as a comfort and support. The receiving teacher makes them welcome, and when they return to the nurture group at the end of the day, perhaps for 'tea' or a story, they talk about what they have done and might show their work. All these supports help them over the difficult early stages.

The Boxall Profile

Record-keeping is an important feature of nurture-work and central to this is the Boxall Profile, until 1998 known as the Diagnostic Developmental Profile (Bennathan and Boxall 1998). This was developed over several years in partnership with teachers, their co-workers and head teachers in ILEA schools which had nurture groups; it involved extensive discussion and frequent reappraisal.

For the first two years of the nurture groups, records of the children had taken an anecdotal form but teachers soon began to express a need for a better way of assessing children referred to the nurture groups. They wanted something which would quantify their impressions, that would alert the class teacher to features to look for and would provide a means of evaluating progress. The behaviours recorded by the teachers were in some cases the characteristics shown by normal young pre-nursery children, and were assumed to persist in older children because early developmental needs had not been met; in other cases the maladaptive behaviours seemed to be an attempt by a poorly organized and ill-supported child to meet the demands of everyday life in school, sometimes at the level of survival.

Work on the profile began in 1972. The behavioural characteristics of children in the nurture groups that were reminiscent of behaviour seen in normally developing children in the pre-nursery years were cast in the form of descriptive items. These were derived from teachers' and helpers' observations, either verbal contributions at meetings, in discussion, or recorded in their notes, or from impressions picked up on visits to the groups. They were discussed at nurture group meetings in terms of developmental expectations of pre-nursery children and were arranged in what was felt to be a developmental order. Teachers, helpers and head teachers all had a part in this. A contribution of one of the helpers stands out vividly. A toddler-like item was under discussion: 'engages in random investigation about the room (picks things up, shakes them, etc. but does not use them)'. 'Is into everything', the helper immediately said and this description remained part of the profile.

All the items discussed at this stage were normal features when seen in the young pre-nursery child but not all were normal in the school setting, where they could be disastrous. It seemed helpful, therefore, to pull out from this continuum features that remained positive as the child grew older, e.g. 'makes eye contact', and to add descriptions of adaptive, organized and constructive behaviour at a more autonomous level, features seen in a competently functioning school-age child, e.g. 'abides by the rules of an organized group game in the playground or school hall (interacts and cooperates and continues to take part for the duration of the game)'. These items formed section I of the profile. All the other items were either normal characteristics of the pre-nursery child that were maladaptive in the school setting, or they reflected more complex deviance. These items formed section II of the profile.

A viable profile emerged from these early discussions and was in use for a number of years. In 1978, the Research and Statistics Branch of ILEA, with funding support from the DES, undertook a statistical analysis of the data. In preparation for this, more intensive work was done on the items of the profile, involving teachers in schools unfamiliar with nurture work.

Two sections

Section I of the profile is named 'Developmental Strands'. It provides a description of the personal and social development of the school-age child from three to eight years, and gives helpful information about the class as a whole. The characteristics noted are those of the developing child that reflect or contribute to a constructive learning process, and they can be scored by the teacher from knowledge of each child in the course of ordinary school life. The statistical analysis indicated that these 34 descriptive items fell into two broad clusters, described as 'Organization of experience' (for example, 'makes appropriate and purposeful use of the materials/equipment/toys provided by the teacher without the need for continuing direct support') and as 'Internalization of controls' (for example, 'Looks up and makes eye contact when the teacher is nearby and addresses him by name, i.e. heeds the teacher').

Section II is named the 'Diagnostic Profile'. The statistical analysis of the 34 non-adaptive items drew them into three clusters, namely:

1. Self-limiting features, e.g. 'avoids, rejects or becomes upset when faced with a new and unfamiliar task, or a difficult or competitive situation'.
2. Undeveloped behaviour, e.g. 'restless or erratic; behaviour is without purposeful sequence, continuity or direction'.
3. Unsupported development, e.g. 'lacks trust in the adults' intentions and is wary of what they might do; avoids contact or readily shows fear'.

Section II shows areas of deviant behaviour that inhibit or interfere with the learning process, and in conjunction with Section I gives clear pointers to those children who would be well placed in the nurture group, those who need other skilled intervention and those who can be helped by appropriate support in the ordinary class.

Conclusion

The work done in the nurture groups is based on the attachment of the child to the teacher and helper at an early level of dependency. Through interaction at this level an expectation of ongoing support is established: the child trusts and teacher and helper build on this trust; the children accept the demands made of them because they are safe in their keeping. The approach is essentially an educational one for it is forward-looking and is concerned with every aspect of early learning. The focus is thus not on problems, but on growth and the conditions which facilitate growth. Clearly, the younger the child, the better the support provided by the whole school and the greater the involvement of the parents, the more likely is this growth to be initiated and maintained.

Those who have been closely concerned with this project have no doubt at all that growth and well-being can be fostered in children whose life situation is difficult and in many cases appalling beyond, belief. The underlying hypothesis is a very simple one and can be implemented intuitively without the need for a lengthy theoretical training. The anxiety of the teacher and the helper is thereby reduced and they are enabled to draw maximally on their own resources; they are not inhibited by the feeling that somewhere there are experts who know better. They are self-reliant and secure in their own autonomy, have a clear sense of direction and a rough idea of the possibility of success with the different kinds of problems.

The work is thus approached with confidence and, because they give themselves unreservedly to the children, they draw on energies that were previously untapped. Teacher and helper have a greater sense of identity in their role, feel they are using themselves fully and, like all parents, they grow with the children. All work hard, but the stress is constructive, not frustrating; they give a great deal but are amply rewarded by the affection of the children and the joy of their progress. The relief to the other teachers is considerable; they become willing and interested partners in the children's development and cooperate in the process of reintegrating them into the ordinary class. The nurture group is also a help to the children who remain in the ordinary class, for the teacher has more time for them and their lessons are not disrupted by inappropriate behaviour.

For a group to function well and to be an integral part of the school it is essential that the principles underpinning nurture work are accepted and its complex and demanding nature is understood by all the staff members and others concerned with the school. The children in the nurture group are then valued members of the school, and the teacher and helper are also held in high regard. When this happens, the ethos of the school changes; optimism is generated, there is mutual understanding and support and concerted, constructive effort which benefits the whole school.

Reference

Bennathan, M. and Boxall, M. (1998) *The Boxall Profile: Handbook for Teachers*. Maidstone: AWCEBD.

Chapter 14

Theorising 'circle time'

Janice Wearmouth

Introduction

In recent years various forms of 'circle time' have increased in popularity in schools in many countries (Lang, 1998). Lown (2002) explains the popularity of circle time in the UK in a number of ways:

- It aims to enhance self esteem which, as many educators have recognised, is crucial to the learning process (Bruner, 1996; Lawrence, 1987; Mosley, 1996)
- Circle time activities focus the pastoral curriculum and thus support students' entitlement to a broad, balanced curriculum (QCA, 2000)
- Central government in England recognises the potential of circle time to address some of the emotional needs of young people (DfEE, 2000; TTA, 1999)

However, a vagueness exists about what 'the essential characteristics or purposes of the process should be' (Lang, 1998, p 3). Lown (2002, p 93), for example, merely describes how, during this period, students and their teacher sit together in a circle 'to share ideas, feelings and games/activities about one or more social/emotional/curricular issues'. This lack of clarity necessarily affects 'any research endeavouring to investigate outcomes' (Lown, 2002, p 94). Further, it results in 'difficulty in defining good practice and offering appropriate training' (Lang, 1998, p 3) especially when 'the sensitivity of the issues it can involve has led to anxiety about the preparation of those using circle time' (ibid).

This chapter outlines the range of curricular functions served by circle time, the theoretical underpinnings of some of these, and evidence of the efficacy of the technique, and explores implications.

The role of circle time

Sitting together in a circle to discuss group issues is a tradition embedded in a number of cultures (Lang, 1998; Mosley, 2001; Schweigert, 1999):

> North American Indians used to sit in a circle with their talking object, often a feather or pipe. Whoever was talking whilst holding the object would not have his train of thought interrupted by others in the circle. Anglo-Saxon monks used to meet in a moot circle to discuss and debate issues affecting their way of life; hence we have the term 'moot point', meaning an unsettled question.
>
> (Mosley, 2001, p 70)

The use of circle time has become very popular in recent years, often, for example in the UK, as a way of 'approaching the task of teaching personal and social skills' (Lown, 2002, p 93). However, across the world, 'circle time' may refer to a range of approaches with a range of curricular aims. Lown's (2002) review of the literature associated with the use of circle time in the UK indicates that this range can include:

- therapeutic functions: raising self esteem (White, 1989; Lang and Mosley, 1993) and cultivating group cohesion (White, 1989)
- cognitive functions: enhancing learning through discussion of emotional, moral, spiritual or social issues (Housego and Burns, 1994), self expression (Cadiz, 1994), problem-solving and decision making(Mosley, 1993)
- social skills: turn-taking and co-operation (Kantor, 1989; Lown, 2002).

Therapeutic functions

The development of self esteem is a very clear theme in the American tradition of using circle time. Lang (1998) traces this tradition to an approach termed 'The Magic Circle' in California in the late 1960s and early 1970s (Palomares and Bell, 1971) in which positive feedback was given to children 'to enhance their feelings about their own ability to manipulate their environment, thus building their self-esteem' (Bessell, 1972, p 4). Lang points to later developments of this work in the publication of *Strategies in Humanistic Education* (Timmerman and Ballard, 1975) built on the assumption that:

> - People are okay; that is, humans are vitally important, worthy of caring, respect and trust;
> - People are their own greatest resource: the seeds of growth and solutions lie inside the grower/problem-solver.
>
> (Timmerman and Ballard, 1975, p 4, cited in Lang, 1998, p 4)

The influence of humanistic psychology (Rogers, 1951; Maslow, 1968) with its emphasis on the counsellor as a source of reflection and encouragement and the potential in everyone for personal growth and self control is clear in the description of 'circle time', as the Magic Circle was later re-named.

> The major goals of circle time are a) to foster self-awareness in children, and b) to build skills of effectively sharing and listening to feelings.
>   The rules of circle time, repeated each session at the beginning, are:
> • Everyone gets a turn who wants one
> • Everyone who takes a turn gets listened to
> (Timmerman and Ballard, 1975, p 15, cited in Lang, 1998, p 4)

Modelling by the teacher and the routine involvement and regular responses of the students enables the establishment of rules on an 'everyone who shares gets feedback, on a here's-what-I-heard-you-say' basis (ibid).

In the UK, a number of programmes of organised circle time activities are in common use, for example Mosley's 'Quality Circle Time' (1993; 1996; 2001) and Bliss, Robinson and Maines' 'Developing Circle Time' (1995). Moss and Wilson (1998, p 13) illustrate a typical circle-time session, aimed at fostering self esteem, as follows:

> *Week Three: Being positive about ourselves and others*
>
> RESOURCES: bean bag, 'magic object', lined paper, pencils
>
> 1. *Icebreaker* – Postman game; objective – to mix pupils up . . .
>
> 2. *Sentence completion game*: objective – for pupils to talk positively about themselves
>
> Sentence topics for this week: 'One of the best days I ever had was . . .'
> 'I feel proud when . . .'
>
> 3. *Discussion*: Use bean bag for 'hands up' discussion.
>
> Teacher questions: Last week we practised being good listeners. What did we need to do to be a good listener?
>
> This week we are thinking about the things people say about others. How can people make you feel bad by what they say?
>
> What kinds of things might make people feel good?
>
> How do you feel when people say nice things to you?
>
> 4. *Main activity*: Compliment letter: objective – for pupils to write positive statements about each other and to read positive statements about themselves.
>
> 5. *Follow-up discussion*: Sentence completions – 'Reading my compliments letter made me feel . . .
>
> 6. *End game*: General Post.

Like Timmerman and Ballard, Mosley (2001) links her version of circle time to theories related to self esteem from humanistic psychology, citing Rogers (1951, 1983):

> Rogers' approach centres on two theories: that inherent in the individual is the capacity for self-understanding and the positive ability to reorganise self structure, and there are core conditions which, if created by educators and therapists, will facilitate the individual's inherent abilities. 'The therapist/educator must be genuine or concerned . . . must possess unconditional positive regard . . . and experience an empathetic understanding of the client's internal frame of reference and endeavour to communicate this experience' (Rogers, 1951). Given Rogerian conditions, students have the capacity to reorganise their self-perceptions and acquire a more positive self-esteem.
>
> (Mosley, 2001, p 73)

Mosley also uses other theoretical frameworks, such as symbolic interactionist theory (Mead, 1934), to explain the development of self esteem in circle time activities, noting Mead's description of the self as a 'social entity formed by appraisal from others' (Mead, 1934, p 158).

> Essential to Mead's contribution is the assertion that the self cannot be reorganised or reconstituted into a more positive one without altering the social relations of the self to others. Circle Time fulfils this criterion because the group – in Mead's term, the 'generalised other' – is bound by groundrules based on respect, valuing and reflecting back to participants a positive reflection of their selves.
>
> (Mosley, 2001, pp 71–2)

A further thread in Mosley's version of circle time is its 'potential to encourage spontaneity, creativity, imagination, non-verbal communication, fun and reflection' (Mosley, 2001, p 71). This thread can be traced back to the work of J.L. Moreno (1889–1974) in the development of psychodrama where there is an emphasis on 'spontaneity, creativity and action' (McLeod, 1998, p 194). In Moreno's (1946) view:

> People co-act with each other, and this sense of mutuality or reciprocation is known within psychodrama as *tele*. . . . Participants in psychodrama groups act out problem situations in their lives, using fellow group members to enact the roles of significant others.
>
> (McLeod, 1998, p 194)

Development of cognitive and social skills

The development of cognitive skills – language, problem-solving and attention – as well as metacognitive skills associated with self control, have been associated with the kind of circle time activities in the UK described by Moss and Wilson (1998) above, and as practised, for example, in Mosley's 'Quality

Circle Time'. Lang (1998, p 8) notes claims of academic/cognitive outcomes of circle time relating to attainment targets in the English National Curriculum:

> At all levels circle time covers many of the components of English Attainment target 1 in speaking and listening. These include taking turns, knowing when to stop talking and wait for another's response and listening attentively in a group situation. Circle time enables children to participate as listeners and speakers and facilitates the whole process of communication.
>
> (Curry and Bromfield, 1994, p 8, cited in Lang, 1998, p 8)

A cognitive focus has also been associated with circle time activities in the United States, outside the humanistic tradition described above, in which instructional procedures are embedded to promote specific aspects of the regular academic curriculum, for example literacy learning (Majsterek et al, 2000; Wolery et al, 2002). Majsterek et al have reported gains in phonological awareness among groups presented with specifically targeted activities embedded into circle time sessions. Wolery et al found that children with learning and/or behaviour difficulties could learn sight words to criterion when teachers embedded instruction into circle time activities in a summer day camp.

Mosley (2001) links the development of cognitive skills in circle time activities to social learning theorists, for example Bandura (1977) and Meichenbaum (1977). Social learning theory focuses on behaviour patterns that individuals develop in response to environmental stimuli. Some social behaviours may be rewarded by praise and encouragement from teacher and peers in circle time and, therefore, be reinforced. Others may have unpleasant consequences and be less likely to occur again. Social learning theory emphasises the importance of cognitive, that is thinking, processes. Individuals are seen as able mentally to represent situations, foresee the likely consequences of their actions and alter their behaviour accordingly (Atkinson et al, 1981). Learning by observation and the role of models in demonstrating specific behaviours is crucial to the learning process. In circle time, teachers and peers have important functions both in providing positive feedback in order to encourage the desired behaviours, and in acting as role models.

Social-learning theory provides another framework within which to understand the acquisition of social skills such as turn-taking, listening to others and co-operation that are claimed to result from circle time (Kantor, 1989; Lown, 2002):

> In the Open Forum phase of Circle Time, children are encouraged to offer help in the form of 'Would it help if I . . .' or 'Would it help if you . . .'. This strategy gives the opportunity for children to offer a form of feedback gently. When a child says to another, 'Would it help if you didn't call him names first/stopped hacking at football/started to ask people if you can join in their games?' these suggestions are

all a way of giving feedback without blame or pressure. The recipient is encouraged to listen and then give a considered response . . ..

(Mosley, 2001, p 74)

The socio-cultural perspective of Vygotsky (1962) and Bruner (1996) can also be seen to support the kind of socially-mediated learning that takes place in some circle time activities. Bruner (1996) notes that individual human meaning-making is situated in a social context as well as in the prior conceptions that learners bring with them into new situations. New learning is a product of the 'interplay' between them. Participation in the student community during circle time has the potential to be 'transformative' both to participants and to the group (Bruner, 1996).

Evidence of efficacy

Claims have been made about the potential of circle time for developing self esteem, and improving cognitive and social skills, as discussed previously. Mosley (2001, p 70) observes that, in her experience, circle time, is 'a powerful vehicle for change'. However, there appears to be little systematic, rigorous, empirical research into circle time. Lown (2002, p 102), for example, comments on 'the huge gap that exists in the area of research'. Lang (1998) concurs with this view:

So far there has been almost no evaluative research into circle time in the UK and its benefits are presented either as acts of faith or as common sense.

(Lang, 1998, p 9)

Partly, as noted above, the paucity of systematic research relates to lack of clarity about what constitutes circle time in the first place. A small-scale, controlled evaluation (Frederickson and Turner, 2003) of the Circle of Friends intervention (Newton and Wilson, 1996) to improve the social acceptance of classmates with special needs indicated that the approach had positive effects on social acceptance. However, few changes were obtained on other measures of perception or behaviour.

Conclusion

The increasing use of circle time in schools as a group activity designed to resolve conflict, encourage social skills, promote personal well-being or encourage cognitive skills has its roots in a number of cultures, ancient and modern. Considerable lack of clarity remains around what comprises 'circle time' and the rationale underpinning circle time techniques, and little systematic research into the efficacy of the technique exists.

Nevertheless, one of the prime responsibilities of schools is to support the construction of young people's sense of Self through an acknowledgement of personal agency and the development of self esteem (Bruner, 1996). It is essential, therefore, to examine the contribution of school practices to this area of personal development. Further, the kind of socially-mediated learning that takes place in some circle time activities appears to be particularly powerful. Given the claims that circle time may enhance both the development of self esteem and socially mediated learning, there is a need for:

- 'a clear definition of the circle time activity, combined with clarity regarding the particular psychological processes being targeted for gain' (Lown, 2002), and
- more systematic rigorous evaluative research to 'identify the actual benefits of circle time', achieve 'a clearer understanding of the variables that make a difference' (ibid), and define good practice in training teachers to handle the technique competently.

References

Atkinson, R L, Atkinson, R C, Smithy, E E and Bem, D J U (1981) *Introduction to psychology* (11th ed), London: Harcourt Brace

Bandura, A (1977) *Social learning theory*, New York: Prentice Hall

Bessell, H (1972) *Human development program: level III activity guide*, California: IPEC

Bliss, T, Robinson, G and Maines, B (1995) *Developing Circle Time*, Bristol: Lame Duck

Bruner, J (1996) *The culture of education*, London: Harvard

Cadiz, S M (1994) 'Striving for mental health in the early childhood center setting', *Young Children*, 49(3), pp 84–6

Curry, C and Bromfield, C (1994) *Personal and social education for primary schools through circle time*, Stafford: NASEN

Department for Education and Employment (DfEE) (2000) *Educational psychology services (England): Current role, good practice and future directions*, Annesley, Nottingham: DfEE

Frederickson, N and Turner, J (2003) 'Utilizing the classroom peer group to address children's social needs', *Journal of Special Education*, 36(4), pp 234–46

Housego, E and Burns, C (1994) 'Are you sitting too comfortably? A critical look at "circle time" in primary classrooms', *English in Education*, 28(2), pp 23–9

Kantor, R (1989) 'First the look and then the sound: creating conversations at circle time', *Early Childhood Research Quarterly*, 4(4), pp 433–48

Lang, P (1998) 'Getting round to clarity: What do we mean by circle time?' *Pastoral Care*, (September), pp 3–10

Lang, P and Mosley, J (1993) 'Promoting pupil self-esteem and positive school policies through the use of circle time', *Primary Teaching Studies*, 7(2), pp 11–15

Lawrence, D (1987) *Enhancing self esteem in the classroom*, London: Paul Chapman

Lown, J (2002) 'Circle Time: the perception of teachers and pupils', *Educational Psychology in Practice*, 18(2), pp 93–102

Majsterek, D J, Shorr, D N and Erion, V L (2000) 'Promoting early literacy through rhyme detection activities during Head Start 'Circle-Time', *Child Study Journal*, 30(3), pp 143–52

Maslow, A (1968) *Toward a psychology of being*, New York: Van Nostrand

McLeod, J (1998) *An introduction to counselling*, Buckingham: Open University Press

Mead, G H (1934) *Mind, self and society*, Chicago: University of Chicago Press

Meichenbaum, D (1977) *Cognitive behavior modification*, New York: Plenum Press

Moreno, J L (1946) *Psychodrama* (2nd ed), New York: Beacon House

Mosley, J (1993) *Turn your school round*, Cambridge: LDA

Mosley, J (1996) *Quality Circle Time*, Cambridge: LDA

Mosley, J (2001) 'Some theoretical underpinnings of "Circle Time"', pp 70–5 in J Mosley *Quality Circle Time in the primary classroom*, Wisbech: LDA

Moss, H and Wilson, V (1998) 'Circle Time: Improving social interaction in a Year 6 classroom', *Pastoral Care*, (September), pp 11–17

Newton, C and Wilson, D (1996) *Circles of Friends*, Dunstable: Folens

Palomares, U and Bell, G (1971) *An overview of the human development program*, San Diego: Human Development Training Institute

Qualifications and Curriculum Authority (QCA) (2000) *Curriculum 2000*, London: QCA

Rogers, C (1951) *Client centred therapy*, Boston: Houghton Mifflin

Rogers, C (1983) *Freedom to learn in the 1980s*, New York: Macmillan

Schweigert, F J (1999) 'Moral education in victim offending conferencing', *Criminal Justice Ethics*, (Summer/Fall), pp 29–40

Teacher Training Agency (1999) *National special educational needs specialist standards*, London: TTA

Timmerman, W and Ballard, J (1975) *Strategies in humanistic education*, Amherst, Massachusetts: Mandala

Vygotsky, L S (1962) *Thought and language*, Cambridge, MA: MIT Press

White, M (1989) 'The Magic Circle: a process to enhance children's self esteem', *Times Educational Supplement*, (30 June), p 24

Wolery, M, Anthony, L, Caldwell, N K, Snyder, E D, Morgante, J D (2002) 'Embedding and distributing constant time delay in "Circle Time" and transitions', *Topics in Early Childhood Special Education*, 22(1), pp 14–25

Chapter 15

Working with families in a school setting

Vince Hesketh and Sue Olney

Introduction

Most teachers would say that the behaviour of the students in their lessons is the key element to both students' ability to learn and their own professional satisfaction. However, whilst it is recognised that the individual skills of the teacher will be a major influence, there is increasing recognition that the wider dimensions of the child's family and community life have to be taken into consideration when trying to understand and address students' behaviour. In this chapter we will outline a model that helps towards an appreciation of how the interactions of home and school affect children's lives and offer some ideas about ways to create change.

Traditionally, in many countries parents have had very little to do with schools outside formal parents' evenings. Particularly at secondary school level, the only task was to educate children in the academic and vocational areas of the curriculum. If children were thought to experience distress or deprivation at home, school was seen as a refuge; it was not felt to be the teachers' responsibility to engage the family beyond that which related to the curriculum.

In the UK, our understanding of children has gradually shifted since the Maria Colwell Enquiry of 1974. Successive government reports about the needs of children emphasised the importance of professionals being able to understand and work alongside colleagues in other agencies, and within this climate there has been an increasing expectation that schools will participate actively in the assessment and treatment of a whole range of children's needs. Schools now have SENCOs, EMAG teachers and designated teachers for the following areas: child protection, children in public care and young carers. It is now commonplace for counsellors and youthworkers to be actively involved in schools.

Alongside this move towards multi-agency work has come a change in social services departments. In response to consistent criticism that they were too unfocused in their task, they are increasingly discriminating about the work they will undertake. There has been a shift towards assessment rather than treatment on the understanding that other agencies will undertake the bulk of intervention and follow-up work. Most social workers now see themselves as case managers and the co-ordinators of services rather than the principal agent for change. The threshold for social work intervention is rising, leaving much of the preventative work to other agencies and, because the education service touches all children and families, it is inevitable that it becomes a crucial agency for conducting this work. The effect of these two shifts means that schools are now managing children who are in serious distress, a situation that often involves staff in regular liaison with external agencies. In addition, there is an increasing expectation that schools will be the primary agent for change in cases where family difficulties are not regarded by health and/or social services as being serious enough to warrant their intervention.

Ways of thinking about working with families: human beings as part of 'systems'

Sutton (1999) describes a system as having two main features.

> Firstly it is an assembly of parts or components connected together in an organised way; second, the parts of the system affect each other.

A change in one part of the system will facilitate change in another part, and this can be demonstrated in the human body, which is such a system. A broken leg is likely to affect other functioning parts of the body, with the uninjured leg taking more of the weight and crutches putting a strain on arms and hands. As individuals we also operate within other systems in terms of our emotional and social selves, for example the family system, the political system and so on. We are all intimately connected in networks of relationships.

This interaction between parts of the system, where the primary focus is the relationship between the parts, is the premise of systemic psychotherapy, which is more commonly known as family therapy. It also underpins much of the practice within social services and child mental health. As professionals who are 'in loco parentis', there is a legal imperative for teachers to consider their place in relation to the child and his/her parent(s), and for this reason the systemic model is one which fits comfortably with work in schools.

Key concepts

In order to understand a child's behaviour in school, it is important to view it within the context of the many influences on his or her life, ranging from parent(s) and siblings, wider family, neighbours, peers, community and so on. Relationships also occur within other contexts, such as employment/unemployment, poverty/wealth, gender, ethnicity, religion, culture, physical and mental health and family constellation. Within this model, the child's behaviour can be understood to make sense when it is considered in relation to the emotional complexities of the people in his or her system, against which it will have a meaning. In order to facilitate change, it is important to reach an understanding about this meaning and we therefore need to begin with a hypothesis to explain the child's behaviour.

Much of human behaviour is carried out at an unconscious or sub-conscious level and it is the purpose of most types of psychological intervention to help the recipient to gain an understanding of his or her responses. A number of key concepts form the principles of systemic therapy. In order to show how they might help us to form a hypothesis to explain a child's behaviour, we will describe a case vignette to which each of twelve concepts can be applied. This case is based on a family with whom we worked but the names have been changed to protect their confidentiality.

Case vignette: Ann

Ann, a 15-year-old girl in year 10, started to attend school less frequently, saying that she was suffering from panic attacks when she was in lessons.

Ann lived with her father Mr Jones, and her younger brother, Steven, aged 12. Her mother died of cancer when Ann was 10 and Mr Jones was clearly still grief-stricken. He too experienced panic attacks and his relationship with Ann could be described as being excessively dependent on her. This meant that Ann, who was a quiet, timid girl, had very little social life.

At the time of the referral, Mr Jones was suffering from a hernia, which was due to be operated on. He was very frightened about this prospect as he associated hospitals with his wife's death. He worried he might not survive surgery.

A description of the work undertaken with Ann can be found at the end of the chapter. It had the effect of helping Ann to become more confident and assertive about her own emotional and social needs, which lay outside the family. However, this change in Ann created difficulties in her relationship with her father, who interpreted her different behaviour as lacking in thought and consideration for the other members of her family.

1. Family members do their best

This statement may seem controversial but it is a liberating premise to assist us in understanding the complex motivations and behaviours shown by human beings. To help to comprehend this idea, we might consider incidents in our lives when we have acted in a way which was intended to be harmful. Most of us can identify times when we have hurt others, but in the context of the dilemmas of the moment the intention would not have been to cause harm. By adopting this belief, we become more cautious about making judgements and we avoid categorising parents, children or colleagues as being either good or bad. If we apply this principle to the case vignette it is possible to argue that, whilst Mr Jones was open to criticism in terms of his dependence on Ann, he had ensured that both his children grew up in a loving and stable home.

2. Life-cycle transitions

As we move from birth to death, we are continually negotiating different patterns of relationships. Most families adjust to this struggle within their own resources but are more likely to have serious difficulties when several life-cycle events coincide. For example, the birth of a baby coinciding with the death of a grandparent and the migration of a family member to a different part of the country, all of which could take place within a short time frame. When children present with behavioural difficulties it is sometimes a reflection of the life-cycle dilemmas that members of the family are trying to negotiate.

It is often useful, when attempting to arrive at an understanding of what is happening within the family, to ask the question 'Why now?' In the case of the Jones family, Ann was making the transition from child to teenager with an increasing number of demands being made on her from friends in terms of conducting a social life away from the family. In confronting surgery, it could be argued that Mr Jones was rekindling the life-cycle transition which occurred when his wife died.

3. Losses and gains of change

In our culture, change is often considered to be a positive step with the negative aspects being ignored. Within this model, we have to consider that there are positives and negatives to staying as we are and positives and negatives to changing.

The gain for Ann in staying as a timid school refuser would be that she could continue to enjoy a close, loving relationship with her father, in which she was highly valued. However, the loss in not changing would be that she would sacrifice a 'normal' social life with friends and it may become difficult for her to commit to a sexual relationship later on.

On the other hand, when change occurred, she gained a sense of freedom to both pursue her identity and learn to cope with the stresses and strains that are intrinsic to the formation of relationships. The loss to her in such a change is that she risked losing the close relationship with her father and the key role she had within the family.

4. All behaviour has a meaning

Our behaviour is not random. A furious argument with a family member before leaving for work often colours our interactions with our colleagues and our ability to show tolerance.

Even the most obscure behaviour, which appears difficult to comprehend, will have a meaning and it is our task to try to understand how it can be 'helpful' to members of the family and the wider system. For example, a child whose behaviour in school appears mindless and random may have the effect of inviting the involvement of an estranged father to meetings in school, rekindling contact between the parents.

By missing school, Ann remained with her father during a time of great anxiety for him whilst at the same time drawing attention to her dilemma and recruiting help in changing her situation.

5. Context defines meaning

The meaning we give to an event or action is defined by the context, or lens, through which it is viewed. Wearing a bikini on a beach is expected and acceptable; wearing the same clothing in an adjacent street is likely to be seen as inappropriate and, in some cases, illegal.

Connected to the above is the idea that each individual sees the world through his/her unique lens. Any one situation is likely to be understood and described differently by observers of that same event. For example, the pastoral Head may privilege the behaviour of Ann's school refusal as a statement of concern about her and her family, while the Education Welfare Officer may privilege the legal context and view her behaviour as an offence. Meanwhile, the family doctor may see Ann's panic attacks as a symptom of mental instability and prescribe medication accordingly. Ann's friends might see her as 'sad' or a 'skiver'.

6. Dilemmas rather than solutions

We operate in a solution-focused culture, which means that we often believe that for every problem there is a solution. However, closer examination suggests that, rather than offering a solution to solve a problem, we simply move from one dilemma to another so that every 'solution' throws up further dilemmas. If we accept this idea, it invites us to adopt a more complex, less simplistic approach to problem solving. As described in the case vignette, the dilemma of her father's panic attacks was resolved only by Ann creating the new dilemma of missing school, thereby inviting the involvement of the professional system.

7. Avoiding the verb 'to be'

It is usually unhelpful to say, 'This *is* a naughty child' because it implies that naughtiness is his prime and only attribute, when in reality he will have many attributes and will only be naughty some of the time. His naughtiness will be connected to a context such as particular teachers, the relationship with his friends or to what is happening at home. It is important, therefore, to focus on the occasions and the context in which the naughtiness occurs. Ann's behaviour put her in the category of a 'school refuser' but such a label would not have offered a way of helping her to change her behaviour. It is not her only attribute and we must be free to consider the whole person. As suggested above, school refusing allowed her to be protective of her father.

8. Mistrust certainty

As soon as we become convinced that we have the answer, we close our minds to other ways of seeing a situation. As suggested above, there are always many ways of reaching an understanding and this idea challenges the commonly held view that the more professional we are, the more certain we should be. There is a paradox here because we need some certainty in order to proceed along a given path, yet we need to remain open to the idea that there are many paths to help us to understand the problem.

9. The parental child

In most families, it is accepted that the parent(s) are in charge and make most of the key decisions about the child's life and the running of the household.

Sometimes, however, children take on the role of a mini-adult within the family and become the helper and confidante of the parent(s) and a carer/controller of other siblings. In many families it is helpful for an older sibling to take charge of younger siblings until the adult comes home from work, provided that at this stage, the parent resumes authority over all the children. The 'parental child' benefits from the importance of his/her role and the closeness with a parent but will often miss out on the freedoms of ordinary childhood. Whilst being the parental child might be seen as a privilege, these children tend to be frightened of the power they may exert within their family and become resentful or scared of the dependency of the parent. On occasions, this may lead to the child becoming aggressive and/or difficult to control. A child is more likely to adopt this role when there are specific difficulties for a parent such as chronic physical or mental health problems, marital violence or addiction. Ann is an example of a 'parental child' who was in danger of remaining permanently in the position of mini-adult in relation to her father and her younger brother.

10. Stages of change

Frequently problems seem to occur in layers. Families may explain the child's difficulties through reference to one problem, for example, panic attacks, peer-group relationships, bullying and so on, and this initial explanation is referred to as the 'presenting problem'. It is essential to address the presenting problem because sometimes this intervention produces sufficient change for the child to feel settled. However, on other occasions the presenting problem masks more complex dilemmas that will not be revealed unless this is tackled. Ann's initial explanation for her school refusal was that she experienced panic attacks in lessons, and this had to be addressed – and thereby eliminated as the sole explanation – in order for the more complex issues about her father to unfold.

It is important to note at this point that the systemic model can produce a feeling in parent(s) that they are being blamed for their child's difficulties and that their explanation of the problem is not being heard. It is crucial, therefore, to listen to their account of what is happening before using the techniques described later in this chapter to explore with them some more complex ideas about what might be happening. In circumstances where it is clear that parent(s) are taking on the burden of guilt and responsibility, it may be important to point out that, just as they may feel intrinsically bound up with the 'problem', so they can be crucial to its resolution.

11. Shifting alliances and 'splitting'

> One of the most common presentations of a school/family problem arises when a child's difficult behaviour in school is denied by the family, who see the school staff as scapegoating the child in a heartless and unsympathetic way. The school in turn is likely to see the parents as irresponsible towards their child and aggressive in their response to the school's complaints.
>
> (Dowling and Pound, 1985)

Children who present difficult behaviour often experience a sense of personal and emotional chaos and the triangular relationship described above can serve to compound this feeling. The tendency, in schools, is for only two sides of the triangle to be actively engaged with each other at any one time. Thus, the parent and child could form an alliance against the school in their mutual criticism of the way in which the child has been treated. However, this construct could just as easily apply to the other sides of the triangle. Examples might be when the child confides to the teacher about his/her unhappiness at home or when the teacher and parent agree that the behaviour of the child in both the school and home setting is not acceptable. The triangle could be further complicated if the alliance is between the teacher and one parent against the other parent.

These alliances often shift, leaving all the participants feeling confused and/or rejected. For example, a child may elicit the sympathy of his/her teacher by attributing poor behaviour to incidents of mistreatment on the part of the parent. However, at a subsequent meeting involving all three people, the parent says the child's behaviour has nothing to do with home but is caused by problems in school at which point the child is likely to remain loyal to the parent. This reversal on the part of the child may leave the teacher feeling confused and/or betrayed.

The phenomenon of shifting alliances provides an opportunity for the child to 'split' the adults (for example, mother from father, parents from school, teacher from teacher, teacher from youthworker/counsellor). When this happens, the adults are often left feeling that one has been labelled 'good' while the other has been labelled 'bad'.

The effect on children when they are allowed to 'split' adults is that they gain too much power and the adults' ability to make them feel safe is considerably reduced. Most children who have this level of power feel frightened as they become elevated to the level of an adult. Often the child will escalate his/her behaviour until the adults can speak with one voice in a way that returns him/her from the position of fearful adult to the status of contained child.

12. Containment

Sometimes what stops us from being able to express our feelings is the fear that the listener will be frightened or rendered powerless by our account. Most of us need to feel emotionally contained by being listened to in a way that both respects our story and holds our anxiety. As the listener, this is particularly important when we hear accounts of extreme distress and abuse. For example, if a manager displays a sense of discomfort and/or is unable to convey a sense of authority when hearing an employee's anxieties/concerns, the staff member is likely to feel uncontained. Similarly, children may feel uncontained when parents cannot provide physical or emotional safety. Parental children such as Ann run the risk of feeling uncontained.

A model for practice

The difficult behaviour that children present in school is often replicated at home, so it is sensible to negotiate a way of addressing it which can be applied both at home and in school. In this way, the child is likely to feel more contained because there is a consistent approach being adopted by all the key adults in his/her life.

Such behaviour is not confined to antisocial behaviours. It could be that the child is a school non-attender or that he presents symptoms of illness. This could be of an emotional kind, such as panic attacks, depression or phobias, or a physical kind such as 'Chronic Fatigue Syndrome'. An increasing number of children are being diagnosed with 'Aspergers Syndrome', attention deficit/hyperactivity disorder (AD/HD), or depression. The nature of the symptom will determine the type of professional involvement that is offered. Difficult behaviour which has been diagnosed as being understood in terms of AD/HD will be treated by the Health Service, while the same behaviour, which carries the label of delinquent, will be treated by Social Services or the Youth Offending Service. The effect of this distinction is that the label rather than the person becomes the focus. If we consider that, in the case of such children, there is a strong possibility that other family members will also be in receipt of professional involvement, it is possible to contemplate a situation in which one family is in contact with a number of different agencies as Figure 15.1 illustrates.

The symptoms of father, son and daughter might be seen as different responses to stress within the family but the professionals involved will inevitably focus on the family member whose behaviour has activated their agency, taking little or no account of the difficulties presented by other family members or the role of other agencies with them.

Whatever the symptoms presented by the child, the model for intervention that is being proposed in this chapter actively considers the three sides of the triangle consisting of home, school and child. The premise is that we should never work with one side of the triangle without including or considering the

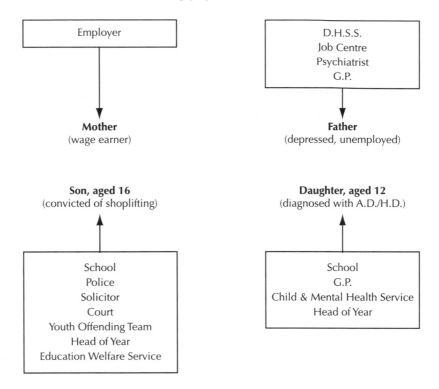

Figure 15.1 Professionals involved with mother, father, son and daughter in one family

other sides and we should always be mindful of the difficulties experienced by other members of the family. The model attempts to understand the fit between all the key people in the student's life and it seeks to create a style of communication with parents and children that encourages a reflective, non-judgemental position.

Process

There is a risk, when establishing family work within schools, that mainstream staff, particularly those involved in pastoral work, will feel disenfranchised. It is important, therefore, to inform staff about the nature and process of the intervention and have clear procedures for referral and feedback to staff. The model described here has been established in one 11–16 mainstream secondary school in England but it will need to be adapted if it is to suit the established way of working within each school, particularly if the school is a primary/junior school.

Stage 1: Referral

The likelihood is that the more staff feel that they have some control of the system, the more they will feel able to support it and this particularly applies to pastoral staff and/or those working with children with special needs. Establishing a clear consultation/referral process is, therefore, of crucial importance to the success of the model, as is the process of keeping staff informed of the progress of the child.

In the secondary school previously mentioned, referrals come through a 'Provision and Review' meeting which takes place on a weekly basis and involves the Heads of Year and appropriately trained key staff working within the Inclusion Department. In another school, this might be the SENCO and other staff who have a responsibility for behaviour. A member of the senior management team chairs the meetings; in terms of decision-making, it is important that this task falls to someone in authority within the school who has been trained appropriately for the task.

The purpose of the Provision and Review (P&R) meetings within the school is to discuss children who are causing concern and may need to be referred for more intensive input. The purpose is also to review the progress of children who have already been referred. Brief notes are taken by the chairperson and distributed widely to key members of staff. A copy is displayed on the staff notice board. These notes are not intended to be a substitute for the more detailed information that should be produced at reviews but are a way of keeping staff up-to-date.

Within the model outlined in this chapter, the family work is carried out as part of the 'Support Programme'. In the event that the members of the P&R Group feel that it is appropriate to refer a child to this programme, the Head of Year will contact parents to get their consent. It is important that this task is carried out by the Head of Year because it respects the relationship that may already be established between that staff member and the parent(s) and it also enables the staff member who is most familiar with the parent(s) to explore their hopes and reservations about the programme. Furthermore, it conveys the message to the family that mainstream staff actively support the referral.

Stage 2: The support programme

Parents are invited to an initial meeting to explain the programme. Often this is attended by one of the parent(s). It is an opportunity to agree which family members might attend in future. This list should include the child but could also consist of biological and non-biological parents and/or other siblings. The frequency and timings of the meetings is agreed, usually weekly or fortnightly, and a discussion takes place about how each meeting will be recorded, suggestions about which are outlined in more detail later under the section entitled 'Feedback'. Agreement is reached about the people to whom copies of this record are sent. It is important to establish whether any other external agencies are involved with the family, for example, Social Services, Health and so on. Often the first meeting is with the parent(s) alone, which respects their position as senior members of the family and enables them to 'tell their story' without the possible restrictions that might be imposed with children being present.

At this stage it is important to listen to an explanation of the child's difficulties, as presented by the parent(s) and/or the child. As explained under No. 10 of 'Key Concepts', it is essential that the 'presenting problem' is heard in order to facilitate further progress.

Stage 3: Forming a hypothesis

At the first two or three meetings with parent(s) and child, the focus is on information gathering. It is important to hear their respective accounts of their relationships in order to begin to form an understanding about how the child's behaviour may fit with the family's history and the pattern of communication between them. The Key Concepts are a useful guide in forming a hypothesis that connects the child's behaviour in school with relationships at home and relationships within the school. For example, in a family where both parents grew up in a culture in which school was not valued, the child may mirror those same values because he is receiving a message (whether explicit or implicit) that school is not something to be respected. Alternatively, a child from a high-achieving academic background may fear failure and create circumstances in which failure is guaranteed as a way to avoid the expectations of a successful parent. Our initial hypothesis may not be useful and we must remain open to many ways of understanding the dilemma.

Stage 4: Exploration of meaning

This stage may take more time and require further sessions to explore the meaning of the family's beliefs and behaviours and to reach an agreement about what is in the best interest of the child. Sometimes the process of enabling the parent(s) and child to reflect on these meanings and the impact on their daily lives is enough to create sufficient change to enable the child to be more settled in school. A key ingredient of this process is providing a respectful and non-judgemental context in which to have these conversations (see Key Concept No. 1: 'Families do their best').

Stage 5: Sustaining change

Once change has started to occur and the child and/or parent(s) feel more settled, it is tempting to assume that the problem is solved. However, change is always accompanied by losses as well as gains (Key Concept No.3) and it is often necessary to maintain regular meetings to sustain this change over time. Sometimes the child will see the value in parent(s) being supported by the school and fear a withdrawal of that support if a significant improvement occurs. In such cases, the role of the support worker may be to offer containment (Key Concept No. 12) to parent(s), which increases their confidence and empowers their parenting. If we withdraw too soon, the child may escalate his behaviour in order to ensure that we do not withdraw the support for the parent(s). We therefore need to respect the pace of change and, where possible, allow the parent and child to dictate the ending of the work.

Techniques

Circular questioning

Most family therapists adopt a proactive stance in their work with clients. They have developed a raft of questions that are aimed at generating new information. Such knowledge enables both the therapist and the family to reflect on what has been said in a way that may create new connections and/or understandings for all involved. This method differs from conventional counselling, where the stance of the professional tends to be more passive.

There are losses and gains to either method but asking questions tends to produce a more dynamic conversation and often helps those involved to feel more at ease. A central feature of the questioning technique is to ask open-ended questions based on the feedback from the answer to the previous question. Families tend to find this method respectful because it requires intense listening on the part of the therapist to the feedback given to each question. Closed questions often lead to a 'yes/no' answer which gives very little feedback to inform the next question.

The following dialogue is an example of circular questioning, using open questions which are based on answers:

Teacher: What do you think about Ann's panic attacks, Mr Jones?
Mr Jones: Well, I think she gets them from me.
Teacher: Where do you get your panic attacks from?
Mr Jones: I've had them ever since my wife died.

The effect of this conversation is that it allows us to develop a more extensive conversation about the effect on Mr Jones of his wife's death.

Among the specific techniques of questioning, there are a few that are particularly useful for those new to this way of working.

- **Triadic questions**: asking one person to comment on another person within the same meeting, for example,
  Q: Ann, what do you think your Dad feels about you not going to school?
  Q: Mr Jones, what do you think about what Ann has said?
- **Most/least questions**:
  Q: Who in the family is most upset by your behaviour?
  A: My Dad.
  Q: How does he show that he is upset?
  A: By crying and having panic attacks.
  Q: If you started going to school regularly, do you think that your Dad's panic attacks would increase, decrease or stay the same?
- **Future questions**:
  Q: Imagine that in three months' time, things in your family were much improved. Describe how they would be.
  Q: How would this affect your relationship with your Dad?
  Q: How would it affect your Dad's relationship with your brother?

The aim of circular questioning is to encourage families and professionals to be reflective and for families to develop their own way forward. For example, questions to Mr Jones are designed to encourage him towards an understanding that Ann's behaviour is linked to his own anxieties. The effect of her behaviour is that it has given him an opportunity to explore some of his concerns with staff at school and this process may be enough to reduce his anxiety, which in turn liberates Ann to return to school.

Our usual tendency when confronted with a family's dilemmas is to make statements in the hope that we can provide a solution, but this can have the effect of making the recipient feel that they are on the receiving end of a lecture and are thereby deskilled. The circular questioning technique opens dialogue rather than closes it.

Recording information and giving feedback

One way of helping parents to feel valued and included in discussions and decisions is to write a summary of the discussion. This could take the form of a letter or a proforma that includes space to record both progress as well as future action.

By writing to the parent(s) we make them central to the process and we give them an opportunity to reflect further on the conversation. This process also meets professional obligations to record such meetings and allows us to send copies to key professionals within the school and relevant agencies.

Maintaining an open dialogue with other key players apart from the family is one of the ways of reducing the likelihood of unhelpful alliances occurring (see Key Concept No. 11: Shifting Alliances and Splitting). Writing to parent(s) also gives us the opportunity to offer our reflections following the meeting. We often have useful thoughts in the calmer moments following an emotional session and it can be helpful to convey these observations to the family in the written feedback. Furthermore, it also allows us to emphasise themes that we think might be most useful, especially highlighting positive aspects of parenting.

Case vignette returned

A description of the intervention with Ann

The initial meeting took place between the support teacher and Ann's father. Mr Jones explained Ann's reluctance to attend school as her fear and embarrassment about the panic attacks she was experiencing in lessons, something with which he identified because he had been in receipt of medication for similar symptoms for several years. This piece of information prompted the support teacher to ask when the symptoms first appeared, which opened the door to a conversation about the death of Mrs Jones and how the individual members of the family had coped with this event.

The support teacher formed the hypothesis that Ann's behaviour was explained by her role in the family, which was to support her father in a way that filled the gap left by her mother's death. The panic attacks from which Mr Jones suffered had increased when he learned that he would need an operation to remove a hernia but questioning revealed that these attacks reduced when Ann was in the house.

The support teacher realised that these issues would need to be addressed in order to clear the way for further work. Mr Jones was a self-employed painter and decorator so a timetable was created for Ann that allowed her to stay at home during the times that her father was not working. For his part, Mr Jones reorganised his working hours to accommodate these changes. Ann was also given a 'time out' card, which allowed her to leave a classroom when she started to feel the symptoms of the panic attack coming on.

In the meantime, with the permission of Mr Jones, the support teacher contacted the family doctor and the bereavement service, which had been a lifeline to Mr Jones in the aftermath of his wife's death.

The effect of this support was that Ann returned to school and her panic attacks reduced. However, a year later Ann and her father were re-referred for quite a different reason. The earlier discussions about the family's situation gave Ann the chance to reflect on her position in relation to her father and enabled her to reconnect with her friends at a time when the development of a social life was high on her agenda. Ann had given herself permission to be a more 'normal' teenager but this change had created difficulties in her relationship with her father, who felt abandoned by her. This highlights that there were losses as well as gains to the initial change and that change often occurs in stages (Key Concepts 3 and 10).

Ann's response to her father's reaction was to escalate her behaviour so that she became a 'stroppy' teenager. Mr Jones felt abandoned by Ann and he felt increasingly frustrated and angry. Without Ann to turn to he directed his needs to other parents experiencing similar dilemmas with their own children. Ann could thereby stop being a substitute for her mother and develop her own life.

Conclusion

Children presenting problems in school not only experience distress but they absorb large amounts of staff time and are a source of worry, both to parent(s) and sometimes to their peers. Whilst there will always be some children who cannot be maintained in mainstream school, it is hoped that the model we have outlined in this chapter offers a way of understanding a child's behaviour in school within the complex set of relationships around him and supports the child, the parent(s) and the teachers to make the necessary adjustments to allow the child to flourish both at home and in school.

References

Dowling, J. and Pound, A. (eds) (1985) 'Joint interventions with teachers, children and parents', in E. Dowling and E. Osborne *The Family and the School: A Joint Systems Approach to Problems with Children*, London: Routledge.

Sutton, C. (1999) *Helping Families with Troubled Children: A Preventive Approach*, Chichester: John Wiley and Sons.

Chapter 16

Antecedent control of behaviour in educational contexts

Ted Glynn

Introduction

There has been a recognition within applied behavioural research of particular dimensions of antecedent control of human behaviour (Risley, 1977; McNaughton, 1980; Glynn, 1982). These dimensions comprise the ecological context or the characteristics of settings within which contingencies of reinforcement operate to shape and maintain behaviour. Research reviewed in this paper suggests that such ecological conditions, or setting events, may exert just as powerful control over human behaviour in developmental and educational situations as do contingencies of reinforcement. Further, in many child development and educational contexts such as classrooms, playgrounds, daycare and residential institutions setting events may be more amenable to modification and hence may yield more efficient strategies for changing behaviour than strategies relying on contingencies or reinforcement alone.

It is important to note that antecedent control has been conceptualised in different ways. First the physical properties or stimulus objects present in an environment can in themselves influence human behaviour. The presence of brightly coloured moving objects over an infant's crib might be expected to affect the infant's rate of looking. However, both Kantor (1970) and Bijou & Baer (1978) distinguish between stimulus objects and stimulus functions. For example, Kantor (1970) argues that particular objects can acquire specific functions for an individual neonate as soon as interactions are established with those objects and particular response functions are built up. While the correspondence between stimulus and response in simple reflex behaviour depends on biological evolution, in more complex behaviour situations there is a psychologically evolved mutuality of stimulus and response functions. Those individual response functions may be facilitated or impaired by situational or setting factors. For example using the model of Kantor and of Bijou & Baer it could be predicted that an infant's rate of vocalisation in response to a given stimulus (toy) might be strongly influenced by the presence or absence of a parent who usually reinforces the infant for all vocalisation. Similarly, the rate of child questions and parent responses might vary according to whether child and parent were at home, or in a public setting, e.g. seated on a bus. Increased responding in both these examples, while partly resulting from reinforcement contingencies applied by the adult, *also* results from the availability of the adult as a cue for responding in the particular setting. The essentials of these examples appear to be captured in Bijou & Baer's (1978) definition: '… A setting event influences an interactional sequence by altering strengths and characteristics of the particular stimulus and response functions involved in an interaction' (p. 6).

Wahler & Fox (1981) note that Bijou & Baer (1978) have extended the definition of setting events to cover not only the concurrent presence of a stimulus condition or events (e.g. adult presence as a setting event for interaction) but also to cover two further possibilities. The first extends the definition of setting events to include stimulus-response *interactions* (e.g. presence of an adult playing with a child, so that the adult-child play could be a setting event for cueing and reinforcing child-initiated language). The second possibility includes as setting events stimulus (or stimulus and response) events which occur totally separate in space and time (i.e. may immediately precede, rather than merely overlap with), the stimulus response relationship they influence (e.g. children will display more on-task behaviour following a rest period, than following a period of vigorous activity (Krantz & Risley, 1977)).

The conceptual framework provided by Kantor (1970), Bijou & Baer (1978), and Wahler & Fox (1981) thus suggests three different classes of antecedent control of human behaviour, concurrent stimulus events, concurrent stimulus-response events, and prior stimulus or stimulus-response events. Many different educational contexts provide clear opportunities both to describe and to manipulate variables within each of these classes of antecedent control.

Concurrent stimulus events

Three important studies examined the effects of large-scale differences in physical environmental variables between schools. Barker & Gump (1964) carried out a broad-scale examination of the relationship between high school size and pupil participation in extra-curricular activities. While numbers of available extra-curricular activities increased as the size of schools increased, as expected, actual rate of participation *decreased*. Increased numbers of activities available did not result in increased participation. Barker & Gump argue that with small numbers there was a greater social pressure on individuals to participate in the smaller number of activities available. Within the context of a small school perhaps, the importance of participation of any one pupil to the success of the activity was much more salient than with the anonymous context of a larger school.

In contrast to the Barker & Gump findings Gill (1977) reported no significant effects on pupil behaviour or achievement of being taught in either conventional classrooms or variable-space (open-plan) classroom settings. Gill reported that differential *teacher* behaviours outweighed the simple effects of the different settings. Teacher behaviour would seem to be a very powerful factor influencing pupil behaviour, capable of overriding the effects of physical environmental (architectural) variables. One further descriptive study by Russell & Bernall (1977) demonstrated clear correlations between rates of appropriate and inappropriate child behaviour at home and time of day, day of week, and rainfall (i.e. child inappropriate behaviour was greater around 3.30–5.00 pm on Fridays, and on wet days rather than dry days). The findings of Barker & Gump, and Russell & Bernall point up interesting and important relationships between physical and temporal environmental variables and human behaviour. While these findings have clear implications for the design and management of school and home environments such variables are not easily or readily altered or manipulated experimentally.

Several further studies illustrate the powerful behavioural outcomes arising from the operation of more easily manipulable physical environmental variables. Quilitch, Christophersen & Risley (1977) conducted an analysis of children's use of a wide range of educational toys in child care contexts, and demonstrated that in a free choice situation specific toys varied widely in the amount of child use they occasioned. Risley (1982) has argued for a process of environmental distillation referring to the need to successively select children's play materials according to their ability to engage children at high rates. O'Rourke (1978) reports that merely supplying additional sports equipment and play materials resulted in increased rates of participation and decreased rates of disruptive behaviour on the playground of a large urban Intermediate School. However these effects were not as lasting as those reslting from supplying additional adults to initiate and participate in children's games.

Other studies have manipulated physical environmental variables within individual classrooms, for example by systematically altering seating patterns. Krantz & Risley (1977) demonstrated that disruptive behaviour during story time and during teacher demonstrations could be reduced just as effectively by providing more space between children as by implementing a positive reinforcement contingency for appropriate attending behaviour. Wheldall *et al.*

(1981) found that in two separate classrooms on-task behaviour was consistently higher when children were seated at desks arranged in rows than when they were seated at group tables. Wheldall (1982) reports further data which confirm these findings in three separate classes in a special school context. In these classes on-task behaviour was twice as high when children were seated individually in rows than when they were seated at group tables. However, Wheldall also reported that important increases in teachers' positive comments and decreases in teachers' negative comments occurred when children were seated individually in rows.

Clark (1982) reports data in support of Wheldall's findings. Clark found that individual seating arrangements resulted in increases of on-task behaviour, over the level of on-task behaviour while pupils were seated at group tables and while they were working on a carpeted floor. This pattern was replicated in a variable-space classroom with two groups of children who experienced the different seating arrangements in a different order. Although data from both the Wheldall and Clark studies demonstrate clear effects of seating arrangements on child behaviour, Wheldall's data suggest that this effect may be at least in part mediated through an indirect effect on teacher behaviour. Wheldall (1982) argues that teachers may find it easier to praise and refrain from disapproval when children are seated in rows. Perhaps this results from pupils' on-task behaviour being easier to *monitor* in the rows condition. The task of scanning and discriminating on-task from off-task behaviour may be less complex when children are seated in rows.

Some evidence in support of the claim that changes in seating arrangements affect child behaviour through indirect effects on teacher behaviour is provided in a study by Moore (1980) who demonstrated that the location of children's seats markedly affected the number of questions they were asked by the teacher. In a subsequent study in progress, Moore (1982) reports that switching individual children's seating position from areas receiving either high or low rates of teacher interaction resulted in changes in the rate of interaction in both the predicted directions. This type of manipulation is readily accomplished within individual classrooms with a minimum of effort.

Although seating arrangements can clearly influence the rate of on-task behaviour, their effect on academic work output is not convincing. Neither of the studies reported by Wheldall include data on rate of academic work completed. Clark (1982), however, monitored both rate and accuracy of completed maths problems in her study and found that neither of these measures varied according to change in seating arrangements. This is consistent with other findings that increases in on-task behaviour do not necessarily result in increased academic output (Marholin & Steinman, 1977; Henderson, 1976; Glendinning, 1978). Hence, seating arrangements may be a functional ecological variable for attentional behaviours rather than academic output *per se*. It is possible that certain seating arrangements are setting events for high rates of teacher praise for behaviours such as sitting still and working quietly.

One common summary theme emerging from several studies of the behavioural effects of physical environmental stimulus variables on child behaviour is that these effects commonly appear to be mediated through the effects on the behaviour of other people present in the setting. School size influenced participation rates, Barker & Gump argue, because of the greater social pressure to participate generated within small schools.

Thus, it would appear that effects on the behaviour of target individuals of changes in specific stimulus setting events are frequently associated with changes in the behaviour of other people present. However, these changes in the behaviour of other people are not explicitly planned, or programmed, as is the case with studies of the second type of setting event.

Concurrent stimulus and response events

The introduction of other people, for example encouraging adults into a pre-school free play context, can influence children's behaviour in two ways. First, familiar adults are likely to have become generalised discriminative stimuli for reinforcement such that child behaviours previously performed and reinforced in the presence of adults (but currently not displayed, or displayed only at a low rate in that pre-school context, e.g. naming objects) will be reinforced in the new context. Secondly, those behaviours specific to the pre-school setting but which have not previously occurred, or have occurred only at a low rate without the presence of adults (e.g. use of climbing equipment), are likely to be cued, prompted and reinforced by the adults. In this way interacting adults can extend antecedent and consequent control over child behaviour. Through these two processes adult presence can be seen both to provide additional opportunities to perform behaviours appropriate to the setting *and* to increase rates of reinforcement for those behaviours. Thus encouraging familiar adults into a pre-school setting may be expected to have a stronger and more lasting effect on child behaviour than either changing the physical stimulus properties of the setting (e.g. introducing new equipment) or merely reinforcing appropriate child behaviour as it occurs.

Several studies of meal-time settings provide clear demonstrations of the effects of the presence of adults on child behaviour. In a pre-school setting, Frewin (1980) manipulated the effects of a physical stimulus change (open display of jigsaw puzzles, versus stacking them together) and introducing an adult into the jigsaw area. Frewin's data show that the adult's presence resulted in more children entering the jigsaw corner, than did displaying the jigsaws, though both manipulations increased the number of children present over baseline rates. Glynn, Glynn & Lawless (1979) examined the amount of different foods eaten and the number of second helpings requested by five children at a family evening meal. Parents either ate their own meal with their children or ate their meal at a later time, leaving the children to eat without adult company. A similar set of menus was presented within each of the four conditions. All children ate more food and required more second helpings when parents ate with them and the effect was greatest for the young children. Baker (1980) describes a child in a day care setting who was a problem eater and who was not responding to systematic procedures for prompting and reinforcing eating. However, Baker found instead that having an adult sit with the child and engage him in conversation during the meal-time resulted in his eating three times as many spoonsful of food as he did on days when the adult supervised from a distance. The two conditions were alternated frequently over three weeks, with the same consistent results. O'Rourke (1978) demonstrated that introducing additional participating adults into a large urban intermediate school playground effected a greater rate of child participation in appropriate activities and a lower rate of disruptive behaviour than did introducing additional play equipment. The effect of the 'adults present' condition was also more lasting than the effect of supplying additional equipment. In these three studies, introducing adults increased the rate of performance of behaviours already occurring in the setting (eating and engagement with play equipment).

Some further studies are of interest because they not only introduced an interacting adult into a target setting, but in addition required the adult to provide a concurrent model of specific target behaviours appropriate to that setting. Haskett & Lenfestey (1974) studied the pre-reading behaviours (e.g. turning pages in books) of six children in a pre-school setting. Two procedures were compared, introducing stacks of new books (a change in stimulus materials) and introducing adults who modelled individual interested reading of these books (without attempting to engage children's attention or 'read to' the children). Introducing new books resulted in brief increases in pre-reading behaviour in several of the children, whereas introducing the adult models resulted in large and consistent increases in pre-reading behaviours in all of the children. This study was followed up by Pluck (1980), who examined the effects of concurrent teacher modelling of appropriate recreational reading behaviour during classroom recreational reading time in a primary school. Recreational reading involved children selecting their own library books and reading silently for 20 minutes. On different days the teacher either sat on a chair at the front of the room modelling reading her own book silently and with enjoyment or alternatively occupied herself with some other tasks (marking or preparation of work or tidying the room). Observational data show that children's rate of engagement in silent reading was higher on days when the teacher modelled recreational reading than on days when she performed other tasks. Further the five least competent readers were found to have a mean on-task behaviour of 33% on no-modelling days and 65% on teacher modelling days. The corresponding figures for the five most competent readers were 70 and 85%. Interestingly, the mean number of teacher comments contingent on children's inappropriate behaviour on the no-modelling days was 5.0 while the corresponding figure on concurrent modelling days was 1.0. Pluck's data are consistent with previous findings that some setting event effects on child behaviour may be mediated through changes in adult behaviour. In this case acting as a concurrent model for target appropriate behaviour may have reduced the teacher's opportunities to monitor and respond to inappropriate child behaviour. This study raises some interesting questions. What opportunities do schools provide for children to see competent adult models performing with enjoyment the target academic behaviour they are instructing? How often do children see adults enjoying silent reading? Do they see adults engaged in and enjoying writing tasks or engaged in maths work? It is unlikely that concurrent modelling of academic behaviours by adults occurs in schools as often as concurrent modelling of physical education and sporting skills. An important area of research to be explored is the analysis of the effects of concurrent modelling of target behaviours on children's *academic* performance. Interestingly several graduate student parents who study and write regularly at home have commented that their young children frequently ask to be allowed to write or engage in academic tasks concurrently with their parent's own writing.

Another setting event of major importance in child development and education is the one to one setting in which an adult and child spontaneously interact over a shared task or activity. This context is regarded as a powerful setting event for the naturalistic learning of language (Bruner, 1977; Risley, 1977). McNaughton (1980) notes that such setting events which operate on both adult and child behaviour are frequently child initiated and have an affective and child-directed basis. This type of child initiated interaction with an adult over a joint task unfortunately does not often occur in the school context.

In school environments, similar one to one contexts frequently arise though they are not typically child initiated. These occur for example when children read from a reading text to an adult. The important implications of this setting for the three-way interaction between teachers, readers and reading tasks have been discussed extensively (McNaughton, 1980). McNaughton (1981) presents data to show that the reading behaviour of low progress readers can function as a setting event for instructor behaviour that maintains dependent error correction strategies in these readers. Specifically, teachers in one intensive descriptive study of low progress readers attended to a high rate (74%) of low progress reader's errors with *immediate* intervention, most frequently in the form of providing models (supplying the correct word rather than providing a prompt, or simply pausing). In a second experimental study, teachers reduced their rate of error attention when low progress readers independently increased their reading accuracy, as a result of earlier tutoring sessions. Thus the behaviour of a low-progress reader in a one-to-one reading context can be seen to function as a concurrent stimulus-response setting event for instructor behaviours which leave the reader more dependent on external help.

Within the same one-to-one oral reading context it is also possible for specific instructor behaviours to function as setting events for particular dependent or independent error correction strategies in readers. McNaughton & Glynn (1981), for example, provide data to show that requiring instructors to delay their attention to errors clearly resulted in marked gains in readers' rates of self-correction of errors and gains in reading accuracy. Thus, one-to-one settings are important because of their potential to influence both instructor and learner behaviour.

Conditions of extended external control or 'maintained instructional dependence' (McNaughton, 1981) occur for all children in some situations. In many classrooms teachers initiate almost all instructional interactions with children and these interactions occur under tight stimulus control (i.e. they take place at set times, involve extended interactions with tightly specified stimulus objects or materials and generally occur in group contexts). Thus the opportunities for any one child to be sharing an activity with an adult are limited. The conditions under which much classroom instruction takes place can be seen as counter to the notion of training under, 'loose control' over acquisition, which Stokes & Baer (1977) and McNaughton (1980) argue is important for the generalisation of behaviours beyond the confines of the original training setting.

In contrast with instructional interactions at school, instructional interactions in some home settings can be seen (potentially at least), as more often child initiated, typically brief and occurring under loose stimulus control. That is, in the home, instructional interactions are likely to take place at a wide range of different times, involve brief interactions with a variety of stimulus object and materials and are much more likely to occur as one-to-one interactions with an adult. These 'loose' setting events appear to be much more suitable for the process of incidental teaching as described by Hart & Risley (1975, 1980) and also to be more likely to promote generalised learning than those obtaining in school settings. Elsewhere the need for research to exploit the advantages of both home and school settings for teaching academic skills has been argued (Glynn, 1982). Arndt (1980), for example, reports a study in which the rate of words written by a seven-year-old girl was between two and a half and three times as high in story writing at home as it was in story writing at school.

Prior stimulus or stimulus-response events

The effect of prior exposure to simple or complex stimulus events is readily illustrated in numerous studies of modelling. A classic study in this area is that of Bandura, Ross & Ross (1963) who demonstrated that prior exposure to a film in which an adult modelled specific aggressive responses towards a doll resulted in young children subsequently displaying these same responses towards an identical doll in a playroom. The efficacy of modelling as a clinical procedure is demonstrated in the following two studies. Bandura, Grusec & Menlove (1967) compared the effects of modelling and systematic desensitisation in the treatment of dog phobia in young children. Children either participated in a typical desensitisation programme in which over repeated sessions, they were slowly moved closer to a dog in a playroom, or they watched a similar-age peer model engage in playful interaction with a dog. All three groups were tested with the target child and the dog in both a neutral and a 'party' context. In both contexts, children who had viewed the child model were markedly less fearful and approached the dog more closely than children who had received the desensitisation procedure. In the second study, Lahey (1971) reported that the use of descriptive adjectives by young children in a Head Start programme was substantially increased by a procedure in which target children watched same aged children model a high rate of descriptive adjectives in their answers to teacher questions.

Prior exposure to a model is also frequently included as a component of programmes of parent training or staff training in the use of behaviour management procedures. However, analyses of the effects of separate training components, e.g. modelling and feedback are seldom carried out. One study which examined the effects of modelling on its own was that of Gladstone & Spencer (1977) who modelled the delivery of positive reinforcement (praise) in the context of training retarded adults in self-care skills. Aides were found not only to increase their use of positive reinforcement when supervising subjects in the setting where the modelling took place, but also to generalise this gain to other settings. It is interesting to note that there appear to be no studies comparing the effects of prior modelling with concurrent modelling in training of staff or parents to implement behavioural procedures. Various studies in which modelling formed part of a training package suggest that instructions and modelling components on their own have little influence on behaviour unless complemented by the provision of performance feedback. However, the unprogrammed finding noted by Glynn, Vaigro & Lawless (1982) suggests that concurrent modelling may be a worthwhile procedure for facilitating staff implementation of behavioural procedures.

Less well-known than the effects of simple modelling which involves prior presentation of stimulus material are the effects of prior stimulus response setting events. Krantz & Risley (1977) demonstrated that children's rate of attention to the teacher or to a story book during story reading was clearly affected by the type of preceding activity the children were engaged in. When story reading followed a quiet rest period children's attention was consistently higher and the time taken to settle and rate of disruption were lower than when story reading followed a period of vigorous activity. In the context of one-to-one oral reading Wong & McNaughton (1980) systematically monitored reading accuracy and rate of self-correction of errors of a seven and a half-year old low-progress reader. This child read a different unfamiliar text each session. Wong & McNaughton found that in sessions which had been preceded by a brief prior discussion of the main events, outcomes and unfamiliar words in the story to be read, this reader's accuracy and self-correction were markedly higher than in sessions where the prior discussion had not occurred. This simple but powerful procedure is commonly used as part of beginning reading programmes in many schools.

In the area of social learning, Fowler & Baer (1981) describe an interesting outcome from children's exposure to a prior stimulus-response setting event. First, pre-school children increased their rate of sharing in an early session following the introduction of contingent reinforcement dispensed at the end of that session. They did not increase sharing in a later session where no reinforcement was dispensed. Next, reinforcement contingent on sharing in the early session was delayed until the end of the later session. However no reinforcement was provided contingent on sharing in the later session. Not only did the rate of sharing continue to remain high in the early session but sharing during the later session also increased. Further analyses showed no changes in teacher or peer social attention contingencies in the later session and no systematic association between sharing in the later session and the number of points obtained. The authors argue that instructions given at the beginning of the school day came to set the occasion for sharing in both early and later session. When reinforcement had occurred after the early session it is likely that children discriminated that sharing in the later session would not be reinforced. With the delay of reinforcement till after the later session the discrimination about when sharing would be reinforced is likely to be blurred. Thus under conditions of delayed reinforcement, the authors argue that instructions about behaviour early in the school day came to set the occasion for sharing in both early and late sessions.

Wahler & Graves (1982) cite an interesting study by Simon, Ayllon & Milan (1982) which reports behavioural contrast effects across settings, resulting from manipulation of token reinforcement contingencies in other settings. The maths performance of seven children was monitored in three different classrooms, each with a different teacher. Following baseline sessions without token reinforcement, a phase in which tokens could be earned at the rate of one per correct response was introduced which produced clear increases in all three settings. Then tokens were withdrawn from two settings, but maintained in the third. Response rate dropped in the first two settings but doubled in the third. When tokens were reinstated in all settings, response rates increased in the first two settings and dropped in the third. Wahler & Graves argue that when these children were subjected to extinction in two settings, they performed in the third setting as if the reinforcement schedule had changed. In this way, the prior extinction experience had served as a setting event in a similar way to that of the prior instruction in the study on sharing by Fowler & Baer (1981).

Conclusions

In summary, there is an impressive range and variety of evidence to demonstrate the power of antecedent control over adult and child behaviour in educational contexts. The studies reviewed provide clear examples of the behavioural effects of all three types of setting event (concurrent stimulus events, concurrent stimulus-response events, and prior stimulus or stimulus-response events). Several tentative conclusions and research suggestions emerge about each.

(1) Antecedent control through the manipulation of physical stimulus events may influence behaviour in two ways. The first influence is direct, through the availability of new stimulus materials – as in the case of providing additional toys, and the second is indirect, as is the case where the physical stimulus events affect the behaviour of other people present, who in turn influence the behaviour of target children. The indirect effects seem to apply to large-scale physical stimulus changes (e.g. school size), to small-scale physical stimulus changes (e.g. location of a pupil in a classroom), and to temporal changes (e.g. the time at which stimulus changes are introduced). Of the studies reviewed, only one major research did not find the commonly reported changes in behaviour attributed to physical stimulus variables (Gill, 1977). Nevertheless, Gill reports that individual teachers within classrooms of each architectural type studied (conventional and open plan) varied so greatly in their behaviour, that physical environmental differences were overridden. Clearly the behaviour of adults and other persons exerts a powerful influence, even in contexts where manipulation or intervention is confined to physical stimulus changes.

(2) The presence of an *interacting* adult is a powerful setting event, as it combines elements of antecedent and consequent control of child behaviour. Introducing interacting adults into educational settings resulted in changes not only in those behaviours likely to have been previously reinforced in the presence of the adult, but also in behaviours specific to the setting into which the adult is introduced. Several studies suggest that behaviour change resulting

from the presence of an interacting adult may be more effective than that resulting from stimulus changes alone (O'Rourke, 1978; Baker *et al.*, 1982).

Concurrent modelling, where a competent performer provides a continuous model of desired target behaviour in educational contexts, appears to be another powerful form of antecedent control over child behaviour, deserving of closer research attention (Haskett & Lenfestey, 1974; Pluck, 1980). It would be interesting to explore the effects of providing, in a classroom context, concurrent modelling of written expression or working at mathematics problems.

(3) The one-to-one instructional setting where adult and child (competent performer and learner) interact over a joint task is of major importance educationally (McNaughton, 1980). Errors made by low-progress learners may set the occasion for *increased* external intervention ('help') by the competent learner. The competent performer's high rate of immediate external assistance may, in turn, restrict the learner's opportunity to learn independent problem solving and self-correction skills.

(4) Where instructional interactions are child initiated and free to occur over a wide range of times, in the presence of a wide variety of different stimulus events, as is the case in incidental teaching episodes (Hart & Risley, 1975, 1980), learning of academic and social skills takes place under 'loose' stimulus control. Learning under such conditions of 'loose' stimulus control is likely to enhance maintenance and generalisation of skills (Stokes & Baer, 1977). Wahler & Fox (1981) have argued that setting event influences have clear implications for the acquisition, maintenance and generalisation of skills, particularly in parent training contexts and recommend increased research attention to these issues.

(5) Extension of the term setting events to cover prior stimulus or stimulus-response events and their effects on subsequent behaviour highlights some further interesting research questions. For example, it is important for those involved in remedial or therapeutic interventions with teachers and parents to explore the behavioural outcomes of advance planning, organization and sequencing of educational activities in home and school contexts as illustrated by Krantz & Risley (1977). Another important question is the analysis and manipulation of prior setting events which may prevent people from benefitting from available contingencies of reinforcement, or from implementing and maintaining a programme of behaviour change.

(6) In contrast with behavioural intervention strategies based on manipulation of contingencies of reinforcement, setting event control over behaviour appears to be much more readily exploitable (McNaughton, 1980). Setting event intervention can be frequently implemented in advance of, or even concurrent with, the occurrence of target behaviour. Contingency management intervention must await the occurrence of target behaviour, which might more effectively have been prevented or minimized. When teachers or parents are required to

implement response-contingent behaviour change strategies, such strategies have to be implemented in competition with other demands or personal needs, e.g. housework or presenting new teaching material or relaxation.

Better environmental design and scheduling of activities for adults and children following any of the suggestions from studies reviewed in this chapter may reduce the frequency with which we resort to remedial contingency management programmes for adult-child interactions that have gone wrong.

References

Arndt, T. (1980) Effects of timing and feedback on output and legibility in story writing, *unpublished term paper*, University of Auckland, Department of Education.

Baker, M. (1980) The effect of adult conversation on amount of food eaten by a preschool child in a daycare setting, *unpublished term paper*, University of Auckland, Education Department.

Baker, M., Foley, M. F., Glynn, T. & McNaughton, S. (1982) The effect of adult proximity and serving style on eating and social behaviours of preschoolers, University of Auckland, Department of Education, in preparation.

Bandura, A. R., Grusec, J. E. & Menlove, F. L. (1967) Vicarious extinction of avoidance behaviour, *Journal of Personality and Social Psychology*, 5, 16–23.

Bandura, A., Ross, D. & Ross, A. (1963) Imitation of film-mediated aggressive models, *Journal of Abnormal and Social Psychology*, 66, pp. 3–11.

Barker, R. G. & Gump, P. V. (1964) *Big School, Small School* (Stanford University Press).

Bijou, S. W. & Baer, D. M. (1978) *Behavior Analysis of Child Development* (Prentice Hall, New Jersey).

Bruner, J. (1977) Early social interaction and language acquisition, in: Schaffer, H. R. (Ed.) *Studies in Mother-Infant Interaction* (New York, Academic Press).

Clark, R. M. (1982) The effects of changing seating arrangements on pupil and teacher behaviour in an open-plan unit, *M Soc Sci. thesis (Psychology)*, University of Waikato.

Fowler, S. A. & Baer, D. M. (1981) 'Do I have to be good all day?' The timing of delayed reinforcement as a factor in generalization, *Journal of Applied Behaviour Analysis*, 14, pp. 13–24.

Frewin, J. (1980) The effect of arrangement of materials and adult presence on number of children present at an activity area in a day care setting, *unpublished paper*, University of Auckland, Education Department.

Gill, W. M. (1977) Classroom architecture and classroom behaviours: a look at the change to open-plan schools in New Zealand, *New Zealand Journal of Educational Studies*, 12(1), pp. 3–16.

Gladstone, B. W. & Spencer, C. J. (1977) The effects of modelling on the contingent praise of mental retardation counsellors, *Journal of Applied Behavior Analysis*, 10(1), pp. 75–84.

Glendinning, S. (1978) Reinforcement of attentiveness and academic performance in an adjustment class, *unpublished MA thesis*, University of Auckland, Department of Education.

Glynn, T. (1982) Building an effective teaching environment, in: Wheldall, K. & Riding, R. (Eds) *Psychological Aspects of Learning and Teaching* (London, Croom Helm).

Glynn, T., Glynn, V. & Lawless, S. (1979) A behavioural approach to nutrition: how we influence what children eat, *Proceedings of the Nutritional Society of New Zealand*, 4, pp. 110–130.

Glynn, T., Vaigro, W. & Lawless, S. (1982) A self management strategy for increasing implementation of behavioural procedures by residential staff, *paper presented at the Fifth National Conference on Behaviour Modification*, Surfers Paradise, Queensland, May.

Hart, B. & Risley, T. R. (1975) Incidental teaching of language in the preschool, *Journal of Applied Behavior Analysis*, 8(4), pp. 411–420.

Hart, B. & Risley, T. R. (1980) *In vivo* language intervention: unanticipated general effects, *Journal of Applied Behavior Analysis*, 13(3), pp. 407–432.

Haskett, G. J. & Lenfestey, W. (1974) Reading-related behavior in an open classroom: effects of novelty and modelling on preschoolers, *Journal of Applied Behavior Analysis*, 7(2), pp. 223–241.

Henderson, M. (1976) Increasing appropriate classroom behaviour and academic performance by reinforcing correct work alone, *Psychology in Schools*, 12(2), pp. 195–200.

Kantor, J. R. (1970) An analysis of the experimental analysis of behavior, *Journal of the Experimental Analysis of Behavior*, 13, pp. 101–108.

Krantz, P. J. & Risley, T. R. (1977) Behavioral ecology in the classroom, in: O'Leary, K. D. (Ed.) *Classroom Management: the successful use of behavior modification*, 2nd ed (New York, Pergamon Press).

Lahey, B. B. (1971) Modification of the frequency of descriptive adjectives in the speech of Head Start children through modelling without reinforcement, *Journal of Applied Behavior Analysis*, 4(1), pp. 19–22.

McNaughton, S. S. (1980) Structuring settings for learning academic skills: applications to oral reading, *Behaviour Therapy in Australia, Proceedings of the Third Australian Conference on Behaviour Modification*, pp. 306–315, Melbourne, May.

McNaughton, S. (1981) Low progress readers and teacher instructional behaviour during oral reading: the risk of maintaining instructional dependence, *The Exceptional Child*, 28(3), pp. 167–176.

McNaughton, S. & Glynn, T. (1981) Delayed versus immediate attention to oral reading errors: effects on accuracy and self correction, *Educational Psychology*, 1(1), pp. 57–65.

Marholin, D. I. & Steinmann, W. M. (1977) Stimulus control in the classroom as a function of the behavior reinforced, *Journal of Applied Behavior Analysis*, 10(3), pp. 465–478.

Moore, D. (1980) Location as a causal factor in the unequal distribution of teacher questions: an experimental analysis, *Behaviour Therapy in Australia, Proceedings of the Third Australian Conference on Behaviour Modification*, pp. 316–324, Melbourne, May.

Moore, D. W. (1982) Variation in teacher question rate as a function of position in the classroom, *paper presented at the Fifth National Conference on Behaviour Modification*, Surfers Paradise, Queensland.

O'Rourke, M. (1978) Play equipment and adult participation: effects on children's behaviour, in: Glynn, T. & McNaughton, S. (Eds) *Behaviour Analysis in New Zealand*, pp. 36–57 (Department of Education, University of Auckland).

Pluck, M. (1980) The effect of modelling (response facilitation) by classroom teacher on children's recreational reading, *unpublished term paper*, University of Auckland, Education Department.

Quilitch, H. R., Christophersen, E. R. & Risley, T. R. (1977) The evaluation of children's play materials, *Journal of Applied Behavior Analysis*, 10(3), pp. 501–502.

Risley, T. R. (1977) The ecology of applied behavioural analysis, in: Rogers-Warren, A. & Rogers-Warren, S. F. (Eds) *Ecological Perspectives in Behavior Analysis* (Baltimore, University Park Press).

Risley, T. R. (1982) Behavioural design for residential programmes, *keynote address to Fifth National Conference on Behaviour Modification*, Surfers Paradise, Queensland.

Russell, M. B. & Bernal, M. E. (1977) Temporal and climatic variables in naturalistic observation, *Journal of Applied Behavior Analysis*, 10(3), pp. 399–405.

Simon, S. J., Ayllon, T. & Milan, M. A. (1982) Behavioural compensation: contrast-like effects in the classroom, *Behavior Modification* (in press).

Stokes, T. F. & Baer, D. M. (1977) An implicit technology of generalization, *Journal of Applied Behavior Analysis*, 10, pp. 349–368.

Wahler, R. G. & Fox, J. J. (1981) Setting events in applied behavior analysis: toward a conceptual and methodological expansion, *Journal of Applied Behavior Analysis*, 14, pp. 327–338.

Wahler, R. G. & Graves, M. G. (1982) Setting events in social networks: ally or enemy in child behavior therapy, *unpublished paper*, Child Behavior Institute, University of Tennessee.

Wheldall, K. (1981) Concluding comments: 'A before C' or the use of behaviour ecology in classroom management, in: Wheldall, K. (Ed.) *The Behaviourist in the Classroom. Aspects of Applied Behavioural Analysis in British Educational Contexts*, chapter 14, Educational Review Offset Publications. No. 2 (University of Brimingham).

Wheldall, K. (1982) A positive approach to classroom discipline, in: Wheldall, K. & Riding, R. (Eds) *Psychological Aspects of Learning and Teaching* (London, Croom Helm).

Wheldall, K., Morris, M., Vaughan, P. & Ng, Y. Y. (1981) Rows versus tables: an example of the use of behavioural ecology in two classes of eleven year old children, *Educational Psychology*, 1(2), pp. 171–184.

Wong, P. & McNaughton, S. (1980) The effects of prior provision of a context on the oral reading proficiency of a low progress reader, *New Zealand Journal of Education Studies*, 15(2), pp. 169–179.

Chapter 17

Motivation theory and the management of motivation to learn in school

Neil R. Hufton and Julian G. Elliott

Introduction

Where governments have introduced prescribed curricula and coupled these with some form of high-stakes accountability, as in England and Wales since 1988, the practical problem of motivating many students to learn in schools has moved centre-stage. It seems rather less certain that motivation theory has yet evolved fully to address this problem. Indeed, from this point of view, there are arguably a number of deficits in much current theory of motivation.

Perhaps the principal set of deficits arises from a failure to recognise that there may be an important distinction to be drawn between motivation in wider life and motivation to learn in school. Though we may see schooling as a preparation for life, we can overlook the ways in which much learning in school cannot be like learning from life. As a result, motivation theories which might be thought to apply to learning in and from wider life, may not be easily applicable to, or appropriate for, learning in school.

To give a foretaste of our concerns, we might cite in evidence Yair's (2000) and Seifert's and O'Keefe's (2001) claims, arising from extensive surveys of motivational projects, that to bring about high motivation, learning tasks set for students should consistently exhibit authenticity; foster student choice, agency and autonomy; and provide the opportunity to acquire higher-order skills. Most teachers would probably agree that where students can choose and direct their learning in relation to 'real life' tasks which involve the learner in some valued personal development, motivation tends to be high. What is much less certain is that such tasks could form anything like a regular 'diet', for all aspects of prescribed curricula, and within the cost limits constraining publicly funded schooling.

There are at least the following important differences between learning in school and in wider life:

- Learning in school is preparatory for, rather than motivated by, the opportunities and exigencies of life. In many state systems, schools are obliged to attempt to foster, impartially, in all students of prescribed ages, a pre-specified range of knowledge, skill and understanding. To the extent that the attempt is unsuccessful, not only the student, but also the school can be held to have failed.

  The 'curriculum' for learning in and from wider life is much more defined by an individual's opportunities for, interest in, and perceived advantage from learning. It may often be possible for individuals to avoid unattractive fields of learning. Unlike school learning, much of which may be aimed at very generalised, distant and imprecise goals, and where intermediate goals (such as passing a French test) can be perceived as artificial, learning in wider life is more likely to be perceived as having clear, real and credibly achievable intermediate and final goals.

- Schools and classes are learning groups of involuntary members who have been assembled as a group (a) predominantly for purpose of learning and (b) in order to minimise the costs to the state of providing for learning. But schools and classes are not simply aggregates of individuals. They are also social psychological arenas, within which individual differences are ascribed influential local labels. The motivational effects of how students see things, and interact with each other, are part of what has to be managed to motivate learning in school. Further, the process of learning in a learning group is an interactive social process over time. As teachers know only too well, the compliance, interest and engagement of the group in learning have to be continuously managed as a precursor to individuals' learning.

  Learning in wider life will very rarely involve involuntary group membership, and may often not involve formal group membership at all. Whilst it may often be social, involving casual or chosen informants and informal or formal instructors, it will rarely take place where either influential labelling, or the need to manage learners' compliance, impinge as motivational issues affecting the individual learner.

- Though schooling need not involve learning in prescribed sequences, it may often be uneconomic or unreliable to manage learning in any other way. As a result, learners may quite often find themselves being asked to engage with material which they have so far felt neither interest in, nor any need to learn.

It is hard to imagine learning in wider life which was not motivated by an individual's interest in, or need to learn, something specific.

- Given their 'case-load' of learners, managers of learning in schools can very rarely, perhaps never, either be sufficiently acquainted with, or give the necessary time to sustain support for, individual students' self-initiated movements in interest and engagement. Of course, teachers do give individuals help with learning, but more commonly in relation to 'set' topics – for which teachers are prepared – than to learners' personal interests.

In wider life, where learners want to learn from other people, they can seek out someone who can help with their specific learning interest or need. With such a person, it will commonly be possible for the learner to detail and clarify his or her current state of knowledge, skill or understanding sufficiently to maximise the likelihood of receiving focused help.

It is because of these differences that it is possible to find much currently accepted motivation theory highly informative and suggestive, but still be uncertain about how it applies.

Extrinsic or intrinsic motivation?

Consider one of the oldest distinctions – that between extrinsic and intrinsic motivation. The idea of extrinsic motivation seems relatively straightforward. Individuals are said to be extrinsically motivated when they engage in tasks in order to receive some kind of reward, or avoid some kind of punishment. For example, a student who completed reading a novel, in order to gain a badge from a teacher, would count as extrinsically motivated. However, we should note that the badge has to count as a 'reward' in the eyes of the student, for it to serve as an extrinsic motivator. Equally, for would-be motivators, to be confident that the badge will count as an extrinsic motivator, they must share some sufficient understanding with those to be motivated, of operative contextual norms and how they are socio-culturally mediated. Only then will the notions of 'reward' and 'punishment' be unproblematic.

That we cannot always know what count as 'rewards' and 'punishments', or that what has counted in the past will continue to do so, is well recognised. In schools, this may be particularly the case for 'rewards', where these have tended to be symbolic, rather than material. As Deci, Ryan and Koestner (1999) have stressed, much depends on the meaning attached to the reward. Thus, 'gold stars' that motivated 'X' at 6 years old may be construed as 'babyish' by 'X' at 8 years old. On the other hand, if 'X' first meets 'gold stars' at 10 years old, they may motivate.

Research interest has focused less on the effects of habituation to extrinsic rewards and more on what is called the 'overjustification hypothesis'. This asserts that where reliance is placed on extrinsic rewards, their withdrawal will tend to reduce motivation (Lepper & Greene, 1978). So, for example, where students have become accustomed to work hard to earn 'stars', placed on a classroom wall-chart for all to see, discontinuing that form of reward may reduce the motivation of those who were motivated by it. Further, in a meta-analytic review, Deci, Ryan and Koestner (1999) found that expected rewards could reduce intrinsic motivation, so that gaining the 'star' could become more important than mastering, or developing any depth of interest in, what was to be learnt. They also found that unexpected rewards, for example handing out chocolate bars to a class which had really worked hard on a project, only retained their motivational power as long as students did not become habituated to expecting such 'unexpected' rewards. Though rewards may have success in controlling behaviour, they may forestall the individual's capacity to self-motivate and self-regulate and thus have unintended negative long-term effects. As Covington and Palladino (1999) observe, '... if someone has to pay me for doing this, then it must not be worth doing for its own sake' (p.2).

Perhaps the least controversial definition of intrinsic motivation is as that motivation to engage in tasks for which there is no obvious external reward or punishment. In other words, intrinsic motivation is most easily defined as 'not-extrinsic' motivation. However, the notion becomes more problematic when attempts are made to give it some positive content. For example, Deci and Porac (1978) have argued that intrinsic motivation is a basic human need to achieve competence and self-determination, but it is possible to think of instances of intrinsic motivation where neither of these goals seems aimed at. On another account, individuals are held to be intrinsically motivated when they engage in a task purely for its own sake. On these accounts, students who read unprescribed novels with no bearing on their prescribed studies, could count as intrinsically motivated. However, it is extraordinarily difficult to forecast what goals completing the reading of a novel might fulfil for any individual. Reading a novel purely for sake of doing so might count as 'odd'. Of course, a young person might deservedly have a strong sense of accomplishment the first time he or she read a whole novel right through. For more experienced readers, a novel might be read as an alternative to boredom in a period of enforced idleness, or in order to be able to present oneself as a more educated or cultivated person in the future, or in order to understand unfamiliar situations or persons better, or as part of a self-therapy for some sense of under-development or inadequacy. There are no doubt many other possible goals. What they all have in common is the location of the act of completing the reading of, not just any, but some particular novel, in the life history, current situation and future anticipations of the reader.

As the discussion above implies, the distinction between extrinsic and intrinsic motivation is not quite as clear-cut as might at first seem. Extrinsic motivation depends upon a person's evaluating something as either a 'reward' or a 'punishment', in their larger meaning system. Being intrinsically motivated does not rule out envisaging the possibility of attaining a goal that one will count, in some sense, as a 'reward', or as avoiding 'punishment'.

From the point-of-view of the management of motivation, it seems that we learn that misplaced reliance on extrinsic motivators has the potential to be counter-productive. What we learn about intrinsic motivation is that it can lead to valuable and productive engagement with learning, but that it is so deeply embedded in individuals' life histories, current situations and future anticipations, that it may be very difficult to initiate and sustain by anyone other than the individuals themselves. The implication of this, for schools, is that teachers might experience great difficulty in finding ways to engage or increase students' intrinsic motivation to learn something.

Expectancy × value theory

Eccles and her colleagues (see: Eccles & Wigfield, 1995) have developed a model which, on the face of it, seems indifferent to the distinction between extrinsic and intrinsic motivation. Based on work by Atkinson (see: Atkinson, 1964), they proposed the 'expectancy × value' model. 'Expectancy', based on prior learning and experience, is an individual's realm of the practicable possibilities attainable by individual effort, together with the likelihood of advantage resulting from its expenditure. For example, in considering whether to learn a foreign language, you might take into account your past experience as a language learner, some estimate of the time it could take, whether you could give that time and how you envisaged using that language, once learnt. 'Value' is an attribute of anticipated goals. Eccles proposed four distinct types of value: attainment value (the importance of the task), intrinsic value (the interest of the task), utility value (the usefulness of the task), and cost (the need for personal investment in the task). On this model, the strength of any specific motivation is the outcome of an interactive weighing up between the in-principle possibility of doing something, a self-perception of personal competence to do that thing, the likelihood of actually succeeding in doing it, the investment of time, energy and resource, and the worthwhileness of the gains to be made if it is done. So if you wanted to learn German because you hoped to holiday independently in Germany, your motivation would relate to some estimate of how much German you needed to learn, of how quickly you expected to able to learn, of where and with whom you would use your German. Your 'motivational calculus' would, of course, be quite different if you wanted to read scholarly books about education in German! Eccles and her colleagues have found that both students' expectancies for success in the future, and their achievement values, are predictive of their choices, behaviours, and learning in academic settings (Eccles, 1983; Wigfield & Eccles, 1992; 2000).

Expectancy × value theory may be very helpful for exploring and understanding individuals' specific motivations. There is also the possibility of managing motivation by manipulating the value elements in the model. In some cases one can see how this might be done. For example, one might not be able to alter someone's sense of the 'importance' and 'utility' of learning French verbs, but one could try to increase motivation by making an easy (less 'costly') game (higher 'interest') of such learning. However, for the wider management of motivation to learn in school, as the above example implies, there is likely to be a problem with individuals' persistence in holding the values they attach to the 'importance' and 'utility' of specific goals. In wider life, goals are unlikely to be sought unless they are valued above some threshold of importance and utility. Also, in wider life, it may often be a matter of indifference whether achieving valued goals will bring extrinsic or intrinsic satisfactions. But, in the world of school, perceptions of the importance and utility of specific learning goals belong in the relatively unmanipulable realm of intrinsic motivation.

Self-efficacy, self-confidence and self-esteem

The concept of 'self-efficacy' is owed to Bandura (1986). Important further work, more specifically in the field of educational psychology, has been done by Schunk (see Schunk, 1991). For any individual, self-efficacy is domain-related. Individuals with high self-efficacy approach tasks, including new tasks, with the confidence that they know, or will be able to find, a way to succeed in them. For example, one might be quite confident in embarking on learning a new language, but very diffident about one's ability to learn to play the guitar. Individuals may vary in the range of domains across which they feel self-efficacious.

Low self-efficacy is frequently associated with poor self-confidence and poor self-esteem, and all of these with poor motivation and engagement with learning. It might then be thought that raising self-confidence and self-esteem could help raise self-efficacy and improve motivation, engagement and achievement. However, this may not follow. Relations between self-efficacy, self-confidence and self-esteem seem likely to be complex. Several studies (Keys, Harris & Fernandes, 1997; Stevenson & Stigler, 1992) have reported a tendency for U.S. and English youngsters to take a more roseate view of their abilities than actually warranted by their achievements. Conversely, our comparative studies (Elliott et al., 1999; 2001; Hufton et al., 2002b; 2003) found that Russian children performed at a higher level than their U.S. and English counterparts, but reported markedly lower self-perceptions of their ability.

We found that children's academic self-perceptions were closely related to how they thought their teachers saw them (Elliott et al., 1999, 2001). In the U.S. and England, 9- and 10-year olds thought that their teachers had rather higher opinions of them than was the case, whereas in Russia, teachers had higher opinions of the children than the children thought they did. These differences seemed likely to reflect differences in pedagogical practice. As Alexander (2000) has pointed out, U.S. and English teachers' concern to maximise children's sense of self-esteem can result in praise for mediocre and acceptance of poor work (see also, Damon, 1995). Russian teachers are far more likely to voice criticism of poor performance. One might anticipate that the more critical stance of their teachers and Russian youngsters' lower levels of academic self-esteem would reduce their motivation to learn. However, it did not appear that young Russians' engagement with, or enjoyment of, school, or their self-efficacy was in any way reduced.

From the point-of-view of managing motivation to learn in school, there seems yet more to understand in this field of motivation theory. Clearly, some young people very much need support for their self-confidence and self esteem – to be in a sustained climate of positive regard – but above some, as yet unidentified, threshold, general and unreflective support for individuals' self-confidence and self esteem may be counter-productive for their achievement and, indeed, foster their disrespect for those who too indiscriminately support them.

Attribution theory

In relation to achievement motivation, attribution theory is concerned with the reasons that students attribute for their attainment of specific academic outcomes. Thus, if students receive poor grades, they could attribute this to lack of effort, lack of ability, poor instruction, luck, or teachers' dislike of them. Weiner (1985) has presented a comprehensive model of human motivation, from an attributional perspective. On his model, learning (including mis-learning) from prior experience influences the kind of attribution an individual will normally tend to make. Such attributions can be classified as being more or less stable over time (stability); more to do with features of oneself, or of external circumstances (locus); and within, or not within, one's power to change (control).

For Weiner (1986), the extent of an individual's 'self-efficacy' depends on interactions between the stability, locus and controllability of their attributions.

Thus, where an individual makes 'external' attributions for success (e.g. task difficulty, or luck), motivation to persist is likely to be reduced (Weiner, 1979). By contrast, where a learner makes 'internal' attributions to such characteristics as high ability, or hard working, there is more likely to be increased motivation to succeed. Studies by Blatchford (1996), Lightbody et al. (1996) and Gipps and Tunstall (1998) have indicated that English children tend to attribute success in school to internal rather than external factors. But here, 'control' becomes important. How much effort they make is normally within individuals' control, but they may feel they can do nothing to alter what they perceive as a fixed quantum of 'innate' ability. Thus, a child who construed failure as the result of a lack of innate ability would be more likely to reduce future engagement in learning than one who construed failure as down to not working hard enough. In support of this, Stevenson and Stigler (1992) saw the emphasis upon effort, in Pacific Rim countries, as key for high motivation and educational performance. In the U.S., by contrast, children were thought more likely to attribute success to fixed ability. Without contradicting this latter point, more recent work by Steinberg (1996) seemed to reinforce the wider primacy of effort, in that those U.S. children who did emphasise effort also tended to achieve higher levels of performance than did those who stressed ability. In further reinforcement, Gipps (1996) and Reynolds and Farrell (1996) have argued that, where children from Western countries such as England and the U.S. are under-motivated, it may be because they attribute success to ability and not to how hard they work.

The message for the management of motivation to learn in school might then seem to be that we should discourage children (and, if necessary, their teachers) from thinking of ability as an innate characteristic and encourage them rather to think of capability as acquired through the expenditure of effort. However, whilst such a change in students' and teachers' thinking might well prove beneficial, there are reasons to doubt that it would, on its own, be sufficient to make great improvement in motivation to learn in school.

In our recent work in England, the U.S. and Russia, we found that, contrary to the research cited above, English and U.S. 10-year olds made strong attributions to effort, whereas Russian 15-year olds were finally more likely to attribute success to ability (Elliott et al., 1999; Hufton et al., 2002b). However, we do not seek so much to challenge earlier research, as, rather, to interpret it in context. Thus, though U.S. and English youngsters emphasised effort, their actual workrate was significantly lower than the Russian (Elliott et al., 1999). Quite reasonably, U.S. and English youngsters thought they were working hard if they were matching or exceeding the learning demand made of them in their schools and/or achieved by their schoolmates. But the learning demand made by English and, more so, U.S. schools was relatively modest, both quantitatively and qualitatively, when compared with the Russian. It seemed that, given the modest demand, more effort might well have made considerable difference to success in England and the U.S, whereas, in Russia, where the learning demand was higher, and where many youngsters could not have safely exceeded their current work-rate, 'a talent' for the subject was seen as finally influential.

As already indicated, it might well be advantageous if it became normative for students to attribute achievement to effort. However, a mere change of attribution may have little effect on achievement. What our experience of Russian schooling highlights is that there may also be a need for a change in the amount and kinds of effort put forth. Unlike in England and the U.S., where the key pedagogical relationship is taken to be between teaching and learning, education in Russia, as in many northern European countries, presupposes a 'didactic triangle' of teaching-studying-learning (see: Uljens, 1997; Kansanen et al., 2000). Young Russians do not expect to learn without studying and one of the reasons for their high average work-rate is that most of them expect to study a topic until they have achieved something near the best possible level of knowledge, skill or understanding, for them. What lies unnoticed in current attribution theory is that the notion of 'effort' is not only socio-culturally relative, but differently relative in different cultures. In England and the U.S., it seems predominantly relative to the need to compete successfully with others. In others, including Russia, it is much more relative to the learning demands of schooling.

In terms of the management of motivation to learn in school, it seems that, beyond seeking a change in their attributions, we may need to attempt to change students' thinking about the goals of study. We may also need to think about the ways in which our assessment regimes encourage a definition of effort as relative to others' achievements, rather than as a means for the achievement of valued learning.

Goal orientation theory

Goal orientation theory differentiates between two types of goal individuals may pursue when they engage in academic tasks: either 'mastery goals' (also referred to as 'ego goals', 'ability goals', and 'relative-ability goals'), or 'performance goals' (also referred to as 'learning goals' and 'task goals'). Students are said to pursue mastery goals when their prime concern is with improvement, personal learning and growth – mastering the task at hand – rather than comparisons with others; they are said to pursue performance goals when their prime concern is to demonstrate competence relative to others.

Within 'performance goals', researchers have further distinguished between 'performance-approach' and 'performance-avoid' goals (Elliot & Harackiewicz,

1996; Middleton & Midgley, 1997). A student who has a 'performance approach goal' would be concerned to appear more competent than others. He or she might put up their hand often to answer questions, or volunteer information, in class. A student who has a 'performance-avoid goal' would be concerned to avoid looking less competent – at worst, 'dumb' or 'stupid' – in comparison with others.

There is very large agreement that students with 'mastery goals', that is, those who, for whatever reasons, seek personal understanding of subject matter, will tend to do well in education (see: Ames & Archer, 1988; Anderman & Maehr, 1994), a phenomenon that has been observed in even very young children (Turner & Johnson, 2003). There has been much more debate about the role of 'performance goals'. Some of this debate no doubt arose because, until the mid-1990s, researchers did not distinguish between 'approach' and 'avoid' goals, so that mixed results emerged from research. Currently, encouraging students to outshine their peers is perceived as, at best, a problematic teaching strategy. Some recent research (see Elliot, McGregor & Gable, 1999) does suggest that, where students are encouraged to adopt 'approach' goals this may foster learning in some situations. However, where performance goals are emphasised, other students' defensive adoption of 'avoid' goals is likely to be detrimental for their motivation and achievement. Thus, in fostering performance goals, schools may risk both over-emphasising extrinsic motivation for successful students and reducing motivation amongst those not able to compete. Other negative effects, such as an increase in, and peer tolerance of, academic cheating, may be unwittingly fostered (see Anderman, Griesinger & Westerfield, 1998).

Covington (1998) has written particularly forcefully about the 'double bind' that an over-reliance on performance goals may generate for students. In highly competitive educational systems, as in the U.S. and, in different ways, England, schools effectively define success in terms of outperforming others. According to Covington, for U.S. students the most important motivation to learn is to demonstrate one's ability to others and to avoid failure. Further, U.S. teenage culture prides effortless success and is often dismissive of those who are seen to be trying too hard (see also: Damon, 1995; Cheney, 1993). Consequently, many U.S. children must find a balance between being seen by their peers to try too hard – with the risk of looking incompetent if they fail – and not trying hard enough – risking the disapproval of teachers and parents. In attempting to preserve '… a sense of dignity in school' students engage in a series of 'ruses and artful dodges' that 'reflect a primordial struggle for self-protection so elemental that many students are prepared to sacrifice even good grades for the sake of appearances' (Covington, 1998, p. 100). In English schools, as we found in our research (Hufton et al., 2002b), students also have to strike a balance. They have to find some way of making the effort to achieve, without appearing to infringe work-rate norms amongst their schoolmates. Our evidence would suggest that quite large numbers of students err in the direction of complying with work-rate norms, at the expense of making the effort for success. Also, amongst those who are not the highest achievers, but who do seek success, many may conceal their effort, engage in judicious displays of disaffection and adopt strategies of modesty and self-deprecation to retain the affiliation of their peers.

Of the theories we have reviewed so far, goal-orientation is probably the most perceptively alive to the experience of learning in school. Covington (1992, 1998, 1999) in particular reminds us of the very powerful effect that peer processes and norms may have upon individual motivation (for an interesting link between goal theory and avoidance behaviours, see Turner et al., 2002). He explains why the peer generation of motivationally beneficial norms may be ruled out by educational policies that place students under heavy competitive pressure. Thus the messages from goal orientation theory for the management of motivation to learn in school might be that schools have to find ways of managing peer effects on motivation and that this may only be possible if peer competition is not fostered, at least beyond some maximum. Unfortunately, although pointing up the need, and specifying a possible pre-condition, goal-orientation theory does not deal with how peer groups might be managed so as to increase individuals' motivation

Situational interest

It is now accepted that mastery and performance goals are not mutually exclusive and recent commentaries (e.g. Pintrich, 2003; Harackiewicz et al., 2002) have suggested that there may be a variety of complex interactions between these, which, in turn, are likely to be influenced by contextual factors. Though deploying a different terminology, Hidi and Harackiewicz (2000) have recently made a parallel move in the possible development of motivation theory for schooling. They have suggested that it might be possible to secure a sufficient motivation to bring about valuable learning in school, without having to attempt to evoke intrinsic motivation, but equally without relying solely, or crudely, on extrinsic motivators. They go further and suggest that if a student were to sustain a sufficient motivation to reach some learning threshold, then intrinsic motivation might become engaged.

Hidi and Harackiewicz (2000) distinguish 'individual interest' from 'situational interest'. As discussed above, the problem with individual interest is that, though it can generate powerful motivation, little is known about how to inculcate or nurture it. Hidi and Harackiewicz (2000) feel that in rightly vaunting the significance of individual interest, intrinsic motivation and mastery goals for motivation to learn, motivation theorists may have become reluctant 'to recognise the potential additional benefits of external interventions, situational interest and performance goals' (p. 167). They fear that this could risk depriving educators of some important means of motivating children who do not 'have interests that are easily adaptable to school settings and academic learning' (p. 157). Situational interest can be elicited by conditions and/or stimuli in the environment that focus attention and generate affect. What they propose is that schools should look for ways to maximise the effects of 'situational interest'.

Hidi and Harackiewicz (2000) cite examples from research where situational interest was influential. Schank (1979) suggested that situational interest could cause learners to focus attention, draw more relevant and better contexted inferences and integrate new information with prior knowledge. More recently, Benton et al. (1995), Schraw et al. (1995) and Wade, Buxton and Kelly (1999) looked at text-stimulated situational interest and found that ease of comprehension, novelty, surprise, vividness, intensity, character identification and reading for a purpose increased interest and produced superior comprehension and recall. Cordova and Lepper (1996) found that where instructional materials and processes evoked meaningful contexts and required more useful or personally relevant learning, situational interest could be engaged. Isaac et al. (1999) found that working with or alongside others may also increase situational interest. Sansone et al. (1999) found that students could independently generate and use strategies, including 'games', to make boring tasks more interesting.

Hidi's and Harackiewicz's point, in citing these findings, is not that any is particularly impressive on its own, but that the maintenance of situational interest may involve the combined influence of a number of perhaps small but practically manipulable factors. The key problem, for trying to motivate through situational interest, is that, though interest may well be 'caught', it may not be 'held'. What it would help for educators to know is how to compose 'constellations', or 'blends' of situational motivators which promote a sufficient engagement of individual interest to bring about, in turn, an adequate measure of intrinsic motivation. Hidi & Harackiewicz would not rule out the possibility of including some tangible rewards in such constellations. They argue that motivation research which focused on 'relatively short-term and relatively simple activities' (p. 159) may have failed to throw light on the combined role of sets, or sequences of rewards, either in stimulating initial situational interest, or in aptly invigorating long-term, complex and effortful engagements, where 'dependence on external feedback continues throughout development' (p. 168). They conclude that 'a combination of carefully administered external rewards and situationally interesting activities may be one of the most realistic approaches to educational intervention' (p. 159).

Conclusion

From our experience of Russian schools, we would agree that a focus on 'situational interest' may well be important for the management of motivation to learn in schools. We have little doubt that Russian teachers, though they value individual interest, centrally rely on stimulating situational interest, through the effective teaching of pedagogically-researched topics and activities, the variety and pace of their lessons and their encouragement of co-operative learning in and out of class. We also have good evidence that a high proportion of students, initially 'caught' by situational interest, are then 'held' by the development of a sufficient individual interest to bring about sustained worthwhile learning, and increasingly, as they mature, the pursuit of mastery goals. We think it very likely that approaches to teaching that aimed to stimulate and sustain situational interest could increase the likelihood of similar outcomes in the English context.

However, we think Hidi and Harackiewicz may not take sufficient account of classroom-, school- and system-level preconditions for the sustained promotion of situational interest. In Russia, we found a nexus of supportive interactions between: readiness for schooling; continuity of compulsory education in the same school; continuity of contact with the same teachers; lesson structure; students' perceptions of the role of study in learning; the design of text-books to support study; families' understanding of and support for the school and teachers; and freedom to use assessment pedagogically. (For a more detailed discussion, see: Hufton & Elliott, 2000; Hufton et al., 2003). No aspect of the schooling process, at least at the time of our research in the late 1990s, undermined or cancelled any other.

By contrast, within the current English system we suspect that frequent, external assessment and the 'streaming' of students in schools, by demotivating some students to the point where teachers cannot foster sustained situational interest, conflict with the aspiration to provide all with an 'entitlement' curriculum. In saying that, we are not attacking streaming, or current assessment arrangements, as such. Our point is to note that 'a nexus of supportive interactions' between its manifold elements does not mark the English schooling system. We agree with Alexander (2000) that schools are essentially embedded in and expressive of the culture of the societies that provide them. We would consequently actively caution against any direct imitation of the Russian approach. We would, however, advocate serious investigation of and reflection upon the ways in which aspects of the schooling process – whether generated at the level of the system, the school, or the classroom – are co-operatively aligned to maximise motivation to learn. No doubt, teachers might give serious address to stimulating situational interest at the level of the classroom and the school, but this may not produce major gains, if their efforts are effectively contradicted at the level of the system.

References

Alexander, R. J. (2000) *Culture and Pedagogy: international comparisons in primary education.* Oxford: Blackwell.

Ames, C. & Archer, J. (1988) Achievement goals in the classroom: students' learning strategies and motivation processes. *Journal of Educational Psychology, 80,* 260–267.

Anderman, E. M., Griesinger, T. & Westerfield, G. (1998) Motivation and cheating during early adolescence. *Journal of Educational Psychology, 90,* 84–93.

Anderman, E. M. & Maehr, M. L. (1994) Motivation and schooling in the middle grades. *Review of Educational Research, 64,* 287–309.

Atkinson, J. W. (1964) *An Introduction to Motivation.* Princeton, NJ: Van Nostrand.

Bandura, A. (1986) *Social Foundations of Thought and Action: a social cognitive theory.* Englewood Cliffs, NJ: Prentice Hall.

Benton, S. L., Corkill, A. J., Sharp, J., Downey, R. & Kramtsova. I. (1995) Knowledge, interest and academic writing. *Journal of Educational Psychology, 87,* 66–79.

Blatchford, P. (1996) Pupils' views on school work and school from 7–16 years. *Research Papers in Education, 11(3),* 263–288.

Cheney, L. (1993) Hard work, once as American as apple pie. *Wall Street Journal.* 5th December.

Cordova, D. I. & Lepper, M. R. (1996) Intrinsic motivation and the process of learning: beneficial effects of contextualization, personalization and choice, *Journal of Educational Psychology, 88,* 715–730.

Covington, M. V. (1992) *Making the Grade: a self-worth perspective on motivation and school reform.* Cambridge: Cambridge University Press.

Covington, M. V. (1998) *The Will to Learn: a guide for motivating young people.* Cambridge: Cambridge University Press.

Covington, M. V. & Palladino, K. (1999) An approach/avoidance interpretation of the relation between intrinsic and extrinsic motivation. Paper presented at the American Educational Research Association Conference, Montreal.

Damon, W. (1995) *Greater Expectations.* New York: Free Press.

Deci, E. L., Ryan, R. M. & Koestner, R. (1999) A meta-analytic review of experiments examining the effects of extrinsic rewards on intrinsic motivation. *Psychological Bulletin, 125(6),* 627–668.

Deci, E. L. & Porac, J. (1978) Cognitive evaluation theory and the study of human motivation. In M. L. Lepper & D. Greene (Eds), *The Hidden Costs of*

Reward: new perspectives on the psychology of human motivation, 149–176. Hillsdale, NJ: Erlbaum.

Eccles, J. S. (1983) Expectancies, values and academic behaviors. In J. T. Spence (Ed.) *Achievement and Achievement Motives*, 5–146. San Francisco, CA: Freeman.

Eccles, J. S. & Wigfield, A. (1995) In the mind of the actor: the structure of adolescents' achievement task values and expectancy-related beliefs. *Personality and Social Psychology Bulletin*, 21, 215–225.

Elliot, A. & Harackiewicz, J. (1996) Approach and avoidance achievement goals and intrinsic motivation: a mediational analysis. *Journal of Personality and Social Psychology*, 70, 968–980.

Elliot, A., Mcgregor, H. A. & Gable, S. (1999) Achievement goals, study strategies, and exam performance: a mediational analysis. *Journal of Educational Psychology*, 91, 549–563.

Elliott, J. G., Hufton, N. R., Hildreth, A. & Illushin, L. (1999) Factors influencing educational motivation: a study of attitudes, expectations and behaviour of children in Sunderland, Kentucky and St Petersburg. *British Educational Research Journal*, 25, 75–94.

Elliott, J. G., Hufton, N. R. & Illushin, L. (2000) International comparisons – what really matters? In Diane Shorrocks-Taylor & Edgar W. Jenkins (Eds) *Learning from Others*, 79–114. Dordrecht: Kluwer.

Elliott, J. G., Hufton, N. R., Illushin, L. & Lauchlan, F. (2001) Motivation in the junior years: international perspectives on children's attitudes, expectations and behaviour and their relationship to educational achievement. *Oxford Review of Education*, 27(1), 36–68.

Gipps, C. (1996) The paradox of the Pacific Rim learner, *Times Educational Supplement*, 20th December, 13.

Gipps, C. & Tunstall, P. (1998) Effort, ability and the teacher: young children's explanations for success and failure, *Oxford Review of Education*, 24(2), 149–165.

Harackiewicz, J. M., Barron, K. E., Pintrich, P. R., Elliot, A. J. & Thrash, T. (2002) Revision of achievement goal theory: necessary and illuminating. *Journal of Educational Psychology*, 94, 638–645.

Hidi, S. & Harackiewicz, J. M. (2000) Motivating the academically unmotivated: a critical issue for the 21st century. *Review of Educational Research*, 70(2), 151–179.

Hufton, N. & Elliott, J. G. (2000) Motivation to learn: the pedagogical nexus in the Russian school: some implications for transnational research and policy borrowing. *Educational Studies*, 26, 115–136.

Hufton, N., Elliott, J. G. & Illushin, L. (2002) Educational motivation and engagement: qualitative accounts from three countries. *British Educational Research Journal*, 28(2), 265–290.

Hufton, N. R., Elliott, J. G. & Illushin, L. (2003) Teachers' beliefs about student motivation: similarities and differences across cultures. *Comparative Education, 39(3)*, 367–402.

Isaac, J., Sansone, C. & Smith, J. L., (1999) Other people as a source of interest in an activity, *Journal of Experimental Social Psychology, 35*, 239–265.

Kansanen, P., Tirri, K, Meri, M., Krokfors, L., Husu, J. & Jyrhämä, R. (2000) *Teachers' Pedagogical Thinking: theoretical landscapes, practical challenges*. New York: Peter Lang.

Keys, W., Harris, S. & Fernandes, C. (1997a) *Third International Mathematics and Science Study, First National Report, Part 2*. Slough: N.F.E.R..

Keys, W., Harris, S. & Fernandes, C. (1997b) *Third International Mathematics and Science Study, Second National Report, Part 2*. Slough: N.F.E.R..

Lepper, M. R. & Greene, D. (1978) Overjustification research and beyond: toward a means–ends analysis of intrinsic and extrinsic motivation. In M. R. Lepper & D. Greene (Eds) *The Hidden Costs of Reward: new perspectives on the psychology of human motivation*, 109–148. Hillsdale, NJ: Erlbaum.

Lightbody, P., Siann, G., Stocks, R. & Walsh, D. (1996) Motivation and attribution at secondary school: the role of gender. *Educational Studies, 22(1)*, 13–25.

Middleton, M. J. & Midgley, C. (1997) Avoiding the demonstration of lack of ability: an underexplored aspect of goal theory. *Journal of Educational Psychology, 89*, 710–718.

Pintrich, P. R. (2003) Multiple goals and multiple pathways in the development of motivation and self-regulated learning. In L. Smith, C. Rogers & P. Tomlinson, *Development and Motivation: joint perspectives*. Monograph Series II: Psychological Aspects of Education. *British Journal of Educational Psychology, 2*, 137–153. Leicester: British Psychological Society.

Reynolds, D. & Farrell, S. (1996) *Worlds Apart? A Review of International Surveys of Educational Achievement Involving England*. London: H.M.S.O.

Sansone, C., Wiebe, D. J. & Morgan, C. (1999) Self-regulating interest: the moderating role of hardiness and conscientiousness, *Journal of Personality, 67*, 701–733.

Schank, R. C. (1979) Interestingness: controlling inferences, *Artificial Intelligence, 12*, 273–297.

Schraw, G., Bruning, R. & Svoboda, C. (1995) The effect of reader purpose on interest and recall. *Journal of Reading Behavior, 27*, 1–17.

Schunk, D. H. (1991) Self efficacy and academic motivation. *Educational Psychologist, 26*, 207–231.

Seifert, T. L. & O'Keefe, B. A. (2001) The relationship of work avoidance and learning goals to perceived competence, externality and meaning. *British Journal of Educational Psychology, 71*, 81–92.

Steinberg, L. (1996) *Beyond the Classroom: why school reform has failed and what parents need to do*. New York: Touchstone Books.

Stevenson, H. W. & Stigler, J. W. (1992) *The Learning Gap: why our schools are failing and what we can learn from Japanese and Chinese education*. New York: Summit Books.

Turner, J. C., Midgley, C., Meyer, D. K., Gheen, M., Anderman, E. M., Kang, Y. & Patrick, H. (2002) The classroom environment and students' reports of avoidance strategies in mathematics: a multimethod study. *Journal of Educational Psychology*, *94*, 88–106.

Turner, L. A. & Johnson, B. (2003) A model of mastery motivation for at-risk preschoolers. *Journal of Educational Psychology*, *95*, 495–505.

Uljens, Michael (1997) *School Didactics and Learning*. Hove: Psychology Press/Taylor & Francis.

Wade, S. E., Buxton, W. M. & Kelly, M. (1999) Using think-alouds to examine reader-text interest. *Reading Research Quarterly*, *34*, 194–216.

Weiner, B. (1979) A theory of motivation for some classroom experiences. *Journal of Educational Psychology*, *71*, 3–25.

Weiner, B. (1985) An attributional theory of achievement motivation and emotion. *Psychological Review*, *92*, 548–573.

Weiner, B. (1986) *An attributional theory of motivation and emotion*. New York: Springer-Verlag.

Wigfield, A. & Eccles, J. S. (1992) The development of achievement task values: a theoretical analysis. *Developmental Review*, *12*, 265–310.

Wigfield, A. & Eccles, J. S. (2000) Expectancy-value theory of achievement motivation. *Contemporary Educational Psychology*, *25*, 68–81.

Yair, G. (2000) Reforming motivation: how the structure of instruction affects students' learning experiences. *British Educational Research Journal*, *26*, 191–210.

Chapter 18

Addressing emotional and behavioural issues in schools through self management training: theory and practice

Kedar Nath Dwivedi

Behaviour problems and causal mechanisms

Since the early 1960s, the Mental Health Programme of the World Health Organisation has been actively engaged in improving the diagnosis and classification of mental disorders. Thus, ICD-10 (WHO 1992) contains a group of disorders described as 'Behavioural and emotional disorders with onset usually occurring in childhood and adolescence' and includes 'Conduct Disorders', 'Hyperkinetic Disorders', 'Disorders of Social Functioning' and so on. 'Severe problem behaviour' in schools is most often associated with 'conduct disorders' and characterised by a repetitive and persistent pattern of antisocial, aggressive or defiant conduct such as disobedience, provocative behaviour, severe temper tantrums, excessive fighting or bullying, cruelty, destructiveness, stealing, lying, truancy and fire setting. 5.3 per cent of children were found to have conduct disorder in a recent survey (Meltzer et al 2000). These problems are not only common, but are also persistent, difficult to treat, expensive for the society and have poor prognosis (Kazdin 1993, Robins 1991).

Conduct disorders are generated and maintained by a large number of factors in a variety of ecologically nested systems. Important social factors include involvement with deviant peers, drug abuse and psychosocial adversity such as overcrowding, institutional care and so on. Family factors include a family history of criminal behaviour, violence at home, use of physical methods of punishment, child abuse, coercive parenting, ineffective parental monitoring and supervision, providing inconsistent consequences for rule violations, failing to provide reinforcement for prosocial behaviour, family disorganisation, attachment difficulties, marital discord, and so on. School factors include being a 'failing' school, with discipline problems, attainment difficulties, and lack of educational resources. Individual factors include difficult temperament, early separation experience, Attention Deficit Hyperactivity Disorder, *hostile attribution* bias (perceiving hostile intention in others' ambiguous actions), poor social skills, poor learning of prosocial behaviour from experience, academic underachievement and learning difficulties.

The multiplicity of causative factors has also prompted a number of theories that explain the causative mechanisms. For example, the *sociological theory* of 'Anomie' highlights the illegitimate means used by members of a socially disadvantaged delinquent subculture to achieve material goals valued by mainstream culture (Cloward and Ohlin 1960). *Systems theories* emphasise the role of characteristics of various systems (for example, family system, broader social network and social systems) in the causation and maintenance of behaviour problems, for example, confusing and unclear rules, roles, routines and communication in a family or a school. *Social learning* theories examine the role of modelling and reinforcements. Thus, behaviour problems may arise owing to imitation of others' (for example, parents, siblings, peers, teachers, media characters) behaviours. Many children learn to continue their antisocial behaviour as they are positively reinforced by their peer group. Parents or teachers can also reinforce (often negatively) such behaviours by confronting or punishing the child briefly. However, when the child escalates the antisocial behaviour, the parent or teacher may withdraw his/her confrontation or punishment and the child learns that the escalation of antisocial behaviour leads to parental or teacher's withdrawal.

Similarly there are *cognitive theories*. In social situations where the intentions of others are ambiguous, children with conduct disorder tend to exhibit aggressive behaviour. According to *Social Information Processing Theory*, this is intended to be retaliatory because they attribute hostile intentions to others in such situations (Crick and Dodge 1994). According to *Social Skills Deficit Theory* children with conduct disorder lack the skills to generate alternative solutions to social problems and to implement such solutions (Spivack and Shure 1982). *Psychodynamic theories* have highlighted the role of impoverished superego functioning (due to overindulgent, punitive or negligent parenting) and of disrupted attachments. *Biological theories* have explored the role of genetics in several biological functions associated with conduct disorders. For example, autonomic under-arousal can lead to impairment in one's capacity for responding to positive reinforcement that often follows prosocial behaviour or for avoiding punishment associated with antisocial behaviour. Deficits in verbal reasoning and executive functioning are associated with self regulation difficulties (Moffit 1993, Shapiro and Hynd 1995).

Several aspects of prosocial behaviours and conduct disorders, including some of the preventive and promotive initiatives in schools, are already outlined by Dwivedi and Sankar (2004).

Self regulation and emotional competence

Children, in the course of their development, assume responsibility for their own behaviour. Thus, there is an emergence of the capacity for self regulation (Schaffer 1996). Self regulation or self control, in order to refrain from antisocial impulses, is associated with the development of guilt, shame, empathy, conscience and emotion regulation or emotional competence (Buchanan and Hudson 2000, Dwivedi 1993a, Rutter 1980, Walley 1993). One of the important aspects of emotional maturation is its differentiation. Thus, out of the two basic emotional states of contentment and distress a huge variety of specific emotions emerge, such as joy, pride, delight, love, anger, jealousy, guilt, and so on. A study in Oxford, Amsterdam and a remote village in Eastern Nepal revealed a similar developmental pattern of emotional understanding in children (Harris et al 1987).

Similarly children go through several stages before they are capable of having a 'theory of mind', that is, understand things from other people's perspective (Happe 1994). These stages include the following:

- *Joint attention* (to look where another is looking);
- *Inferring goal from gaze* (i.e. understanding that intention can be deduced from behaviour, e.g. gaze);
- *Mentally labelling objects* (first evidence of metarepresentation);
- *Talking about mental states* (e.g. 'You know what? Mummy thought I was asleep but I was just pretending!');
- *Understanding that seeing leads to knowing* (i.e. an awareness of the unique and personal nature of knowledge derived from perception);
- *Understanding the mental–physical distinction* (i.e. distinguishing mental entities from physical ones, e.g. Jane has a biscuit, Harry is thinking about a biscuit, who can eat their biscuit?);
- *Understanding true belief* (e.g. John believes his dog is in his bedroom, Rob believes the dog is in the kitchen, where will John/Rob look for the dog?);
- *Understanding false belief* includes understanding that people will act on their beliefs even if these conflict with reality (if John believes the dog is in the bedroom he will look there even if the dog is in fact in the garden);

- *Understanding the appearance–reality distinction* (when shown an ambiguous object such as a stone egg, children with a mental age of three or over can normally say what it looks like and what it is);
- *Deception* emerges in normal children at around four years of age. By five years most children show deliberate manipulation of others' intentional states and comprehend the nature of deception as deliberately manipulating another's knowledge by giving them a false belief.

Another aspect of emotional maturation involves the development of an increasing capacity to tolerate emotions. In order to facilitate the development of tolerance, parents allow their infants to experience emotions but intervene to protect the child from being overwhelmed by excessively intense or prolonged emotions. Such interventions have a dual function. On the one hand, the child is protected from being traumatised by the overwhelmingly unbearable and shattering emotional experiences, and on the other hand, this enables the child to learn to use by him/herself some soothing, comforting or distracting strategies. This helps the development of an increasing capacity to tolerate emotions through self regulation of emotion. As the babies grow, they can identify with their care givers and can initiate self soothing or comforting interventions themselves, as soon as their emotions begin to exceed their capacity to tolerate. And a good enough mothering person enables the child to exercise such measures for self regulation of their emotional states.

In the beginning, all of emotional expression or its communication is through somatic or massive bodily responses. However, with maturation, motor control, cognitive development and learning, one begins to use various symbolic gestures (such as for initiating comforting, expressing affection, separation, loss, anger and so on) and words. Such a development is heavily influenced by the caregivers helping the child acquire various verbal and non-verbal communication skills and to identify and articulate their feelings and needs. An integral part of good parenting is the great pleasure that the caregivers take in the slightest difference in baby's vocalisations and keep encouraging the growing child to recognise and put their feelings into words rather than just act these out.

Yet another aspect of the development of emotional competence is utilisation. The growing self-awareness enables the child to begin to treat their emotions as signals to themselves so that the emotional energy can be utilised for problem solving, planning and implementing constructive strategies. As the children mature they also learn how to get in touch with their almost hidden feelings and how to explore an apparent complexity of feelings. *Emotions play a central role not only in organising and integrating cognition but also in a variety of mental functions, such as motivation, information processing, memory, behaviour and so on. They appreciate the role of these feelings in a whole range of mental and physical activities and begin to learn to utilise this important channel of influence.*

Emotion dysregulation and causal mechanisms

A whole range of factors can have an influence on the development of emotional competence, for example, the extent of cognitive and motor development, genetic and biological potential, training/parenting and cultural context, and so on. Just as the ability to become dry and clean, (that is urinary and faecal continence) and to walk and talk not only depends upon one's potential but also on the training one receives, for example, toilet training and training in walking and talking, similarly the development of emotional competence is also dependent on the quality of the training that the child receives (Dwivedi 2004).

Sometimes, we meet children who are, as if, emotionally illiterate, who do not recognise more than a few feelings, for example boredom, anger etc. This may be due to poor training. In a study by Denham et al (2002) children's deficits in emotional knowledge assessed at age 3 and 4 predicted subsequent years' aggression. Preschool disruptive behaviour can be associated with a number of later psychopathology including delinquency, school failure and substance abuse. Aggressive children are more likely to have impulsive and hostile attributions of others in social interactions with peers.

Similarly the development of emotional tolerance is dependent on the quality of training. Some parents, because of their own emotional problems, for example jealousy, may have aversion to self soothing behaviours and are unable to convey the feeling to the child that it is all right to assume some possession or control of their automatically controlled parts of themselves. Thus, the affect regulatory functions become inaccessible to such individuals. This can give rise to psycho-somatic illnesses, drug abuse, and total dependence upon partners for sexual arousal, and so on (Krystal 1988).

In order to master the distressing feelings of *separation anxiety (when separated from caregivers)*, there is a normal developmental line of a sequence of certain interactive play proceeding from 'peek a boo' to object tossing, being chased, hide and seek, bye-bye, and so on (Kleeman 1967, 1973). These developmental games promote the growth of confidence and trust in the child that, despite separation, the primary object is still there with whom reunion will occur. Children who have not been enabled in this way to master distressing separation anxiety tend to exhibit disorders of conduct, running away, violence, joy riding and so on in order to engage others in a disguised play. They continue to create situations whereby they might be chased and held.

In times of distress there is a heightened need for soothing contact with the attachment figure. If the stress is too severe or prolonged or the attachment figures are rejecting, or unavailable, then this attachment and proximity-seeking behaviour can become rather indiscriminate and disorganised, appearing even hostile and violent. Even in adults, the desire to reach out and touch someone can become so intense that it can become disguised, confused, hurtful and even fatal. In children too, behind a lot of aggressive and violent behaviours may be a disguised need to make contact with someone (Mawson 1987).

The parents need to keep a close enough eye on a mobile toddler who begins to explore the environment by climbing, running, poking and so on. Because these objects in the environment can also attack, cut, hurt, bite, shout, burn, electrocute, they can be experienced as very frightening by the child. If the parents are neglectful or hurtful themselves, the child may go on engaging in risky behaviours to elicit their concern and may have no other option than to employ the primitive aggressive defences of the jungle, to cope (Willock 1990).

If the caregiver is unable to protect the child from overwhelming emotions, a state of psychic trauma can develop. Trauma means shattering of psychic or ego functions, a state of disorganisation, timeless horror, an unbearable hell, an utter helplessness. The child will grow up dreading such dangerous feelings (for example, of abandonment, rejection etc.). *At the slightest experience of such a feeling, there is a panic of being flooded by it. Therefore, they use various strategies to defend against being overwhelmed by such a feeling.* These strategies include anger, induction of altered states of consciousness either psychologically (through dissociation), physically (e.g. activity, distracting rituals, over-breathing) or chemically.

When a child is faced with intolerable assault, hurt, torture or abuse and is helpless in avoiding or escaping from it, the mental mechanism of dissociation can be induced as a protective device. Such dissociation may manifest as: becoming part of the wall, floating near the ceiling and looking at what is happening, taking imaginary walks, becoming the long hand of the clock, holding breath to stop crying, and other means of inducing self hypnotic trance, dissociation and anaesthesia. This may also lead to identification with the aggressor. When the child grows up and has violent outbursts, these are triggered by the subtle reminders of the hurtful past experience. The process of identification can be so subtle that the child even sounds, talks and appears like the aggressor, as if bewitched or possessed, and may not remember the incident or the feeling of hurt but acts it out as a substitute for memory. The traumatic experiences from the preverbal periods can perhaps be communicated only through action. Thus, within a violent individual is a screaming child feeling hurt.

Why should this be included in an overcrowded agenda of schools?

Emotions have a direct impact on teaching and learning and also on pupil and teacher behaviours which in turn have an impact on the learning environment

(Salzberger-Wittenberg et al 1963). In fact, teaching and learning are rather like being on a roller-coaster of emotions and emotions can range from one extreme to the other. Many teachers and pupils can enjoy it so much that they cannot wait to turn up at school, while some others may feel bored, stressed out or even disgusted. It is the emotional atmosphere that helps learning to sink in deeper. Paying attention to emotional regulation in pupils and teachers has to be seen at the heart of whatever schools are trying to achieve.

Gains from programmes to improve emotional competence can be far-reaching in a variety of areas including educational achievement, health and welfare, prevention of classroom bullying, substance abuse, teenage pregnancy and AIDS, promotion of teacher–pupil relationship, academic performance, school attendance, parent–child relationship, self confidence and self esteem (World Health Organisation 1997). Child mental health is everyone's business, and there is a need for various prevention initiatives to address concerns such as disaffection from school, disruptive, antisocial, bullying and violent behaviours, teenage pregnancy, post-traumatic stress, deliberate self harm, depression, anxiety disorder, eating disorder, school refusal and effect of bereavement, separation, divorce and parental mental disorder and so on (Royal College of Psychiatrists, 2002, Dwivedi 2000a, Dwivedi and Harper 2004, Dwivedi and Varma 1997a, 1997b). Programmes facilitating the development of emotional competence can feed the roots of all such initiatives.

Schools' contributions to the development of emotional competence

Schools have a critical role to play in creating emotionally competent children (Mental Health Foundation, 1999). Policies or programmes for emotional development and well-being are often lacking in schools and emotional development is treated as unnecessary, as an extra, or as something that relates exclusively to children in difficulty (Orbach 1998). Such efforts need to take the form of a whole-school or school ecology approach which may be extra-curricular (such as a mental health promotion initiative), integrated (as part of school curriculum such as PSHE) or infused (as part of academic subjects, such as emotional communication skill as part of language class). The possibilities are countless. Below are some examples.

1. Enhancing parenting skills

Enhancing parenting skills is one of the most important contributory factors in the emotional development of children (Dwivedi 1997a, 2002). Schools can also contribute to the enhancement of parenting skills in their community. For example, in Northamptonshire, in England, one of the schools in collaboration with the then Adult Education Department organised a study day on enhancing parenting skills for the parents of the children of that school. This generated enough momentum for the parents to organise themselves in the form of an association to run regular parenting enhancement events themselves.

2. Professional development of teachers

Schools need to ensure that these issues are also given due priority in the professional development of teachers. For example, in Northamptonshire several schools have participated in a Life Skills Education programme for psychosocial development (Coley and Dwivedi 2004). We started running this programme with the help of funding from the local Health Authority. The programme uses the World Health Organisation (1997) framework and includes areas such as decision-making, problem-solving, creative thinking, critical thinking, communication, interpersonal relationships, self awareness, empathy and coping with emotions and stressors. *The teachers are then able to use the learning in preparing their lessons, responses and behaviours in the school setting. The lessons can be spread over a flexible period of time.* The aim is to help teachers create a learning environment in which experiential and active learning on the above aspects can take place.

3. Helping teachers and other staff with their emotion regulation and behaviour

Teaching has become a very demanding occupation and teachers are often provoked into emotional outbursts that may lead to a harmful effect all round. A regular reflective forum, usually with the help of a competent person from outside, can assist in the process of learning from such experiences (Salzberger-Wittenberg et al 1963).

4. Supporting the students' development of emotional competence and behaviour

The help in this regard can take any form. It can be indirect through routine lessons or lessons designed specially for this purpose. For example, PATHS (Promoting Alternative Thinking Strategies) is a school-based intervention designed to improve children's ability to discuss and understand emotions

(Greenberg et al 1995). Stories, play and enactment can have an enormous impact as well. Direct help can be organised from individuals within the educational setting, from outside agencies or in a collaborative partnership. Such help can be offered individually or in a group setting.

School staff familiar with the development of various aspects of emotional competence and their impact on pupil behaviour can see innumerable opportunities for helping pupils in these matters (Dwivedi 1996). Without such help, many individuals will continue to have violent and destructive outbursts, often because they are unable to make contact with the feelings of hurt in the screaming child within in order to offer any comfort. If they could be helped, the need for dissociation or the identification with the aggressor could diminish.

When emotions become intense they not only break into conscious awareness but their excessive intensity can even trigger a chain of disastrous consequences such as violent or destructive acting out, alcohol and drug abuse and psychosomatic illness. One may feel that such an emotional state is going to be everlasting and may not appreciate the fact that all emotions are only transient. With the help of mindfulness, if one does not fight, indulge or actively avoid, they will just run their course (Dwivedi 2000b).

It may not be too difficult to include such meditative practices in the school by finding a competent helper (Fontana and Slack 2002). Training in mindfulness can harness the emotional energy for creative and constructive purposes, similar to taming a tiger. Some meditative practices, for example from Buddhist teachings, can thus be of enormous help in improving emotion regulation in a variety of ways. By learning to expand one's consciousness, one can become aware of even subtler (otherwise preconscious) emotions and, thus, better manage various mental operations (such as information processing, learning, memory, decision making, creativity, motivation and so on). By early detection of emotional processes, one can promptly initiate coping strategies or interventions before the emotions grow to produce a crippling effect. The inexperienced practitioners are also advised not to dabble in potentially very powerful techniques.

5. Therapeutic use of stories and play

We are all aware of the powerful therapeutic impact of stories, enactment and play on human development, insight, emotion and behaviour (Dwivedi 1997b, 2000c). Stories help in evoking imagination, thereby better engagement. As they also stir-up feelings, they enable learning points to sink in deeper. Stories provide space for reconstructing one's own meanings and allow play-space, so that people can change at their own pace and as and when they are ready. They help to bypass resistance as stories can create a psychological distance and provide an indirect non-confrontational approach to exploration and problem solving. Stories can mirror emotional problems and can point to their roots and solutions. Stories can provide multiple and meta-perspectives, alternative possibilities, new attitudes and belief systems.

There is a huge quantity and good quality of material already available in the literature, so that one can choose what is relevant and use it in one's own creative manner (e.g. Bettelheim 1978, Kale 1982, Barker 1985, Gersie and King 1990, Gardner 1993, Roberts 1994, Dwivedi 1997b). For example, the book *Therapeutic Use of Stories* (Dwivedi 1997b) contains chapters relating to Anger Management (Dwivedi 1997c) and use of stories in school settings (Compton 1997). Day (2002) has described how an innovative project used drama and 'Circle Time' techniques (Mosley, 1996) to broaden children's emotional language and boost their mental health.

6. Mobilising the power of group processes

Although most of school business is conducted in group settings, there is still an enormous potential for mobilising and utilising group processes in schools (Coppock and Dwivedi 1993). Effective group work can enhance self esteem, pro-social skills, emotion regulation, self control, and ability for reality testing. It may help young people learn, at least to some extent, how to give of themselves to others, master narcissistic impulses and rage, delay gratification, cultivate creativity and inculcate the sense of interdependence.

In group work with children and adolescents, a great deal of effort needs to be put into planning, organising, assessing, motivating, reflecting on group work and liaising with others. Groups can be 'open', 'slow open' or 'closed'. 'Open' groups allow the members to join in or leave according to their needs. 'Slow open' groups aim to minimise the disruptive impact of such changes. In 'closed' groups, all participants start together and end the group together. Psycho-educational and homogeneous groups that have a sequential agenda tend to be closed, such as groups for children with encopresis, sexual abuse, and bereavement and so on. Experiential heterogeneous groups can be open or slow open.

In group work, there is a need for a balance between structuring and spontaneity. Group work with children and adolescents is like pottery where you put one hand inside and the other outside. Without the hand inside, the pot is very likely to break. Without the hand outside it will turn ugly. Similarly, in group work there is a need on the one hand for emotional nurturance and support and, on the other, for discipline and boundary-setting. A group full of disturbed children can very easily get into fights, become destructive, defiant, chaotic and unmanageable. Therefore generating group rules with the help of the entire group and meaning business in sticking to these rules are essential aspects of group work (Dwivedi 1993b, 1997d).

Many therapeutic games and exercises (such as group stories, socio-drama, activities and play) that may be difficult to use in an individual or family therapy setting become easy in a group setting. Just as individual therapy or family therapy can make use of any of a variety of theoretical frameworks available, for example, psycho-dynamic, behavioural or social learning, cognitive, systemic and so on, similarly group therapy can also make use of any of these perspectives.

In group work, it is useful to create an atmosphere that enables the psychodynamic phenomena of positive mirroring and merging to emerge. It is through mirroring that a baby feels delighted in the delight of the parent who is delighted in the delight of the baby. Similarly the group and its members can be enabled to be delighted in the delight of each other. As a baby has limited abilities, it is unable to handle the world adequately but can do so through the parents, who appear to become omnipotent and almighty for the baby. A sense of belonging or merging with such an omnipotent being makes one feel equally omnipotent oneself. Similarly the sense of belonging to a group that begins to achieve higher and higher goals fills its members with a sense of confidence and achievement through this process of merging, as the essence of group work is losing and finding oneself.

Cognitive therapy approaches are also extremely useful in group work with children and adolescents, for example, for enhancing emotional management skills such as dealing with jealousy, anxiety, anger, misery and so on. Better behaviour, achievement and popularity have been reported by teachers in targeted children who received training in social skills (Rotheram et al 1982). A significant enhancement of prosocial behaviours and reduction in problem behaviours (both at home and at school) has been found after training through the Interpersonal Cognitive Problem-Solving Programme (Spivack and Shure 1982). Group work using cognitive approaches can be of immense value in anger management training (Feindler and Ecton 1986, Dwivedi 1997c, 1997d, Dwivedi and Gupta 2000). Systemic perspectives can be helpful in exploring interactions between a variety of systems that the children belong to, and the nature of boundaries around various relevant systems and subsystems. Activities, tasks and other interventions can thus be designed to mend defective boundaries which may either be eroded or be too rigid.

Enlisting co-operation of many disturbed young people to participate in group therapy is not easy. The work that has to go into clarifying the purpose and processes of group work cannot be overemphasised, so that group work is not seen as stigmatising or coercive but rather as valuing and enhancing of many aspects of themselves. We ran a group for violent young people in a school on cognitive behaviour therapy lines and called it a 'Keeping Cool' group. This helped in obtaining a great deal of their support for an anger management programme to reduce aggressive behaviour (Dwivedi and Gupta, 2000).

However, it is important to keep in mind not only the potential for the unleashing of the healing power of the group but also of its destructive power. This is why staff engaged in group work must undergo experiential training (such as the Midland Course in Group Work with Children and Adolescents run annually over six days in Northampton). Conducting group work is rather like swimming that one cannot learn just by reading a swimming manual in water.

7. Creating space for reflection

In Sanskrit, there are two words: *Sukha and Dukha. Sukha* means Happiness and *Dukha* means Misery or Suffering. If we look at their epistemology, *Kha* means space, *Su* means good and *Du* means bad. Therefore, *Sukha* is good space and *Dukha* is bad space. Here space is in the sense of clearance between the hub and the axle of a wheel. Therefore, if we can create a space of awareness and reflection around our experiences, processes, and interactions, this will lead to happiness, otherwise they lead to misery. In a classroom situation, if the teacher is too busy getting on with academic work and is unable to create space of awareness and reflection around the incidents in the class, children will miss out on opportunities for learning from these incidents and experiences.

References

Barker, P. (1985) *Using Metaphors in Psychotherapy*. New York: Brunner/Mazel.

Bettelheim, B. (1978) *The Uses of Enchantment*. London: Penguin Books.

Buchanan, A. and Hudson, B. (Eds) (2000) *Promoting Children's Emotional Well-being*. Oxford: Oxford University Press.

Cloward, R. and Ohlin, L. (1960) *Delinquency and Opportunity*. Glencoe, IL: Free Press.

Coley, J. and Dwivedi, K. N. (2004 in press) Life Skills Education through schools. In: Dwivedi, K. N. and Harper, P. B. (Eds) *Promoting Emotional Well Being of Children and Adolescents and Preventing their Mental Ill Health*. London: Jessica Kingsley Publishers.

Compton, C. (1997) Stories used therapeutically with children in educational settings. In: Dwivedi, K. N. (Ed.) *Therapeutic Use of Stories*. London: Routledge.

Coppock, C. and Dwivedi, K. N. (1993) Group work in schools. In: Dwivedi, K. N. (Ed.) *Group Work with Children and Adolescents*. London: Jessica Kingsley Publishers.

Crick, N. and Dodge, K. (1994) A review and reformulation of social information processing mechanism in children's social adjustment. *Psychological Bulletin*, 115, 74–101.

Day, P. (2002) Classroom drama: Acting for emotional literacy. *Young Minds Magazine*, 61, 22–23.

Denham, S. A., Caverly, S., Schmidt, M., Blair, K., Demulder, E., Caal, S., Hamada, H., and Mason, T. (2002) Preschool understanding of emotions: Contributions to classroom anger and aggression. *Journal of Child Psychology and Psychiatry*, 43(7), 901–916.

Dwivedi, K. N. (1993a) Emotional development. In: Dwivedi, K. N. (Ed.) *Group Work with Children and Adolescents*. London: Jessica Kingsley Publishers.

Dwivedi, K. N. (Ed.) (1993b) *Group Work with Children and Adolescents*. London: Jessica Kingsley Publishers.

Dwivedi, K. N. (1996) Facilitating the development of emotional management skills in childhood: A programme for effective self regulation of affect. In: Trent, D. R. and Reed, C. A. (Eds) *Promotion of Mental Health*, 6. Aldershot: Ashgate.

Dwivedi, K. N. (Ed.) (1997a) *Enhancing Parenting Skills*. Chichester: John Wiley.

Dwivedi, K. N. (Ed.) (1997b) *Therapeutic Use of Stories*. London: Routledge.

Dwivedi, K. N. (1997c) Management of anger and some Eastern stories. In: Dwivedi, K. N. (Ed.) *Therapeutic Use of Stories*. London: Routledge.

Dwivedi, K. N. (1997d) Group work with violent children and adolescents. In: Varma, V. P. (Ed.) *Violence in Children and Adolescents*. London: Jessica Kingsley Publishers.

Dwivedi, K. N. (Ed.) (2000a) *Post Traumatic Stress Disorder in Children and Adolescents*. London: Whurr.

Dwivedi, K. N. (2000b) Mindfulness in mental health. Transcultural Mental Health On-Line. http://www.Priory.com/psych/mindfulness.htm.

Dwivedi, K. N. (2000c) Therapeutic powers of narratives and stories, *Context*, 47, 11–12.

Dwivedi, K. N. (2002) Culture and personality. In: Dwivedi, K. N. (Ed.) *Meeting the Needs of Ethnic Minority Children*. London: Jessica Kingsley Publishers.

Dwivedi, K. N. (2004 in press) Emotion regulation and mental health. In: Dwivedi, K. N. and Harper, P. B. (Eds) *Promoting Emotional Well Being of Children and Adolescents and Preventing their Mental Ill Health*. London: Jessica Kingsley Publishers.

Dwivedi, K. N. and Gupta, A. (2000) Keeping cool: Anger management through group work. *Support for Learning*, 15(2), 76–81.

Dwivedi, K. N. and Harper, P. B. (Eds) (2004 in press) *Promoting Emotional Well Being of Children and Adolescents and Preventing their Mental Ill Health*. London: Jessica Kingsley Publishers.

Dwivedi, K. N. and Sankar, S. (2004 in press) Prevention of conduct disorder. In: Dwivedi, K. N. and Harper, P. B. (Eds) *Promoting Emotional Well Being of Children and Adolescents and Preventing their Mental Ill Health*. London: Jessica Kingsley Publishers.

Dwivedi, K. N. and Varma, V. P. (Eds) (1997a) *Depression in Children and Adolescents*. London: Whurr.

Dwivedi, K. N. & Varma, V. P. (Eds) (1997b) *A Handbook of Childhood Anxiety Management*. Aldershot: Arena Publishers.

Feindler, E. L. and Ecton, R. B. (1986) Implementing group anger control treatment for agencies and institutions. In: *Adolescent Anger Control: Cognitive-Behavioural Techniques*, pp 54–85. New York: Pergamon Press.

Fontana, D. and Slack, I. (2002) *Teaching Meditation to Children*. London: Thorsons.

Gardner, R. A. (1993) *Storytelling in Psychotherapy with Children*. Northvale, New Jersey: Jason Aronson.

Gersie, A. and King, N. (1990) *Storymaking in Education and Therapy*. London: Jessica Kingsley Publishers.

Greenberg, M. T., Kusche, C. A., Cook, E. T. and Quamma, J. P. (1995) Promoting emotional competence in school-aged children: The effects of the PATHS curriculum. *Development and Psychopathology*, 7, 117–136.

Happe, F. G. E. (1994) An advanced test of theory of mind: Understanding of story characters, thoughts and feelings by able autistic, mentally handicapped and normal children and adults. *Journal of Autism and Developmental Disorders*, 24, 1–24.

Harris, P., Olthof, T., Terwogt, M. M. and Hardman, C. E. (1987) Children's knowledge of the situations that provoke emotion. *International Journal of Behavioural Development*, 10(3), 319–334.

Kale, M. R. (1982) *Pancatantra of Vishnusharman*. Delhi: Motilal Banarasi Das.

Kazdin, A. E. (1993) Treatment of conduct disorder: progress and directions in psychotherapy research. *Development and Psychopathology*, 5, 277–310.

Kleeman, J. A. (1967) The Peek-a-boo Game. Part I: Its origins, meanings and related phenomena in the first year. *Psycho-analytic Study of the Child*, 22, 239–273.

Kleeman, J. A. (1973) The Peek-a-boo Game. Part II: Its evolution and associated behaviours especially bye-bye and shame expression during the second year. *Journal of American Academy of Child Psychiatrists*, 12, 1–23.

Krystal, H. (1988) *Integration and Self Healing*. Hillsdale, New Jersey: The Analytic Press.

Mawson, A. R. (1987) *Transient Criminality: A model of stress induced crime*. New York: Praeger.

Meltzer, H., Gatward, R., Goodman, R. et al (2000) *Development and Wellbeing of Children and Adolescents in Great Britain*. London: Stationery Office.

Mental Health Foundation (1999) *The Big Picture: Promoting children and young people's mental health*. London: The Mental Health Foundation.

Moffit, T. (1993) The neuropsychology of conduct disorder, *Development and Psychopathology*, 5, 135–151.

Mosley, J. (1996) *Quality Circle Time*. Cambridge: LDA.

Orbach, S. (1998) Emotional literacy. *Young Minds Magazine*, 33, 12–13.

Roberts, J. (1994) *Tales and Transformations*. New York: Norton.

Robins, L. N. (1991) Conduct disorder. *Journal of Child Psychology and Psychiatry*, 32, 193–212.

Rotheram, M. J., Armstrong, M. and Boorraem, C. (1982) Assertiveness training in fourth and fifth grade children. *American Journal of Community Psychology*, 101, 567–582.

Royal College of Psychiatrists (2002) *Prevention in Psychiatry*. CR 104. London: Royal College of Psychiatrists.

Rutter, M. (1980) Emotional development. In: Rutter, M. (Ed.) *Scientific Foundations of Developmental Psychiatry*. London: William Heinemann Medical Books Limited.

Salzberger-Wittenberg, I., Henry, G. and Osborne, E. (1963) *The Emotional Experience of Learning and Teaching*. London: Routledge & Kegan Paul.

Schaffer, H. R. (1996) *Social Development*. Oxford: Blackwell.

Shapiro, S. and Hynd, G. (1995) The psychobiological basis for conduct disorder. *School Psychology Review*, 22, 386–402.

Spivack, G. and Shure, M. (1982) The cognition of social adjustment: Interpersonal cognitive problem-solving thinking. In: Lahey, B. and Kazdin, A. (Eds) *Advances in Clinical Child Psychology*, 5, 323–372. New York: Plenum.

Walley, M. (1993) Empathy and prosocial development. In: Dwivedi, K. N. (Ed.) *Group Work with Children and Adolescents*. London: Jessica Kingsley Publishers.

Willock, B. (1990) From acting out to interactive play. *International Journal of Psychoanalysis*, 71 321–324.

World Health Organisation (1992) The *ICD-10 Classification of Mental and Behavioural Disorders*. Geneva: WHO.

World Health Organisation (1997) *Life Skills Education for Children and Adolescents in Schools*. WHO/MNH/PSF/93.7A.Rev.2. Geneva: WHO.

Chapter 19

Why bully?

Ken Rigby

Introduction

Broadly we can distinguish between three kinds of explanations sometimes advanced for the things we do. Since time immemorial people have given credit or discredit to gods or demons that have come, often unbidden, into their lives and got them to do creditable or discreditable things. Others have rejected such supernatural explanations and viewed their actions as a consequence of the kind of biological organism they are or (through evolution) have become. Still others have seen their behaviour as a response to the environment, physical, social and cultural, in which they live and the ways in which the environment has operated upon them to condition them to act the way they do.

These views or perspectives are not necessarily mutually exclusive. A person may see no contradiction between being religious, recognising biological and evolutionary influences on behaviour and attributing actions to previous learning and the demands of specific situations. Or for that matter taking an existential position and asserting that to bully or not to bully is a matter of free will. Yet the differences in perspectives do excite controversy.

Supernature

The belief that beings with supernatural powers can and do influence human behaviour is to be found in the literature and folklore of every culture. In Western countries the notion that supernatural forces operate in people's lives derives largely from traditional Christianity. In the Old Testament God and the Devil are seen to be in competition for human souls, inspiring and corrupting by turns. The Ancient Greeks saw gods and goddesses at work everywhere; the Romans made a point of propitiating the more powerful ones. The view that people can be cursed or bewitched is less evident in contemporary society than, say, in the 17th century when the witches of Salem in North America were seen as 'possessed' and appropriately despatched. But the belief that the Devil can order people to do evil things is still not without its believers. At the trial of Peter Sutcliffe, the Yorkshire Ripper, who was found to have murdered 13 women in a year-long reign of terror in the north of England during 1980, the accused testified that he had heard voices that told him that he must seek out and kill prostitutes who deserved to die.

To some this perspective provides a satisfying explanation for bullying conceived as evil. This view becomes more plausible when we reflect upon the nature of some malicious forms of bullying whereby an individual may continue to derive intense and seemingly incomprehensible satisfaction from the spectacle of another person being hurt without cause. To others this explanation for bullying can appear as mere superstition or even a cop-out: 'The Devil made me do it.'

Nature

Bullying may be understood as an inevitable part of the struggle that is inseparable from existence.

To what extent, we may ask, can we understand bullying in the light of evolutionary theory?

From an evolutionary perspective 'social dominance' holds centre stage. All creatures are programmed, as it were, to seek to acquire the necessary resources to survive. Because resources are limited, creatures are forced to compete with each other, as Darwin (1859) argued they must. From this perspective, bullying may be seen as one means by which more powerful creatures get what they need. Not, one should emphasise, the only means, but the one systematically employed by those we call bullies.

We cannot dispute that 'dominance' is the primary goal that the bully seeks. But we may question whether energy invested by Bully A to dominate Victim B is always, or even typically, the means by which the bully gains access to 'necessary' resources. If we look now, mundanely, at what the schoolyard bully gets out of the bullying it may turn out to be such things as lunch money, a favour, admiration from a gallery of watchful fans; maybe enhanced security as he/she rises in the school pecking order – hardly necessary resources. We might nevertheless choose to see in this behaviour vestiges of a strategy employed by those primitive ancestors who ensured the bully's survival.

Patricia Hawley (1999) in her interesting paper 'The Ontogenesis of Social Dominance: A Strategy-Based Evolutionary Perspective' argues that the kind of behaviour that we might call bullying (she calls it 'coercive behaviour') can be understood from an evolutionary perspective. She sees it as a largely unsuccessful adaptation to the conditions of modern life. There are, she suggests, other more effective ways of achieving dominance, that is, by cooperative and pro-social means. And this, she maintains, is what more complex and highly evolved organisms, such as humans, eventually (mostly) come to realise. As children grow older and more mature they begin to see that pro-social means rather than anti-social means are in fact more likely to produce the coveted goal of social dominance among their peers. Thus the aggressive, pushy, bossy, bullying toddler develops in time into the pro-social schoolboy or schoolgirl and subsequently into the even more socially cooperative adolescent.

Central to the evolutionary perspective is that it is in our nature to strive to be socially dominant, bullying being one primitive expression of that need. Put simply: if our ancestors had not been dominant we wouldn't be here. We come from a long line of successful dominators. It is in our blood, our guts, our brains, our genes. If this is so, we would expect to see in every human interaction evidence of a desire or intention to become elevated relative to someone else. If we watch people even in friendly encounters, say at a party, we will doubtless often find some evidence to support this view. Notice how people introduce themselves, how they drop clues to their importance, the gossip they engage in. But if we are to sustain this theoretical position to apply to all interactions, we will need considerable recourse to paradox. We may argue – if we are sufficiently perverse – that humility is always a mask or a ploy to support a subtle form of self-aggrandisement: Christ washing his disciple's feet being a cynical means of establishing dominance through a dramatic show of self-abasement. Wedded to the position that human beings invariably seek to establish dominance in their social sphere – one way or another – we stretch credulity to its breaking point.

It's in the genes

Behavioural geneticists are constantly reminding us that a high proportion of the characteristics that guide our behaviour is inherited. They draw largely on studies showing a greater similarity in the characteristics of identical twins – who have the same genetic make-up – compared with non-identical twins. There is strong evidence that identical twins are much more similar in personality than non-identical twins even when members of the 'identical' pair have been brought up in different home environments and the non-identical twins have experienced the same home environment. Such studies have led to the claim that approximately half the variation in personality characteristics between individuals is genetic in origin. Some of what is heritable may be described as 'direct' – for example, a nervous disposition. Some can be viewed as 'indirect', as when a person is treated in a particular way because he or she is known to have a nervous disposition.

We should ask whether the kind of qualities associated with bullying others or being bullied could, to some degree, be inherited. The answer appears to be 'yes', although only one study to my knowledge has made use of twin studies to examine whether the tendency to bully is to any degree heritable. In a study by O'Connor *et al.* (1980) mothers of identical twins (n = 54) and mothers of fraternal twins (n = 33) rated their children (mean age eight years) on their tendency to bully others, using a six-item measure of good reliability. The identical twin correlation (.72) was significantly higher than the fraternal twin correlation (.42). This difference was interpreted as indicating substantial genetic influence upon the tendency to bully others.

We can add to the specific finding of O'Connor *et al.* results from numerous studies that have shown that aggressiveness is to a substantial extent inherited. Besides this, there are studies that have shown that characteristics less obviously associated with being a bully or being a victim are also significantly heritable. These include introversion–extraversion, anxiety, stability, social competence, self-esteem, cooperativeness, impulsiveness and empathy. No-one is claiming that this is all there is to it. It would be foolish, for instance, to argue that social competence and self-esteem are unaffected by experiences with others. But what is inherited, it is argued, can have a major influence on how one treats, and is treated by, others.

The environment

In common usage the environment is that by which we are constantly surrounded or the conditions under which we live. It is everything except us. But how can 'everything' be broken down so that we can gauge environmental effects of this kind or that kind on anything? On bullying for instance. Admittedly somewhat arbitrarily we will exclude the sun, the moon and the stars (to the chagrin of astrologers) and identify these aspects:

- the home environment
- the school and the peer group
- the neighbourhood.

The three aspects of the environment listed above have figured individually or jointly in an increasing number of studies of bullying and have become the foci of a number of different perspectives that will now be described and examined.

The home environment

The home is generally recognised as making the deepest and most enduring contribution to the way children think, feel and behave both in their homes and outside their homes. Commonly the word 'nurture' is used to describe this function. 'Nurture' has a positive ring about it. It has the same root as 'nourishment'. It is what helps us grow, physically and psychologically. Those who provide the nurturing are usually biological parents, mother and father, although 'caregivers' may include single parents, foster-parents, siblings, grandparents, uncles and aunts and, indeed, anybody else who may play a part in the rearing of children. Close contact tends to be more continuous and intimate with babies and very young children and for that reason is often thought to have greater impact and significance in the nurturing process. The question naturally occurs: does the way the child is nurtured really have an enduring effect on its subsequent behaviour, more especially in the way it relates to members of the family – and also to non-family members in the bigger, wider world which is entered, as a rule, when the child goes to school? Can the way the child is nurtured reduce its chances of becoming a bully, a victim or a bully/victim in later life?

The answer to the question about whether a child can be reared so as to be less likely to become a bully or a victim in the family is probably 'yes'. We know that some parents monitor their children's behaviour in the home quite carefully and seek to promote cooperation between their charges. Generally they do it simply by administering appropriate rewards and punishments, and, with persistence, manage to influence, if not entirely control, the way their children behave towards others – *in the home*.

The question of whether a child can be so reared as to reduce his or her chances of being involved in bully/victim problems outside the home is a contentious one, despite the fact that over the last ten years or so a great deal of research has been undertaken to find out. We must be careful in considering what it tells us and what it doesn't tell us.

This I think is solid and indisputable. There is indeed a link between what parents and families do in the home and the behaviour of their children at school with their peers, and that includes being a bully and/or being a victim in encounters with other children. Notice that we are talking here about a statistical relationship. There are definable ways of parenting and definable ways in which families function (more later about how these may be defined) which are significantly related to the involvement of children in bully/victim problems at school.

This is an important discovery. But it does not necessarily mean what we would like it to mean. We have discovered an association; we have not yet established to everyone's satisfaction the nature and direction of a causal relationship. We will see later that the meaning of the association is in dispute. But for the moment let us accentuate the positive. If such a relationship as I am claiming did not exist, then it would be time to quit worrying about how parenting might affect a child's peer relations. An association does not prove a cause, but it does make the discovery of a causal relationship possible. And, moreover, it does give us a clue as to which children are 'at risk' of bullying or being bullied.

The association between parenting and children's interpersonal behaviour

It is useful to examine in a little detail what the research literature tells us about the relationship between parenting and children's behaviour at school. In an examination of 83 studies conducted between 1939 and 1998 on the relationship between parenting and the behaviour of children, Schneider (2000) has provided overwhelming evidence that the two are related.

The studies show that aggressive parenting and aggressive behaviour on the part of children with their peers are related. Here are some examples:

> Sears *et al.* (1953) found that the more severely boys (aged 3–5 years) were punished for aggression by their mothers, the more aggressive they were at preschool.

> Eron *et al.* (1963) reported that children aged eight years who were exposed to high-intensity punishments behaved more aggressively with their peers.

> Larzelere (1986) found that among children between 3 and 17 years of age, aggression towards peers at school was more common among children who (according to their mothers) had been spanked more frequently, especially if 'reasoning' was not incorporated into the disciplinary action.

> Pettit, Dodge and Brown (1988) reported that children aged five years with mothers who used restrictive discipline were more aggressive with their peers.

> Pettit *et al.* (1991) reported that children aged three to five years were more aggressive with their peers if their mother engaged in coercive and intrusive interactions with them.

> Strassberg *et al.* (1992) found that the more parents used aggressive strategies to deal with conflicts, the more aggressively the child behaved with peers.

Although aggressive behaviour by parents is the main variable that has been reported as correlating with children's behaviour with peers, permissive parental behaviour also appears to be related.

> Sears (1961) found that among 12-year-old children, high levels of permissiveness were correlated with anti-social aggression.

> Levy (1966) reported that among children with ages ranging from 4–16 years, mothers rated as 'overindulgent' tended to have more aggressive children.

Some studies have focused on children with high levels of interpersonal competence and popularity with peers. Such children are rarely bullied and tend to be non-aggressive. Here again there are numerous studies that report parenting correlates, for example:

> Austin and Lindauer (1990) reported that better-liked children (aged nine to ten years) were less controlling, less directive and less intrusive.

> Hart, Ladd and Burleston (1990) noted that for two groups of students (aged five to seven and nine to ten years) more popular children had mothers who were disinclined to use power-assertive disciplinary methods.

> Pettit *et al.* (1991) reported that higher levels of social competence among five-year-olds were found when their mothers were more responsive in their interactions with their child.

> Henggeler *et al.* (1991) reported that among eight-year-olds, those children who were most popular with their peers had fathers who were most receptive to solutions to problems that they (the children) proposed.

> Strassberg *et al.* (1992) reported that among five-year-olds, the more popular children had parents who use least aggression in resolving conflicts.

Although the studies summarised above do not deal with bullying per se, they do deal with qualities in children that are related to bullying, e.g. being aggressive or having low social competence and being unpopular with peers. Moreover, the bulk of these studies employed measures of parenting behaviour from one source, e.g. direct observation or interviews with parents, and measures of peer relating from another source, e.g. self-reports from children or peer reports from other children who knew them. This enabled the researchers to avoid one of the weaknesses in conducting research of this kind, that is reliance on information obtained from one source only. Admittedly, the correlations between the measures of parenting and children's behaviour are generally not high (often between .2 and .3) but the fact that there are so many studies producing consistently significant results in relation to children in widely different age groups should convince us that the association is a reliable one. Although there is plenty of room for other, non-parenting influences to play a part, we do have, I think, a prima facie case for believing that what parents do and how children behave outside the home with other people are connected in some way.

You may have noticed that research emphases have been on what mothers do. To some extent this is understandable. Generally they form closer relations with children and play a more nurturing role. Sadly, fathers are generally neglected in these studies – and it matters. A further area of concern is the common practice of not discriminating between the effects of parenting and family functioning on boys and girls. This also matters, as there are grounds for supposing that boys and girls may react differently at times to the same treatment from their families (Rigby, 1993, 1994). Finally, there is a dearth of studies that are longitudinal in nature. Such studies are exceptional, but there is one. It deserves a paragraph.

In 1997 the first prospective study of early family experiences of boys who were both aggressive and bullied during their middle childhood years was undertaken by Schwartz *et al.* (1997) in the USA. Mothers of 198 5-year-old boys were interviewed to ascertain how the children had been treated by their parents. Some 3 years later a group of 16 children was identified as 'aggressive victims'. The researchers were able to show that these children differed from others in having experienced at an early age more punitive, hostile and abusive family treatment than other groups. Unlike studies in which measures of parenting and children's behaviour are undertaken at about the same time, a prospective study of this kind enables one to infer that the aggressive behaviour of children is not a cause of the parenting and quite possibly an effect. That the effect of aggressive parenting should show up among children often referred to in the bullying literature as bully-victims is particularly interesting, as these children have been shown in a number of studies to be the most psychologically distressed of all bully/victim sub-groups (see Zubrick *et al.* 1997).

Early attachment and young children

Some of the research on possible effects of parenting has been theory driven. Much of the research has focused upon the early years of the relationship between the caregiver and the child. The close attachment or bonding of mother and child has received tremendous emphasis. There was a time when not a moment was to be lost in getting the newborn baby safely, securely in its mother's arms. The theory of attachment, as proposed by John Bowlby (1969), is as follows. The attachment relationship that develops between the primary caregiver – usually, but not always, the mother – and an infant over the first few years of life lays the foundation for an 'internal working model' that continues to influence the child's future development throughout the lifespan. Needless to say, if this is true, how a child relates to its peers will be in part determined by the nature of the attachment – or the failure of the attachment – in the first few years of life.

It would seem to follow that children involved in bully/victim problems would have a different history of attachment from those who are neither bullies nor victims. There is some evidence consistent with this view. It should be explained that it is possible to categorise infants according to how they react when they are reunited with their primary caregiver after a brief and usually unhappy period of absence. Most children are glad to see her and show it. These are the securely attached. Others may ignore her, scream loudly and angrily or even push her away. In 1987 Troy and Sroufe reported that children who at 18 months had shown signs of insecure attachment, being anxious/avoidant or anxious/resistant, were more likely than others to be involved in bully/victim problems at age four to five years. Smith and Myron-Wilson (1997) have reported other studies supporting this finding, although it is fair to say that some developmentalists have come to different conclusions, for example Lamb and Nash (1989) who write: 'Despite repeated assertions that the quality of social competence with peers is determined by the prior quality of infant–mother attachment relationships, there is actually little empirical support for this hypothesis.' (Cited in Harris 1998, p. 152).

One of the things that commends this line of research is that the early testing of subjects in these experiments makes it unlikely that the behaviour involving bullying (being victimised or victimising others) has been learned from the peer group. But what we do not know is how the children who acted so insecurely as infants would have acted with a different caregiver. Perhaps the insecurity was inherited. We know that anxiety is a characteristic that is to a substantial extent heritable. The crucial factor may be the inherited nature of the child, not the treatment from a caregiver. Until we partial out the genetic factor the theory must remain speculative and controversial.

It would, of course, be unthinkable to allocate babies at random to 'care-givers' who would provide or not provide the conditions likely to bring about secure attachment. The best we can do is to draw upon the experimental work of Harlow and Harlow (1962) who did in one experiment deprive baby rhesus monkeys of contact with any other animal, the consequence of this extreme treatment being lifelong social maladjustment. This is certainly consistent, up to a point, with attachment theory. But in another experiment, baby rhesus monkeys were allowed other babies to be with (no mother). Although the mother-deprived babies were distinctly unhappy, there were no signs of subsequent social maladjustment. For those who think you can extrapolate from one species to another, it would seem that the identity of the carer and even the role of the carer may not be so crucial after all.

Further implications of parent–child relationships

The general notion that unsatisfactory relationships with parents constitute a root cause of unsatisfactory relations with one's peers has been accepted by a number of researchers, including several who have specialised in the study of aggressive and bullying behaviour between children. Two main questions have been addressed: what are the parental antecedents of being bullied by peers at school, and what are the parental antecedents of bullying others at school? More recently researchers have been concerned with the question of how parental behaviour may account for some children being both bullies and victims.

A study conducted by Olweus (1993) in Sweden with adolescent schoolboys and with their parents suggested that the mode of parenting was a significant factor. The boys were assessed by a number of their peers according to how frequently they were bullied by other students. Subsequently, interviews were conducted with the mothers and fathers of the students (aged 13–16 years) included in the sample. Olweus's analyses indicated that in addition to being generally physically weaker and more passive than other students, the children who were victimised most often were: (i) overprotected by their mothers; and (ii) distant from their fathers, who were critical of them.

Some studies have attempted to describe the relationships between involvement in bully/victim problems at school as bully or as victim or as both and prior relations with parents. One instrument that appears suitable for such an inquiry is the Parental Bonding Instrument (the PBI) devised by Parker *et al.* (1979). This is a questionnaire in which respondents are asked to describe their parents and how they have been treated by them in the past. There are two sub-scales to the measure; one assesses the quality of care received by the respondent from a male and a female caregiver in the family (usually a mother or father) and the other the degree of control that each exercised over him or her. An example of an item to assess parental care is 'speaks to me in a warm and friendly voice'; an example of parental control is 'tries to control everything I do'.

The PBI was administered in Australia to adolescent students (769 boys and 663 girls) between the ages of 12 and 16 years, together with reliable self-report measures of tendencies to bully others and tendencies to be victimised by others (Rigby, Slee and Martin 1999). (We also included in this study measures of mental health and psychological extraversion – for reasons to be made clear later.) Our main interest here is whether the students' appraisal of their parents related to their reports on their involvement in bully/victim problems. We found that most of the correlations between measures of parental bonding and self-reports of involvement as a victim or as a bully were small but statistically significant.

Even though the correlations are small and several do not reach an acceptable level of statistical significance, they are all in a direction that suggests that parental care *may* have the effect of reducing the tendency to bully and also the tendency to be victimised by peers, whilst high levels of parental control may have the opposite effect, that is, increase the tendency for children to bully others and also the tendency to be bullied by others. There is some limited support here for the claim made by Olweus that parental control (or over-protection) of boys by mothers can increase the likelihood of them being victimised. It is also suggested by these results that over-protection of girls by fathers may have a similar effect.

Here we may pause and examine some possible alternative interpretations of these results. First, the PBI items are framed in the present tense, and it may be the case that the parents' perceived behaviours do not have a long history.

Adolescence we know is a time when children are particularly critical of parents and especially sensitive to being 'controlled'. Further, it may be that negative and controlling attitudes of the parents are in some cases at least a response to negative behaviours on the part of the child. Finally, we come back to the old bugbear of research of this kind, and ask: could the actions and reactions of child and parents be determined by other factors that are attributable to a common genetic source? For example, both parents and children may share a disposition that makes them get mad at each other.

Perhaps the modest correlations can be accounted for if there are enough pairs of parents and offspring who are extraverted and also mentally distressed. Fortunately, it was possible to take this possibility into account by controlling for each child's level of extraversion and mental distress. Much as expected from previous studies, we did find that extraverts were more likely to bully and introverts to be bullied. We also found that the more mentally distressed had a tendency to be involved in bully/victim incidents. What happened when extraversion and mental health of children were controlled was that some associations remained significant for girls but not for boys. Girls who felt less well cared for were prone to bully. Girls who felt highly controlled by parents were prone to bully too, leading one to conclude that a high level of parental control combined with a low level of care may well be a recipe for bullying by girls. We should add that over-controlled girls were also more likely than others to experience peer victimisation. For boys we are left with the conclusion that parental influence – as assessed by the PBI – may well be negligible as far as peer bullying among adolescents is concerned.

Research conducted in Italy by Baldry and Farrington (1998) has contributed further to our knowledge about relationships between parenting and children's peer relations. Their work was with children between the ages of 11 and 14 years in a middle school in Rome. As in the Australian study, an anonymous self-report questionnaire was used to identify bullies and victims. To assess parenting practices a number of questions were asked of the students about their parents. Their answers led to parenting practices being categorised as 'authoritarian', e.g. if the student answered yes to this question: 'Do your parents always decide things for you?', or 'authoritative', e.g. saying yes to: 'At home do you have the possibility to say what you want?' In addition there were measures to assess how punitive parents were and the extent to which parents got along, e.g. whether they quarrelled and argued a lot.

They also found that in comparing children categorised as 'bullies' as opposed to 'non-bullies' the former were more likely to report having parents who were relatively authoritarian, punitive, not very supportive and inclined to disagree with each other. They reported that victims and bully/victims also tended to have authoritarian parents. Somewhat surprisingly, the 'pure' bully (who bullies but is not bullied in return) did not appear from this analysis to have parents with such negative characteristics. In some respects this study provides results similar to those of the Australian study, especially in suggesting that perceived high parental control is associated with being a bully and with being a victim – although it may be recalled that in the Australian study this finding applied specifically to girls. (It is a pity that the Italian results were not examined separately for boys and girls, since differences could well have emerged.)

Again, we are faced with some uncertainty in interpreting these results so as to establish causal links. Could uncontrolled genetic factors have accounted for the associations that have been suggested? As in the Australian study some factors were employed to control for other influences, some of which may have a partial genetic basis. These included self-esteem and perceived social competence, both of which have been shown to have some significant heritability. Analyses showed that with these factors controlled (as well as gender) having authoritarian parents was significant for bully/victims vs neither and for victims vs non-victims and for 'only victims' vs non-victims. Bullies vs non-bullies were distinguished by having low-supportive and highly punitive parents.

Family relationships and bullying

Some might say that we are focusing in an unduly narrow way in picking out (or picking on) parents as possible causal agents in explaining bullying. Perhaps the family may be a more appropriate unit on which to base an analysis. In England a rather ingenious method was used to examine how children categorised on the basis of peer reports saw their families (Bowers, Smith and Binney 1992). These researchers utilised the Family-Systems Test (Gehring and Wyler 1986) to assess structural aspects of families. This is a figure placement technique in which children place small wooden dolls representing family members on a chequer board so as to 'make a picture of their family' showing 'how close everyone feels to each other'. In addition, one to three blocks can be placed under each figure to show 'how powerful they are'. Unlike many questionnaires and interview procedures, this is a procedure that really engages children's attention. The subjects in their study were children between the ages of 9 and 11 years. Bullies, victims, bully/victims and controls (neither bullies nor victims) were identified by peer nomination. It was found that bullies tended to place significantly greater distance between representations of family members, suggesting a low level of cohesiveness in their families. Unlike children not involved in bullying, both bullies and victims tended to see their fathers as much more powerful than their mothers. This suggests that such children are more likely to come from families whose structure is highly patriarchal. One further characteristic of victims was noteworthy. They were significantly more likely than others to clump all family figures together, with no clear separation between any of the figures. This suggested that their families were very high in cohesiveness: arguably too high, suggesting a degree of enmeshment consistent with over-protectiveness of each other. The finding that bullies and victims, though similar in some respects, come from families differing greatly in cohesiveness is a particularly interesting one, all the more so since it was replicated in a similar study conducted in a different culture by Berdondini and Smith (1996) in Italy.

Family functioning and bullying

If a family as a total unit functions badly, individual members, it may be argued, are likely to be affected in ways that may influence how they behave outside the family. According to Roelefse and Middleton (1985) there are six major dimensions of family functioning that are of particular relevance to adolescents. They maintain that 'good family functioning' is evident when these conditions are fulfilled:

(1) There is a coherent family structure with members accepting each other according to clearly defined and consistent roles, e.g. as authoritative parents and respectful children (Structure).
(2) Within the family, individuals can express themselves freely (Affect).
(3) There is good, clearly understood communication between family members leading to them addressing problems together constructively (Communication).
(4) Control is exercised in a democratic rather than authoritarian manner (Control).
(5) Positive values such as personal honesty are transmitted from parent to child (Value).
(6) There is a sense of positive connection with the world outside the family (External systems).

In general, then, knowing about a young person's parenting and family background does provide some indication of whether that person is more likely or less likely than others to be involved in a bully/victim problem at school. We may draw some confidence in this belief by noting that research conducted in different countries, for example, Norway, Australia, Italy and England, points to similar conclusions. But note too that the connections revealed by research are not strong and are open to alternative explanations. They certainly do not provide strong support for those who might lay the blame for bullying squarely on parents.

Peer group pressure and bullying

There can be no doubt that the peer group can be a powerful influence on how children behave. This can readily be observed in the way they speak, for instance. As Harris (1998) points out, the children of migrant families soon learn to speak like other kids, not like their fathers and mothers with accents they brought from their former country. They opt to wear the clothes other kids wear, not what their parents like. Their interests and hobbies are, by and large, the interests and hobbies of their peers. They have a drive to fit in, to be like the others.

For those who need convincing of the powerful influence of the peer group we have the famous experiment of the robber's cave (Sherif *et al.* 1961) conducted over 40 years ago but still cited today, remarkably enough, in social psychology texts for students. Perhaps its longevity is due to a dearth of significant studies of real life behaviour that are rigorously experimental and also revealing. In this study, boys were randomly allocated to two groups – genetic considerations thereby cancelled out – and on a summer camp allowed to develop a group identity, with a little encouragement. They were given names – the Rattlers and the Eagles – and encouraged to compete. In next to no time the group members were welded together, true believers in their destiny, which, in due course, included the vilification of their rivals. Whenever they could, they engaged in abusing members of the other group, physically and verbally. According to the experimenters, an outsider would have seen these boys as 'wicked, disturbed and vicious bunches of youngsters'. Clearly aggressiveness among boys can be stimulated and maintained through the creation of a group identity, especially if members of a group are directed towards seeing themselves as different and superior to another group. This may explain the bullying of 'outsiders'.

If we are interested in explaining individual behaviour in the area of bullying it is better to speak of 'peer groups' rather than 'the peer group'. There are groups that encourage bullying and groups that do not. Some groups glory in bullying. Several years ago I interviewed a likeable young boy of about nine years old whose background I knew nothing about at the time, who cheerfully told me that he had a gang that specialised in bullying. Each day the group identified a potential victim in the playground and gave him or her – no gender bias – absolute hell. If the child was likely to put up a serious fight, then the bullying, usually physical, was undertaken by the group. When the victim was 'weak', one member of the group was delegated to do the bullying and the rest watched. Such specialisation is rare, but the promotion of a group identity that can lead to bullying someone is not uncommon. They may or may not have some interests that draw them together, for example, a liking for a violent sort of sport that goes with a tough guy image, or an obsession with computing which can be (not always) the preserve of the more introverted, who may accordingly be labelled as 'computer nerds'. We have seen that some bullying is in fact perpetrated collectively by groups and even orchestrated on occasions by individual leaders.

But whilst we can see that peer pressure may lead children to bully others and thereby promote or uphold a satisfying image of being tough, it does little to explain how some children come to be victims. It is unlikely (but not impossible) that a child may identify with a group that is being victimised and thereby bring victimisation on himself or herself. If this happened we would be inclined to look for the unusual motivation of those who wish to suffer the fate of the oppressed, or alternatively, for signs of pathology. And it begs the question of why some children for whom the idea of being tough is attractive do not bully others.

There is as yet little empirical evidence relating to the importance of different kinds of social influences that operate on children to incline them to engage or not engage in bullying. But there is one useful study that has examined social influences affecting the tendency to bully among early adolescents in the USA (see Espelage, Bosworth and Simon 2000).

Espelage *et al.* undertook their study at a large middle school, the data being gathered using anonymous questionnaires from 1361 students in grades 6, 7 and 8. Unlike some measures of bullying tendencies the scale they used was broad in content and psychometrically reliable. The extent to which individuals bullied others was inferred from estimates they made of how frequently they had engaged in the following behaviours over the previous 30 days:

* Called other children names.
* Teased other students.
* Said things about students to make other students laugh.
* Threatened to hit another student.
* Pushed, shoved, slapped or kicked other students.

Negative peer influence was assessed by asking students how many friends they had who: (i) were involved in gang activities; (ii) had hit or threatened someone; (iii) suggested that the student do something against the law; and (iv) damaged or destroyed property.

Adult influence thought likely to discourage aggressive behaviour was assessed by asking respondents to think about adults they spent most time with and indicate how many tell them: (i) if another student hits you, hit them back; (ii) if another student wants to fight, you should try to talk your way out of a fight; (iii) if another student asks you to fight, you should tell a teacher or someone older; (iv) fighting is not good, there are other ways to solve problems.

Parental and family influence centred upon two areas in which it has been claimed that bullying behaviour may be encouraged in families, namely by parental punishment and lack of family attention and support. Respondents were asked to estimate how often they had been hit by parents for breaking rules and how much time they spent with family members and talked and engaged in activities with them.

Finally, respondents were asked to indicate how much gang activity there was in their neighbourhood and how safe they felt.

Using a statistical technique of multiple regression analysis to assess the unique influence of each of the above factors produced very interesting results. Each of the factors contributed significantly to predicting the self-reported frequency of bullying. Their order of importance, as inferred from the amount of variance in the bullying scores attributable to each factor, was as follows:

(1) Absence of positive adult models.
(2) Low level of neighbourhood safety.
(3) Little or no time spent without adults being around.
(4) Negative peer influence.
(5) Being spanked at home by parents.

By far the most powerful influence on bullying behaviour according to this analysis was the absence of positive adult models as indicated by reports of spending little or no time with adults. This is precisely what William Golding (1954), author of *Lord of the Flies*, would have predicted. In the absence of adults the young adolescents on Golding's mythical island begin to engage in the most violent, and indeed lethal, form of peer victimisation. With the arrival of adults, the normal world reasserts itself again.

Physical punishment is the least powerful of the inferred influences, but its contribution to bullying was as predicted. Aggressive parenting and aggressive peer relating went together. Importantly, the study draws attention to a factor often neglected in studies of bullying, namely what goes on in the wider community, beyond the home and beyond the school: the neighbourhood. Where there is a low level of perceived community safety, there would appear to be more bullying going on among children at school. This raises the question of whether it is fair to say, as Randall (1996) has suggested, that bullying is – at least to some extent – imported into the school from the community.

We should acknowledge, as the authors do, the limitations of the study I have described. It relies heavily on student judgements of the intensity of different kinds of social influences. Yet despite these shortcomings, we may be persuaded that adult influence on whether a child engages in bullying is greater than those who attribute overwhelming influence to peer pressure would have us believe.

A further study which enables us to examine the possible contributions of peer and adult pressure to bully others focused upon the degree to which adolescents believe that their peers and adults encourage them to engage in bullying others (Rigby 1997). In that study respondents were asked in an anonymous questionnaire to indicate whether they thought nominated persons would support them in bullying someone. Those nominated included mothers, fathers, close friends and teachers. Not surprisingly, only a minority of students saw others approving of them bullying someone. There was nevertheless a big contrast between the perceptions of how they thought their close friends and adults would react. Up to 15 per cent thought that their friends would approve of at least one kind of bullying they might engage in. This is about three times the proportion who thought that adults might support them. This suggests that the influence of peers, especially close friends, may be crucial in some cases.

However, when we look at the ratings provided by students on how much they care about the judgements others may make of them if they bullied someone, we see that on average students cared more about what parents would think than what their peers thought of them. Students were asked to say on a seven-point scale from 'a great deal' to 'not at all' how much they would care about the judgements others might make about them if they bullied someone. This provided a measure of how much influence over their bullying behaviour respondents thought each of the rated persons had. Most students indicated that they cared a good deal: on average they scored above 4, the mid-point indicating neutrality. But notice that both boys and girls cared *less* about what their peers thought than about what their parents thought. Teachers were seen as the least worth taking notice of.

We might ask whether there was any relationship between how the students thought they were being influenced by others and the extent to which they engaged in bullying others. The answer is yes: significant correlations (.34 for boys and .32 for girls) were found between a measure of self-reported bullying behaviour and reported influence from others (see Rigby, 1997, p.215, for further details).

Both the study by Espelage *et al.* (2000) and that of Rigby (1997) suffer from a failure to control for genetic influences. A recent ingenious study conducted in Texas, USA, by Loehlin (1997) has overcome this problem, and although it did not assess bullying per se, it did examine related behaviour as indicated through personality measures. The research question was whether members of 839 late-adolescent twin pairs who shared more friends were more similar in personality than those who shared fewer friends. By comparing results for identical twins (330 pairs) with results for non-identical pairs (509 pairs) it was possible to control for genetic influence. Respondents were asked: 'Do you and your twin have the same or different friends?' They could answer by choosing one of the following answers:

(1) All of my friends are also my twin's friends.
(2) Most of my friends are also my twin's friends.

(3) Some of my friends are also my twin's friends.

(4) Few or none of my friends are also my twin's friends.

In addition, respondents completed a reliable personality test, the California Psychological Inventory. One of the dimensions assessed was of particular relevance to bullying: namely, dominance, a construct reflecting the extent to which respondents sought to act in a dominating way. (One would expect bullies to be strongly motivated to dominate.) In general, twins who indicated that they had relatively few friends in common – and were assumed to have been influenced by peers differently/have different friends – were more different on the measure of dominance. The obtained correlations (0.19 for identical and 0.20 for non-identical twins) between the measure of dominance and having different friends were small but statistically significant – and remarkably similar for the two sorts of twins, suggesting that genetic influences interacting with choice of similar or different friends was unimportant.

Second, the study enabled one to examine the possible effects of parents treating one twin in a pair differently from another. To obtain a measure of how similarly or differently parents treated the respondents, parents (usually mothers) were asked to rate their parenting of each twin in terms of the attention they paid to each and the discipline they applied. The question here was whether differences in treatments were related to differences in personality. In general the correlations suggesting parental influence were lower than those suggesting peer influence. For dominance the obtained correlations though positive were smaller (.07 for identical twin pairs and .04 for non-identical twin pairs). This result may be interpreted as giving some support for the view that by late adolescence the influence of peer group is stronger than that of the parents on dominance. Yet in some areas of personality – for example socialisation – the correlations relating to parental influence are higher than those for peer influence. Hence, it seems that parents may have more influence in some areas but not in others. The author, John Loehlin, concludes cautiously that the study gives 'mild support' for the view that peers shape personality more than parents do. But quite appropriately he calls for further research in this area. As far as bullying is concerned, it would be good to see, incorporated in such a study, a better measure of bullying than 'dominance' which, as I have argued earlier, may be achieved by non-bullying methods, especially among more mature students in late adolescence. The finding that 'socialisation' is more closely related to parental than peer influence – even in late adolescence – suggests that a relatively long-term effect on the tendency to act in a socially responsible manner is certainly possible.

Conclusion

In seeking to explain why people bully a variety of factors have been suggested. Some of the explanations are extremely general, their purpose being to explain why there is a tendency to bully in human nature. These include explanations that take a religious or supernatural view of the causes of human behaviour and posit a force for evil that we are not always able to resist. Alternatively, the urge to bully others, especially as children, is seen as implanted through an evolutionary process that has enabled us to survive. Such general explanations for bullying are difficult, if not impossible, to evaluate.

Other explanations have sought to explain why some people bully or are bullied more than others. These include explanations that attribute bullying tendencies (and sometimes the tendency to be bullied by others) to genetic factors; to the early home environment; to the peer group; and to the wider community. Evidence has been piling up in support of each of these explanations. However, because the influences alluded to above operate together, the unique effects of each needs to be disentangled from that of others. And this unfortunately has rarely been done.

As we have seen, currently we have a good deal of evidence obtained from diverse sources – the USA, England, Italy and Australia, for instance – that the involvement of children in bully/victim problems is related to the kind of parenting they have experienced and the sort of family life they have had. This has led many people to assume that inadequate parenting and dysfunctional family life cause bullying or at least constitute a causal influence. However, as we have seen, other explanations for the association are possible. Increasingly, the claim that parenting is directly responsible for a child's involvement in bully/victim problems at school is being challenged, principally by behavioural geneticists and by social psychologists who emphasise the importance of the peer group as a causative influence in accounting for the way children behave towards each other.

Despite the challenges to the view that parents may influence their children to become bullies or victims, it would be premature to abandon this viewpoint. One may concede that some children who are inclined to bully others might actually elicit cold and/or over-controlling behaviour from their parents and that their behaviour may contribute to the dysfunctionality of a family. One may concede that genetic influences on a child's behaviour may (for better or worse) frustrate attempts by parents to shape their child's behaviour. One may concede that a child's peers – and the influence of the neighbourhood – may have an important effect on how that child behaves. And yet, it is still conceivable that under some conditions parental influence on how a child relates to others, both inside and outside the home, could be important. One might expect parental influence to be greatest under extreme conditions, for example where parenting is highly abusive. It may also be the case that the effects of parenting on the way children relate to others are greatest in the early years of schooling and attenuate as the years pass by and other influences increasingly take effect.

References

Austin, A. B. and Lindauer, S. K. (1990) 'Parent-child conversation of more-liked and less-liked children.' *Journal of Genetic Psychology 151,* 5–23.

Baldry, A. C. and Farrington, D. P. (1998) 'Parenting influences on bullying and victimisation.' *Criminal and Legal Psychology 3,* 237–254.

Berdondini, L. and Smith, P. K. (1996) 'Cohesion and power in the families of children involved in bully/victim problems at school: an Italian replication.' *Journal of Family Therapy 18,* 99–102.

Bowers, L., Smith, P. K. and Binney, V. (1992) 'Cohesion and power in the families of children involved in bully/victim problems at school.' *Journal of Family Therapy 14,* 371–387.

Bowlby, J. (1969) *Attachment and Loss,* Vols 1 and 2. New York: Basic Books.

Darwin, C. (1859, 1871) *The Descent of Man.* London: John Murray.

Eron, L. D, Walder, L. O., Toigo, R. and Lefkowitz, M. M. (1963) 'Social class, parental punishment for aggression and child aggression.' *Child Development 34,* 849–867.

Espelage, D., Bosworth, K. and Simon, T. (2000) 'Examining the social context of bullying behaviours in early adolescence.' *Journal of Counselling and Development 78,* 326–344.

Gehring, T. M. and Wyler, I. L. (1986) 'Family–System–Test (FAST): A three dimensional approach to investigate family relationships.' *Child Psychiatry & Human Development 16,* 235–248.

Golding, W. (1954) *Lord of the Flies.* London: Faber and Faber.

Harlow, H. F. and Harlow, M. (1962) 'Social deprivation in monkeys.' *Scientific American 207,* 136–146.

Harris, J. R. (1998) *The Nurture Assumption.* New York: Free Press.

Hart, C. H., Ladd, G. W. and Burleston, B. R. (1990) 'Children's expectations of the outcomes of social strategies: relations with sociometric status and maternal disciplinary styles.' *Child Development 61,* 127–137.

Hawley, P. H. (1999) 'The ontogenesis of social dominance: a strategy-based evolutionary perspective.' *Developmental Review 19,* 97–132.

Henggeler, S. W., Edwards, J. J., Cohen, R. and Somerville, M. B. (1991)

'Predicting changes in children's popularity: the role of family relations.' *Journal of Applied Developmental Psychology 12*, 205–218.

Lamb, M. E. and Nash, A. (1989) 'Infant–mother attachment, sociability and peer competence.' In T. J. Berndt and G. W. Ladd (eds) *Peer Relationships in Child Development*. New York: Wiley.

Larzelere, R. E. (1986) 'Moderate spanking: model of deterrent of children's aggression in the family?' *Journal of Family Violence 1*, 27–36.

Levy, D. M. (1966) *Maternal Overprotection*. New York: Norton.

Loehlin, J. C. (1997) 'A test of J. R. Harris's theory of peer influences on personality.' *Journal of Personality and Social Psychology 72*, 1197—1201.

O'Connor, M., Foch, T., Todd, S. and Plomin, R. (1980) 'A twin study of specific behavioral problems of socialisation as viewed by parents.' *Journal of Abnormal Child Psychology 8*, 189–199.

Olweus, D. (1993) *Bullying at School*. Cambridge, MA: Blackwell Publishers.

Parker, G., Tupling, H. and Brown, L. B. (1979) 'A Parental Bonding Instrument.' *British Journal of Medical Psychology 52*, 1–10.

Pettit, G. S., Dodge, K. A. and Brown, M. M. (1988) 'Early family experience, social problem solving patterns and children's social competence.' *Child Development 59*, 107–120.

Pettit, G. S., Harrist, A. W., Bates, J. E. and Dodge, K. A. (1991) 'Family interaction, social cognition, and children's subsequent relations with peers and kindergarten.' *Journal of Social and Personal Relationships 8*, 383–402.

Randall, P. E. (1996) *A Community Approach to Bullying*. Stoke on Trent: Trentham Books.

Rigby, K. (1993) 'School children's perceptions of their families and parents as a function of peer relations.' *Journal of Genetic Psychology 154*, 4, 501–514.

Rigby, K. (1994) 'Psycho-social functioning in families of Australian adolescent schoolchildren involved in bully/victim problems.' *Journal of Family Therapy 16*, 2, 173–189.

Rigby, K. (1997) 'Attitudes and beliefs about bullying among Australian school children.' *Irish Journal of Psychology 18*, 2, 202–220.

Rigby, K., Slee, P. T. and Martin, G. (1999) 'The mental health of adolescents, perceived parenting and peer victimisation at school.' Unpublished paper.

Roelefse, R. and Middleton, M. R. (1985) 'The Family Functioning in Adolescence questionnaire: a measure of psycho-social family health.' *Journal of Adolescence 8*, 33–45.

Schneider, B. H. (2000) *Friends and Enemies: Peer Relations in Childhood*. New York: Oxford University Press.

Schwartz, D., Dodge, K. A., Pettit, G. S. and Bates, J. (1997) 'The early socialization of aggressive victims of bullying.' *Child Development 68*, 665–675.

Sears R. R. (1961) 'Relation of early socialisation experiences to aggression in middle childhood.' *Journal of Abnormal and Social Psychology 63*, 466–492.

Sears, R. R., Whiting, J. W. M., Nowlis, V. and Sears, P. S. (1953) 'Some child rearing antecedents of aggression and dependency.' *Genetic Psychology Monographs 47*, 135–234.

Sherif, M., Harvey, O. J., Hood, W. R. and Sherif, C. W. (1961) *Intergroup Cooperation and Competition. The Robber's Cave Experiment*. Norman, OK: University Book Exchange.

Smith, P. K. and Myron-Wilson, R. (1997) 'Parenting and school bullying.' *Clinical Child Psychology & Psychiatry 3*, 405–417.

Strassberg, Z., Dodge, K. A., Bates, J. E. and Pettit, S. (1992) 'The longitudinal relation between parental conflict strategies and children's sociometric standing in kindergarten.' *Merrill-Palmer Quarterly 38*, 477–493.

Troy, M. and Sroufe, L. A. (1987) 'Victimization among preschoolers: Role of attachment relationship history.' *Journal of the American Academy of Child & Adolescent Psychiatry 26*, 166–172.

Zubrick, S. R., Silburn, S. R., Gurrin, L., Teoh, H., Shepherd, C., Carlton, J. and Lawrence, D. (1997) *Western Australian Child Health Survey: Education, Health and Competence*. Perth, Western Australia: Australian Bureau of Statistics and Institute for Child Health Research.

Chapter 20

Pressure, stress and children's behaviour at school

John Cornwall

Introduction

Do we put up with too much stress and pressure as part of our everyday lives, in schools, at home and in the adult world of work? Is stress a necessary part of our lives and, if so, how much is necessary? Why is stress generally regarded as an adult thing? Is it, and should it be, a part of children's lives? What effect does stress in schools and classrooms have on children's learning and future achievements? Where is the dividing line between acceptable challenge and overwhelming pressure? Is academic attainment a true indicator of future success or happiness? What effect does academic pressure have on children's long term health? Going to school can be enlightening or damaging for children and young people and there are whole batteries of questions associated with stress, pressure, children's health, development and learning. This chapter explores some aspects of stress and its management in learning environments, such as nurseries, schools and colleges. It cannot answer all of the many difficult questions but examines some ideas that might promote a more human and humane approach to schooling, teaching and learning.

The physical and mental consequences of overwhelming pressure or stress are well documented (e.g. Gray 1987; Stroh 1971; Smith and Cooper 1996; Cartwright and Cooper 1997; Fontana 1989). The negative effects of stress (Yerkes-Dodson Law – see Figure 20.1) on exam performance (Yerkes 1921), on teaching effectiveness (Dunham 1983), on working performance (Cartwright and Cooper 1997) or sporting achievement (Hardy 1988; Bakker *et al.* 1990) are also well known. The athlete who has 'peaked' in performance or the professional who has 'burnt out' are becoming common parlance. Research and discourse over the past seventy years clearly indicates the important effects of

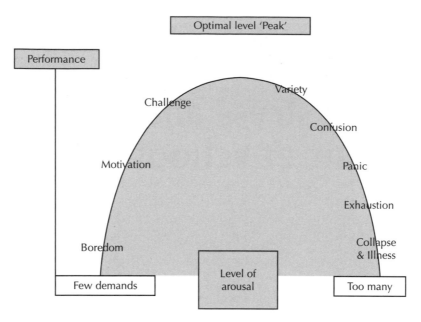

Figure 20.1. An illustration of the Yerkes-Dodson Law.

anxiety, stress and pressure on attention, learning, psychological health, academic performance and self-actualisation (e.g. Yerkes 1921; Maslow 1968; Stroh 1971; Gray 1987). There are clear relationships between stress and motivation (Maslow 1954) and between stress and significant life events and lifestyles (Fontana 1989; Bailey 1994). Similarly, the role of attribution and locus of control in coping with success and failure links with life events. For example, the degree to which a child or young person blames or congratulates themselves for failures or successes will have a great impact on their learning (Rotter 1954; Lawrence 1987) and potential for achievement. They will also be affected by a range of cognitive factors (see later) and possibly subject to learned helplessness (Seligman 1975; Bandura 1989) through demoralising experiences. A child's self-esteem and self concept (Lawrence 1987; Fontana 1989) are also involved in positive or negative responses to stress. It is now also accepted that stress affects the activity of our immune systems. Short-term stress can downgrade or upgrade our immune system activity but chronic or intense stress can impair the immune system and its functioning (Evans *et al.* 1997), causing both short- and long-term health problems. As well as a physical 'emergency reaction', causing biochemical changes in the body, there are long-term biological changes brought forth by prolonged stress (Gray 1987). These are what can cause significant short- and long-term health problems.

Great skill is needed to set up realistic challenges for the child but ones that don't become stressful and counter-productive. Teacher's expectations (e.g. Rosenthal and Jacobson's classic research, 1968) and an individual's personal response to rewards and punishments or to those who inflict them will affect the balance of stress or stimulation. Teacher's decisions and realistic or informed appraisal of a situation are absolutely crucial. Over arousal, through excessive stimulation or challenge, can lead to stress and stress induced behaviour as well as to a significant decrease in performance (see Figure 20.1). These are complex and sensitive areas that are not considered in the current debate about 'standards' or in the current rush to make the teacher a mechanical deliverer of curriculum. It is possible that the 'politicisation' of education is responsible for the increasing stresses upon pupils. Only sometimes is this made worse by individuals' behaviour in classrooms or by classroom practices.

Previous work on stress, childhood and behaviour

Hitherto most of the work on stress, with some notable exceptions (e.g. Leach 1992; Varma 1973; Wolff 1981), relates to adult stress. There has been a fair degree of research and valuable discussion about teacher stress that clearly links their stress to both their working conditions on a grand scale (Dunham 1983; Cole and Walker 1989; Mills 1995) and personal disposition or personality types. Children share these working conditions and also have specific and additional pressures of their own to contend with. There is good reason for continuing to examine the causes and consequences of stress as a result of the school environment. Disaffection and disruption may have much to do with a negative reaction to the 'structural functionalist' view of pupils as being trained and selected to fit their 'place' in society (Meighan 1981). Working with pupils defined as having emotional and behavioural difficulties, like other special educational needs, is a complex and interactive process. In education, particularly with respect to pupils with emotional and behavioural difficulties, thinking has moved away from the assumption that problems are associated within an individual and more recognition has been given to the effects of the social environment upon the learning, attitudes and behaviour (Bandura 1977). This change of thinking emphasises the value for teachers of establishing a conceptual framework in which to consider different explanations for emotional and behavioural difficulties (Smith and Cooper 1996). The construct of 'stress' may provide such a framework, or at least part of one, not just for pupils with special needs, but for all pupils.

There is still an assumption abroad that stress is an adult 'thing' and does not really apply to children. After all, what have they got to be stressed about? What responsibilities do they carry? Their decisions are less important because they are young. Their fears and anxieties are not as potent as adult fears and anxieties because we can protect them from 'reality'. They are part of a cultural myth of happy, endless childhood, reinforced by stereotypes of children in TV adverts and superficial literature or media presentation.

> It is also important to recognise that our perceptions of childhood undergo constant change and are in many ways ambivalent and contradictory. For many adults, childhood is imbued with a rather romanticised notion of innocence – a period free from responsibility or conflict and dominated by fantasy, play and opportunity. Yet for many children of all cultures and classes the dominating feature of childhood is powerlessness and lack of control over what happens to them.
>
> (Lansdown 1994)

Childhood is far from 'the carefree time for loving, laughing and learning' (Leach 1992). It is certainly not like that for most children all of the time. If we reflect back to childhood, all of us have probably experienced extreme pressures and stress, albeit short term in most cases. For a significant number of children, stress has become a way of life or else a permanent feature of their lives that could limit their capacity for growth and learning. Some children will have constitutional difficulties that can turn the normal pressures of school life into extremely stressful situations. Other children are the victims of conditions brought about by adults through their inability to cope with their own lives, to moderate their own behaviour or to understand a child's viewpoint. These assumptions about model childhood are very much linked with a readiness to dismiss young people's behaviour as 'naughty' or 'bad'. These behaviours could be regarded as symptoms of stress (see Figure 20.2) and as a normal, emotional or even rational response to impossible circumstances.

Our world is changing rapidly and one of the tensions for pupils and teachers resides in an outdated view of education and teaching in a rapidly changing world. These tensions affect a large proportion of pupils in the education system, not just those with 'special' difficulties defined in medico-educational terms. Figure 20.2 illustrates some of the causes, including constitutional disorders that could result in stress and its accompanying emotional and behavioural difficulties. It would be foolish to ignore the weight of research evidence that links stress and academic performance, health risks or challenging behaviour in schools. Understanding the factors and issues of stress in children can help us to support a child's full development whilst at school and understand some of the behaviour that is labelled 'naughty', 'uncooperative', 'dysfunctional' or 'bad'.

Conscious reactions to excessive pressure are intended to maintain self-esteem and stability of personality in the face of insane and unreasonable demands. Unconscious reactions to stress and unrealisable demands are more complex, involving sensory, motor or visceral responses or even the whole immune system. They can have far reaching consequences leading to ill health

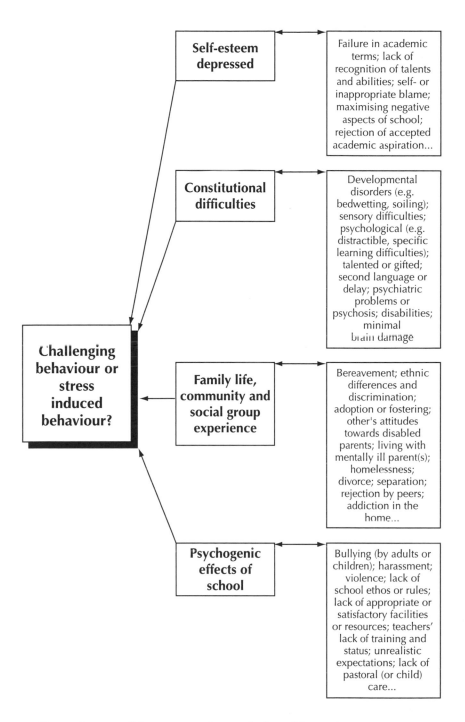

Figure 20.2. Illustrating possible sources of stress induced behaviour.

and even death. What are the characteristics of the education system that affect the health and well-being of children? Hard-line attitudes involving too much reliance on discipline and behavioural management are beginning to re-emerge. Fixed rewards and sanctions (although hopefully more rewards than sanctions!) do not deal with the causes of challenging behaviour. There is an obvious link between stress and its emergence in challenging behaviour. There are also many children who are quietly suffering and trying to succeed in a school system that does not acknowledge individual or emotional needs. The psychogenic effect of schools (McGuiness 1993) is a nettle that remains to be fully grasped (see Figure 20.2).

Political drums, personal battles

Is the rise in the number of school exclusions (Parsons 1996) since the inception of the 1988 Education Act just a coincidence? The ethos of a school can make learning and school life an enjoyable and celebrated experience or make it full of nasty surprises and a constant battle to escape disapproval. For some children, school is an adventure; for other children school is a nightmare. In the current hard political education milieu, curriculum content and measures of school effectiveness are narrowing with consequent squeezing out of a broader, more liberal view of education (Raven 1997; Kelly 1990; Lindsay 1997). It is becoming increasingly difficult to preserve a humane view of children's learning, or to practise teaching methods, that recognise the inherent uniqueness of each child and the way they make sense of the world around them. Teachers are under pressure to produce results and drive up so-called standards in large classes, overcrowded rooms, noisy and often stressful working environments. Schools that have formerly been concerned with the wider outcomes of education are now concentrating exclusively on exam performance (Raven 1997). The effect of this is to deny pupils who possess any of the wide variety of hugely important talents which do not show up on traditional examinations, and more recent standardised tests, the opportunity to develop or to get recognition for these talents.

> What we are witnessing is a world-wide reinforcement of a move towards widespread acceptance (of the kind most desired by fascists) of the right of others to dictate what one will do and what one will learn, of the right of others to issue demeaning and degrading orders and expect compliance, and of the right of authority to test one, assess one's 'integrity' according to their standards, and allocate one's life chances on the basis of criteria they have established.
>
> (Raven 1997, p. 4)

Each of us will respond to challenges and difficulties in our lives in distinct ways and with varying degrees of emotional involvement. One person's stimulation or pressure is another person's stress and anxiety.

> Psychological stress is a relationship between the environment and the person.
>
> (Lazarus and Folkman 1984)

Stress can be short or long term and can challenge an individual beyond their own perceived capacity to deal with life circumstances. An individual begins to feel overwhelmed and unable to control events around them or are increasingly driven by them. A person can also put themselves under stress through their own demands or expectations of themselves. These expectations are usually a result of a number of factors including conditioning and upbringing in youth and early years. These drives and expectations may have started in trying to please teachers in the nursery, and later in school. A child may well be very sensitive to the expectations of others but have little ability to assert their own needs and exert control over their circumstances. How do they protect themselves from overwhelming pressure to succeed?

Although some children experience permanent stresses due to constitutional disorders or emotional difficulties it can be argued that adult sensitivity to stress is important in all aspects of schooling and for all pupils.

> Indeed it can be argued that stress is most likely to be evident during periods of most rapid change. And since childhood is the period during which we develop most rapidly, then a strong case can be made for stress being especially prevalent in children.
>
> (Varma 1973)

Behavioural difficulties, conduct disorders and **challenging behaviour** are apparently on the increase in our schools. Are these obvious and apparent symptoms of stress? Could it be that education provision is just not equipped to deal with the rapid changes taking place in our society as a whole and little to do with a collapse of moral standards? This places children under greater and greater stress over a period of years as the gap between what they need and what they get in schools becomes wider and wider. Could it also be that our expectations of both behaviour and academic standards in school have changed immeasurably over the past thirty years or so? Is the gap between what pupils can attain and what is expected of them widening to the extent that a significant proportion of pupils are voting with their feet and pulling out? Or, is the gap between the kind of behaviour and free expression that young people see around them on TV, in films, in their communities and the conformity that is expected in schools irreconcilable in young minds? Another possibility has to do with the ethos of schooling. Schools have been very hierarchical and authoritarian structures since the 1800s. Are they changing? Is education itself in a state of flux and about to re-define itself? If so, there will be stress on teachers and pupils that have to do with the way the system is changing.

Recognition of stress in children and young people

An individual's defence or coping mechanisms are intended to maintain the stability or integrity of the personality. If these defence or coping mechanisms are counter-productive they can end in creating further problems. Hence the medical consequences. Medical models require considerable interpretation and extension to make them useful in educational and social terms. In this instance, I hope that the reader will make the links between behaviour described as 'challenging' and yet emanating from a child or young person's stress and coping responses.

- **Repression** occurs when a child puts experiences that cannot be dealt with away into the unconscious mind in such a way as to become inaccessible to further conscious thinking. This can be shock reaction to traumatic and stressful events or it can be simple lapses of memory.
- **Regression** can occur when a child is under stress and reverts to behaviour reminiscent of an earlier stage of development (e.g. bedwetting or thumb sucking).
- **Denial** allows the individual to falsify or change experience to reduce emotional discomfort (e.g. stealing and vigorously denying it). Often, the more forceful the reality proffered, the more vigorous become the denials.
- **Displacement** allows an individual to shift anxieties or negative, perhaps aggressive, feelings from one person to another. For example, instead of expressing the feelings to brother or father, a child may 'take it out' on a class mate.
- In some cases, pent up stress and anxiety can take the form of **reaction formation** where, simply put, unwelcome feelings or anxieties are turned into their opposite (e.g. over-attention, solicitude, being too 'goody goody').
- **Projection** is different from displacement in that, instead of simply 'taking out their feelings' on somebody else, a person will go further and actually perceive the other person as being hostile, aggressive or indifferent. One's own unacceptable impulses are attributed to someone else, hence escalation in aggressive situations where each is attributing the hostility to the other!

There are various ways in which children and adults may choose an escape route when under stress. Escape routes can be useful but can also be counter-productive in many situations. Children and adults can experience **isolation of feelings** where they become detached from their own everyday experiences but remain attached to other's actions or experiences. A child may mess himself or hit another child but be revolted or angry when another child does the same thing. **Flight into fantasy, ritualistic behaviour** and **intellectualisation** or **rationalisation** can all become defence mechanisms to ward off anxiety and repress unwelcome feelings. We must be careful here because there is a thin dividing line between taking the path of unhelpful defence mechanism and what is called **sublimation** (Wolff 1981) where a child or young person allows full creative use of the primitive impulses induced by stress and turns them into positive social action. This often leads to diminution of guilt and is rewarded, raising self-esteem and confidence. It is easy to see how the two pathways are very near each other but can have totally different effects on an individual. One child or young person's sublimation can become another's nightmare and desperation. It has been shown that unqualified positive regard from teachers and adults, where children are concerned, goes a long way to enhancing self-esteem and reducing stress (Charlton and Hunt 1993).

Assessing whether a child or young person is under stress is not a simple matter and requires observation and objectivity as well as considerable insight, empathy and intuition. There are no set patterns of behaviour that can be classified purely as stress. Nor are there obvious or easily identified sources of stress. Sometimes, the apparently obvious may be misleading, such as a child living in relative poverty. There may well be stresses but these may be offset by a loving and caring family or parent or sibling. Sometimes a child who appears to be extremely talented may be exerting sustained stress upon themselves by having taken on board other people's expectations too much. Each child or young person will respond differently to stress. We may be looking for extreme changes in life circumstances or sudden changes involving uncharacteristic behaviour. It is likely that a child who has been under stress for a prolonged period of time will have developed various defence mechanisms. Many of these may well be identified as unacceptable behaviour in the school or classroom. It is helpful to identify the behaviour and then look beyond into some of the underlying causes of that behaviour.

| **Cognitive effects** | • attention and concentration decrease. Powers of observation diminish;
• distractibility increases and the thread of what is said or happening is lost;
• memory span reduces and even familiar material cannot be recalled;
• response speed decreases and pupil may try to make up for this by guessing or making snap decisions;
• error rate increases. For example, when a child has a specific learning difficulty – they will tire more easily and errors will increase;
• powers of organisation and planning deteriorate – conditions or requirements cannot be accurately assessed or positive moves planned; |

- reality testing becomes less efficient and critical powers reduced. Child can become more detached from what is happening and become irrational (even if only temporary).

Emotional effect
- Physical and psychological tensions increase – muscles become tense, simple movements can become difficult, teeth clench, emotional outbursts may increase and so on ...;
- can manifest in physical pains or maladies (e.g. headache, tummy ache, existing aches are magnified ...) through inhibited emotions;
- some personality changes can occur (easygoing child may become irritable, caring child indifferent ...) and existing personality traits can become amplified (e.g. over-sensitive, over-anxious ...);
- a child may sink into depression and apathy. Feeling that nothing matters and there is nothing worth doing. They are powerless to influence anything in their surroundings. These are generalised negative thoughts and deactivated emotions;
- self-esteem lowers as feelings of worthlessness and incompetence increase.

General behavioural effects
- Speech problems may appear or increase (e.g.
- stuttering, stammering or hesitancy);
- interest and enthusiasms (i.e. personal enthusiasms) may decrease or disappear in a general feeling of inability to affect anything positively;
- absenteeism and avoidance increases (e.g. more often finding ways of avoiding tasks or activities);
- energy levels may be low or fluctuate rapidly;
- sleep patterns may be disrupted and disturbed;
- general feeling that nobody likes me or cares about what I do;
- excessive tendency to blame (outwardly others – or inwardly self);
- unpredictability or uncharacteristic behaviour may develop through out-of-control emotions.

(Constructed by the author with extracts from Wolff 1981, Gray 1987, Fontana 1989 and Evison 1988)

Children are in the early stages of development of their language and their ability to express themselves verbally. Establishing friendships is also something of a hit and miss process until children have learned a fair degree of tolerance and begun to be able to visualise from another's viewpoint. We can apply this knowledge to, for example, a counsellor's viewpoint about the characteristics of people who are likely to be under stress:

> Overstressed people '... tend to be the persons who find that they cannot state ... that they are unhappy with particular issues and therefore tend to be the persons who internalise their resentment about their physical environment, their workload.'
>
> People '... who have not developed friendship or other systems ... to express difficulties ... [or] receive help'.

(Ridgeway 1988)

A humane response to stress?

In the same way that the symptoms of stress can be divided into cognitive, emotional and general (including physical), so we could do this with stress management strategies. Some of these, children might do naturally or for themselves, or with some encouragement. Some may need to be demonstrated and learned in order to generate stress management type behaviour. An effective and affective social skills programme will contain many of these elements.

Cognitive methods
- active recognition and description of negative emotions and moods whenever they occur (helping the child to describe their feelings – not internalise them);
- verbal feedback about the pupil's own (perhaps rigid) responses and blocks to questions, to other pupils or to tasks. Helping children to reframe and redefine their experiences;
- noting small successes in work or in other activities. Sometimes actively finding these;
- recognise, describe and encourage pupil to recognise their own natural methods of diffusing or disrupting stressful situations (e.g. telling a joke, laughing, giggling, changing the subject, asking for help ...);
- helping pupil to recognise when their own attention or concentration is reducing through stress or pressure. Encourage and allow them to switch attention (most children do this naturally enough!) briefly and productively;
- take care about 'loading on' pressure in academic situations. It can very quickly become counter-productive. A relaxed mind will work better;

- children need skills to help them plan in both the short and the long term. When under stress, it is helpful to be able to plan the next step or to see what the longer term results might be.

Emotional strategies

- celebrating mastery experiences. Encouraging and working from strengths is a good technique for building up a child's personal resource kit to apply to the next difficult or challenging situation;
- positive attention switching means helping a child or young person to switch their attention. Feelings tend to follow the focus of attention – think of something pleasant and feelings will often follow;
- interrupting 'out of control' feelings (aggression, panic) and giving support. Showing how to get support when these feelings begin to emerge;
- supportive relationships minimise and mitigate stress whether they are natural or specifically set up;
- good relationships between teachers, parents or carers can reduce a child's anxieties and stress.

General behavioural or physical strategies

- natural physical movements interrupt and disrupt stressful
- situations – yawning, stretching limbs and body, shaking hands or feet, laughing …;
- inhibited feelings leading to anger and hatred need 'safety' to let go outside of normal situations. Children often do this in soft play areas, ball pools or bouncy castles;
- children (particularly very young children) derive great security from predictable routines – regular events that cannot be anticipated will heighten stress levels.

(Adapted and extended from material by Fontana 1994, Evison 1988 and Leach 1992)

Considering stress as one way of looking at the behaviour of children and young people brings forward the importance of relationships in their widest sense and including home and the community. Teaching and learning is not just about curriculum content but about the process of acquiring and using knowledge, skills and understanding. Successful teaching is not just about measuring attainment against arbitrary and pseudo-developmental standards but about establishing a relationship between the teacher, the learner and his or her environment. As is often the case, discussion is long on the causes and assessing these but shorter on remedies. Many of the remedies lie in the hands of those that have power in the education system. Teachers have power over pupils in the classroom but there are many more people who wield power to change the system outside the classroom. Politicians, education managers (including Headteachers), education research and the purveyors of good practice (e.g. Ofsted Inspectors, school consultants) have great power over the quality of pupils' lives. The current political educational milieu can be stress producing. For example:

- an over emphasis on 'didactic' teaching methods where there is potential for a 'power through knowledge' relationship;
- emphasis on pure content without the skills and the possibility of using or generalising this knowledge content effectively outside school;
- a surfeit of fairly arbitrary and demanding external 'standards';
- a general lack of understanding about, or unwillingness to accept, the 'affective' nature of learning;
- limiting and ageing physical environments, overcrowded and noisy classrooms;
- too much content squeezed into too little time;
- little consideration for the 'interactive' nature of learning and effective teaching;
- insufficient appreciation of the impact of social mores in the classroom and insufficient means to change schools to respond to broader changes in society.

Children and young people who express their stress reactions in outward and 'challenging' ways are those most likely to get away from the stress in the short term but whose lives may be socially damaged in the long term, for instance, by being excluded. Those who cannot express the effects of stress through outward behaviour may not be such a problem in the short term but may end up suffering from illnesses, both physical and mental, in the longer term. A child or young person may well succeed academically but questions have to be asked. What is the cost of academic success and conformity to a very competitive system? At what point should teachers modify the pressures exerted by the education system on children and young people in order to preserve their health and well-being in the long term? At what point is it worth losing health and well-being for academic attainment and the illusory promise of success later in life?

In the 1980s Mr Justice Coleman said that employers should not be excluded from responsibility for the risk of psychiatric damage to their employees through the scope of their 'duty of care' (Lazarus and Folkman 1984). At the turn of the century, shouldn't legislators and managers be held responsible, as part of their 'duty of care', for the psychiatric well-being of pupils and students? As well as an overview of the global causes of stress in children at school, there is a need for insight and empathy from professionals because stress is not something that is easily classified with obvious and 'standard' symptoms or responses. It is as unique as the individuals who experience it and it can show itself in many ways.

Competent and inspirational teachers know the infinite variety of personalities, perspectives and circumstances of their pupils and the massive impact of cultural and social influences that pervade the classroom. We still attempt to measure individual needs as deficiencies against fixed, and often discriminatory labels. The concept of stress as something that is imposed upon individuals by the organisation of schooling and the political systems that drive it is not far fetched or radical. If there is anything to be learnt from the literature and research on 'stress' and stress management, it is that it often generates challenging behaviours and disaffection, resulting in exclusion or rejection of schooling and education. On the positive side, proper recognition of the whole learning process as interaction and as a human activity can lead to many benefits. Amongst these benefits are accelerated learning; proper application of emotional intelligence and later adjustment; appreciation of multiple intelligences and individual talent or 'giftedness'; a feeling of valued education in a caring society; a reduction of difficult or challenging behaviour and consequent exclusion or marginalisation. A significant number of these benefits to statutory schooling seem to be eluding us at the moment.

Issues

1. Do we put up with too much stress and pressure as part of our everyday lives, in schools, at home and in the adult world of work? Is stress a necessary part of our lives and, if so, how much is necessary?
2. Why is stress generally regarded as an adult thing? Is it, and should it be, a part of children's lives? What effect does stress in schools and classrooms have on children's learning and future achievements?
3. Where is the dividing line between acceptable challenge and overwhelming pressure? Is academic attainment a true indicator of future success or happiness? What effect does academic pressure have on children's long-term health?

Sources and references

Bailey, R. (1994) *LISA: Lifestyle Information and Stress Analysis*. London: Warwick IC Systems. Centre of Advanced Learning.

Bakker, F. C, Whiting, H. T. A. and van der Brug, H. (1990) *Sport Psychology: Concepts and Applications*. London: John Wiley & Sons.

Bandura, A. (1977) *Social Learning Theory*. Englewood Cliffs, NJ: Prentice Hall.

Bandura, A. (1989) Perceived self-efficacy in the exercise of personal agency. *The Psychologist*. Vol. 2, p. 411–24.

Cartwright, S. and Cooper, C. L. (1997) *Managing Workplace Stress*. London: Sage Publications.

Charlton, T. and Hunt, L. (1993) Towards pupil's self-image enhancement: The EASI teaching programme. *Support for Learning*, No. 8, August.

Cole, M. and Walker, S. (1989) *Teaching and Stress*. Milton Keynes: Open University Press.

Dunham, J. (1983) Occupational Stress. In A. Paisley (ed.) *The Effective Teacher*. London: Ward Lock.

Evans, P., Clow, A. and Hucklebridge, F. (1997) Stress and the immune system. *The Psychologist*. Vol. 10, No. 7, July.

Evison, R. (1988) Effective Stress Management = Management of Inappropriate Negative Emotions. *The Occupational Psychologist*. British Psychological Society. No. 6, December.

Fontana, D. (1989) *Managing Stress*. London: The British Psychological Society and Routledge.

Gray, A. G. (1987) *The Psychology of Fear and Stress* (2nd ed.). Cambridge: Cambridge University Press.

Hardy, L. (1988) The Inverted-U Hypothesis: a catastrophe for sport psychology. Paper presented at the British Psychological Society Annual Conference, Leeds. April.

Kelly, A. V. (1990) *The National Curriculum: A Critical Review*. London: Paul Chapman.

Lansdown, G. (1994) Children's Rights. In B. Mayall (ed.) *Children's Childhoods: Observed and Experienced*. London: Falmer Press.

Lawrence, D. (1987) *Self-Esteem in the Classroom*. London: Paul Chapman.

Lazarus, R. and Folkman, S. (1984) Psychological stress is a relationship between the environment and the person. In *Stress, Appraisal and Coping*. New York: Springer.

Leach, P. (1992) Young Children Under Stress (Section 1). *Starting Points 13: Practical Guidance for Early Years Workers*. London: NEYN.

Lindsay, G. (1997) Open Dialogue: Peer Review (of Raven, J.). *BPS Education Section Review*. Vol. 21, No. 2, p. 19.

Maslow, A. H. (1954) *Motivation and Personality* (2nd ed.). New York: Harper and Row.

Maslow, A. H. (1968) *Toward a Psychology of Being* (2nd ed.). New York: Van Nostrand.

McGuiness, J. B. (1993) *Teachers, Pupils and Behaviour: A Managerial Approach*. London: Cassell.

Meighan, R. (1981) *A Sociology of Educating*. London: Holt, Rinehart & Winston.

Mills, S. (1995) *Stress Management for the Individual Teacher: Self study modules for teachers and lecturers*. Lancaster: Framework Press Educational Publishers.

Parsons, C. (1996) Permanent Exclusions from School: A Case Where Society is Failing Its Children. *Support for Learning*. Vol. 11, No. 3, pp. 109–12.

Raven, J. (1997) Education, Educational Research, Ethics and the BPS. The British Psychological Society. *Education Section Review*. Vol. 21, No. 2, p. 3.

Ridgeway, C. (1988) Stress: A counsellor's viewpoint. *The Occupational Psychologist*. British Psychological Society. No. 6, December.

Rosenthal, R. and Jacobson, L. (1968) *Pygmalion in the Classroom: Teacher Expectation and Pupils' Intellectual Development*. New York: Holt, Rinehart & Winston.

Rotter, J. B. (1954) *Social Learning and Clinical Psychology*. Englewood Cliffs, NJ: Prentice-Hall.

Seligman, M. E. P. (1975) *Helplessness: On Depression, Development and Death*. San Francisco: W. H. Freeman.

Smith, C. J. and Cooper, P. (1996) Emotional and Behavioural Difficulties: Theory, Practice and School Effectiveness. *Emotional and Behavioural Difficulties*. Vol. 1, No. 1, Spring, p. 3.

Stroh, C. M. (1971) *Vigilance: the Problem of Sustained Attention*. Oxford: Pergamon Press.

Varma, V. P. (ed.) (1973) *Stresses in Children*. London: University of London Press Ltd.

Wolff, S. (1981) *Children Under Stress* (2nd ed.). Harmondsworth: Penguin Books Ltd.

Yerkes, R. M. (ed.) (1921) Psychological examining in the United States army. *Memoirs of the National Academy of Science*, 15.

PART 4
Medical perspectives

Chapter 21

Attention Deficit Disorder as a factor in the origin of behavioural disturbance in schools

Maurice Place, Jo Wilson, Elaine Martin and Jessica Hulsmeier

Introduction

Although it may be tempting to think that 'children behaving badly within school' is a recent phenomenon, it is far from the truth. Nevertheless, concern about misbehaviour within schools has been steadily increasing, with growing rates of formal exclusion (Social Exclusion Unit, 1998), and continuing calls for the examination of the role of specialist provision in trying to respond to this group of children's needs (Croll & Moses, 1998).

The factors which influence these behavioural difficulties have been intensively sought within the child, the family, the classroom, the school and even in the child's peer group. The conclusions drawn from this work have been wide-ranging and varied. The interventions which have been urged have been equally broad in their scope, ranging from improving teacher authority and developing the process of 'Assertive Discipline' within the classroom (Canter & Canter, 1992) to encouraging more structured family management regimes and changing the child's own psychosocial functioning through therapeutic mechanisms such as groups and counselling (Langham & Parker, 1989).

Over a similar period, there has been an emerging body of research looking at whether poor concentration, impulsivity and motor restlessness form a distinct clinical entity, and at the impact which such a condition could have upon both general behaviour and educational functioning. It has proved difficult to endorse the concept that these form a single mental disorder because so many factors may produce such a pattern of problems. In Britain, the diagnosis of Hyperkinetic Disorder detailed in the International Classification of Diseases (Edition 10) (World Health Organisation, 1992) has traditionally been used to define the disorder, although increasingly the diagnostic category of Attention Deficit Hyperactivity Disorder, detailed in the American Diagnostic and Statistical Manual of Mental Disorders (DSM IV) (American Psychiatric Association, 1994), is being quoted, especially by families. Table 21.1 shows the features which make up this diagnostic category

Table 21.1 Attention Deficit Disorder (American Psychiatric Association, 1994)

A) Either
Six (or more) of the following symptoms of *inattention* have persisted for at least 6 months to a degree that is maladaptive and inconsistent with developmental level:
  (a) often fails to give close attention to details or makes careless mistakes in schoolwork, work, or other activities
  (b) often has difficulty sustaining attention in tasks or play activities
  (c) often does not seem to listen when spoken to directly
  (d) often does not follow through on instructions and fails to finish school work, or chores (not due to oppositional behaviour or failure to understand instructions)
  (e) often has difficulty organising tasks and activities
  (f) often avoids, dislikes, or is reluctant to engage in tasks that require sustained mental effort (such as schoolwork or homework)
  (g) often loses things necessary for tasks or activities (eg toys, school work, pencils, books)
  (h) is often easily distracted by extraneous stimuli
  (i) is often forgetful in daily activities
  or
Six (or more) of the following symptoms of *hyperactivity/impulsivity* have persisted for at least 6 months to a degree that is maladaptive and inconsistent with developmental level:
  (a) often fidgets with hands or feet or squirms in seat
  (b) often leaves seat in classroom or in other situations in which remaining seated is expected
  (c) often runs about or climbs excessively in situations in which it is inappropriate (in adolescents this may be subjective feelings of restlessness)
  (d) often has difficulty playing or engaging in leisure activities quietly
  (e) is often 'on the go' or often acts as if 'driven by a motor'
  (f) often talks excessively
  (g) often blurts out answers before questions have been completed
  (h) often has difficulty waiting turn
  (i) often interrupts or intrudes on others (eg butts into conversations or games)
B) Some hyperactive-impulsive or inattentive symptoms that caused impairment were present before 7 years of age.
C) Some impairment from the symptoms is present in two or more settings.
D) There must be clear evidence of clinically significant impairment in social or academic functioning.
E) The symptoms do not occur exclusively during the course of another condition.

and recognises three subtypes of Attention Deficit Disorder: impulsive, hyperactive and combined; the last of which is close in elements to the Hyperkinetic Disorder.

Reviews of the studies exploring the existence of a specific disorder have come to differing conclusions, ranging from doubts about the usefulness of thinking of it as a mental disorder (British Psychological Society, 1996) to forceful assertions that there is now a satisfactory degree of external validation for this diagnostic category to be accepted as a distinct entity (Cantwell, 1996). These differing conclusions clearly pose a challenge to professionals, particularly when faced with a difficult pupil who finds it hard to stay settled and to concentrate on set tasks. The matter is further complicated as, in common with most disorders, there is a continuum of difficulty which makes decisions in borderline situations very difficult.

Accepting the existence of ADHD, however, does identify a significant group of pupils, although the differing definitions and methods of assessment have produced wide variations in prevalence. The DSM IV (American Psychiatric Association, 1994) estimates the prevalence to be 3% to 5%, but there have been reports which suggest it to be as high as 17% (Cohen, Cohen & Kasen, 1993). Work using current definitions suggests that the problem may be present in about 0.5% to 1% of the school population (Taylor & Hemsley, 1995). Such a prevalence would suggest that a considerable number of children would be potentially at risk of having the disorder, and poses a very significant question: 'What contribution could such difficulties be making to the disruptive and challenging behaviour being reported within schools?'. Certainly it has been suggested for some time that there is a link between ADHD and conduct problems (Laufer & Denhoff, 1957), and there are indications that when both are present the effects are greater than either exerts on its own (McArdle, O'Brien & Kolvin, 1995).

A considered view on whether ADHD is a distinct entity is particularly important as focused interventions, in particular drug treatments, have been used in children with attention problems for some time. Most studies reporting on the use of stimulant drugs are American in origin, and indicate that they can reduce the overactivity and impulsivity which the child shows, as well as improving overall attention levels (Wilens & Biederman, 1992). There is work to suggest that such treatments also increase the pupil's academic productivity, as well as improving cognitive functioning and recall (O'Toole, Abramowitz, Morris & Dulcan, 1997), and teachers regularly report that medication gives the opportunity to work more effectively with the pupil in the areas of appropriate classroom behaviour and social skills.

As has been highlighted, professional opinion about the value of the concept of ADHD is somewhat polarised, and is intensified by the high level of media coverage and the often vociferous demands of parents to have their children's difficulties diagnosed as ADHD. Although the concept of ADHD can be useful in a clinical setting, should it actually be a serious consideration when trying to respond to difficult pupils within the educational system? To explore this question, all of the pupils attending an EBD provision were surveyed for the prevalence of psychiatric disorder in general, and ADHD in particular. Children whose behavioural difficulties are sufficiently extreme to cause their removal from mainstream schooling often find themselves in specialist educational establishments, as attempts at inclusion can be highly disruptive to their peers. If ADHD is a factor in the behaviour of some of these children, it should be prevalent in the population of any school for children with EBD.

Method

The sample consisted of all the 85 children attending one local authority's special day school provision for children with emotional and behavioural disorders in the north-east of England. The provision caters for children under the age of 13 years who have severe difficulties within mainstream schools and are within the average range of intelligence. It is the only such provision within the authority. In line with most schools catering for such children in the United Kingdom, admission is restricted to children who have a Section V Statement of Special Educational Needs, criteria which reflect the severe level of problems that a child must be experiencing before admission is considered. Each child on the school roll in January 1997 was asked to take part and, if agreeable, his or her parents were approached for permission for their child to participate in the study. All agreed. Staff at the school were all made familiar with the focus of the study, but no specific information about mental health issues was offered during its course, other than when necessary to help with the management of individual children.

All the pupils were screened using the teacher version of the Ontario Child Health Scale (OCHS) (Boyle, Offord, Racine, Fleming, Szatmari & Sanford, 1993) which measures, in a standardised instrument, the emotional and behavioural functioning of pupils aged 5 to 16 years. The scale was one of the first to be specifically designed to map to a formal diagnostic classification system, and has demonstrated good internal consistency (all estimates > 0.74) and test-retest reliability (all estimates > 0.65). There are subscores for 'conduct disorder', 'oppositional disorder', 'over-anxious disorder' and 'depression', as well as ADHD. The validity of using the instrument in a UK population has been examined, and its ability to detect disorders using current diagnostic criteria has been confirmed (Place, Martin, Wilson & Hulsmeier, 1999).

The 85 children attending the school ranged in age from 8.5 to 13.4 years, with a mean age of 11.5 years. Of these only three were girls. The nine class teachers were each asked to complete the revised OCHS for every child in their class. In addition each child was assessed by psychiatric interview, which was independent of the teacher assessment process, and information was gathered from the parents using a semi-structured format which gathers details of the children's functioning in terms of both their behaviour and their inner world (Place, Framrose & Willson, 1985). The child and parental interview information was then considered by one of the authors (MP) who was unaware of the teachers' views of the children. If either informant indicated that a symptom was present, its severity was noted and it was included in the diagnostic process for that index child. These symptom profiles were then used to formulate DSM IV (American Psychiatric Association, 1994) diagnoses.

The educational attainments of all the children were assessed; in the younger children by completing the Individual Reading Analysis (Vincent & de la Mare, 1989); with older children being assessed using the Wechsler Objective Reading Dimensions (WORD) (Wechsler, 1993). In addition, the medical and educational histories of the children were examined.

Results

All the children had educational Statements, and the mean reading ability was 38 months below the chronological ages (standard deviation = 24.5 months); 75.4% had reading abilities which were at least two years behind their chronological age. It is a criterion of admission that the child's behaviour should be too difficult for a mainstream school to cope with, and it was therefore not surprising to find that all the children's records showed a catalogue of behavioural difficulties over a long period within their mainstream school. These usually involved frequent defiance towards teaching staff, disruption of classroom activities and a refusal to complete set work. Aggression, both verbal and physical, featured in their histories as did overt temper tantrums. Teacher information and detailed behaviour records were available on all children, but six of the families did not attend the assessment interviews.

The psychiatric formulations made for each child showed that 86% had at least one psychiatric disorder, with high rates for each of the specific diagnostic categories (Table 21.2). To help give a sense of scale to this level of psychopathology, these results are compared with the rates of disturbance found in recent, community surveys of children. As is evident from this comparison, the level of disturbance found within this sample population is far in excess of that in the general population, and this high level of difficulty was mirrored in the parents' responses, confirming that the difficulties are pervasive and not confined to one particular sphere of the children's lives.

Table 21.2 The frequency of disorders within the school and comparison with rates found in community surveys

	Present Study				Published Population Studies	
	Teacher Questionnaire			Psychiatric Formulation		
	Mean	Std Dev (N = 85)	% above cut-off	% with disorder (N = 79)	% with disorder	Study
Conduct disorder	5.13	3.52	36	46	5.5	Offord et al, 1987
					10.8	Fergusson et al, 1993
Oppositional defiance	9.64	4.52	31	29	1.3	McGee et al, 1992
					5.7	Anderson et al, 1987
Depression	8.74	4.33	34	24	1.4	McGee et al, 1992
					4	Whitaker et al, 1990
Over-anxious	4.68	2.77	20	11	2.4	Bowen et al, 1990
					2.5	MGee et al, 1992
Attention Deficit	15.02	6.54	65	70	5–10	Szatmari et al, 1989
					1–3	McArdle et al, 1995

It might not seem surprising to find such levels of disturbance in this group of children, for their behaviour had caused sufficient concern to prompt placement in a special setting. It needs to be borne in mind, however, that the decisions about placement were made because of their behaviour within school, and never in response to a diagnosed psychiatric problem. It is clear from the results that they have high rates of disturbance, particularly with regard to ADHD. Over half of them also had depression, and only two of those with depression did not also have a diagnosis of ADHD. As might be expected, their self-esteem and self-confidence tended to be low, although the evaluation did not allow any causal link to be made between these features.

Discussion

Part of the problem in establishing the validity of ADHD as a distinct diagnosis has been that difficulties with poor concentration, restlessness and impulsivity can emerge in particular situations for reasons other than the presence of an intrinsic disorder. For example, in school there may be a pattern of 'not settling to task', 'frequently leaving the seat', and 'disturbing other children'. Even when their families have few concerns about behaviour, careful analysis and assessment often reveal that the child has previously unrecognised educational problems, which can be specific difficulties or possibly a more generalised inability to cope with school work.

Alternatively, problems may emerge primarily at home, with parents complaining of persistent defiance and disobedience; friction with siblings; destructiveness; or even fire-raising. In school, problems may be few, particularly when the pupil is with relatives or family friends, and such behaviours would appear to indicate that the child's problems arise as a consequence of exposure to chronic family adversity rather than from any intrinsic difficulties. Such contrasting pictures probably form distinct subgroups of the attention deficit spectrum (Elliott & Place, 1998), and need to be distinguished from the pervasive type of problem where the child's poor attention and over-activity usually began very early in life, and in which the genetic component is particularly strong compared to other forms of psychopathology (Rutter, Silberg, O'Connor & Simonoff, 1999). The vulnerabilities which this genetic loading suggests will be influenced by psychosocial factors and, if these lead to the emergence of troublesome behaviours in the young child, it is highly likely that conduct problems will emerge in later childhood (Stevenson, Richman & Graham, 1985). Other problems, such as depression, are also far more frequent in these children (Bird, Canino, Rubio-Stipec, Gould, Ribera, Sesman, Woodbury & Huertas-Goldman, 1988) and even if initially there are few family difficulties, the continued effects of impulsivity and poor compliance prompt their gradual emergence. This complex mix of psychiatric problems is very potent in lowering children's self-esteem and can easily cause them to give up on academic strivings (Puig-Antich, Kauftman, Ryan, Williamson, Dahl, Lukens & Todak, 1992).

Such findings stress how significantly educational difficulties may be influenced by those aspects of a child's life which are not immediately visible to the outside observer. This is especially true of ADHD, which is well recognised as being associated with poor school performance (Faraone, Biederman, Lehman, Spencer, Norman, Seidman & Kraus, 1993). In their eight-year follow-up of such children, Barkley and his colleagues (Barkley, Fischer, Edelbrock & Smallish, 1990) found that hyperactivity greatly increased the risk of academic failure, and doubled the chance of the child being suspended. If there was also conduct disorder, the risk of suspension increased fourfold over the controls. Results such as these suggest that major educational and behavioural difficulties are commonly associated with this disorder, and being aware of its potential presence can assist when determining how best to respond to children who are demonstrating challenging behaviour.

Focused interventions such as behavioural programmes (Abramowitz, 1994) and social skills training within the school setting (Connors, Wells & Erhardt, 1994) are important elements of intervention with such pupils. Parental efforts which focus upon peer interactional tasks (Cousins & Weiss, 1993) and help given to a child's family to create a more settled environment (Anastopoulos, Shelton, Du Paul & Guevremont, 1992) can also contribute to a positive improvement in a young person's functioning. In addition to such approaches, it has been suggested that reducing the child's 'distractibility' and 'over-activity' with stimulant medication would improve his or her performance by between 30% and 60% (Millichap & Fowler, 1967). Stimulants also appear to have a positive impact upon the young person's social interaction (Whalen, Henker & Granger, 1990), and can improve his or her overall classroom performance (Du Paul, Barkley & McMurray, 1994). The medication can, however, prompt the emergence of headaches and greater emotionality in some children. Deterioration in control of co-existing epilepsy and an exaggeration of pre-existing tic disorder may also render such treatment inappropriate. Consequently, the question of how to determine which children should be considered for medication arises. In severe cases, the relevance and value is usually clear, but in children with multiple problems such decisions can be challenging. Some assistance with this conundrum is now available by using the decision tree which was recently published as part of the European clinical guidelines for Hyperkinetic Disorder (Taylor, Sergeant, Doepfner, Gunning, Overmeyer, Mobius & Eisert, 1998).

This sample of children demonstrated the full range of difficulties from challenging behaviour to poor social skills. It is also relevant to note that, prior to the study, only seven of the children were known to have attention problems and therefore, for the majority, it was their acting out behaviour which was seen as their principal difficulty. Consider, for instance, George who, throughout his school career, had been volatile, irritable and abrasive in his relationships with peers. His temper outbursts had increasingly led to apparently uncontrollable incidents of physical aggression where he wept and screamed with rage. Academically, he rejected all work out of hand, usually complaining that it was too difficult, or hurling it aside without a glance. Identification of his attention deficit disorder resulted in his being started on an appropriate stimulant medication regime, which was closely medically monitored with close co-operation between his mother and the school to ensure compliance. As a result, his pattern of difficulties ceased, although he was initially tentative and seemed wary of trusting his new-found control. Gradually, however, he gained confidence, became more relaxed, began to smile regularly, and to mix with the other children with obvious pleasure. George began to make any complaints appropriately, and often with evident good humour. He was amenable to handling strategies and was able to talk about his responses in a calm and settled way.

Robert provides a more dramatic example. He had shown levels of physical and verbal aggression which had defeated his parents, teachers and his fellow pupils. He could apply himself to work but only with an intensity that erupted into furious impatience if he was evenly slightly distracted. He sneered at peers, sought adult attention constantly, and was always restless and fiddling with any equipment within reach. His response to the stimulant medication regime was immediate and he became visibly relaxed and began to display a previously unseen side to his nature: he became thoughtful and considerate of others. He showed a growing ability to control his behaviour, discuss his responses and initiate friendships; something that previously he had not been thought capable of.

Although these examples display a dramatic change in behaviour, it could be questioned whether such outcomes could not simply be the response to the special educational regime. This is unlikely to be the case, however, since these pupils had been within the setting for some time without any such improvement being evident. With both pupils, staff had employed a range of handling strategies over a period of time, but nothing had produced any consistent improvement in behaviour. The response to medication was immediate and evident in all of the school settings. Possibly more significantly, however, was that the changes emerged immediately after the drug regime was introduced. It is, of course, tempting to believe that perhaps every difficult child could be helped by the introduction of such regimes, and this has certainly been the trend in America and has given rise to a concern that medication is being overused (Kolata, 1996). Such concern has prompted the British Psychological Society to urge that medication should not become the first line treatment for such problems in the United Kingdom (British Psychological Society, 1996). There are also concerns that medication is merely sedating a difficult child, and that manifest improvements in functioning and attainment, not docility, should be the markers used to judge the efficacy of medication. When trying to determine the appropriatenesss of using medication in any situation, it is necessary to balance the perceived benefits against the potential dangers of the regular use of a powerful drug especially for ADHD. In this case, once established, medication tends to be maintained but regular reviews and periods without medication should ensure that it is discontinued as soon as it is no longer helpful.

With the increasing press interest and the growth of parental pressure groups, there is an obvious danger that over-prescription of stimulant medication will emerge in the United Kingdom. Such a development clearly raises concerns about the level of certainty needed in the diagnostic process before those involved can be confident that medication is appropriate. On the other hand, is the 'American experience' prompting too great a level of caution and consequently depriving children of treatment that might greatly aid their educational progress and personal development? The balance to be struck is between the effects of taking stimulant medication for a lengthy period and the changes in functioning which are likely to emerge. The speed of action of the stimulant means that it is quickly evident to both teachers and parents what benefits might accrue, and that its potential part in the programme of intervention can be balanced against the known risks and problems. The experience from this small sample was that the recognition of the presence of psychiatric problems (ADHD in particular) and an appropriate response to them, results in tangible educational gains and improves the child's ability to respond positively to effective handling and to access the curriculum.

Conclusion

The study highlights the potential for major psychiatric problems, and particularly Attention Deficit Hyperactivity Disorder, to contribute to children's behavioural and educational difficulties. Screening for such disorders in highly vulnerable populations can identify those children who need to be examined in greater detail, with the likelihood that effective intervention may have a tangible effect not only upon their behaviour, but also on their academic performance.

References

Abramowitz, A. J. (1994) 'Classroom interventions for disruptive behavior disorders', *Child and Adolescent Psychiatry Clinics of North America*. 3, 343.

American Psychiatric Association (1994) *Diagnostic and Statistical Manual of Mental Disorders (DSM IV)* (4th Edition). Washington DC: American Psychiatric Association.

Anastopoulos, A. D., Shelton, T. L., Du Paul, G. J. & Guevremont, D. C. (1992) 'Parent training for attention deficit hyperactivity disorder: its impact on parent functioning', *Journal of Abnormal Child Psychology*. 21, 581.

Barkley, R. A., Fischer, M., Edelbrock, C. S. & Smallish, L. (1990) 'The adolescent outcome of hyperactive children diagnosed by research criteria-I. (An 8 year prospective follow-up study)', *Journal of the American Academy of Child and Adolescent Psychiatry*. 29, 546.

Bird, H. R., Canino, G., Rubio-Stipec, M., Gould, M. S., Ribera, J., Sesman, M., Woodbury, M. & Huertas-Goldman, S. (1988) 'Estimates of the prevalence of childhood maladjustment in a community survey in Puerto Rico', *Archives of General Psychiatry*. 45, 1120.

Boyle, M. H., Offord, D. R., Racine, Y., Fleming, J. E., Szatmari, P. & Sanford, M. (1993) 'Evaluation of the revised Ontario Child Health Study Scales', *Journal of Child Psychology and Psychiatry*. 34, 189.

British Psychological Society (1996) *Attention Deficit Hyperactivity Disorder (ADHD): a Psychological Response to an Evolving Concept*. Leicester: British Psychological Society.

Canter, L. & Canter, M. (1992) *Assertive Discipline*. Santa Monica: Lee Canter Associates.

Cantwell, D. P. (1996) 'Classification of child and adolescent psychopathology', *Journal of Child Psychology and Psychiatry*. 37, 3.

Cohen, P., Cohen, J. & Kasen, S. (1993) 'An epidemiological study of disorders in late childhood and adolescence-I (Age and gender-specific prevalence', *Journal of Child Psychology and Psychiatry*. 34, 851.

Connors, C. K., Wells, K. C. & Erhardt, D. (1994) 'Multi-modal therapies: methodological issues in research and practice', *Child and Adolescent Psychiatry Clinics of North America*. 3, 361.

Cousins, L. S. & Weiss, G. (1993) 'Parent training and social skills training for children with attention deficit hyperactivity disorder. How can they be combined for greater effectiveness?', *Canadian Journal of Psychiatry*. 38, 443.

Croll, P. & Moses, D. (1998) 'Pragmatism, ideology and educational change: the case of special educational needs', *British Journal of Educational Studies*. 46, 11.

Du Paul, G., Barkley, R. & McMurray, M. (1994) 'Response of children with ADHD to methylphenidate: interaction with internalizing symptoms', *Journal of the American Academy of Child and Adolescent Psychiatry*. 33, 894.

Elliott, J. & Place, M. (1998) 'Attention deficit disorder and hyperactivity', in J. Elliott & M. Place, *Children in Difficulty*. London: Routledge.

Faraone, S., Biederman, J., Lehman, B. K., Spencer, T., Norman, D., Seidman, L. J. & Kraus, I. (1993) 'Intellectual performance and school failure in children with attention deficit disorder and their siblings', *Journal of Abnormal Psychology*. 102, 616.

Kolata, G. (1996) 'Boom in Ritalin sales raises ethical questions', *New York Times*. 15 May, p.8.

Langham, M. & Parker, V. (1989) *Counselling Skills for Teachers*. Lancaster: Framework Press.

Laufer, M. & Denhoff, E. (1957) 'Hyperkinetic behavior syndrome in children', *Journal of Pediatrics*. 50, 463.

McArdle, P., O'Brien, G. & Kolvin, I. (1995) 'Hyperactivity: prevalence and relationship with conduct disorder', *Journal of Child Psychology and Psychiatry*. 36, 279.

Millichap, J. & Fowler, G. (1967) 'Treatment of minimal brain dysfunction syndromes', *Pediatric Clinics of North America*. 14, 767.

O'Toole, K., Abramowitz, A., Morris, R. & Dulcan, M. (1997) 'Effects of methylphenidate on attention and non-verbal learning in children with ADHD', *Journal of the American Academy of Child and Adolescent Psychiatry*. 36, 531.

Place, M., Framrose, R. F. & Willson, C. (1985) 'The classification of adolescents who are referred to a psychiatric unit', *Journal of Adolescence*. 8, 297.

Place, M., Martin, E., Wilson, J. & Hulsmeier, J. (1999) 'Validating the Ontario Child Health Scale in a UK population', *European Child and Adolescent Psychiatry*. 8, 255.

Puig-Antich, J., Kauftnan, J., Ryan, N. D., Williamson, D. E., Dahl, R. E., Lukens, E. & Todak, G. (1992) 'The psychosocial functioning and family environment of depressed adolescents', *Journal of the American Academy of Child and Adolescent Psychiatry*. 32, 244.

Rutter, M., Silberg, J., O'Connor, T. & Simonoff, E. (1999) 'Genetics and Child Psychiatry-II: Empirical research findings', *Journal of Child Psychology and Psychiatry*. 40, 19.

Social Exclusion Unit (1998) *Truancy and Social Exclusion* (cm 3957). London: The Stationery Office.

Stevenson, J., Richman, N. & Graham, P. (1985) 'Behaviour problems and language abilities at three years and behavioural deviance at eight years', *Journal of Child Psychology and Psychiatry*. 26, 215.

Taylor, E. & Hemsley, R. (1995). 'Treating hyperkinetic disorders in children', *British Medical Journal*. 310, 1617.

Taylor, E., Sergeant, J., Doepfner, M., Gunning, B., Overmeyer, S., Mobius, H. J. & Eisert, H. G. (1998) 'Clinical guidelines for hyperkinetic disorder', *European Child and Adolescent Psychiatry*. 7, 184.

Vincent, D. & de la Mare, M. (1989) *The Individual Reading Analysis*. Windsor: NFER-Nelson.

Wechsler, D. (1993). *Wechsler Objective Reading Dimensions (WORD)*. London: The Psychological Corporation.

Whalen, C., Henker, B. & Granger, D. (1990) 'Social adjustment processes in hyperactive boys: effects of methylphenidate and comparison with normal peers', *Journal of Abnormal Child Psychology*. 18, 297.

Wilens, T. E. & Biederman, J. (1992) 'The stimulants', *Psychiatric Clinics of North America*. 15, 191.

World Health Organisation (1992). *The ICD-I 0: Classification of Mental and Behavioural Disorders: Clinical Description and Diagnostic Guidelines*. New York: WHO.

Chapter 22

Approaches to autism

Kieron Sheehy

Introduction

Autism is a complex developmental disability that occurs, typically, during the first three years of life and is approximately four times more common in boys than girls. It was first described by Leo Kanner (1943), who named the pattern of behaviour he observed in a small group of young children 'early infantile autism'. He chose the term 'autos' (self) to describe the children's apparently 'inward looking' behaviour. A little later, and separately, Asperger (1944) wrote an account of some older children that overlapped, to some extent, with Kanner's ideas. Asperger also used the term 'autistic' in his description.

This chapter aims to outline criteria by which autism is recognised in individuals and discusses some of the common approaches to addressing behaviour identified as 'autistic' together with their theoretical underpinnings.

Recognising autism

Kanner (1943) developed a list of five characteristics to define the group of children he observed.

- The inability to relate to and interact with people from the beginnings of life
- The inability to communicate with others through language
- An obsession with maintaining sameness and resisting change
- A preoccupation with objects rather than people
- The occasional evidence of good potential for intelligence.

(Waterhouse, 2000, p.15)

Much later Wing and Gould (1979) identified a broader group of 'autistic' children. This group (about 15 in 10,000) showed a 'triad of impairments', having a significant impairment in social interaction, communication and imagination. These children experience difficulties in both verbal and non-verbal communication, and in important aspects of their play activities.

However, the common stereotype of children with autism as possessing islets of great ability, possibly influenced by films such as *Rain Man*, is misjudged. Whilst such *idiot savant* skills do exist in some people (for example the author has taught children and adults with such skills as rapid calendar calculating, drawing skills or notable mathematical aptitude), only a small minority would fall into this group. Eighty per cent of children with autism score below 70 on the psychometric tests of intelligence (Peeters and Gilberg, 1999) and increasingly severe general learning difficulties are correlated with an increasing occurrence of autism. Consequently, a high proportion of children with autism have severe or profound learning difficulties and it becomes difficult to separate out the effects of autism and those of having profound learning difficulties (Jordan, 1999).

The diagnostic criteria

Today, diagnostic criteria are used to identity children with autism. Diagnostic criteria are a profile of symptoms and characteristics that typify a particular syndrome and differentiate syndromes from each other. The Diagnostic and Statistical Manual created by the American Psychiatric Association (DSM, 2003) outlines the diagnostic criteria for autism and Asperger's syndrome. These are shown below:

The DSM IV criteria for autistic disorder

A. A total of six (or more) items from (1), (2), and (3), with at least two from (1) and one each from (2) and (3)
(1) qualitative impairment in social interaction, as manifested by at least two of the following:
a) marked impairments in the use of multiple nonverbal behaviors such as eye-to-eye gaze, facial expression, body posture, and gestures to regulate social interaction
b) failure to develop peer relationships appropriate to developmental level
c) lack of spontaneous seeking to share enjoyment, interests, or achievements with other people, (e.g., by a lack of showing, bringing, or pointing out objects of interest to other people)

d) lack of social or emotional reciprocity (note: in the description, it gives the following as examples: not actively participating in simple social play or games, preferring solitary activities, or involving others in activities only as tools or 'mechanical' aids)

(2) qualitative impairments in communication as manifested by at least one of the following:

a) delay in, or total lack of, the development of spoken language (not accompanied by an attempt to compensate through alternative modes of communication such as gesture or mime)

b) in individuals with adequate speech, marked impairment in the ability to initiate or sustain a conversation with others

c) stereotyped and repetitive use of language or idiosyncratic language

d) lack of varied, spontaneous make-believe play or social imitative play appropriate to developmental level

(3) restricted repetitive and stereotyped patterns of behavior, interests and activities, as manifested by at least two of the following:

a) encompassing preoccupation with one or more stereotyped and restricted patterns of interest that is abnormal either in intensity or focus

b) apparently inflexible adherence to specific, nonfunctional routines or rituals

c) stereotyped and repetitive motor mannerisms (e.g. hand or finger flapping or twisting, or complex whole-body movements)

d) persistent preoccupation with parts of objects

B. Delays or abnormal functioning in at least one of the following areas, with onset prior to age 3 years:

(1) social interaction

(2) language as used in social communication

(3) symbolic or imaginative play

C. The disturbance is not better accounted for by Rett's Disorder or Childhood Disintegrative Disorder

The DSM IV Diagnostic Criteria for Asperger's syndrome

A. Qualitative impairment in social interaction, as manifested by at least two of the following:

(1) marked impairments in the use of multiple nonverbal behaviors such as eye-to-eye gaze, facial expression, body postures, and gestures to regulate social interaction
(2) failure to develop peer relationships appropriate to developmental level
(3) a lack of spontaneous seeking to share enjoyment, interests, or achievements with other people (e.g. by a lack of showing, bringing, or pointing out objects of interest to other people)
(4) lack of social or emotional reciprocity
B. Restricted repetitive and stereotyped patterns of behavior, interests, and activities, as manifested by at least one of the following:
(1) encompassing preoccupation with one or more stereotyped and restricted patterns of interest that is abnormal either in intensity or focus
(2) apparently inflexible adherence to specific, nonfunctional routines or rituals
(3) stereotyped and repetitive motor mannerisms (e.g., hand or finger flapping or twisting, or complex whole-body movements)
(4) persistent preoccupation with parts of objects
C. The disturbance causes clinically significant impairment in social, occupational, or other important areas of functioning
D. There is no clinically significant general delay in language (e.g., single words used by age 2 years, communicative phrases used by age 3 years)
E. There is no clinically significant delay in cognitive development or in the development of age-appropriate self-help skills, adaptive behavior (other than social interaction), and curiosity about the environment in childhood
F. Criteria are not met for another specific Pervasive Developmental Disorder or Schizophrenia

Note that the key difference between the two syndromes is in the area of cognitive and language development. The term Autistic Spectrum Disorder encompasses children with autism and those with Asperger's syndrome (for a thoughtful discussion of differential diagnosis see Jordan (1999)). The common feature is possessing the triad of impairments, usually accompanied by repetitive patterns of activities. This spectrum encompasses a very wide range of children, some of whom have no spoken language, or others who talk with considerable skill but do not understand the social rules of conversation.

Explanations of autism

There have been many competing theories put forward to explain the patterns of behaviour found in autism. Most prominent in recent years have been theories that address the way in which children with autism think in social situations. These 'theory of mind' explanations propose that the key feature of ASD (in contrast to other learning difficulties) is the child's difficulty in understanding and interpreting the mental states of others. One example might be predicting the beliefs or intentions of other children. The majority of children with autism fail simple tests whose solution requires them to guess what another child is thinking. However, not all children with autism fail such tests or lack social understanding. This has become a fruitful but complex area of research. (see Baron-Cohen, 1995). There are a growing number of accounts written by young people with autism and these often highlight pervasive anxiety and fear as common experiences of being in an unpredictable world (Jones, Zahl and Huws, 2001).

Interventions

A focus of this chapter is a consideration of some established methods of teaching children with autism. The following examples are selected to illustrate three general levels of approach: behavioural, cultural and social.

Behavioural approaches

Applied Behavioural Analysis (ABA) is built on behavioural methods such as breaking identified tasks into small, discrete, 'teachable' steps reinforcing appropriate behaviours, and using highly structured intensive teaching strategies.

ABA usually selects developmentally appropriate behaviours as teaching targets. These can range, for example, from maintaining eye contact to complex responses such as social interaction. Initially each skill is taught separately. It is analysed and broken down into small steps. As each step is taught, the gradual fading of prompts acts to ensure successful completion of the learning tasks. This success is then positively reinforced by consequences that are reinforcing for the individual child. The use of 'discrete trial training', that is, teaching an identified behaviour through a stimulus (instruction)–response model, has become a primary method within the behaviourally-based interventions for teaching children with autism.

Once a specific skill has been mastered successfully it can then be mixed into the teaching of other skills. Redirecting the child towards appropriate behaviours that can be positively reinforced has been found to be most effective in managing inappropriate aggressive behaviour (Lovaas, 1981). Therefore this approach emphasises expanding the child's repertoire of appropriate behaviours. Inappropriate behaviour is not reinforced and an analysis is made of the individual's environment based on the hypothesis that there are likely to be conditions that maintain the behaviour (Green, 1996).

The Lovaas method

The Lovaas Method (Lovaas, 1987) has remained influential in education since its original development. Lovaas was a behaviour analyst who pioneered the use of Applied Behavioural Analysis (ABA) with autistic children, and the ABA procedures that he developed are often referred to as Lovaas therapy.

The key assumptions of the Lovaas approach (Lovaas, 1987; 1996) are

1. Autism is characterised by behaviours that are detrimental or destructive to the child and/or those around him or her.
2. The search for 'underlying causes' of autism may be theoretically misguided and is irrelevant to developing effective therapy.
3. Learning plays a central role in the autistic child's failure to acquire 'desirable' behaviours (such as physical contact with others), and in his/her acquisition of 'undesirable' behaviours (repetitive behaviours that may be injurious or antisocial, such as head banging, destruction of objects, taking off clothes in public, etc.). Therefore behaviour modification is an appropriate technique for changing these behaviours.
4. The key to behaviour modification therapy is to analyse the child's behaviour into 'manageable' components that can be individually tackled.
5. An important extension of this approach (introduced in the 1980s) is training parents to carry out the therapy themselves at home.

(Roth, 2002, p.297)

Thus, in this approach parents are trained to become the primary therapists and children receive one-to-one tuition. The tuition delivers a behavioural teaching programme, usually in the child's own home. Early intervention programmes for children with learning disabilities are recommended as they have the potential to produce major positive changes in development and consequently reduce the need for later interventions (Sheehy, 1993).

Results from early evaluations of the method proved very positive (Lovaas, 1987). For example, 47 per cent of the children who had been taught using the Lovaas method consequently achieved placement within mainstream schools. This was achieved by only 2 per cent of two comparable groups, who received alternative therapies.

Colin's story

'Colin's Story' (McKay, Keenan, and Dillenburger, 2000) gives a clear account of an ABA programme carried out, initially, by parents. The following is a description of Colin's behaviour before beginning the programme.

> He was extremely active, and if restrained (e.g. holding his hand, carrying him, or using a child harness) he became extremely upset and it became a thoroughly aversive situation for the whole family. He depended on routines, for example, he became upset if his mother, Laura, varied the route to the nursery school, even if she parked the car in a different place. In nursery school he refused to join in story time or planned activities, preferring solitary repetitive play with toy cars, water, and sand. However, he adjusted quickly to routines such as those used for going to school, having a break at school, or going home. At home he was seldom still and the parents had to lock the windows and internal doors. He did not respond to his name, he slept little, waking frequently and was very difficult to settle in bed again.
>
> (McKay, Keenan and Dillenburger, 2000, p.64)

Reports from educational and health professionals described Colin as presenting with language delay, being egocentrically preoccupied, lacking the urge to engage socially, obsessiveness and having poor adaptation to change. In line with the diagnostic criteria mentioned above, Colin's behaviour was seen as falling within the umbrella term of Autistic Spectrum Disorder. When Colin was nearly four years old his mother began a parent training programme in ABA. After only one year she had taught her son the skills he needed successfully to begin primary school education.

In class, after three years he was beginning to contribute to discussions without prompting and his academic attainments were comparable to those of his peers. His social interactions had also shown great improvements and Colin was attending the same local school as the rest of his family. (For a detailed account of ABA techniques and Colin's story see Keenan, Kerr and Dillenburger, 2000.)

The Southampton Childhood Autism Programme (SCAmP)

An emerging project within the UK is The Southampton Childhood Autism Programme (SCAmP). This is an intensive early intervention ABA approach. Influenced by Lovaas's original model of 40 hours' tuition per week, the SCAmP intervention funds up to 30 hours per week of tuition from tutors (funded by the Local Education Authority), with parents contributing up to 10 hours of additional time per week, over a two year period [http://www.scamp.soton.ac.uk/]. This contribution offers significant support to families for whom a '40 hours' commitment might have previously been a barrier to participation. At the time of writing, 11 UK LEAs are involved, or becoming involved, in SCAmP. In terms of helping children begin school, a transitional period is envisaged.

> Initially, the child is taught at home to develop skills that are designed to enable him/her to be integrated successfully, with or without support. Assuming these are acquired successfully and are being used functionally, the Supervisor, Senior Supervisor and Consultant may suggest the child can begin to be integrated in nursery/school. School inclusion is a long process and it may be achieved gradually; initially a child may only go for brief sessions every week, accompanied by a trained ABA tutor who acts as a 'shadow'.
>
> (http://www.scamp.soton.ac.uk/FAQ.htm#SchoolIntegration)

Precision teaching

Within classroom settings ABA has influenced the development of precision teaching (PT) approaches. As with other ABA approaches, target behaviours are identified, the teaching interaction (instruction and response) is analysed and progress in learning recorded. The teacher implements a programme of instruction that concentrates on improving the pupil's performance in a particular skill or task. It is concerned with observable and, therefore, measurable behaviours. The pupil's performance is stated as a behavioural objective. This has three components:

- *Action* – what the pupil needs to do
- *Conditions* – a description of the important conditions under which the pupil's performance should occur
- *Criteria* – an indication of what is defined as success for the activity (for example, spelling 4/5 c-v-c words accurately).

Kerr, Smyth, and McDowell (2003) describe implementing precision teaching within the classroom:

> While some practitioners might baulk at the thought of measuring progress on top of teaching and managing the behaviour of a class of students, the procedures involved are not so complex and can be easily introduced within currently existing classroom structures. The product of measurement within PT is generally the number of responses within a standard unit of time (e.g., the number of words a child reads out aloud in a 2 minute period). By plotting the rate of performance, learning pictures in the form of charts can be created. This allows practitioners to scrutinise the learning picture/path for each child at each instructional level. One variable of importance in the teaching process as evident from the learning pictures is the number of responses (correct and incorrect) that each child makes. Related to this is the fact that repeated opportunities to engage in or practice behaviour to a fluency level prove extremely valuable for children with autism.
>
> (Kerr, Smyth, and McDowell, 2003, p.400)

ABA techniques are commonly criticised on the ethics of using explicit rewards and leaving any 'underlying' problems untouched. Other issues are that ABA techniques such as 'time out' from reinforcing conditions are easily misused, that the use of aversives (for example, mild slapping, verbal reprimands) is ethically unsustainable (Lovaas and Favell, 1987), and that ABA techniques treat children 'mechanically'. In considering these points it is worth emphasising that modern versions of this approach do not use aversive methods (Jordan and Jones, 1999) and that precision in one's teaching need not necessarily be construed as mechanistic. Further, whichever way we react to a child's behaviour, there will be consequences. An ABA approach presents a model for understanding the effect that our interactions may have on children and vice versa.

Overall, ABA has been well evaluated, partly because it is built on the observable and measurable learning of children. Hence data is readily forthcoming and evaluative studies are usually well controlled enabling influences such as placebo effects and maturation to be ruled out (Dempsey and Foreman, 2001).

Birnbrauer and Leach (1993), for example, followed up an ABA approach, the Murdoch Early Intervention Program, two years after it began. Whilst half of the Murdoch group made significant progress in terms of compliance and cooperativeness, they made little progress in social play or reducing self-stimulatory behaviour. However, more recently Hall (1997), in reviewing ABA studies, found that overall stereotypical behaviours decreased and that language and social initiation skills increased.

Cultural approaches

The TEACCH approach

ABA makes an assessment of the child's current behaviours, defines what the child needs to learn and then teaches the child these behaviours using a focused behavioural strategy. The TEACCH approach (Treatment and Education of Autistic and related Communication handicapped CHildren) is built on a broader view of autism and its interventions reflect this breadth.

TEACCH began in North Carolina, USA with a focus on teaching self-care skills and managing inappropriate behaviour (TEACCH, 2003) and it draws upon a combination of approaches in the way it teaches. As with some ABA methods parental involvement is an important element, although in the UK, TEACCH is more commonly found within schools than pre-school settings (Jordan and Jones, 1999) and hence parental involvement as TEACCH practitioners is not common.

TEACCH's unique approach is that it considers the way the child 'reads' their environment, rather than looking simply for environmental stimuli that might trigger particular behaviours. TEACCH considers the environment in terms of how the child will be able to interact and learn from it, and how the child him/herself will see the environment. Therefore a TEACCH-influenced classroom places a large emphasis on physically structuring the room to facilitate learning interactions within it. The child's learning experiences are usually cued through associated visual or concrete signals. This may include putting specific activities within specific classroom locations and signalling the transitions between activities through explicit schedules. Schedules are presented in formats appropriate for each child, for example using pictorial or symbolic representations of activities and events. A picture or an object could be set out on a TEACCH board to help the person structure space, concepts, tasks and activities (Roth, 2002). These visual timetables can make the child's day understandable and predictable and consequently reduce the child's anxiety. The strategy also lessens the amount of processing of spoken language that is required.

Children's programmes include both group and individual activities. The individual activities typically occur at the child's own workstation within the class, separate from the class group. This way of working endeavours to meet and address key features of autism such as a need for predictability and the clarification of social messages. In this way the TEACCH classroom might be described as prosthetic, as its design and structure support the particular needs of individual children. A full TEACCH programme runs throughout the day and encompasses all aspects of the curriculum, including play and leisure activities. In the latter children may choose activities that they themselves prefer, rather than imposed 'play' activities that the children may not enjoy. In this respect, and in its design, TEACCH is tuned into the culture of being autistic. In an ABA approach such activities might be given to reinforce preceding 'appropriate' behaviour. In TEACCH there is a feeling for the child as a person with activities of value to him/herself, although (as with ABA) in the longer term TEACCH aims to broaden the child's range of leisure skills. In the UK, for example, schools using TEACCH usually combine it with other approaches such as ABA and Music Therapy (Richardson, 2000).

Positive outcomes have been reported for children being taught through TEACCH programmes, in terms of their adaptive behaviour, perception, motor and cognitive performances, and independence skills (Panerai, Ferrante, and Caputo, 1997). However, evaluative investigations of TEACCH have, so far, lacked control groups (Dempsey and Foreman, 2001) and rarely have they contained explicitly matched comparisons with alternative approaches (Jordan and Jones, 1999). Thus it remains unclear exactly, in empirical terms, what gains children make from inclusion in this programme.

The Higashi School

As its name suggests the Higashi approach originated in Japan. (Higashi translates as 'East'). There is now a Higashi School in Boston, which has attracted students and considerable interest from parents and teachers in the UK. The approach is based on Daily Life Therapy ('Seikatsu Ryouhou'), a 24-hour curriculum developed by the late Dr. Kiyo Kitahara. A key aspect of her approach is exercise. The use of physical activity is seen as a means to reduce anxiety, gain stamina, establish rhythm and routines, (Quill, Gurry and Larkin, 1989, cited in Dempsey and Foreman, 2001) and also reduce aggression and frustration. In support of the latter, there is evidence to suggest that vigorous physical exercise, as well as improving movement co-ordination, may indeed help to reduce anxiety by releasing endorphins, consequently reducing aggressive behaviour, hyperactivity, and self-stimulatory behaviour including self-harm (Richardson, 2000).

The Higashi curriculum is based on the pupil's chronological age and includes activities of daily living, music, craft and the development of play. A major tenet of Daily Life Therapy is that children's education should be conducted in an environment of 'normality' and in the Tokyo school pupils with autism are educated alongside their mainstream peers. In contrast (owing to state legislation) the Boston school caters solely for pupils with autism (Gould, Rigg and Bignell, 1991). Higashi education is based on three tenets:

1. to stabilize emotions though a predictable environment and within in which the child can begin to develop independence;
2. to develop a rhythm of life and well-being through vigorous exercise; it does this through repetition of tasks, strict schedules and intensive physical activity;
3. to stimulate intellectual and cognitive growth through a broad and age-appropriate curriculum that allows individual interests and talents to flourish, taking into account any modifications necessary for each individual child.

(http://www.bostonhigashi.org/html/faq.html)

Unlike the approaches mentioned so far, Dr Kitahara's begins from the basis of group dynamics. There is a systematic focus on developing interactional skills and children can practise these emerging skills within a predictable daily routine. The Boston school now includes 'an overlay of the American system (e.g. individual educational plans and the use of computers)' (Jordan and Jones, 1999). There is a day school and fully residential programme. The pattern of each day is identical and the pace of the group is determined by the slowest member. This can lead to some children waiting quietly for considerable periods of time. Whilst this type of waiting is an important feature of DLT, it may not translate easily into the UK. For example Gould, Rigg, and Bignell (1991) noted that children could wait for up to 35 minutes before beginning an activity.

A questionnaire based on parental ratings of 'Pre-school and now' comparisons of 80 children found that 'more life skills essential for self-esteem and social interaction, such as improved eating, drinking, sleeping, toilet training, and reduced self-injurious behaviour and physical aggression towards others, developed significantly with Daily Life Therapy than with TEACCH' (Richardson, 2000). A report for the National Autistic Society made some positive comments about the Boston school's approach.

> In essence DLT is a scheme which successfully eradicates adverse behaviours and prepares a pupil for, but does not offer, a broader curriculum …

> … There is little doubt that UK teachers would benefit from studying DLT and incorporating the best and most positive aspects into their broader curricula. The physical education and music section of DLT produce a high level of achievement in the pupils and with it improved confidence and self esteem …
>
> (Gould, Rigg, and Bignell, 1991, p.11)

There has however been very little controlled and evaluative research into 'Daily Life Therapy' and it would be difficult to transfer the approach into other cultures without extensive training.

Social interactive approaches

Intensive Interaction

The child with autism can be seen as being 'outside the culture', unable or struggling to tune into the meanings that are embedded within our social world. Learning to understand what things mean cannot be accomplished alone and interactive approaches use interpersonal relationships to build and develop this meaning. In the Higashi approach the group is a starting point. In interactive approaches it is the dyad, the interaction between two people that develops the social interactions from which human abilities are constructed. In contrast to the approaches mentioned so far, Gary Ephraim (1997) argued that people with learning disabilities needed to learn fundamental communication and social abilities in a naturalistic way. They could do this, he proposed, through the interactive play that occurs between parents and children. This interaction would encourage an underpinning social development, rather than the development of isolated and socially 'disembedded' skills.

One social approach that adopts this strategy is 'Intensive Interaction' (Nind and Hewett, 2001). This method trains teachers to help children gain the experience of what it is to be social. In line with Ephraim's suggestions, the teacher adopts a strategy based on early child development to construct a shared experience with the child. Intensive Interaction sets out to enhance social and communication abilities rather than to reduce stereotyped behaviours per se. However, findings from two studies of Intensive Interaction (Nind and Kellett, 2002) report the reduction of such behaviours.

> The aim of Intensive Interaction was to enhance the social and communication abilities of the young people who had severe learning difficulties and ritualistic behaviour and to find a meaningful way of interacting with them. The approach is based on the style of caregiver–infant interaction that facilitates child/learner involvement and control over the social environment. Rather than focusing on changing the behaviour of an individual with learning difficulties, practitioners of Intensive Interaction focus on seeking to establish rapport and communication in ways that an individual finds meaningful. The working premise is that through the development of relationship other development will follow, facilitated by the skilled scaffolding of interactive experiences.
>
> (Nind and Kellet, 2002, p.270)

The approach was originally designed for children with profound and multiple learning difficulties, whose development would be at a pre-verbal and often pre-intentional developmental level. The key elements of the approach are:

- responding to the behaviour of the child with autism 'as if' they had an intentional purpose
- adjusting one's own behaviours to establish social interplay and rapport
- allowing the person with autism to 'take the lead' in social interactions
- using rhythm and timing to give the interactions flow
- allowing the sessions to be enjoyable.

The approach is flexible in that the communicative principles it is built on can be applied in specific Intensive Interaction sessions or during other parts of the day. The following example indicates the playfulness of the approach.

> Kris, a young adult with autism, is roaming around the classroom, repeating sounds to himself. Lindsey, his teacher, approaches, face on, and places her hands on his shoulders, squeezing playfully and saying in a playful, rhythmic, almost daring tone, 'Are you going to play with me? Are you? Go on, go on!' Kris turns his head to the side and continues with his vocalising. The sounds indicate that his mind is elsewhere, the impact is blocking. Lindsey places her hand over his mouth, on and off, on and off, immediately changing the nature of the sound. This initiates a known game in their repertoire. Kris narrows his eyes in a frown of concentration, dips his head forward slightly and becomes interested. There is a visible switch of mood as a half-smile appears. After a few seconds Kris becomes silent …
>
> … The game continues with phases of wandering and intermittent playful exchanges, Lindsey commentating on their joint actions, placing her hand over his mouth during his vocalising and giving him sideways cheery hugs. At one point Kris allows himself to be guided into a corner where he can be completely still; he relaxes, leaning against the wall and enjoys a burst of the nose-pressing game. On this occasion Kris enters into

the turn-taking, putting his head forward each time to trigger the turns of his teacher; he becomes fully engaged, smiling and daring to look. There is tension in the playful atmosphere and then he pushes forward. They enjoy some more turns on the move, this time less intense, until his mood changes, his movements become quicker, his expression becomes more distant and Lindsey does not attempt to resume the game.

(Nind, 2000, p.39)

The meanings of the interactions are negotiated, in situ. The child is not expected to learn the adult's meaning or the adult to immediately guess those of the child. The ritualised games that are characteristic of early child development provide a structure and a social environment for the child to explore (Nind, 2000). The adult enhances the interactions by using elements of early caregiver–infant interactions. These might include adjusting the rhythm of the interaction, creating mutually enjoyable 'games' and through this responding contingently, imputing intentionality to the actions of the child. By engaging in interactions that the child him/herself finds enjoyable and meaningful the child can begin to 'learn how to learn' socially.

The essence therefore of the approach is to build on and use natural processes rather than contriving artificial learning situations. In the examples of approaches given so far, the TEACCH approach brings the physical environment 'closer' to the child's world and develops a physical scaffold to their learning; the Higashi method, although using routines, does not move as 'close'. There is also a continuum concerning the degree of control that the child with autism has over the educational interactions in which they are engaged. Intensive Interaction is at one end point, and ABA is at the other.

The flexibility and negotiation required by the 'Intensive Interaction' is found in other social approaches to autism, for example those based on music (Prevezer, 2000), ICT (Tjus and Heimann, 2000) or a multisensory curriculum (Longhorn, 2000). All would see learning being promoted when the teacher starts from where the child is developmentally and creating enjoyable and interactive experiences. Other approaches for children who rarely initiate social interaction, apparently lacking interest in other people, also suggest that an adult can 'carry the load' of an interaction in order to encourage and teach the child to take their first steps in initiating and interacting socially, through shared attention with another person (Janert, 2000).

These same principles emerge again in social approaches for older, more socially engaged, children. Newsom (2000) describes working with teenagers with Asperger's syndrome, and how she used humour to develop both social empathy and flexibility of thinking. Her approach included tackling the use of metaphors. The use of metaphor is engrained so deeply in our communication that we fail to notice it, yet it can completely confuse and appear bizarre to children with ASD. Newsom's use of humour in teaching metaphor indicates a way of approaching a difficult concept.

James happily learned about 50 metaphors by heart, and then began to use them in real conversation situations: the first time in a 'what if' exchange about 'suppose there were burglars next door', with a triumphant 'we could dash in and catch them red handed!' ...

[after nine months]

... James' new flexibility with words was helping his tolerance of difference: on one occasion I handed him a drink in a mug which I immediately realised from his face he didn't like; but instead of handing it back (or shouting as he might have done two years previously), he took a drink from it, saying thoughtfully 'you can't judge a drink by the mug' – that's like 'you can't judge a book by its cover'.

(Newsom, 2000, p.96)

Newsom also used visual correspondences, such as painting emotions or sounds, to help the children move beyond concrete representations and inflexible judgements about correctness. Puns and plays on words were explored and explained. This led to some children being able to 'get' the shifts in perspective embedded in jokes and create their own. As with other approaches Newsom often moved the material 'closer' to the children's interests. For example, in exploring ironic humour she used the book *Fungus the Bogeyman*:

a further reason why *Fungus* has been so popular for bright autistic children is probably that much of it is in the form of a spoof information book. Where ordinary children may be helped by a storyline to make the informational bits more palatable, for autistic children it is usually the other way around: information is what they like best, and stories about people need too much social empathy to be very rewarding ... this is a format which they are ready to enjoy.

(Newsom, 2000, p.99)

The examples chosen in this section indicate the importance of reciprocal social interactions in developing learning. This is a fundamental principle that underpins work with a wide range of children and contexts. Social scaffolding is seen as being at the heart of learning. Rigorous evaluation of many social approaches is rare but there is a growing body of research which demonstrates significance changes in children's social development following Intensive Interaction (Nind, 1996; 2000; Nind and Kellet, 2002).

Conclusion

This chapter has outlined criteria employed to identify autism and a number of explanatory theories, reviewed some approaches used in the education of children with autism and grouped them as behavioural, cultural and social. Each offers a different perspective on pedagogy and autism. Each agrees that this process should begin early and that significant progress is achievable.

There is considerable debate as to which strategies are most appropriate and hence empirical evaluative evidence has been offered for each, where it exists. Across these approaches some features of good practice emerge (expressed in varying degrees), and these have been supported by others elsewhere (for example Iovannone et al, 2003; Powers, 1992; Powell, 2000; Jordan and Jones, 1999). These features are:

- individually based support for children and their families;
- pedagogy that is based on an underlying model of learning, applied consistently;
- the child's learning environment, social and physical, is made comprehensible to them;
- the curriculum is tailored to the child's cognitive and social requirements;
- problem behaviour is treated functionally, although each of the approaches discussed would respond to this in a different way;
- planned integration and inclusion with peers.

The inclusion of children with ASD in mainstream settings requires both whole-school planning and a degree of preparedness and flexibility in school staff (Simmonds, 1993). The actual teaching approach adopted will depend on the child's age and development and might encompass behavioural, cultural or social approaches. Awareness of this range is essential. Children with autism, or ASD, are so varied that

> it is quite likely that an approach may appear ineffective when tested across a full group, yet might be useful for particular individuals.
>
> (Dempsey and Foreman, 2001, p. 113)

Until the long-sought 'definitive teaching method' arrives (if it ever does) teachers will need to choose and evaluate their pedagogical approaches with respect to the progress of the children that they teach. This type of monitoring is a feature of good teaching practice but it needs to include the potential exploration of alternative teaching approaches. This is particularly challenging in the field of autism for, as we have seen, different approaches carry with them different assumptions about the nature of learning.

References

Asperger, H. (1944) in Waterhouse, S. W. (2000) *A Positive Approach to Autism.* London: Jessica Kingsley.

Baron-Cohen, S. (1995) *Mindblindness: an Essay on Autism and Theory of Mind.* London: MIT Press.

Birnbrauer, J. S. and Leach, D. J. (1993) The Murdoch Early Intervention Program after 2 years. *Behaviour Change*, 10, 63–74.

Dempsey, I. and Foreman, P. (2001) A Review of Educational Approaches for Individuals with Autism. *International Journal of Disability, Development and Education*, 48(1), 104–116.

DSM (2003) *Diagnostic and Statistical Manual of Mental Disorders DSM-IV-TR* (Text Revision). Task Force on DSM-IV, American Psychiatric Association.

Ephraim, G. (1997) Intensive Interaction. Paper presented at the Annual Conference of the British Psychological Society Division of Clinical Psychology Special Interest Group (Learning Disabilities), Abergavenny.

Gould, J., Rigg, M. and Bignell, L. (1991) *The Higashi Experience*. A report on a visit by NAS staff to the Higashi School in Boston. The National Autistic Society.

Green, G. (1996) Early behavioral intervention for autism. In C. Maurice (Ed.), *Behavioral Intervention for Young Children with Autism* (pp. 29–44). Austin, TX: Pro-Ed.

Hall, L. J. (1997) Effective behavioural strategies for the defining characteristics of autism. *Behaviour Change*, 14, 139–154.

Iovannone, R., Dunlap, G., Huber, H. and Kincaid, D. (2003) Effective educational practices for students with Autism Spectrum Disorders. *Focus on Autism and Other Developmental Disabilities*, 18(3), Fall, 150–165.

Janert, S. (2000) *Reaching the Young Autistic Child: Reclaiming non-autistic potential through communicative games and strategies*. London: Free Association Books.

Jones, R. S. P., Zahl, A. and Huws, J. C. (2001) First-hand accounts of emotional experiences in autism: a qualitative analysis. *Disability & Society*, 16(3), 393–401.

Jordan, R. (1999) *Autistic Spectrum Disorders: An introductory handbook for practitioners*. London: David Fulton Publishers.

Jordan, R. and Jones, G. (1999) Review of research into educational interventions for children with autism in the UK. *Autism*, 3(1), 101–110.

Kanner, L. (1943) Autistic disturbances of affective contact. *Nervous Child*, 2, 217–250.

Keenan, M., Kerr, K. and Dillenburger, K. (2000) *Parents' Education as Autism Therapists. Applied Behaviour Analysis in Context*. London: Jessica Kingsley.

Kerr, K. P., Smyth, P. and McDowell, C. (2003) Precision teaching children with autism: helping design effective programmes. *Early Child Development and Care*, 173(4), 399–410.

Longhorn, F. (2000) Multisensory education and learners with profound autism. In S. Powell, (Ed.) *Helping Children with Autism to Learn*. London: David Fulton Publishers, 27–38.

Lovaas, O. I. (1981) *Teaching Developmentally Disabled Children: The ME book*. Austin, TX: Pro-Ed.

Lovaas, O. I. (1987) Behavioural treatment and normal educational and intellectual functioning in young autistic children. *Journal of Consulting and Clinical Psychology*, 55, 3–9.

Lovaas, O. I. (1996) cited in Roth, I. (2002) The autistic spectrum: from theory to practice. In N. Brace and H. Westcott (Eds) *Applying Psychology*. Milton Keynes: Open University, 243–315.

Lovaas, O. I. and Favelle, (1987) Protection for clients undergoing aversive/restrictive interventions. *Education and Treatment of Children*, 10, 311–325.

McKay, L., Keenan, M. and Dillenburger, K. (2000) in M. Keenan, K. P. Kerr and K. Dillenburger, *Parents' Education as Autism Therapists: Applied Behaviour Analysis in Context*. London: Jessica Kingsley.

Newsom, E. (2000) Using humour to enable flexibility and social empathy in children with Asperger's syndrome: some practical strategies. In S. Powell, (Ed.) *Helping Children with Autism to Learn*. London: David Fulton Publishers, 94–106.

Nind, M. (1996) Efficacy of Intensive Interaction: developing sociability and communication in people with severe and complex learning difficulties using an approach based on caregiver–infant interaction. *European Journal of Special Needs Education*, 11, 48–66.

Nind, M. (2000) Intensive Interaction and children with autism. In S. Powell, (Ed.) *Helping Children with Autism to Learn*. London: David Fulton Publishers, 27–38.

Nind, M. and Hewett, D. (2001) *A Practical Guide to Intensive Interaction*. Kidderminster: BILD Publications.

Nind, M. and Kellett, M. (2002) Responding to individuals with severe learning difficulties and stereotyped behaviour: challenges for an inclusive era. *European Journal of Special Needs Education*, 17(3), 265–282.

Panerai, S., Ferrante, L. and Caputo, V. (1997) The TEACCH strategy in mentally retarded children with autism: a multidimensional assessment. Pilot study. *Journal of Autism and Developmental Disorders*, 27, 345–347.

Peeters, T. and Gilberg, C. (1999) in Roth, I. (2002) The autistic spectrum: from theory to practice. In N. Brace and H. Westcott (Eds) *Applying Psychology*. Milton Keynes: Open University, 243–315.

Powell, S. (2000) *Helping Children with Autism to Learn*. London: David Fulton Publishers.

Powers, M. (1992) Early intervention for children with autism. In D. Berkell (Ed.) *Autism: Identification, education, and treatment*. Hillsdale, N.J.: Erlbaum.

Prevezer, W. (2000) Musical interaction and children with autism. In S. Powell, (Ed.) *Helping Children with Autism to Learn*. London: David Fulton Publishers, 50–62.

Richardson, H. (2000) Outcomes of Three Educational Interventions for British School Children with Classical Autism: A Comparative Study. Paper presented at ISEC 2000 University of Manchester, UK.

Roth, I. (2002) The autistic spectrum: from theory to practice. In N. Brace and H. Westcott (Eds) *Applying Psychology*. Milton Keynes: Open University, 243–315.

Sheehy, K. (1993) Preventing disabilities in children: Active intervention in the developmental process. In J. Rothman and R. Levine (Eds), *Prevention Practice*. New York: W.B. Saunders.

Simmonds, C. (1993) The Asperger Student in a Mainstream Setting. In *Children with Asperger Syndrome*: A collection of papers from two study weekends run by The Inge Wakefield Trust 1992–1993. The National Autistic Society.

TEACCH (2003) Treatment and Education of Autistic and related Communication handicapped CHildren. On-line at http://www.unc.edu/depts/teacch/teacch.htm [ACCESSED 9.12.03].

Tjus, T. and Heimann, M. (2000) Language, multimedia and communication for children with autism: searching for the right combination. In S. Powell, (Ed.) *Helping Children with Autism to Learn*. London: David Fulton Publishers, 78–93.

Waterhouse, S. W. (2000) *A Positive Approach to Autism*. London: Jessica Kingsley.

Wing, L. (1991) Asperger's syndrome and Kanner's autism. In Frith, U., (Ed.) *Autism and Asperger Syndrome*. Cambridge: Cambridge University Press.

Wing, L. and Gould, J. (1979) Severe impairments of social interaction and associated abnormalities in children: epidemiology and classification. *Journal of Autism and Developmental Disorders*, 9, 11–29.

Index